Hoover Institution Publications

THE ARMS RACE
AND SINO-SOVIET RELATIONS

THE ARMS RACE
AND SINO-SOVIET
RELATIONS

Walter C. Clemens, Jr.

THE HOOVER INSTITUTION ON WAR,
REVOLUTION AND PEACE

Stanford University · Stanford, California

1968

The Hoover Institution on War, Revolution and Peace, founded at Stanford University in 1919 by the late President Herbert Hoover, is a center for advanced study and research on public and international affairs in the twentieth century. The views expressed in its publications are entirely those of the authors and do not necessarily reflect the views of the Hoover Institution.

Hoover Institution Publications [72]

© 1968 by the Board of Trustees of the Leland Stanford Junior University

Library of Congress Catalog Card Number: 68–21253

Printed in the United States of America

For my Mother and Father

Acknowledgments

A great debt is owed to a number of conferences and publications that have served as stimuli for the present work and as foundations on which it could build. In 1963 the U.S. Arms Control and Disarmament Agency (ACDA) initiated two studies in which the author was privileged to take part, a summer study organized by Columbia University and published as Alexander Dallin and others, *The Soviet Union and Disarmament* (New York: Frederick A. Praeger, 1965), and an eighteen-month study carried out at the Massachusetts Institute of Technology, published as Lincoln P. Bloomfield, Walter C. Clemens, Jr., Franklyn Griffiths, *Khrushchev and the Arms Race: Soviet Interests in Arms Control and Disarmament, 1954–1964* (Cambridge, Mass.: The M.I.T. Press, 1966). In 1964 ACDA sponsored another summer study, published as Morton H. Halperin and Dwight H. Perkins, *Communist China and Arms Control* (New York: Frederick A. Praeger, 1965). The same agency sponsored a third conference in 1966 aimed at bringing together the insights developed in the course of the previous two summer studies of Soviet and Chinese policies. The essays prepared for that conference have been published as Morton H. Halperin, ed., *Sino-Soviet Relations and Arms Control* (Cambridge, Mass.: The M.I.T. Press, 1967). Several of the chapters in the present volume appeared in that symposium after being published first in *Orbis*, X, No. 1 (Spring 1966). Chapter VIII derives from an article published initially in *The China Quarterly*, October–December 1967.

The author benefited greatly from criticisms of his research and from discussions of other papers at the 1965 summer study, and was encouraged by Dennis J. Doolin and Karol Maichel of the Hoover Institution to proceed with the present work, which derives in part from earlier research conducted on *Khrushchev and the Arms Race;* from a study undertaken for the M.I.T. International Communism Project in 1965; and from research supported in 1966 by the M.I.T. Center for Space Research. During 1966–68 the work has been funded and facilitated by the Boston University Graduate School and the Department of Government. A number of Boston University students also contributed to the book, both by their comments on the arguments presented and by their assistance with aspects of its preparation. Particular thanks go to Ronald H. Linden, Charlene Morris, and Edward J. White.

For their criticisms and suggestions, the author wishes to express his great debt to William E. Griffith, Morton H. Halperin, Raymond L. Garthoff, Jerome B. Wiesner, Lincoln P. Bloomfield, Francis J. Rendall, Uri Ra'anan, Homer A. Jack, Ralph J. Thomson, and Edward Drachman; to the participants in the 1965 conference on Sino-Soviet relations and arms control; to the Joint Harvard-M.I.T. Arms Control Seminar; and to the many other scholars and government officials who have reviewed parts of the manuscript. Much of the policy analysis derives from the discussions and recommendations of the National Citizens' Committee for the White House Conference on International Cooperation, November 29–December 2, 1965, and from the work of the Steering Committee, Educational Campaign to Halt Nuclear Weapons Spread, United Nation Association—U.S.A. Messrs. Milous Vejvoda, Jouri Barinov, and Nandasiri Jasentuliyana of the U.N. Secretariat have been particularly kind in helping to locate U.N. documentation. The facilities of the Harvard University Russian Research Center and the International Communism Project, M.I.T., have yielded much useful material.

In a real sense this study of contemporary Soviet and Chinese arms policy is also a direct outgrowth of work begun at the Hoover Institution in 1959. The author is deeply indebted to the Hoover Institution for continuing support and for publication of this volume.

This book is dedicated to my Mother and Father, whose support and encouragement over the years have had a profound influence on this work, probably deeper and more meaningful than any of us know. Heartfelt thanks to them and to all members of my family for their understanding and patience throughout this project. A special note of thanks to my wife Diane, who, as before, has helped to think through many problems of the analysis.

Contents

PART FOUR
THE OUTLOOK

TABLES

FIGURES

MAP

Abbreviations

ABM	antiballistic missile defense
ACDA	U.S. Arms Control and Disarmament Agency
ASW	antisubmarine warfare
BAMBI	ballistic missile boost intercept
CIA	U.S. Central Intelligence Agency
CMEA	Council of Mutual Economic Assistance
CPR	Chinese People's Republic
CPSU	Communist Party of the Soviet Union
DIA	U.S. Defense Intelligence Agency
DOSAAF	*Dobrovol'noe obshchestvo sodeistviia Armii, Aviatsii i Flotu*—Voluntary Society for Cooperation with the Army, Air Force, and Navy
ENDC	Eighteen-Nation Disarmament Committee
EURATOM	European Atomic Energy Community
FOBS	fractional orbit bombardment system
FRG	Federal Republic of Germany
GCD	general and complete disarmament
GDR	German Democratic Republic
IAEA	International Atomic Energy Agency
ICBM	intercontinental ballistic missile
IRBM	intermediate-range ballistic missile
JCP	Japanese Communist Party
LASA	large aperture seismic array
MIRV	multiple individually-guided reentry vehicles
MLF	multilateral nuclear force
MOL	manned orbiting laboratory
MRBM	medium-range ballistic missile
NCNA	New China News Agency
OCAM	Organisation Commune Africaine et Malgache
PKI	Indonesian Communist Party
PLA	People's Liberation Army
PVO	*Protivovozdushnaia oborona*—anti-air defense
SAMBIS	sea-based antiballistic missile intercept system
SCMP	Survey of the Chinese Mainland Press
SDV	strategic delivery vehicle
SLBM	submarine-launched ballistic missile

THE ARMS RACE
AND SINO-SOVIET RELATIONS

Introduction

"The atomic bomb does not adhere to the class principle—it destroys everybody within the range of its devastating force." With these words the Soviet Communist Party statement of July 14, 1963, attempted to epitomize the differences between its own outlook and that of Peking on central issues of war and peace. The Soviet leaders, to be sure, had not turned to "Bible-reading and psalm-singing," as Peking charged on November 19, 1963. Nor had the Chinese leaders proved themselves anxious for a global nuclear war, as the Kremlin averred. Despite their distortion and exaggeration, however, the polemics—paralleled by Soviet and Chinese actions—indicate that the nuclear issue has been a profoundly agitating factor in Sino-Soviet relations for more than a decade. Considering the underlying elements conditioning these frictions in the past, it seems likely that arms control developments will both shape and be shaped by Sino-Soviet relations for more than a decade to come.

The present work examines the interface of two problems usually considered separately—arms control and Sino-Soviet relations. It is hoped that the analysis of each problem and the search for the relationship between them may contribute both to the study of arms control and to the field of communist studies. The concept of arms control, of course, is very broad, embracing not only negotiations for the limitation and reduction of arms, but the management of military power in such a way as to reduce the chances of war, to lower the damage if war occurs, and to contain the cost of military competition. The notion of arms control is closely related also to political applications of military power, whether used to support an alliance, to press for diplomatic concessions, to sap the adversary's will, or to overcome his resistance to a relaxation of tensions. When the Bolsheviks embarked on their disarmament campaign in the 1920s, arms control negotiations were seen as a defensive weapon in the short run, but as an offensive instrument for the long run. Disarmament, for them, was the continuation of revolution by other means. This approach has been modified in different ways by the contemporary governments in Moscow and Peking. While their analysts continue to spurn the term "arms control," however, it is clear that Chinese—no less than Soviet and East European leaders—have come to appreciate the wide uses to which they can put the management of military power, in senses familiar to Western strategists, and disarmament diplomacy, as suggested by Lenin and elaborated by his successors.

The present study attempts to provide an analytical history of arms control and related issues in Sino-Soviet relations from the early 1950s through the mid-1960s. It seeks to clarify the historical record, reconstructing not only the nature of Soviet and Chinese policies on these matters, but also the driving forces that have conditioned the words and deeds of Moscow and Peking.

We now know, partly as a result of the revelations of the Sino-Soviet polemics, that one of the major factors in the deterioration of relations between Moscow and Peking—perhaps the decisive cause—has been the Kremlin's handling of the nuclear issue. Soviet policy appears to have been contradictory, for at the same time Russian diplomats were antagonizing Peking by edging toward a nuclear test ban with the West, Moscow was attempting to keep China as an ally by extending to her significant nuclear assistance—atoms for war as well as for peace. These contradictions manifested themselves even during the uneasy honeymoon between the communist giants in the mid- to late 1950s. The seeming paradoxes in Soviet policy may have resulted from a calculated double game—a strategy that sought to freeze the membership of the atomic club while ensuring China's good will or at least her dependence on Moscow. The famous subjectivism of the Soviet Party Chairman may also have played a role, leading the USSR down contradictory paths without full consideration of the consequences. It seems possible, in fact, that elements of both calculation and behavioral response patterns combined to shape Soviet policy. Whatever the respective weights of such elements, it is clear that we have here an important case study of the manner in which arms control issues may impinge on alliance relationships, while depending for their outcome on cohesion or disintegration of the alliance.

As the Soviet leaders gave increasingly serious consideration to the signing of a test ban treaty with the West, they were aware from Chinese warnings that such a step could provide a last straw shattering all semblance of communist unity. Not surprisingly, the Moscow Treaty in 1963 triggered a new and more intensive stage in the struggle for power within the communist movement and for influence in the third world. For about a year it also supplied momentum to other arms control negotiations and contributed to a sense of détente in Moscow's relations with the West.

With China's entry into the nuclear club in October 1964, coincidental with the fall of Khrushchev in Moscow and with escalating conflicts in Southeast Asia, arms control problems had to be viewed in a new context. China's nuclear potential was for the time being far from developed, but the political and military pressures generated by her first tests sharply enhanced the prospects that a series of additional states would decide to go nuclear. Not only did China's atomic program make horizontal proliferation more likely, but it added significantly to the upward thrust by the superpowers in the development and procurement of defensive and offensive weapons. At the same time that Peking's incipient arsenal threatened to accelerate the arms race, it sharpened the urgency for negotiations to stave off new rounds of arms competition that could involve the entire world, large and small powers alike.

The outcome of these negotiations depends upon a number of variables. Given the scope of the present study, we can mention many of them only in passing. Among the key variables, however, the attitudes and actions of the Soviet and Chinese governments will surely play important roles. What force or configuration of forces has been shaping Moscow's and Peking's policy and will continue to shape it in the years ahead? The factors that condition most immediately their decisions on arms control and related foreign policy matters appear to be of a military-strategic nature. These, in turn, depend heavily upon economic and technological developments. The economic base—including the ability of each regime to satisfy consumer wants as well as foreign policy needs—also conditions its attitude toward risk-taking, since it helps determine attitudes toward the existing order and the direction of change. In sum, although ideological, cultural, and personality factors play important roles that must be recognized, a materialist interpretation appears to be the most useful approach in analyzing Soviet and Chinese decisions in these crucial areas of foreign policy. Since ideology is among other things an action program, it is hardly coincidental that a comparison of the doctrinal stands taken by Moscow and Peking on war, peace, revolution, and arms control indicates a broad consonance between these views and the perceived material needs of each government. On the other hand, while objective forces arising from the material environment condition long-term trends and determine the perceived challenges and opportunities of the moment, voluntaristic factors will be particularly salient in crisis situations.

While the present study is primarily historical, it may contain also implications both for Western policy-makers concerned with arms control and/or the communist world. Clearly, absolute prediction of Soviet or Chinese policy is not possible; but an improved understanding of the way the Kremlin and Peking have responded to certain pressures and opportunities in the past may be at least suggestive of their probable responses to alternate worlds of the future.

The range of issues discussed herein is outlined in Fig. 1, "Framework for the Study of Communist Arms Control Policy." While the outline may be used to visualize the factors bearing on Chinese as well as on Soviet policy, it is more relevant to the latter, since almost half the categories concern relations with the West, in which Moscow has been more immediately engaged than Peking. The fundamental dichotomy shown in the outline is that between policy—"declaratory" and "actual"—and the conditioning factors shaping these words and deeds. By making this distinction it may be possible to avoid one-sided interpretations that result from taking communist statements at face value or examining primarily the presumed determinants of Soviet attitudes toward disarmament. The approach here has been to examine both these sets of parameters and their sub-set components. Some chapters deal with one aspect or sub-set of the total problem, such as declaratory policy on arms control, while other chapters treat the interaction of several different factors. While some aspects are treated in detail, others—such as the use of military threats for diplomatic bargaining—are mentioned only in passing, usually with a reference to more detailed studies.

The present work has sought to construct and to interpret a vital and interesting segment of contemporary history. Some of the materials analyzed have been discussed in the public and scholarly press, while other materials, particularly those relating to more recent events, may be less familiar. Four levels of analysis have been attempted: first, to bring forward in time the study of problems, such as arms control negotiations, already analyzed for earlier periods; second, to present in a single monograph a synthesis of what is known about Sino-Soviet relations on the one hand, and arms control developments on the other; third, to sort out and clarify existing hypotheses; and fourth, to evaluate existing hypotheses and to develop new ones where appropriate.

The ingredients for this reconstruction and interpretation are diverse. Two main sources of documentation have been used: the Sino-Soviet polemic and the record of the arms control negotiations. Students of communist affairs owe a great debt to the Chinese leadership because, in the words of Moscow's statement of August 21, 1963, the

> government of the People's Republic of China, disregarding its duty as an ally and abusing the relations of trust existing among the socialist countries, has embarked upon the road of making public classified documents and information relating to the defenses of the countries of the socialist community. . . .

The Kremlin added that Peking had presented "the facts tendentiously, in a distorted light." But Moscow also told its side, which was amplified in additional material released by other Communist Parties, most notably, those of Albania, Yugoslavia, and Italy. Materials of this nature are often not available to historians for decades, and in the case of communist states, perhaps never.

The record of arms control negotiations constitutes another important source of information, not only about the formal proposals and agreements reached, but about the attitudes of the negotiating partners. Changes in bargaining posture or even in style may reflect a far-reaching change in the substance of a nation's policy. Additional sources of documentation and analysis have come from a wide range of primary and secondary materials dealing with military, political, economic, and cultural affairs, in the Western and nonaligned as well as in the communist worlds. Scholars and government officials from a number of countries have also discussed the problems of this study with the author, helping to correct and supplement the results of library research. The methodology used is an adaptation of that employed in earlier studies of Soviet policy, studies that pointed to the great influence of China upon Moscow's arms control strategy. No doubt the conclusions offered here—both as to facts and to interpretations—will be subject to modification as a result of more refined modes of analysis, of additional materials that may come to light, and of the perspective of time.

It would ultimately be desirable to study Soviet and Chinese arms control policies in a much broader framework than can be explicitly done here. Such a framework would: (1) root these policies more firmly in the domestic political, social, and economic circumstances of each country; (2) evaluate them in terms of the historical behavior patterns and culture of each; (3) compare them with the policies of other states at similar stages of industrial and political development; and (4) go deeper into the interaction patterns that would reveal the extent to which Soviet and Chinese policies are reactions to those of other states, rather than simply self-generated initiatives. Finally, the analysis should be anchored in a more rigorous and penetrating theory of international relations: one that would enable us better to grasp the interfaces between the structure of the international system; the transnational forces, both objective and subjective, that shape it; the interaction of domestic and foreign policy considerations; and the product of these dimensions—the ends and means by which states pursue their objectives and the way in which the international system operates at different periods in time.

FIGURE 1

Framework for the Study of Communist Arms Control Policy

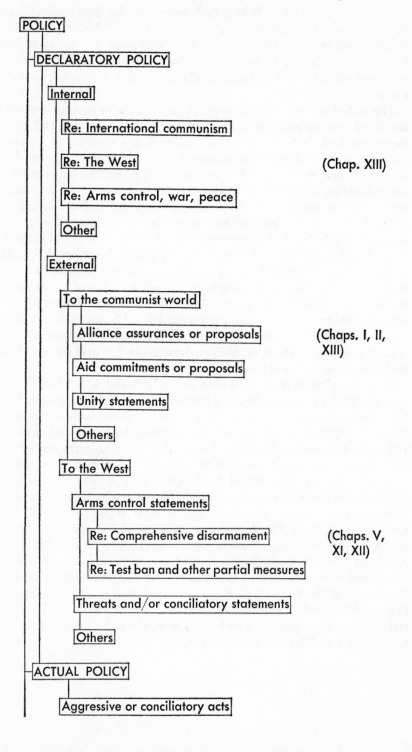

Steps to inhibit or spread nuclear weapons (Chap. I)

Arms controls (uni-, bi-, or multilateral) (Chaps. IV, V)

UNDERLYING FACTORS (Chap. XIV)

Strategic-military (Chaps. IV, VIII, IX, X, XII, XIV, XV)

Balance of power (present and anticipated)

Conventional

Strategic

Strategic doctrine (Chap. XIII)

Alliance commitments (Chap. VI)

Economic (Chap. XIV)

Rate and direction of growth

Defense burden

Public and elite pressures

External political (Chap. VI)

Relations within the communist world

Conflict (frontiers, leadership, doctrine, etc.)

Cohesion

Relations with the West

The third world (Chaps. VII, IX, X)

Internal political and sociological (Chaps. XII, XIV)

Elite relations

Public pressures

Part One

THE DYNAMICS OF CONFLICT, 1950–63: MOSCOW'S TWO-FRONT DILEMMA

I

A "Most Puzzling Aspect" of Sino-Soviet Relations

The main problems of the present work derive from what one authority terms "the most puzzling aspect of the whole range of Sino-Soviet relations":

> Basically the question to be asked is: did the Chinese receive practical Soviet aid in building up their military atomic capability from 1957 onwards, and if so, why did the Soviet Government deliberately set about helping its gigantic neighbor to become an atomic power, especially since in 1957–58 the Soviet Union was putting forward at Geneva nonproliferation and nuclear test ban proposals? There is, at the present, no satisfactory answer to these questions. . . .[1]

Two seemingly contradictory courses were pursued by Moscow: nuclear aid to China simultaneous with serious efforts to negotiate a nuclear test ban. A host of subsidiary questions follows: How much and what kind of aid? Over what time period? How much interest in a test ban? Under what conditions? How soon was it expected to be achieved? Finally, what was Peking's appraisal of Soviet policy—its assistance program to China and its flirtation with the West?

The outsider who attempts to unravel these enigmas must beware of seeking too rational an explanation for Soviet behavior. Indeed, one of the few comments made by a communist official regarding a study of Khrushchev's arms control policy was that the book worked too hard to find a logical explanation for disarmament proposals that were churned out perfunctorily by the middle echelons of the Soviet foreign ministry.[2] On balance, it seems more likely that Moscow's policy on arms and arms control actually has been approved and even dictated at a very high level (especially in the Khrushchev period), but the caveat against excessive expectations of rational planning is well taken.

Two frameworks have been proposed for analyzing policy-decisions: one emphasizing the logic of the situation, and the second seeking generalizations about the usual behavior pattern of specific actors as they have responded to similar situations in the past.[3] The first approach assumes that the actors are rational and that, if the alternatives as they saw them can be known, their motives and aims may be reconstructed. If the motives appear irrational in the light of existing information, the analyst should seek and even hypothesize other alternatives, recasting his explanations in the light of additional findings. The second approach lays less stress on rationality than upon behavior trends likely to be repeated in recurring situations.

These two approaches need not be antithetical, of course; they may rather complement one another. In any case, both methods dictate a careful search for factual data about the circumstances in which certain decisions were taken. With this principle in mind we shall attempt to review the basic evidence regarding the apparently contradictory aspects of Moscow's nuclear policy toward China and the West. We shall then have a basis for considering the available explanations of Soviet policy and for assessing them in terms of the logic of the situation and relevant behavior patterns.

At the outset, however, five major hypotheses attempting to explain the "most puzzling aspect" of Sino-Soviet relations should be summarized, even though they are evaluated later in more detail. The first three explanations posit an underlying rationale behind Moscow's aid to China and the Soviet diplomatic search for a nuclear test ban. The first theory argues that Soviet assistance to China's nuclear program was part of a larger strategy aimed at enhancing Soviet controls through a Far Eastern version of the Warsaw Pact. A second theory posits that Moscow employed its aid program to purchase China's support for the Soviet test ban policy. A third theory argues rather that the Kremlin played a kind of double game: it provided assistance for China's own nuclear production capability while seeking a test ban with the West that would serve as a justification for halting Russian aid.

A fourth and fifth theory assume that Soviet policy had little rhyme or reason. The fourth argues that the contradiction in Soviet policy resulted from the existence of two factions within the Kremlin—one favoring aid to China, the other championing a test ban and possibly détente with the West. A fifth theory contends that, even if Soviet policy were the product of a unified strategy, it was badly conceived and even more ineptly applied. Finally, there is a sixth viewpoint that denies the existence of the contradiction analyzed by the other theories. One variant of the argument holds that Moscow did not supply significant nuclear aid to China (at least during 1957–59). A second variant contends that whatever the facts about the Soviet assistance program, it cannot be proved that the Kremlin seriously wanted or expected a test ban during the years 1957–59. In part to refute this sixth approach, and to establish the facts by which to evaluate the first five theories, we shall review the main points known about Moscow's nuclear assistance and test ban policies, especially within the time frame of 1955–60.

SOVIET SCIENTIFIC AND MILITARY AID TO CHINA

Beginning in late 1954[4] the Soviet regime gave Peking tangible signs that it would assist China's nuclear program in a number of ways, although neither side may have been clear as to the possible contribution of "atoms for peace" to "atoms for war." The Khrushchev-Bulganin mission to Peking in late 1954 committed Russia to transfer to exclusive Chinese control the joint Soviet-Chinese stock company for the mining of "non-ferrous" metals established in Sinkiang Province under the terms of a 1950 agreement between Stalin's Russia and the new communist regime in China. More important, Stalin's successors in 1955 committed themselves to aid China in peaceful nuclear research and development. Partly to counter President Eisenhower's "Atoms for Peace" proposal, Moscow in January 1955 launched a major new program of "scientific and technical assistance" to China and other communist-bloc nations for the development of "atomic energy for peaceful purposes." The Kremlin promised to supply its allies with research reactors and with the "necessary amount of fissionable materials for research purposes."

In February 1955 a chemical separation plant was set up in Sinkiang with Soviet aid, although the Russians for the time being probably returned the enriched fuel to their own reactors. In April an Institute for Atomic Energy was established in Peking, and Moscow agreed to supply it with an experimental heavy water reactor. In 1956 the first Chinese scientists arrived at the Joint Institute for Nuclear Research organized by the Soviets in Dubna, near Moscow, to cooperate with scientists from the entire communist bloc.[5] Later in 1956 Moscow announced its "First Five-Year Plan for Foreign Aid," which provided for development of 39 atomic centers in China.

By mid-1957 ten Chinese scientists were engaged in research in high-energy physics at Dubna. The state of Chinese science was reported to be "dreary" in 1957, but Soviet and Chinese scientists jointly lectured in China on nuclear science in that year. Teaching and research in nuclear physics spread, and some industrial use of isotopes began. More important, the research reactor and cyclotron promised by Moscow in 1955 commenced operation near Peking in 1958. Also in 1958 there was established in China another Institute of Atomic Energy Research, under the leadership of a former collaborator of Frederic Joliot-Curié, who has testified to the "financial and material resources" provided by the Chinese Communist Party to the research there. Indeed, a Draft of Twelve-Year Plan for the Development of Science and Technology, drawn up between January and December 1958, defined 57 specific priorities, the highest of which were peaceful uses of atomic energy, electronics, and jet propulsion technology.[6]

In October 1957 Moscow seems to have undertaken another commitment, which came to light only in 1963, to aid China's nuclear program. The primary source is a Chinese statement made during the heated polemic that followed the signing of the nuclear test ban treaty:

> As far back as June 20, 1959, when there was not yet the slightest sign of a treaty on stopping nuclear tests, the Soviet Government unilaterally tore up the agreement of new technology for national defense concluded between China and the Soviet Union on October 15, 1957, and refused to provide China with a sample of an atomic bomb and technical data concerning its manufacture.[7]

The accuracy of the Chinese revelation has not been specifically challenged or confirmed by Moscow, although the Kremlin has indicated that it did refuse sample atomic bombs to Peking. Further, Moscow has accused China of "making public classified documents and information relating to the defenses of the countries of the socialist community. . . ." Thus, at least by implication, the Kremlin has acknowledged that the Chinese allegation is generally accurate, although Moscow adds that Peking has presented "the facts tendentiously, in a distorted light."[8]

Since the Chinese statement does not indicate the precise nature of the 1957 agreement except to say that it concerned national defense, it is not necessarily true, as some have concluded, that "Moscow promised to furnish Peking one or several samples of the Russian A-bomb and to supply scientific information to help with the construction of the bomb."[9] The eventual Soviet refusal to provide a sample bomb may have violated the spirit but probably not the letter of the October 1957 agreement.

The circumstances surrounding the October 15, 1957 pact give rise to a number of questions, some of them suggesting that the agreement may have been equivocal in some important respects. What we do know is that a large delegation of Chinese scientists headed by the president of the Chinese Academy of Sciences was in the Soviet Union from October 18, 1957 (three days after the pact is supposed to have been signed)[10] to January 18, 1958, and that during this period agreement was reached for joint Soviet-Chinese scientific research in 1958–62 on 122 different items. Later reports indicated that the key fields in this research would be physics and the peaceful uses of atomic energy.[11]

A hint that military matters also were involved in these negotiations came on November 6, 1957, when a high-level Chinese military mission left for Moscow without prior publicity. Mao Tse-tung, too, was in Moscow in November for discussions with Khrushchev prior to the Conference of Communist and Workers Parties. However, the different emphases in speeches by Defense Ministers P'eng Teh-huai and Malinovsky on November 27, 1957—after the "Moscow Declaration" of the Conference had been signed—suggested that the Kremlin may not yet have committed itself to providing nuclear weapons to China.[12]

A key element in the reconstruction of Sino-Soviet relations during this period is the strategic debate within China, particularly in 1957–58. The technological backwardness of China, combined with the proximity of a Soviet Russia that was both friend and foe, created a tension within the Chinese leadership as to whether they should attempt to rely on Soviet aid (depending of course upon the terms) or upon a bootstrap development of China's own military and economic potential. Beginning in 1954–55 the Peking hierarchy seemed to become alert to the qualitative impact of nuclear-missile technology upon modern warfare. In 1955–56 they debated whether China should attempt to acquire this technology by a long-term process of developing her own resources or whether she must and should buy some modern weapons abroad. Party leaders, including the leaders of the Defense Ministry, downgraded the urgency of interim defense measures in favor of a slower but fuller development of the country's industrial capabilities, relying for a time on the Soviet deterrent. The General Staff, on the other hand, argued the necessity of acquiring immediately well-trained and well-equipped forces in being, including a modern air force and air defense. Either course would require the cooperation of the Soviet Union, but the first plan would entail only temporary dependence upon Russia, pending China's own breakthrough to self-sufficiency. The second approach, however, could make China dependent upon Moscow's good will for a longer period, since it would purchase present security by foregoing some of the means needed for self-development. This debate apparently culminated in 1956 in a high-level decision to pursue economic development as the critical need, while relying on a transitional military strategy that depended heavily upon the Soviet nuclear shield.[13]

The underlying rationale of this 1956 decision seemed consistent with a military training program promulgated in January 1958, implying that China could and should depend upon modern weapons acquired from

Russia. It stressed the importance of incorporating "Soviet advanced experience" in the "development of modern military techniques and military science" and of coordinating "various branches of the Army in combat under the modern conditions of atom bombs, chemical warfare and guided missiles. . . ." But after an interim period in which the new program was not approved or even heard of again, a new strategic line was proclaimed in mid-1958 that turned the January program on its head. "Dogmatism" in the blind reliance on foreign experience, experts, and textbooks was condemned. Slavish reliance on the Soviet Union (by name) was said to have a harmful effect on China's military modernization. Man—not technology—was termed the decisive factor in modern war. A series of official statements in early and mid-August 1958 made the point that China should not and could not rely on outside military aid, but ought to carry out her own research in the newest technology, even while mobilizing the masses. The validity of Mao Tse-tung's strategic ideas from the 1930s was reaffirmed for the contemporary era as the "Great Leap Forward" endeavored to establish a national militia organized in communes.[14]

The existence of this debate and its final resolution in favor of autarky are not disputed. As we shall see, however, the debate is subject to diverse interpretations. The decision to rely on China's own efforts could mean that Russia had refused to meet Peking's demands for military assistance, whether in the nuclear, the missile, or in some other field. Alternatively, it could mean that Russia was proposing certain arrangements which Peking—perhaps Mao himself—decided would give the Russians too much control over China. A third hypothesis is that precisely because Peking was satisfied with Russia's aid in one area—that of China's own efforts in nuclear development and/or missilry—Peking rejected Soviet suggestions of intensified collaboration in other domains, e.g., a joint naval command.

In any event, the first public indication by Peking that China intended to produce her own nuclear weapons came in May 1958.[15] The announcement could have been geared to the commencement of operation in September 1958 of the nuclear reactor promised to China in 1955, although the process by which this reactor built up the requisite plutonium stockpiles would be lengthy, taking at least five years, and would require a Russian blank check to use irradiated fuel rods for that purpose.[16] It is perhaps more likely that the announcements, if meant as realistic predictions, were based on some new Soviet aid commitment in late 1957 or early 1958. It might have taken one of three main forms: (a) an outright transfer of nuclear weapons; (b) stationing of Soviet weapons to China under joint control; or—most likely—(c) the initiating (or intensification) of Soviet scientific and technological assistance to China's nuclear weapons program.

The first two possibilities are most unlikely, for Russia was never ready to transfer atomic weapons to unilateral Chinese control, and Peking—at least after the spring of 1958—was quite unwilling to consider sharing control over major weapons systems on Chinese soil.[17] Hence the Chinese expectation must have been based on a belief that China, with whatever Soviet aid was available, would produce her own nuclear weapons. (Morton Halperin has speculated that the Chinese might have expected to explode their own bomb by 1960 had the Soviets promptly and systematically fulfilled their obligations under the 1957 agreement.)[18]

The official U.S. estimate of Moscow's aid to China's nuclear program has been summarized by President Johnson:

> At first, in the nineteen fifties Russia helped the Chinese. This assistance in the spread of nuclear weapons may now be regarded with some dismay today in Moscow. We believe that this help was ended in 1960 as the quarrel among the Communists grew sharper. Soviet scientists and technicians left suddenly, with the blueprints under their arms. Unfinished facilities were left standing, and expected supplies were cut off.[19]

Although President Johnson placed the final cutoff date in 1960, the Chinese have asserted that the Soviets unilaterally abrogated the defense technology pact on June 20, 1959. Two aspects of the Chinese charge are patently untrue. One is that the Soviet action took place when there was not the slightest sign of movement toward a test ban treaty. In reality, as we shall see, Western officials were highly optimistic about achieving a treaty in the near future. The second distortion in the Chinese position is that the Russians violated the treaty as a "presentation gift" at the time the Soviet leader went to the United States for talks with Eisenhower in September. Western officials have denied that the Russians told them of the Soviet action in 1959—either before, during, or after Khrushchev's visit. Further, the invitation to Khrushchev to visit the United States was not extended until July—and only then because of a misunderstanding between the President and Under-Secretary of State Robert Murphy.[20] A third aspect of the Chinese charge—that the abrogation took place "not long after" Russia's attempt to impose unreasonable demands upon China in 1958—is also misleading, since fourteen to sixteen months separated the two events.[21] Finally, an additional source of information derived from an interview with Khrushchev indicates that the nuclear issue was not entirely settled when he visited Peking in September 1959 after his meeting with Eisenhower at Camp David. According to the interview broadcast by NBC Television on July 11, 1967, Khrushchev

recalled his 1959 meeting with Mao Tse-tung in Peking during which the
Soviet leader said he had refused to supply nuclear arms to China and
for which he took credit for maintaining world peace. Mao, for his part,
was reported to have said: "Comrade Khrushchev, you have only to
provoke the Americans to military action and I will give you as many
people as you wish—100 divisions, 200 divisions, 1,000."

It may be that the bulk of Soviet nuclear aid was suspended in 1959,
particularly that directly associated with a gaseous diffusion plant, but
that other experts working on related fields of military technology did not
leave until 1960. It is known, for example, that of the Soviet experts sent
to China in November 1957, those who specialized in engineering problems of weapons design left Peking in the summer of 1959, while those
who worked on electronics departed in August 1960.

Confirmation of the foregoing estimates and elucidation of some details
were provided by Chinese statements made during the Cultural Revolution. An article "written collectively by the proletarian revolutionaries in
departments under the Scientific and Technological Commission for
National Defense" and published in *Peking Review* (November 3, 1967)
underscored the contention that China's nuclear program had proceeded
since the 1950s in the face of bitter opposition from forces led by "China's
Khrushchev" (presumably Liu Shao-ch'i), who favored instead Chinese
reliance on the Soviet nuclear umbrella.* Heading the defense commis-

---

* The basic theme of Liu Shao-ch'i's policy, as it is interpreted by Cultural
Revolutionaries, is opposition to bootstrap development and reliance on foreign
aid. Thus, an article by Chan Yi-min in *Peking Review* (January 3, 1968) contends
that China's Khrushchev, his agent P'eng Teh-hai, and their like, "did their utmost
to publicize the omnipotence of weapons, of foreign rules and regulations and of
'experts.' They [i.e., Khrushchev, *et al.*] said that in battle the navy relied upon the
tonnage of its vessels, the calibre of its guns and the slide rule." They "advocated
the imperialist and Soviet revisionist road in building the navy, peddled the so-called
experience of the bourgeoisie and revisionists, and imported from abroad whole sets
of foreign dogmas and examples of torpedo-boat engagements and methods of
training." If their ideas had prevailed, the Chinese "armed forces would have
gradually degenerated politically. So we resolutely acted according to Chairman
Mao's teachings and took our own road." This action is claimed to have led to many
victories for Chinese torpedo boats, which the author ascribes to a combination of
sheer courage and the fact that the revolutionaries availed themselves of the aid of
friendly fishermen willing to help out in engagements with enemies off the Taiwan
coast.

While Liu Shao-ch'i apparently wanted more sophisticated torpedo boat operations
than China could immediately provide for herself, he is also castigated for a defeatist
attitude toward a program of building ocean-going freighters. A *Peking Review*
article of January 19, 1968, declares:

Opposing Chairman Mao's revolutionary line, China's Khrushchov and the
counter-revolutionary revisionist Lo Jui-ching propagated the slavish idea of

sion was Chairman Mao, who in 1958 "clearly pointed out: 'I think it is entirely possible for some atom bombs and hydrogen bombs to be made in ten years' time.'" However, the article relates,

> from the very first day the Chinese people began making their own nuclear weapons, the U.S. imperialists and the Soviet revisionist leading clique tried in every way to undermine our efforts. They colluded with each other in viciously attacking us. The Soviet revisionist leading clique also tried to deceive us, saying, "China can rely on Soviet nuclear weapons and there is no need for you to make them." Its purpose was to bind the Chinese people hand and foot. It was a wild attempt to turn the great socialist China into a "docile tool" under its nuclear umbrella. When we saw through the sinister intentions of the Soviet revisionist ruling clique and exposed its true features of big-nation chauvinism, it unilaterally, in June 1959, tore up the Sino-Soviet agreement on new techniques. The following year, in an attempt to smother the development of the most advanced technologies and national economy of our country at one stroke, it went further: it tore up the economic and technical agreement between the two countries and withdrew all its experts.

The thought of Mao Tse-tung, however, divined the solution:

> Confronted by blockade and sabotage organized by the U.S. imperialists and the Soviet revisionist leading clique, in the absence

---

trailing behind others and going at a snail's pace, not trying to break new ground. They said: "While other countries are developing advanced, high-speed vessels, we should for the time being build ordinary, low-speed ones. We shouldn't try to finish all the work which should be left to our children and grandchildren." They viciously attacked the big leap forward, alleging that the shipbuilding industry had over-extended itself. They ordered it to slow down and make way for other projects.
It was at their instigation that the handful of capitalist roaders and bourgeois technical "authorities" insisted that China lacked experience and data for designing large vessels and that it was impossible to leap from building small and medium-sized coastal craft to manufacturing a 10,000-ton ocean-going freighter.

Although bourgeois technical authorities refused to believe in the wisdom of the masses, reflected for example in a complicated crankshaft which the foreigners maintained was faulty, the workers insisted during the Cultural Revolution that the crankshaft be tested again, with the result that it proved to be of good quality.

> The fierce struggle that developed around the building of the *Dong Feng* involved far more than just a single freighter; it concerned the future of China's shipbuilding and shipping industries as well as the direction which China's economic construction should take. It represented a struggle between the political lines of the proletariat and the bourgeoisie on the industrial front. In resisting Chairman Mao's instructions, suppressing the mass movement and trying to undermine the building of this freighter, China's Khrushchov and Co. were in fact aiming at restoring capitalism in China's shipbuilding and shipping industries.
> Their conspiracy fell through as this handful of Party people taking the capitalist road headed by China's Khrushchov were exposed and overthrown in the great proletarian cultural revolution.

of available technical data and scientific instruments and equipment, and of factories and laboratories, and with most of our research workers young people fresh from school, what could we do to gain in the shortest time the knowledge for the designing, making and testing of atom bombs? . . .

A sharp struggle unfolded between the proletarian revolutionary line represented by Chairman Mao and the Right opportunist line represented by China's Khrushchov [*sic*] over the question of whether our great mother-land should develop the most advanced branches of science and technology and whether China should take the road of self-reliance or depend on the Soviet revisionist leading clique in the development of nuclear weapons.

The handful of Party persons in authority taking the capitalist road headed by China's Khrushchov, who were scared out of their wits by the temporary internal economic difficulties, submitted to the pressure of the imperialists and revisionists. Working hand in glove with the Soviet revisionist ruling clique, these capitalist roaders frantically opposed Chairman Mao's proletarian revolutionary line. China's Khrushchov did his utmost to publicize the U.S.–Soviet "atomic stalemate." In a vain attempt to turn China into an appendage of Soviet revisionism, he advocated the dependence of China's national defences on Soviet atomic bombs and tried in a variety of ways to hamper our development of up-to-date science and technology.

Under the correct leadership and with the care and solicitude of Chairman Mao, his close comrade-in-arms Vice Chairman Lin Piao, and Premier Chou En-lai, the revolutionary masses and cadres kicked all the stumbling blocks out of their way and marched courageously forward in the teeth of difficulties.

To achieve this breakthrough in nuclear technology as quickly as possible, our great leader Chairman Mao issued a call to the entire Party and nation: Make great efforts in co-ordination to do this work well. On this order from Chairman Mao, workers, peasants, soldiers, academic circles and trade departments joined into one mighty force. Their song of triumph soared to the skies. On October 16, 1964, the first atomic bomb designed and built by the Chinese people was exploded successfully. The U.S. imperialists' and Soviet revisionists' policy of nuclear monopoly and blackmail and the liquidationism and slavishness of China's Khrushchov on the question of development of nuclear weapons went bankrupt. The revolutionary people of China and the world as a whole greeted with tremendous enthusiasm this great victory for Mao Tse-tung's thought.

Further, according to a report by New China News Agency on August 27, 1967, the opponents of Mao Tse-tung expressed confidence that China might receive military aid from the capitalist countries, if not from the USSR. This report was derived from meetings held at the Scientific and Technological Commission for National Defense and in scientific research institutes of the General Headquarters of the General Staff, of the General Logistics Department, and of the three services in Peking. It charged that Mao's enemies

> spread such capitulationist nonsense as "We can rely on the Soviet Union for long-range guided missiles" and "When it is getting dark in the East, it is getting bright in the West," meaning "We can buy some weapons from the capitalist countries" and so on. . . .
> They also pursued liquidationism in the field of national defense scientific research. On the one hand, they set up obstacles to restrict and strangle the development of national defense scientific research; on the other, they spread rumors and slanders dismissing achievements in that field. Worse still . . . they carried out a whole series of schemes such as deceiving the leadership above while suppressing functionaries below, forming cliques, recruiting turncoats and renegades, and using Khrushchev's method of surprise attack, with the aim of usurping the leadership of the national defense scientific research and of cutting down or dismantling research institutions.

Analysis of the Chinese weapons tests, beginning in October 1964, has provided additional bases for inferences about the nature of Soviet aid in the years before 1960. Taking into account the various ways of producing a nuclear device and the Atomic Energy Commission's analyses of the Chinese tests, scholars have concluded that Peking took a route different from that of the first four nuclear powers, which relied initially upon a plutonium bomb. Rather, China's first two tests exploded a bomb made from enriched uranium. The first stage of the enrichment process was almost certainly carried out in the gaseous diffusion plant in Lanchow; this concentration was probably taken a step further by an electromagnetic process. Because the gaseous diffusion plant, which has extremely complex valves and other equipment, resembles closely a Soviet model and has been known to exist for some years, it is believed to have been built with Russian aid. The electromagnetic process, on the other hand, may well have been developed by the Chinese from blueprints declassified by the United States in 1955 and by the Soviet Union in 1958. Had China wanted, she could have used her reactors to produce plutonium bombs, but that approach would have taken longer. Instead, she probably used her scarce electric resources in the electromagnetic process.[22] One additional possibility must also be considered, however—a method that could either complement or supplant the others: China may have perfected the gas centrifuge process for uranium separation, even though this approach has been explored but not mastered in the West. The 1967 article by the proletarian but scientific revolutionaries, cited earlier, suggests that Maoist ideology might in fact foster innovations of this kind. The writers declare:

> We cannot just take the beaten track traversed by other countries in the development of technology and trail behind them at a snail's

pace. We must break away from conventions and do our utmost to adopt advanced techniques in order to build our country into a powerful modern socialist state in not too long a historical period. This teaching of Chairman Mao's showed the way for our victorious advance and gave us tremendous new spiritual strength.

Soviet aid in building a gaseous diffusion plant must be regarded as a significant step in the development of China's war potential; but Peking could have justified its request for such a plant by arguments stressing its peaceful utilities, namely, for skirting the industrial difficulties involved in producing large quantities of very pure aluminum, graphite, and other reactor materials. Indeed, before Sino-Soviet relations became quite strained, Russian scientists boasted to Western colleagues about the progress in China's nuclear program being made by Soviet assistance. Whatever the extent and kind of aid, however, some Soviet officials have in retrospect indicated privately their regrets that it took place at all. (Several senior Soviet historians and disarmament analysts interviewed in 1967–68, on the other hand, denied that Moscow had given China nuclear aid that could be of military significance. They averred that Soviet assistance was basically of the same type as that provided to East European countries. While their remarks could have been restrained by discretion, these scholars seemed unaware of the Chinese charges about the 1957–59 pact or of any other evidence suggesting that atoms for war as well as for peace had been given to China. If their ignorance was genuine, it might be a comment on the extent to which the Chinese side of the polemics has been restricted in the USSR—restricted to exclude even men with access to those Western publications which documented the Chinese charges rather fully. On the other hand, a formerly high placed Soviet official dealing with science and technology has testified that the alleged pact did exist 1957–59, and that he knew personally at least one of the Soviet physicists sent to China to take part in its implementation.)

SOVIET INTEREST IN A NUCLEAR TEST BAN

The second key element in this Sino-Soviet tangle is Moscow's apparent interest in negotiating a nuclear test ban with the West—an interest, surprisingly enough, echoed and approved in many Chinese declaratory statements in 1957–58. It appears that as early as 1956–57 the Kremlin came to believe that a test ban would be useful to its overall military and political objectives, and, what is more, would be attainable in the not-too-distant future. Two factors led Moscow to the assessment that a test ban, or at least a test moratorium, would enhance its strategic posture vis-à-vis the West. First, since Soviet rockets could carry larger payloads into space than U.S., a test ban would be useful in inhibiting American efforts to miniaturize warheads. Second, a test ban could cramp U.S. plans to develop tactical nuclear weapons of limited explosive yield, minimum radiation effects, and high mobility. Both these objectives could be achieved by a moratorium, which Moscow initiated after concluding a test series in March 1958 and in which Washington and London concurred later that year.[23] But the Kremlin's negotiating record suggests a considerable Soviet interest in going beyond a moratorium to a formal treaty banning all nuclear tests (including those underground), provided intrusion by foreign inspectors could be kept to a low level.

Soviet interest in a nuclear test ban as a separate measure was hinted at for the first time in Moscow's disarmament proposals of May 10, 1955. In China's view, however, Moscow's line altered most significantly in February 1956 when Khrushchev told the Twentieth Congress of the CPSU that Russia would stop testing if other nuclear powers followed suit, adding that "such measures could pave the way of agreement on other more intricate aspects of disarmament." In this manner, Peking has argued, Khrushchev "divorced the cessation of nuclear tests from the question of disarmament."[24] The First Secretary's lead seemed to affect Soviet diplomacy almost immediately, as Gromyko proposed a ban on hydrogen weapons tests as a partial measure which could be implemented without inspection. And in January 1957 Moscow introduced a resolution in the U.N. General Assembly calling for a separate ban on the testing of nuclear weapons. In March 1957 Soviet diplomacy portrayed a test ban as a way of obstructing the spread of nuclear weapons to additional powers. By mid-July the Soviet Union had accepted the Western view on the need for on-site inspection of a test ban. In September 1957—less than a month before the Sino-Soviet defense technology treaty —Moscow proposed in the United Nations that the nuclear powers agree "not to allow the installation of any military units or any types of atomic or hydrogen weapons beyond their national frontiers and not to place these weapons at the disposal of any other States or commands of military blocs."

While this proposal could have been written off as a gambit to complicate NATO policy, the Kremlin showed a more serious view in 1958 when it agreed to hold technical talks with Western experts on the requirements for policing a nuclear test ban. (The resultant agreement called for a worldwide network of test stations, eight of them on Chinese territory.) Soviet acceptance of a British compromise suggestion on the requirements for inspection led Prime Minister Macmillan to predict in

May 1959 that he expected a nuclear test ban treaty to be signed within several months.[25] The Chinese, as Morton Halperin has suggested, may well have been prompted by these developments to reopen discussion with the Soviets about the price the Russians were prepared to pay to ensure Chinese adherence to the test ban treaty.[26]

Various unresolved technical and political issues thwarted agreement in 1959, but the gap between the Western and Soviet positions became considerably narrowed at several junctions during 1960 and 1961. A comprehensive test ban proved unattainable because Western proposals required more extensive controls than Moscow would allow.[27] But both sides proved willing for a time to consider a compromise agreement involving a limited test ban accompanied by a moratorium on underground testing, during which time control systems were expected to be improved so that seismic disturbances could be detected and identified with minimal or no intrusion. The West, however, tended to favor a specific and short-term moratorium, while Moscow preferred one of indefinite or longer duration. On May 3, 1960, for example, the Soviet Union proposed a limited ban with a five-or four-year moratorium, but the West on September 27, 1960, advocated a moratorium of 27 months and on March 21, 1961, a moratorium of three years.[28] After the collapse of the Paris Summit Conference in May 1960, however, political conditions were not favorable to an agreement.

More important, by late 1960-early 1961 the Soviet Union was confronted by a strategic situation quite different from that of 1957–60. Instead of an apparent missile gap in Russia's favor, the East-West balance was being radically and quickly altered by the large number of nuclear delivery systems produced and deployed by the United States, a situation that led Moscow in 1961 to renew atomic testing in the atmosphere. By 1963, however, each side had some ground to claim that a limited test ban was in its own favor: The United States could point to its numerical superiority in strategic delivery systems, while Moscow could refer to its experience in testing giant warheads and its booster capacity to lift such heavy payloads.[29] Despite these perturbations of the early 1960s, however, the fact remains that Moscow showed a serious interest in negotiating a nuclear test ban treaty in the period 1957 to 1960 or 1961.

THE TEST BAN AND SINO-SOVIET RELATIONS

How does one square the evidence of Soviet interest in a test ban as early as 1957 with the Soviet-Chinese defense technology pact of that year? What was the Chinese attitude to indications of Russian interest in a test ban? Did the Soviet Union think that Peking could be persuaded or perhaps pressured to adhere to such a ban?

A case can be made from the public record for the thesis that China supported Soviet policy on a nuclear test ban in 1957–58. A number of statements by Russian diplomats indicated their confidence that Peking would sign a test ban if one were agreed to by the three nuclear powers. China, for her part, gave declaratory support to a number of Soviet initiatives in this period, including the Russian position on a moratorium. On August 31, 1958, a Chinese statement declared that Washington and London should suspend all tests because "the experts at Geneva have found detection possible." Peking added that an "agreement must be negotiated for a permanent ban on the testing of all atomic and hydrogen weapons by all powers." (To be sure, Peking was also quick to support Moscow's temporary resumption of testing in 1958 in view of the West's refusal to suspend testing at the same time Russia did.)[30]

Chinese statements of this kind may of course be interpreted in various ways. Manifest Sino-Soviet harmony on the test ban issue tends to support the theory that Russia's nuclear aid was premised on Chinese acceptance of a test ban. But reasons will be given below, in the discussion of this theory, for not taking at face value the declarations of either side.

In any event, toward the end of 1958 the residue of mutual trust between Moscow and Peking seemed to dissipate. On December 4, 1958, Soviet delegate Tsarapkin objected to the Western position that the proposed test ban being drafted include an article on the accession of other parties. He warned: "You wish to liberate a genie from a bottle whom you will not be able to put back in the bottle and keep under control." Tsarapkin in the preceding weeks had argued that the test ban and control system should be limited to the three powers and that the moral and political force arising from their agreement would be adequate to prevent tests by other states. Shortly afterwards, on January 12, 1959, he modified this position to the extent that a provision on accession was possible so long as the operation of the treaty with respect to the three original parties was not linked to the accession of other states.[31] Still, in June 1959—about a week before Moscow is supposed to have torn up the defense technology pact—a Soviet radio broadcast to North America assailed the "Washington claim" that the test ban under negotiation could not be trusted because China would not be a signatory. The broadcast accused Washington of persisting in this refusal "in order to have an excuse for getting out of all kinds of international agreements."[32]

Sino-Soviet disagreement about the desirability of China's nuclear program seems to have been reflected in the divergent approaches each side took to the question of an Asian atom-free zone.[33] On several occasions in 1958 Peking indicated a reserved and qualified interest in the idea of an atom-free zone in the Far East.[34] But Peking took umbrage at Khrushchev's emphatic remarks on the subject to the Twenty-first CPSU Congress on January 27, 1959. He gave only perfunctory approval of the Rapacki proposals for an atom-free zone and Central European disengagement, but Khrushchev asserted that a "zone of peace, above all, an atom-free zone, can and must be created in the Far East and the entire Pacific basin area."[35] From January to mid-April 1959, Chinese spokesmen either ignored, distorted, or gave qualified support to Soviet advocacy of a nuclear-free Far East. Even this qualified support may have been partially spurred by pressure from the Japanese and Korean Communist Parties and by a common anxiety about increased deployment of U.S. nuclear weapons in the Far East. The most restricted Chinese endorsement of the denuclearized zone concept came on April 18, 1959, when Chou En-lai advocated an area of peace, free of atomic weapons, "throughout the whole of East Asia and the Pacific regions"—an implication that only part of China would be included,[36] and hardly Sinkiang—where nuclear energy facilities are known to be located.

The timing and site of renewed Soviet advocacy of a nuclear-free zone of peace in the Balkans may also have been related to the emerging Sino-Soviet rift.[37] Khrushchev supported such a zone in a May 26, 1959 speech in Tirana—two days before Chinese Defense Minister P'eng Teh-huai arrived there. Khrushchev warned that the Soviet Union might establish missile bases in Albania if the West set up bases in Italy and Greece. This may have been a hint that Moscow would do no more for Peking than establish Soviet bases to defend China in case U.S. rockets were emplaced, for example, in Japan. A speech by P'eng on May 31 approved Khrushchev's idea of a peace zone in the Balkans, but suggested that a Western attack on Albania would provoke a world war.[38]

It appears that the Soviet refusal to give China a sample atomic bomb was one of a series of incidents that made the year 1959 a watershed in Sino-Soviet relations, deepening and hardening the rift so that it was virtually irreparable without a radical change of leadership in Moscow or Peking. The positions taken by the Twenty-first Soviet Party Congress in February appeared to rebuff Peking on two counts: first, with their stress on peaceful coexistence, and second, by claims that the Soviet Union was entering a period of rapid building of the foundations of communism. More important, Soviet dissatisfaction with the leftward turn in Peking coincided with similar feeling by Defense Minister P'eng Teh-huai; and strong evidence suggests that Khrushchev backed P'eng in a challenge to

Mao's authority (which was put down at the Lushan plenum in July and August 1959).[39] To make matters worse, the Soviet Government declared its neutrality in the Chinese-Indian border clashes in September, and Khrushchev journeyed from Camp David to Peking to campaign for a peaceful solution of the Formosan Straits problem.[40]

The economic backdrop to these developments also underscored the importance of 1959 as a turning point. As Griffith has summarized the situation:

> From 1955 to 1956 the Chinese began to repay their debts by substantially increasing their deliveries, whereas the Soviets reduced their exports. . . . Soviet exports to China thus declined markedly from 1956 through 1958, while Soviet-Indian trade jumped more than 500 percent in 1956 and nearly doubled again by 1958. Similarly, the temporary upsurge of Soviet exports to China during 1959 and 1960 again coincided with a simultaneous slump in exports to India.[41]

Finally, after reaching its highest total volume in 1959, Sino-Soviet trade rapidly dwindled,—to such a degree, in fact, that the turnover was less in 1962 than it had been in 1951. A more than 50 percent decline in Soviet exports to China during 1961 was paralleled by a near doubling of exports to India.

Following these developments the Chinese began increasingly to criticize Moscow's pursuit of East-West détente and disarmament. In February 1960 the magazine *China Youth* called disarmament an "impractical fantasy," since the imperialists would never disarm themselves. The Chinese observer at a Warsaw Pact conference in February insisted that since the United States wanted an arms race, "the struggle for general disarmament is a long-term complicated struggle between us and imperialism."[42] In April 1960 came the Chinese broadside entitled "Long Live Leninism!" Imperialism had not changed since Lenin's day, it was asserted, and an attempt to negotiate disarmament or a relaxation of tensions would mislead the people.[43] The U-2 incident seemed somewhat to vindicate the Chinese image of the West. But Moscow continued in the following months to uphold its view that some members of Western "ruling circles" took a sober and reasonable approach to East-West relations. Khrushchev now recalled Soviet specialists from China, sharply reduced Soviet trade with China, and reportedly tried to overthrow the Albanian leadership.

In January 1960 the Chinese Government made explicit that it would not be bound by decisions of other states on arms control. It declared:

> Any international agreement concerning disarmament, without formal participation of the People's Republic of China and the signature of its delegate, cannot of course have any binding force on her.[44]

This view was expressed at a time when the Soviet Union had begun to emphasize general and complete disarmament, but the warning would doubtless apply to the test ban negotiations as well.

PARTS OF A PUZZLE

This review indicates that the sixth argument outlined earlier does not hold up. There really is a serious puzzle regarding Soviet intentions and behavior toward China and the West during the years 1955–60. Some parts of the puzzle are still missing, so that a faithful reconstruction cannot be guaranteed. It must be admitted that the publicly available facts cannot entirely refute those who deny the very existence of what we take to be a contradiction in Soviet policy. On balance, however, strong evidence indicates a conflict if not a contradiction in the Kremlin's position.

To summarize, we have the judgment of official Washington that Soviet nuclear assistance to China continued until 1960; we have the fact of a gaseous diffusion plant and several reactors in China which the Chinese could hardly have started by themselves from scratch. Such aid, especially on the diffusion plant, could by no stretch of the imagination be regarded as minor; nor could it be deemed merely aid on "peaceful uses," since it could yield weapons grade fissionable material. On the other hand, the record does not definitely establish the extent of Russia's voluntary contribution to the Chinese plant. To a degree, the entire argument seems to rest on the assumption that China was technically incapable of building such a plant with its complex pumps and other equipment without external assistance. The plant follows closely a Soviet design; but it is at least conceivable that the blueprints were pirated, and that the Chinese produced a plant which neither Soviet nor Western analysts expected them to complete by their own efforts. Despite these uncertainties, it seems likely that Russia, probably voluntarily, provided aid during the 1957–59 period that proved sufficient to give a large boost to the Chinese indigenous production program.

It seems clear also that the Soviet Government was in fact pushing for a nuclear test ban treaty as early as 1956–57. This proposition is borne out by the facts of Soviet negotiating behavior and by interviews with U.S. diplomats involved in those negotiations, even years after the events in question. To be sure, no absolute proof of Russia's intentions is possible in that no test ban treaty was actually signed until 1963. But this does not gainsay the possibility or refute the evidence that in 1957 Khrushchev believed a test ban not only to be useful to Soviet interests but attainable in a short span.

II
Five Hypotheses, Rational and Behavioral

The preceding chapter indicates there is reasonable ground for holding that Moscow's policies in 1955–60 embodied one or more fundamental riddles. Five major theories have attempted to unravel these enigmas. Before discussing the differences between the theories, however, we should note several points of agreement among them. Most of the theories would concede that Moscow's assistance to Peking was directed in part toward controlling China's military development. Second, most of them agree that whatever commitment Moscow made in October 1957 reflected the Kremlin's desire to obtain Chinese assistance at the November meeting of ruling Communist and Workers Parties. A third point of general agreement is the acceptance of the premise that the Soviet leadership wanted a test ban, but there is disagreement as to whether assistance to China's nuclear program would give Moscow greater leverage for bringing Peking into such a treaty.

A WARSAW PACT FOR THE FAR EAST

The first theory postulates that Moscow's nuclear aid commitment formed part of a larger strategy aimed at establishing a kind of Warsaw Pact arrangement in the Far East.[1] The accord reached on October 15, 1957, may have pledged Soviet assistance to China's indigenous nuclear program, but this undertaking was meant to give Russia a better bargaining position in subsequent negotiations spelling out the details of Soviet rights as well as obligations in China. This theory, it should be noted, places great emphasis on Russia's interest in controlling China's military development through what amounted to on-site inspection and direction. But it also harmonizes with the assumption that Khrushchev wished to make Russia a truly global power in the wake of the first ICBM and sputnik launchings. On a less grandiose scale, however, this theory also suggests that Moscow wished to counter the introduction of U.S. tactical nuclear weapons in Europe by threatening more directly American power in the Pacific. Another variant of the theory suggests that Moscow offered China joint military arrangements as a sop, after refusing Peking's demand for independent control of nuclear weapons.

That Russia did in fact make far-ranging proposals to Peking is certain. The Chinese declared in 1963 that "in 1958 the leadership of the CPSU put forward unreasonable demands designed to put China under Soviet military control."[2] A Chinese spokesman in 1964 spelled out that Russia had tried to rule China by proposing in April 1958 a joint Sino-Soviet fleet and construction of a long-range radar station on the Chinese mainland.[3] Other analysts have suggested that Moscow may have proposed integrated air defense arrangements; joint control of nuclear weapons and advanced delivery systems on Chinese territory; Soviet submarine bases; mutual landing rights in time of war; a jointly controlled broadcasting station.[4] At least some military leaders in both countries may have favored such arrangements. Chinese Defense Minister P'eng Teh-huai, purged in August 1959, may have argued for such a close link with Moscow.[5]

A debate among Chinese strategists in early 1958 over the desirability of such reliance upon Soviet aid seems to have been resolved in February, probably in accord with the views of Mao Tse-tung,[6] with the upshot that Russia's "unreasonable demands were rightly and firmly rejected by the Chinese Government."[7] Perhaps to make its offer more attractive, however, Moscow continued its proposals until April, suggesting ever broader fields of cooperation. China's rejection of the Soviet offer coincided with adoption of the Great Leap Forward program, the underlying principle of which was the feasibility of rapid bootstrap development. Mao may well have reasoned that to accept the Soviet proposals would have meant a return to the extraterritorial concessions for foreigners that had violated China's sovereignty for a century before the last joint enterprises were eliminated in late 1954.

In addition to Chinese documents recording the Soviet proposals, there is substantial evidence that Moscow did in fact give vital assistance to China's missile program from the mid- to late-1950s, the Russians delivering short- and medium-range missiles as well as helping to build production facilities. Large numbers of Soviet military experts traveled to China in November 1957. Among other activities, they helped in setting up a missile test range in northwest China. Some of these personnel were primarily engineers and weapons designers; others were basically electronics experts. Khrushchev himself told Averell Harriman on June 23, 1959 (two days after Moscow allegedly "tore up" the 1957 defense pact) that Soviet rockets had been shipped to China, although he did not specify that they had been put under exclusive Chinese control.[8] In 1961, however, Khrushchev explained that no nuclear warheads or long-range missiles were stationed outside Soviet territory except "perhaps in East Germany."[9]

Soviet participation in the Chinese rocket program may have been stepped up as part of the October 1957 agreement. Some scholars have argued that the October pact dealt exclusively with missiles, and that it was a subsequent dispute over control of the warheads that touched off the disagreements of 1958 and 1959, leading in turn to ideological bickering over theoretical issues of war and peace.

Without denying Soviet involvement in the Chinese missile program or Moscow's attempts to gain bases and controls in establishing bases and other controls in China, it still seems doubtful that these programs were linked to Moscow's nuclear aid program in the manner suggested by the theory under consideration. First, it appears unlikely *a priori* that Moscow would undertake a significant program of assistance to China's nuclear capability on the gamble that this would facilitate a joint program of military cooperation the details of which were still to be arranged. Second, we know *a posteriori* that the sharing arrangements discussed by Soviet and Chinese leaders were definitely and vigorously rejected by Peking in spring 1958, while Soviet nuclear aid continued until 1959 or 1960.

It may very well be true, however, that Moscow offered nuclear assistance to China in the hope that it could better control China's military development through Russian personnel involved in overseeing and contributing to Peking's own nuclear capability. Such "controls," it turned out, proved abortive in the extreme.

THE CONDITION FOR CHINESE ADHERENCE TO A TEST BAN

A second view is that Soviet nuclear assistance to China was conditioned upon an understanding that Peking would support Russia's test ban policy and sign the treaty when it was reached.[10] This argument rests in large part upon the declaratory policies of the Soviet and Chinese governments in 1957–58. Moscow seemed publicly confident that Peking would sign a treaty; and Chinese statements backed Russia's disarma-

ment diplomacy to the extent of denouncing the United States for attempting to block progress toward a test ban by associating it with other
disarmament issues.

This thesis assumes a considerable rapport between Soviet and
Chinese planners on the desirability and likelihood of achieving a test
ban—a degree of consensus that would be most surprising considering
the different stages and interests of the two countries in military, political, and economic affairs. Most problematic, however, is the assumption
that the Soviet Union and Peking would agree to develop China's own
nuclear production capability as the *quid pro quo* for Chinese signature
of a test ban. If the ban were achieved, Peking's atomic program would
come to naught, for its products could not be tested (or demonstrated).
In that case the price for China's signature would seem impossible to
fulfill: either it would be a complete nuclear arsenal handed over without
any Soviet control—a step that would be anathema to Moscow; or it
would mean a joint arsenal—a proposition turned down by Peking in
1958.

How do we account then for the apparent confidence of Soviet negotiators and the diplomatic support given them by Peking? First of all,
both sides sought to paper over their disputes on a number of issues so as
to preserve a common front vis-à-vis the West. They did this so successfully that a study by a Nationalist Chinese professor has found considerable agreement in the views of Peking and Moscow on a whole range of
arms control issues even up to late 1962.[11]

Second, the attitudes of the Soviet and Chinese leaders may have been
shaped in part by the principles of selective perception and denial.[12] Both
sides may have been whistling in the dark; to say the least, they probably
had quite different perceptions of the state of negotiations on a nuclear
test ban. At any rate, they probably deemed it wiser to wait to see
whether a test ban treaty were signed before drawing swords over the
event. The Soviets would naturally prefer not to complicate the negotiations by admitting the need for a concern over Chinese participation.
They would prefer to obtain a tripartite treaty first and then present it to
China as a *fait accompli*. It is notable that many indications of Russian
confidence about Chinese adherence to a test ban are clustered in the
spring and summer of 1957—prior to the defense technology pact.[13]

As for the Chinese, they probably saw the chances of such a treaty as
much lower than those calculated by Moscow. If so, the record shows,
Peking's estimate was also more realistic than Moscow's. Furthermore,
the Chinese may have realized that continuation of Soviet support—
economic as well as military—could be better assured through Chinese
propaganda in favor of Soviet disarmament schemes. Particularly if a test

ban were unlikely to be achieved, it would cost China little to approve the principle of such a treaty. Ostensible Chinese backing for the Soviet moratorium proposal may have derived from the premise that the three nuclear powers would never reach the stage where all were willing to suspend tests at the same time. Peking showed a conspicuous alacrity in backing the resumption of Soviet tests in the fall of 1958 at a time when the West was ready for a moratorium.[14] As soon as the Soviet tests halted and a *de facto* tripartite suspension had begun, the signs of Sino-Soviet disharmony and mutual distrust began to mount.*

Finally, in contrast to manifest Sino-Soviet attitudes in 1957–58, we have a Chinese statement in 1963 indicating serious disagreement between Moscow and Peking as early as 1956.

> From 1946 to 1956, the Soviet Government insisted on the complete prohibition of nuclear weapons. They were correct then and we firmly supported them. In his summary report to the 20th Congress of the Communist Party of the Soviet Union in 1956, the Soviet leader divorced the cessation of nuclear tests from the question of disarmament. Subsequently, they were wrong on certain issues and correct on others, and we supported them in all their correct views. But on July 25, 1963, they went altogether wrong, and it is quite natural that we should resolutely criticize them.[15]

No other documents are available to support this historical retrospection, but the broad picture painted by the Chinese statement is quite plausible and parallels other Chinese grievances dating from the Twenty-second Congress of the CPSU.

A SOVIET DOUBLE GAME

In contrast to the temporary Sino-Soviet harmony postulated by the second theory, a third viewpoint argues that Moscow played a double game, one that entailed huge risks for large gains, one that may or may

* The USSR renounced further testing on March 31, 1958, but the United States and United Kingdom proceeded with a series of tests, terminated however by a proposal by President Eisenhower on August 22 for a tripartite suspension of nuclear testing. The USSR denounced this proposal on October 30, and carried out two tests of relatively unsophisticated weapons on November 1 and 3. From that date until Moscow resumed testing in August 1961 a de facto moratorium on all nuclear testing seemed to prevail, except for the French tests inaugurated in 1960. (See Harold Karan Jacobson and Eric Stein, *Diplomats, Scientists and Politicians: The United States and the Test Ban Negotiations* [Ann Arbor: University of Michigan Press, 1966], pp. 119–120.) Another writer has argued, without providing evidence, that "the Defense Department finally recognized that clandestine testing probably had been occurring in the Soviet Union." (See Earl H. Voss, *Nuclear Ambush: The Test Ban Trap* [Chicago: Henry Regnery, 1963], p. 512.)

not have been completely thought through by Moscow in advance, and one that ended in the worst of several possible worlds.[16]

In 1957, however, Moscow may have conceived of this strategy as a way of achieving the best of two available worlds: maintenance of communist solidarity under Soviet leadership, and maintenance of Soviet strategic interests both on the Eastern as well as on the Western front. In late 1957 the Khrushchev regime could deal with Peking from a position of great strength in most respects. The "anti-party" group challenging the First Secretary had been removed in June, after which Moscow intensified its formal commitment to "peaceful coexistence,"[17] and Zhukov went into political oblivion in October. In August the Soviet Union had made the world's first successful firing of an ICBM and followed this feat in October by Sputnik I. The main trouble spot on the Kremlin's horizon, however, was Eastern Europe. Although ferment there had diminished since 1956, the Kremlin still needed Peking's assistance to bring the champions of polycentrism into line at the November 1957 Moscow Conference of ruling Communist and Workers Parties.[18]

If, as seems likely, China requested more Soviet aid for her nuclear program, four considerations must have been weighed by Moscow's leadership: first, the communist world was in disarray, the Kremlin's leadership increasingly questioned, especially in Eastern Europe; second, China had helped to reduce this disorder and could continue to do so; third, Soviet military force was without peer in the bloc and in some respects was equal to or superior to the West's; and fourth, a nuclear test ban might be advantageous to Moscow for various strategic, political, and economic reasons. Two scenarios followed. *If* Moscow refused to aid China's nuclear program, disorder in the communist world would increase; China might in any case be able herself to make a bomb by the late 1960s. *If* Russia did aid China, Peking could be counted on to bolster Moscow's role in international communism. A Chinese nuclear force would not endanger Russia for the foreseeable future, but would add to the overall strength of communist military froces.[19]

Reasoning along these lines might have led the Kremlin to go to great lengths to purchase Mao Tse-tung's support at the Moscow Conference. When the East and West European Party leaders arrived there, expecting to find Chinese support for polycentrism, they were startled to find that Mao had already aligned with Khrushchev and that the Chinese leader personally championed the formula "the socialist camp headed by the Soviet Union." To be sure, Peking and Moscow were not in idyllic harmony at the conference. The phraseology suggested by China may not even have been to Moscow's liking. Mao was quoted as saying that every snake must have a head, and the Chinese line was probably more anti-Yugoslav than pro-Soviet. Nevertheless, the thrust of China's stand at the conference was to support Russia against the sallies of the Kadars, Gomulkas, and Togliattis seeking a justification for greater autonomy within the movement. This unexpected Chinese posture, it seems safe to presume, stemmed in considerable measure from Peking's satisfaction with the secret Sino-Soviet pact of October 15, 1957. Khrushchev benefited greatly from Mao's support and would have been willing to pay a substantial price—or at least to extend a pledge, the fulfillment of which he could determine over time.

The major type of nuclear aid provided to China by Moscow was assistance to the country's production facilities, including not only reactors but a gaseous diffusion plant, the need for which could be rationalized under "atoms for peace" even though it had tremendous military potential as well.[20] Probably the October 1957 pact provided for an increase in Soviet assistance of this kind. The terms of the agreement may have been general, allowing the Russians a certain leeway in the timing and specific nature of their deliveries.[21] Certainly the pact did not obligate Russia to provide a sample bomb, as some have suggested. But it may have called for the construction of the gaseous diffusion plant in Lanchow, although the pace of this and other possible commitments could have been left to clarification in further negotiations on the basis of experience.

The other fork in Moscow's two-pronged strategy concerned the nuclear test ban negotiations. If a treaty were signed, it might mean that China's own program would not reach fruition. Precisely how a test ban treaty would terminate the Chinese program is not clear, but a number of alternative courses are plausible: (1) Russia could claim that the treaty prohibited her from rendering further aid to China's program. Without Soviet assistance, it may have been supposed, China could not carry her program to fruition. (2) China might be coerced to sign the treaty. Once she had signed the treaty, she would have to break it in order to test her own atomic product. (3) Faced with a *fait accompli*, China might herself volunteer to sign the pact, especially if she obtained some economic, political, or military benefits in exchange. This last *scenario* is not identical with the theory that posits a Sino-Soviet understanding in 1957 that the Russian aid program was conditional upon Chinese support for a test ban. The essential difference is that the image suggested here depicts Peking making the most of a bad deal that it had not anticipated, whereas the other view presumes China would willingly and knowingly step into such a trap.

THE KREMLIN DIVIDED

Whereas the three foregoing explanations seek to find a master plan in Kremlin strategy, a fourth and fifth hypothesis portray Soviet actions as lacking internal logic. The fourth argument holds that the Soviet leadership was itself divided: one faction wanting to aid China, despite the long-run risks involved; the other, for military and/or political reasons, seeking a test ban and better relations with the West. The proponents of aiding China, in addition to being concerned with promoting ideological solidarity, may have sought to build up a second communist nuclear power to balance off British and French nuclear capabilities in the West. Parity of representation, in the 1950s, was ostensibly an important Soviet concern.[22]

The fundamental weakness in this hypothesis is that the Sino-Soviet pact of October 1957 was signed at a moment when Khrushchev's power was at its zenith. In June 1957 the Central Committee had sided with him against the "anti-party group" in the Presidium, and the latter group was replaced by men more to the First Secretary's liking.[23] Marshal Zhukov was replaced in October 1957.[24] Although his ouster did not come until March 1958, Premier Bulganin in late 1957 was in no position to lead any opposition to Khrushchev. Finally, although some Soviet leaders may be notably anti-Chinese,[25] the unfolding of the Sino-Soviet dispute has not revealed any important Soviet leaders as being pro-Chinese, especially if this would have meant opposing the current line of the CPSU.

Another more plausible version of this argument is that the Soviet aid program was not clearly conceived, or that its implications either were not known or were not adequately conveyed to the Kremlin leadership. This interpretation could be based in part on facts cited by Arnold Kramish in a review of *Sino-Soviet Relations and Arms Control* published in *Survival* (December 1967). Kramish reiterates that 1957 was

> a critical year, in the Soviet Union at least, for a reorganization of whatever topics came under the heading of "new technology." It was in that year that the "Committee for New Technology" was replaced by the "State Scientific Technical Committee." It was also a critical year for the reorganization of the Soviet nuclear weapons programme.

Nevertheless, it seems most likely that Russian and Chinese experts alike understood that Soviet aid had important military potential even if its precise significance was not appreciated, and that this information was transmitted to the highest political leaders, who weighed its bargaining importance in considering the defense technology pact.

SUBJECTIVISM

A fifth theory takes us back to the warning against excessive reliance upon retrospective analysis regarding the logic of the situation.[26] Khrushchev and his associates may not have had a master plan, but may rather have muddled through. Such a possibility runs counter to the Marxist-Leninist emphasis on analyzing objective trends so as to anticipate and cooperate with the wave of history. But Khrushchev's personal disposition may have been much more intuitional than rational. At any rate, like many politicians, he may have preferred to concentrate on immediate rather than on distant problems. As Edward Crankshaw has written, Khrushchev

> did not see the insuperable contradictions latent in all his policies. It is to be questioned whether he ever saw them. His mind was agile to a degree, strong, and even supple; but it was not lucid and it was not subtle. Like the minds of many politicians, it was not creative and it was the reverse of contemplative. It was essentially a mind swift in reaction to exterior pressures and stimuli, and when the pressures and stimuli were contradictory, as frequently they were, his reactions were contradictory too.[27]

Khrushchev's inclination, therefore, may have been to extend China military aid without considering the consequence. Or, assuming that he did endorse a double game strategy, he may have dismissed the problem of how to get China to abide by a test ban once it had been signed, preferring to meet that problem when it arose.

Alternatively, it is possible to accept one of the three theories that posit a rational plan, but with the qualification that it was ill-conceived and/or executed. Such a view would amount to a synthesis of the logic-of-the-situation approach and an emphasis on traditional behavior patterns.

THE MIX: LOGIC AND TEMPERAMENT

Of the five explanations presented, a composite of the third and the fifth seems most plausible. The available facts suggest that the Kremlin played a kind of double game. Keeping several alternatives open simultaneously, Moscow appears to have stalled for time, taking some of the edge off Peking's nuclear desires while exploring an arrangement with the West that would prohibit further nuclear testing before the Chinese program could get off the ground.[28] This interpretation assumes that Moscow believed a test ban to be useful not only in terms of the Soviet strategic position vis-à-vis the West, but also attainable within a span of years prior to the time China could test atomic weapons.[29]

But the evidence summarized here fails to give a coherent picture. On the one hand, we are confronted with the fact of Soviet aid sufficient to help build a gaseous diffusion plant from which China could eventually produce weapons-grade uranium. On the other hand, we have signs that Moscow was stalling[30] and that Peking felt impelled as early as mid-1958 to renounce reliance upon the Soviet Union for the modernization of China's strategic capabilities. On balance, it appears most likely that the October 1957 pact dealt primarily with plans for Soviet aid to China's research and development program in atomic energy. At virtually the same time, however, negotiations were under way also for stationing of Soviet forces and equipment in China. The Kremlin was therefore offering both long-range nuclear assistance and immediate military support of a conventional variety. Moscow may even have conditioned—at least in its own mind—the former upon the latter.

More generally, however, the Kremlin probably encountered great difficulty in deciding what minimum commitment to make to China's nuclear program, given the contradictory risks in building up a potential enemy and antagonizing an ally. Such a conflict may have impelled Moscow to temporize from the mid- to the late 1950s. The October 1957 agreement, if it were general in tone, may have facilitated such temporization. Although it probably committed the Soviets in principle to increasing their aid to China's own nuclear program, it may have left unspecified the nature of the technical data to be made available to China, perhaps leaving the substance and the timetable to be ironed out in subsequent parleys. It may well have been the very issues left unresolved by the agreement, perhaps the timetable for Soviet deliveries, that ultimately served as a focal point for the breakdown of the pact. Thus, Moscow's denunciation of the pact in 1959 could have been provoked by Chinese demands for more aid at a quicker rate. The Chinese anxieties naturally mounted as a test ban treaty began to look more imminent and as Khrushchev intensified his campaign to appeal to "sober-minded" leaders in the West.

It is not clear that Moscow entered the pact with the intention of reneging, but contradictory developments may have served to make the Kremlin somewhat amenable to Chinese influence in 1956–57 and then to become more resistant by 1958–59. Once Khrushchev had the November 1957 Moscow Declaration ode to Soviet hegemony in his pocket, his dependence on Mao's good wishes diminished, although it by no means disappeared. Khrushchev's sense that Moscow could afford to lower its payments for Chinese support was probably strengthened by public tribute to an alleged missile gap in Russia's favor. Equally important, the Soviet leadership probably became more wary of Peking precisely because the Chinese appeared to draw more radical conclusions from Soviet space and strategic successes than did the Kremlin.[31] For Mao Tse-tung the ICBM test meant that the balance of forces now favored in an absolute sense the communist camp: the East wind was prevailing over the West wind. Soviet statements, on the other hand, averred only that the balance had shifted relatively to favor the communist bloc. The evidence suggested that Mao, convinced that the overall strength of socialism outweighed that of imperialism, believed the bloc "could now pursue a policy of 'brinkmanship' in selected areas under the cover of the Soviet nuclear shield."[32] Thus it was hardly accidental that Soviet spokesmen began in the fall of 1957 to warn of the dangers of broad escalation from local military conflicts.[33]

From his base of general strength Khrushchev did not need to look kindly on the independent course manifested in China's more forward strategy toward imperialism, the Formosa regime and, domestically, in the economic and ideological innovations of the Great Leap Forward program. All these considerations would lead the Kremlin to caution in implementing whatever nuclear aid commitment it had made in 1957 either because Moscow still hoped to tame the left deviation in Peking or because the Soviets feared an inexorable break with the colossus to the east. Significantly, one of the most authoritative Soviet statements has pointed to 1958 as the beginning year of the Sino-Soviet rift.[34]

On balance it appears that Moscow's nuclear aid program was short-sighted and poorly thought through. If its purpose had been to keep Peking as an ally, Moscow should have been prepared to live with a Chinese nuclear capability even though it could in time endanger Soviet interests and security. Since Moscow appears to have feared this long-term contingency, the Soviet leaders should never have deviated from the precedent established in Eastern Europe of not providing, even to allies, nuclear assistance of military value. If Moscow were playing a double game, as suggested above, it should have been more ready (1) to make concessions to reach a formal test ban treaty with the West at an early date, even if extensive on-site inspection were required; and (2) to work jointly with the West to pressure China and other non-nuclear powers to abide by the test ban and to come to a general agreement on non-dissemination. The irrationality of Moscow's course may, of course, be more obvious as a matter of hindsight.[35] The Kremlin may have taken the position that it could cross the various bridges as it came to them. In the still confident mood of the middle and late 1950s the Soviet leaders may have felt that it was superfluous to make decisions that would alienate China in the near future or that would open Soviet territory to extensive international inspection.

Finally, internal opposition to either or both courses—estranging China and/or permitting inspection—may have been sufficiently strong to deter Khrushchev from attempting to implement either one.[36] It seems unlikely, however, that the contradictions in Moscow's nuclear policy derived fundamentally from the existence of a pro- and an anti-Chinese group in the Kremlin. The defense technology pact of October 1957 was signed at a moment when Khrushchev's power position had been considerably strengthened by the removal of the "anti-party" faction. A step so radical as atomic aid to China could certainly have been vetoed by Khrushchev even if it were being advocated by some other faction to whom he was indebted. It must therefore have been the same man, perhaps in his "subjective" way, who elected both to push for a test ban and to buy Peking's fealty by limited nuclear assistance.

III
Prelude to Schism

Looking back over the years, we see that the issues surrounding the possibility of a ban on nuclear testing became, perhaps as early as 1956, a prime factor in the deterioration of Russian-Chinese relations. Whether one believes the Sino-Soviet dispute hinges on national interest or on ideology, or on both, the prospect of a nuclear test ban has clearly been of profound substantive as well as symbolic importance to the "fraternal" regimes in Moscow and Peking. As a result, the test ban treaty finally signed in 1963 had an impact upon world politics; and, to a more limited extent, affected Sino-Soviet relations to a degree far beyond the immediate arms controls it provided.

During the years 1957–58 the government of Mao Tse-tung moved away from the Bandung spirit to a more belligerent stance, at the same time that Khrushchev's regime was expressing increasing dedication to peaceful coexistence as the main line of Soviet foreign policy. Given this context, a Soviet–U.S. agreement to ban atomic tests could be viewed only with the gravest concern by Peking. From China's perspective, a Soviet decision to sign any major agreement with the United States suggested that Moscow was turning westward, away from alliance with Peking. Ideologically, such a turn would serve to reinforce Mao's growing belief that the Khrushchev government was abandoning world revolution to concentrate on raising to new levels Russia's *embourgeoisement*. Strategically, a Soviet accord with the West would tend to confirm the Kremlin's unwillingness to support China's external policies, particularly in the Taiwan Straits.

In specific terms, a nuclear test ban treaty could threaten China's security on several levels. At the very least it could bring a halt to Soviet aid to Peking's nuclear program and create some legal or moral restraint upon China's future capacity to test nuclear weapons. A test ban might well lead to a U.S.–Soviet nonproliferation agreement, thus increasing the pressures against Chinese entry into the nuclear club. More ominously, a U.S.–Soviet understanding could lead to joint measures to eliminate China's incipient nuclear plant. For all these reasons, any sign of Soviet interest in a nuclear test ban tended, along with other irritants, to undermine the Peking-Moscow axis.

The revelations of the Sino-Soviet dispute point to the nuclear test ban issue as a major factor exacerbating relations between Moscow and Peking as early as the Twentieth Congress of the CPSU in February 1956, when Khrushchev—in Peking's apt expression—"divorced the cessation of nuclear tests from the question of disarmament." After 1956 the Soviet leaders "were wrong on certain [disarmament] issues and correct on others," according to Peking, and China "supported them in all their correct views."[1]

While one cannot take at face value these retrospective Chinese judgments, it seems likely that for reasons outlined above Moscow's first steps toward a nuclear test ban as a negotiable "partial measure" of disarmament did in fact cause Peking serious concern. By 1957 at the latest, the Soviet Government seems to have been interested in a cessation of nuclear testing if not in a formal treaty banning such tests. The Kremlin did give some aid to China's nuclear program; but on June 20, 1959 Moscow "refused to provide China with a sample of an atomic bomb and technical data concerning its manufacture," and "unilaterally tore up the agreement on new technology for national defence concluded between China and the Soviet Union on October 15, 1957."[2]

From 1959 until 1962, Sino-Soviet relations continued to spiral downwards, troubled by disagreement on many issues, one of them being the issue of a nuclear test ban. Did the Soviets appreciate the grave consequences for their relations with Peking that would ensue from formalization of a limited test ban? Surely the answer is affirmative. Moscow must have known that the Chinese would regard the signing of a Soviet–U.S. test ban as a step that could and probably would lead to a superpower conspiracy to keep China out of the nuclear club. According to Peking, China received word from Moscow on August 25, 1962 that the Soviet Government had responded "affirmatively" to Secretary of State Rusk's proposal for a nonproliferation agreement. His proposal stipulated that (1) the nuclear powers refrain from transferring nuclear weapons and technical information concerning their manufacture to non-nuclear countries; and (2) that non-nuclear countries refrain from manufacturing nuclear weapons, seeking them from nuclear powers or from accepting technical information concerning their manufacture.[3]

Moscow's expression of "affirmative" interest in a nonproliferation agreement came in private negotiations at the same time that the Kremlin was making concessions in the open negotiations in Geneva to narrow the gap separating Moscow and Washington from an agreement to end nuclear testing. In fact the Chinese have printed the relevant U.S. and Soviet test ban proposals at Geneva as a kind of documentary corroboration of what may have been an oral communication from Moscow concerning the nonproliferation understanding.[4] On August 27, 1962 the U.S. delegate to the Eighteen-Nation Disarmament Committee (ENDC) stated his government's willingness to agree either to a comprehensive test ban involving on-site inspection or a ban excluding underground tests but without on-site inspection. The Soviet delegate replied on August 29 and again on September 3, 1962, announcing Moscow's readiness to sign a three-environment ban with a moratorium on underground testing "while continuing negotiations on the final prohibitions of such explosions." A similar proposal had been made by Moscow on November 28, 1961, but with the provision that inspection over the underground test moratorium could take place only in the context of a comprehensive disarmament agreement. Moscow's position of August 29–September 3, 1962 seemed no longer to be contingent upon GCD measures being enacted. But on September 5, 1962 Soviet representative Vasily Kuznetsov clouded the issue by reiterating Moscow's support for its stand of November 28, 1961. In any event, the Western delegates rejected the new Soviet overture on principle because, after the sudden Soviet test resumption in 1961, the West would no longer consent to an unpoliced moratorium.[5] But the shift in Moscow's position on August 29, 1962 was described by *Pravda* on the following day as "opening the way to agreement" and was soon thereafter similarly featured by the Soviet publication *New Times*.[6] On October 1, 1962 in Ashkhabad, Khrushchev reaffirmed Soviet willingness to sign an agreement on a partial test ban on the terms articulated by Mr. Kuznetsov.[7]

People's Daily charged on September 12, 1962 that the United States was obstructing the progress of the ENDC by demanding on-site inspections. But the article went on to indicate a deeper concern. The U.S.–U.K. statement on testing, said *People's Daily*, declared that the

> treaty would make it easier to prevent the spread of nuclear weapons to countries not now possessing them. . . . The reason U.S. ruling circles are so interested in preventing what they call nuclear proliferation is not secret . . . . Washington is anxious to tie China's hands in developing nuclear weapons.

People's Daily went on to say that

> only a complete ban on nuclear weapons and the unconditional destruction of all existing nuclear weapons can prevent a nuclear war. . . . The discontinuance of nuclear tests . . . should under no

circumstances become a means by which the United States may achieve and maintain nuclear superiority.[8]

Peking's response to the reported U.S.–Soviet understanding on nonproliferation was to send three memoranda to Moscow—on September 3, 1962, October 20, 1962, and June 6, 1963. Their substance held:

> It was a matter for the Soviet Government whether it committed itself to the United States to refrain from transferring nuclear weapons and technical information concerning their manufacture to China; but that the Chinese Government hoped the Soviet Government would not infringe on China's sovereign rights and act for China in assuming an obligation to refrain from manufacturing nuclear weapons. We solemnly stated that we would not tolerate the conclusion, in disregard of China's opposition, of any sort of treaty between the Soviet Government and the United States which aimed at depriving the Chinese people of their right to take steps to resist the nuclear threats of U.S. imperialism, and that we would issue statements to make our position known.[9]

This "earnest counsel," Peking professed to hope, would lead the Soviet leaders to "rein in before reaching the precipice" so as not to "render matters irretrievable. Unfortunately," however, the Chinese statement goes on, Moscow "did not pay the slightest attention" to China's advice, but proceeded to conclude the limited test ban, "thereby attempting to bring pressure on China and force her into commitments."[10]

Shortly after the Kremlin's message to Peking on nonproliferation, two other events seriously affected Russian-Chinese relations: the Cuban missile crisis and the Chinese-Indian engagement in the Himalayas. From these points in time until the signing of the nuclear test ban treaty in July 1963 the tensions between Moscow and Peking seemed to escalate in three stages amounting to quantum jumps in the dispute. The three main rungs in the Sino-Soviet escalation ladder in 1962–63 corresponded roughly with Moscow's rejections of Peking's thrice-proffered "earnest counsel" to desist from negotiating a nonproliferation agreement. While the evidence is far from complete, it is possible that a cause and effect relationship existed between the general deterioration of Sino-Soviet relations and China's mounting concern that Moscow would reach an entente with Washington on the spread of nuclear weapons.

The first stage in the escalation ran from October 1962 to April 1963, when a series of Communist Party Congresses and front meetings provided a forum for Soviet and Chinese delegates assailing one another openly; and readers of *People's Daily* saw Khrushchev criticized through attacks on Messrs. Togliatti and Thorez.[11] Second, after a lull in April and May 1963, Peking let loose its broadside of June 14, to which

Moscow replied in kind on July 14. While this exchange added a new dimension to the dispute, particularly in naming names instead of using surrogates like Albania or Italy, it was qualitatively surpassed by the polemic initiated by China on July 31, commenting on the test ban initialed on July 25. In William E. Griffith's words, "Peking now opened an overt and all-out attack on Moscow: the Sino-Soviet schism had now clearly occurred."[12] Moscow's reply came quickly—on August 3—and a new chapter began in which both sides released detailed, if distorted, accounts of their hitherto secret conflicts on political, military, and economic affairs. In communist parlance, not only "party" but "state" relations became an issue.[13]

If we trace the relationship in time between these stages and Peking's concern over a U.S.–Soviet nonproliferation treaty, we note that the Kremlin told Peking on August 25 that it had responded "affirmatively" to the U.S. proposal, and China replied privately to Moscow on September 3, 1962. In the ensuing weeks—even while Soviet missiles were being unloaded in Cuba—the Kremlin made concessions to the Western position not only on the test but also on general disarmament (GCD) issues.[14] The second Chinese comment on the Soviet nonproliferation message came on October 20, two days before the United States quarantine of Cuba and almost two months before Khrushchev announced his government would accept "two to three" on-site inspections per year for the control of a comprehensive test ban treaty.[15] The third "'earnest counsel" from Peking that Moscow desist from negotiating a nonproliferation agreement came on June 6, four days before President Kennedy's address at American University and one week before Peking issued its June 14 open letter.[16] While the American University speech no doubt helped to pave the way to the Moscow Treaty, the fact is that private talks among representatives of London, Moscow, and Washington had already led to a three-power agreement that enabled Kennedy to announce on June 10 that "high-level discussions will begin shortly in Moscow looking toward early agreement on a *comprehensive* test ban treaty."[17] Ten days later—on June 20—the "hot line" agreement was signed in Geneva.[18]

IV
Significance of the Test Ban Issue

It is probably impossible to untangle from the web of other key elements, such as Soviet aid to India, the precise role played by the approaching test ban agreement in the deterioration of Russian-Chinese relations. But the importance of the nuclear issue to the Sino-Soviet schism has been noted by Russian and East European as well as by Western commentators. China's complaint that Moscow refused her a sample bomb in 1959 led *Pravda* to declare on August 21, 1963:

> It looks as if annoyance with this policy of the Soviet Union and other socialist states of not spreading nuclear weapons *explains* the attacks of the CPR leaders on the USSR's foreign policy measures aimed at lessening international tensions and consolidating peace, especially their attacks on the nuclear test ban treaty. . . .
> The Chinese leaders abuse the Soviet Union in every way because it has nuclear arms, while the CPR does not have them.[1]

The Soviet journal *New Times* used even stronger language in 1963 and linked Chinese opposition to the "Moscow Treaty" with the Kremlin's refusal to transfer atomic weapons to Peking. It argued that "the desire to get hold of the bomb by every available means seems to be the underlying motive of Peking's attitude to the test ban treaty and of the clamorous campaign against the Soviet Union now being conducted in the Chinese press. . . ."[2]

The possibility that the nuclear test ban talks could lead to a major change in the thrust of Soviet foreign policy was suggested by the presence in Moscow in July 1963 of a high-level Chinese delegation as well as of a Western one. The dramatic parallel with the period of June to August 1939 was striking.[3] In 1963 as in 1939 the Kremlin seemed prepared to ally itself with one camp or the other, and received delegations from two opposing alignments. The analogy with 1939 fails in that

Stalin gave both delegations—the Anglo-French and the German—a hearing before he had Molotov sign with Ribbentrop. The 1963 decision, by contrast, was probably struck before the Chinese or Western diplomats had arrived in Moscow, as evidenced by the tit-for-tat Soviet response on July 14 to the vitriolic Chinese letter of June 14 and by the contrast in the reception accorded the Chinese and Western delegations. The 1939 pact led to much more active collaboration between its signatories than did the 1963 Moscow Treaty, but it ended in war between the two parties. The test ban treaty, on the other hand, served as a reminder—even after the Moscow "spirit" had dissipated—that its signatories feared a nuclear engagement.

If one sought to compare the importance of the nuclear test ban with other issues exacerbating Sino-Soviet relations prior to July 1963, it would be difficult to point to any other that so consistently gnawed at what both sides regarded as their vital interests, whose symbolic and material significance was so great in itself, or whose ramifications penetrated so many other areas of the dispute. The issue of a nuclear test ban—in form and in substance—drove to the very heart of the political, ideological, military, and even the economic factors in the rift. Hence it was not surprising that the signing of the Moscow Treaty seemed to hurtle the two giants of world communism onto a new and qualitatively more serious plateau of controversy.

Personality differences, as between Mao and Khrushchev, could be overlooked if broader common concerns brought the two governments together. Domestic policies—the denunciation of the personality cult in Russia and the "Great Leap Forward" in China—triggered major disagreements; but the threat each side posed to the other's internal stability remained quite remote, even when Moscow in 1959 backed Defense Minister P'eng Teh-huai against the central hierarchy. Territorial disputes could be shelved, as they had been for the most part since Mao's pretensions over Outer Mongolia in his 1954 meeting with Khrushchev.[4] Soviet leadership of the communist movement could be tolerated by Peking so long as China received a sufficient pay-off, e.g., nuclear and other aid.

Similarly, disagreements over risk-taking in foreign affairs could usually be contained, because in most instances neither Peking nor Moscow had a direct stake in the areas contested by the other. The weaker party, China, was hardly in a position to do more than complain if the Kremlin refused to give unlimited support to CPR aims in the Taiwan Straits or the Himalayas. Nor could Peking deter or effectively aid the Soviet Cuban gambit in 1962, except to denounce it after the fact

as "adventurism" made worse by subsequent "capitulationism." Sino-Soviet competition for the allegiance of developing countries was fierce but
offered inadequate grounds for a major break. The Russians could live
with Peking's rather left ideology and foreign policy, at least while the
Chinese dragon's growl exceeded its bite. And in the same way Peking
could stomach the Kremlin line on peaceful coexistence—"conflict *cum*
collaboration"—so long as nothing came of U.S.–Soviet gropings toward
entente.

All these and other factors severely strained the Sino-Soviet relationship, but none in itself constituted either a necessary or sufficient cause
for an overt schism. Taken together, however, their cumulative impact
was such that a final straw could break the back of the alliance. The close
connection in time between the escalation ladder of the dispute and
Peking's protests against a Soviet entente with Washington regarding
arms control suggested even in late 1962 and in the spring of 1963 that a
test ban agreement would have the gravest consequences for Chinese-
Russian relations. The violent Chinese response to the Moscow Treaty
showed that its signing served at least as the occasion and perhaps also as
the immediate cause—the final straw—that brought the schism into the
open.

The importance of the Moscow Treaty probably went still deeper. The
test ban represented symbolically Moscow's joining what Peking deemed
an imperialist conspiracy, not only to try to block China's nuclear program, but to oppose her political advance in the third world. The
Chinese had known since 1959 that Moscow would not continue assistance to Peking's nuclear program. As the Chinese correspondence cited
earlier indicates, Peking purported to fear (perhaps in part for propaganda reasons) that even a partial test ban might lead to a nonproliferation agreement and, what was worse, to coercive measures by Russia and
the West to destroy the CPR nuclear facilities. Finally, the Moscow
Treaty confirmed for Peking that the Soviet regime had, to say the least,
a quite different approach to world revolution from that of Mao Tse-
tung.

If we seek to determine the relative weight of the Moscow Treaty in
bringing on the open schism, two sets of competing hypotheses must be
considered. First, did Moscow sign the test ban because the Sino-Soviet
dispute had become irreparable? Or did the dispute become as severe as
it did because the Kremlin signed the test ban? Figures 2, 3, and 4
suggest the interrelation between (a) Moscow's interest in a nuclear test
ban and (b) the deterioration in Sino-Soviet relations, which lessened
the Kremlin's reluctance to enter arms control arrangements with the
West. The asterisks suggest approximate rank-order changes in the Soviet

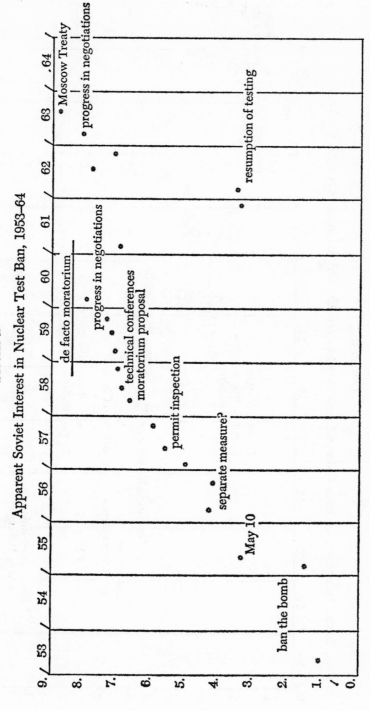

FIGURE 2

Apparent Soviet Interest in Nuclear Test Ban, 1953–64

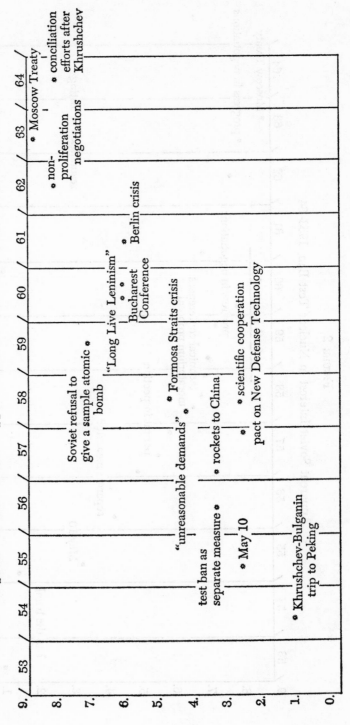

FIGURE 3

Soviet Independence from Chinese Opposition to Arms Control Arrangements with the West

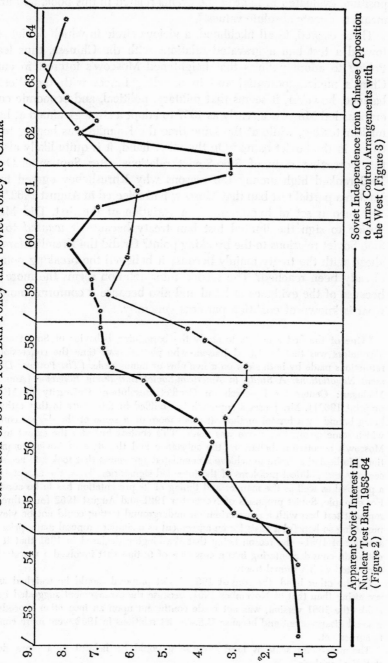

FIGURE 4

Correlation of Soviet Test Ban Policy and Soviet Policy to China

—————— Apparent Soviet Interest in
Nuclear Test Ban, 1953–64
(Figure 2)

———— Soviet Independence from Chinese Opposition
to Arms Control Arrangements with
the West (Figure 3)

position, evaluated in light of the events related in this book, and are not meant to denote absolute values.*

There existed, in all likelihood, a vicious circle in which Soviet moves toward a test ban aggravated relations with the Chinese, thus leading Peking to adopt policies that heightened Moscow's interest in curbing China's nuclear potential and in mending fences with the West. On balance, however, it seems that military, political, and economic considerations led Moscow as early as 1957 to adopt a strategy aimed at halting nuclear testing, while at the same time the Kremlin was hoping to keep China in the Soviet camp.[5] On the other hand, it is quite likely also that the worsening state of Sino-Soviet relations after September-October 1962 ranked high among the reasons why Khrushchev agreed in July 1963 to a partial test ban that Moscow had rejected in August 1962.[6]

A second set of hypotheses is a variation of the first. Did Moscow decide to sign the limited test ban treaty because it *wanted* to drive Sino-Soviet relations to the breaking point? Or did the Kremlin *dare* to go ahead with the treaty mainly because it believed the breaking point had already been reached? The second interpretation seems the more likely because of the evidence at hand and also because it conforms more with what is known of coalition patterns generally.

* One of the first attempts to study the bargaining behavior of Soviet and U.S. negotiators was that by Lloyd Jensen, who plotted over time the concessions and retractions made by both sides on a five plus or minus scale. (*The Postwar Disarmament Negotiations: A Study in American-Soviet Bargaining Behavior* [Ann Arbor, Michigan: Center for Research on Conflict Resolution, University of Michigan, preprint 1962]). Mr. Jensen's approach is modified in this study in that rather than being bound by a formal method, it relies more on a sense of the deeper context in which some negotiating move was made. This context includes the extent to which Moscow's negotiating behavior (the substance and the style of Soviet communications) indicated a desire to achieve a negotiated agreement that took into account the security and political problems of the intended signatories. Thus, the acceptability of a proposal as well as the manner and timing of its presentation has to be considered. For example, Soviet proposals of November 1961 and August 1962 for a three-environment test ban with a moratorium on underground testing could not be viewed as promising so hopeful a basis for an agreement as a similar proposal made prior to the summer of 1961—the reason being that Washington declared in 1961 that it would not again consider entering into a cessation of testing that involved a moratorium as contrasted with a formal treaty.

On the other hand, the August 1962 Soviet proposal should be weighed as more promising than that of November 1961, because the arrangement suggested in 1962, unlike the 1961 version, was not made contingent upon an inspection procedure for general disarmament and because U.S.–Soviet relations in 1962 were more conducive to agreement.

The nine-point scale is used because it could be helpful in a more detailed, statistical analysis.

It was in Russia's interest, so long as Moscow could dominate the communist movement, to have China's grudging and nominal support rather than risk a split of the entire movement, with the splintering and polycentrism it would precipitate. As in the Atlantic community, so in the communist camp, the leading power has preferred to live with autonomy on the part of a major ally rather than lose him—and others—altogether. The vanguard power by his general weight within the alliance can usually get his way: hence his appearance of being more tolerant of diversity than the challenger to his pre-eminence. Paris (since 1958), like Peking (since 1959), seems to have become increasingly rebellious because of the reluctance of the alliance leader to ease its entry into the nuclear club or share its weapons.[7]

For Moscow, of course, much else was at stake in 1963 than the shaky and perhaps doomed alliance with China. The failure of the Cuban adventure, the increasing U.S. strategic lead, the faltering Soviet economy, along with the challenge from Peking—all dictated that Moscow seek a breathing space, at least temporarily, in its political-military competition with the West. If Moscow therefore moved toward accommodation with the United States, it was more in spite of Chinese opposition than because of it. Soviet leaders would have preferred to retain China as an ally and follower, if only nominally. Since the Chinese seemed determined to challenge Soviet hegemony rather than submit to it, Moscow had little to lose and something to gain by coming to terms with Washington, rather than attempting to deal with frontal pressures from East and West simultaneously.

Once Peking openly challenged Moscow's leadership, the Soviets had additional incentives to attempt to ostracize if not excommunicate China from the communist movement. That Khrushchev strove to do this in the year following the Moscow Treaty does not contradict the assertion that he would have preferred to avoid this course. Once the die was cast, both Moscow and Peking endeavored to win support—both in the communist and in the third world—by their interpretation of the war/peace issue.

This analysis of what Peking and Moscow stood to gain or lose by pushing for an open break is corroborated by their respective tactics during the six to eight months prior to the signing of the test ban treaty. During this period it was usually China rather than the Soviet Union that intensified the public polemic, e.g., by the strong criticism of the Soviet withdrawal from Cuba;[8] by the thinly veiled attacks on Khrushchev through criticism of Italian and French surrogates;[9] most important, by the June 14 letter three weeks before Sino-Soviet negotiations were to begin in Moscow; by the open Chinese attack on the Soviet line of peaceful coexistence at the World Congress of Democratic Women which met in Moscow, June 24–29, 1963 (where the Soviet delegation stressed *unity* as well as peace);[10] and by the Chinese motion to "suspend" the Party negotiations in Moscow on July 20, 1963.[11]

But if the Chinese were usually the first to escalate the public polemic, Soviet deeds often served as the catalyst. Peking's analysis of the Sino-Soviet axis naturally became darker as Khrushchev, after Cuba, not only moved toward an understanding with the Kennedy Administration, but began to supply India with more military aid than did the United States.[12] Then, at the East German Party Congress in January 1963, when the Chinese spokesman attacked Yugoslav revisionism, "his voice was drowned out by whistles, boos, shouts and feet-stamping—an insult carefully staged, one must assume, by Khrushchev, who was ostentatiously absent. . . ."[13]

The Rubicon was crossed on June 25, 1963 when the partial test ban was initialed. The last bridge, if one still existed, burned on August 5 when dignitaries from Britain, the Soviet Union, and the United States formally signed the document. A photograph of the Soviet Premier hugging the U.S. representative the day after the initialing ceremony was printed by Peking with the explanation: "Khrushchev Embraces Harriman."[14]

For almost a decade—with the possible exception of the period from the May 1960 Summit meeting to the Cuban missile adventure—Khrushchev had staked the success of his foreign policy on a gamble. He had calculated that Moscow could reach an understanding with "sober forces" in the Western governments, particularly in Washington, that would permit both sides to compete by measures short of war. From roughly 1955 to 1959 the Soviet First Secretary seemed confident that this competition would rapidly "bury" the West, shrinking its sphere of influence by winning the third world for the Soviet camp.

By 1963, however, Moscow seemed satisfied merely to stabilize the political-military situation with the West and cut losses within the international communist movement, accepting (even after Khrushchev's removal) the defection of China. Soviet acquiescence in these limited objectives stemmed from the narrowing of alternatives open to Soviet policy following the Cuban debacle. Rather than essay some other quick-fix to overcome strategic inferiority, Moscow grasped the opportunity implicit in President Kennedy's refusal to exploit aggressively the Soviet retreat. Moscow's mounting tensions with Peking and Russia's stagnating economy made it the more desirable to reach some accommodation with Washington. While the Kremlin had no prospect of overturning the military balance, it could nevertheless rest secure behind its minimum but adequate deterrent.[15]

The significance of the Moscow Treaty extended on many planes far beyond the immediate purpose of prohibiting nuclear testing in three environments. (It was precisely because the three signatories' interest in such tests had declined that the ban became militarily and politically feasible.) The treaty gave a boost to efforts to reach other arms control agreements and, as a result, created a "spirit of Moscow" that proved less transient in East-West relations than had the "Geneva spirit" eight years before. But future historians might well decide that the treaty's greatest impact was registered upon international communism. For the signing of the test ban unleashed a torrent of words and some deeds within the communist movement that left it not only divided but, at least in Europe, fragmented, both in structure and strategy. The now open struggle for power between Russia and China within the movement spilled over into the third world, into relations with the West, and even manifested itself in overt interferences in one another's domestic politics. The net impact was to supplant what some had seen as an age of ideology with a vivid return to the classic struggle of national interests, historically unique, however, in its global scale. These different levels in the meaning of the Moscow Treaty are discussed in the next three chapters.

Part Two

THE MOSCOW TREATY AND OPEN SCHISM, 1963–64

V
Arms Control and East-West Détente

The Khrushchev government came to seek not only a relaxation of tensions with the West, but—moving beyond détente—at least a partial entente. A common understanding ensued between Moscow and Washington permitting parallel courses of action to deal with particular problems, even though competition and conflict persisted in many areas of Soviet relations with the West.

A salient result of the test ban was to heighten the Kremlin's stake in moving further toward arms control agreements with the West and, generally, in perpetuating the spirit engendered by the Moscow Treaty. By the same token the treaty gave Peking cause to intensify its opposition to arms control and détente. Not only was the test ban held by Peking to be an illusion, liable to sap the revolutionary élan of peoples around the world, but it appeared to aim at closing the door of the nuclear club just when China knocked. All parties were aware that Peking's first atomic device could soon be exploded. The more imminent this event, the more intense the conflict between those who sought to raise the Moscow Treaty to the status of general international or at least moral law, thereby increasing the political cost of the Chinese detonation, if not preventing it.

Moscow for the first time made public its opposition in principle to the spread of nuclear weapons,[1] while Peking—even after October of 1964—took the contrary tack, seeking to defend its drive to unlock the atomic genie, despite the growing number of countries adhering to the tripartite treaty.[2] How, the Kremlin demanded rhetorically of Peking, could the Chinese expect Russia to aid their nuclear program without undermining the foundations of Soviet opposition to nuclear spread within NATO, in particular, to West Germany? Why, the Soviets continued, should China even seek her own nuclear arsenal? Such weapons were beyond the economic capabilities of developing countries, Moscow contended, and were after all superfluous, owing to the Soviet nuclear shield which had guarded and would continue to maintain the security of the entire socialist camp.[3]

Thus, the viewpoints of Moscow and Peking grew more polarized. Kremlin propaganda justified the test ban as a vindication of the CPSU "theses" on peaceful coexistence. Peace was now the condition of communist victory, to be achieved by evolution if not revolution. Peking, in contrast, sought to expose the fallacies of partial disarmament measures such as the test ban and called instead for total nuclear disarmament, which, however, would be achieved only by "unswerving struggle," although Peking did call for a heads-of-state meeting of all governments.[4] The Chinese contention was that the "psalm-singing" Khrushchev had been duped. They cited as evidence the many U.S. government claims that the treaty favored America's strategic interests. Soviet propaganda countered by asserting that the treaty favored neither side, but that if either gained, it was the USSR, which already led in the testing of high-yield warheads.[5] Peking pointed also to the several underground tests carried out by Washington immediately after the treaty had been signed; but Soviet news agencies apparently clamped a lid on such information, at least until October 12, 1963, when a broadcast to Italy declared that such tests ran contrary to the spirit of the treaty.[6] Still more difficult for the Kremlin to rebut, Peking threw back in Moscow's face the very objections the Soviets had earlier raised to a test ban without disarmament or, at other moments, to a ban that permitted underground testing.[7]

Any indication that the Moscow spirit was illusory would leave the premises of Khrushchev's policy more vulnerable to Chinese attack. Hence, even while Peking condemned the test ban and the U.S. Senate debated its merits, Moscow appeared to seek additional signs, no matter how inconsequential *per se*, to demonstrate the improved state of its relations with the West and, of less immediate importance, to reduce the risks and the costs of military competition. Among the steps possessing at least a symbolic value, limited arms control measures ranked high. The direct communications link and the test ban treaty proved relatively simpler to formalize than consular exchanges, scientific cooperation, or even East-West trade. Both Moscow and Washington showed some understanding of one another's internal and alliance problems. Moscow did not press the West for a nonaggression pact between the NATO and Warsaw Pact organizations. And both sides came to see that formal treaties might be less feasible than tacit or unilateral measures. This awareness helped account for the Soviet-U.K.-U.S. decision to formalize their declaration of intent not to orbit weapons of mass destruction merely by means of a U.N. Resolution.[8] In Khrushchev's words of December 31, 1963, some measures of arms limitation were possible by "mutual example." Actions such as reductions of defense spending and troop levels could be carried out unilaterally, Khrushchev stated, although a cessation of the arms race as a whole would depend on both sides.[9] Indeed, in mid-December the Soviet Premier announced a reduction in the Soviet military budget, implying a tacit understanding with Washington that the United States would reciprocate. He spoke also of a possible cutback in armed forces personnel.[10] Shortly thereafter, in another field of arms control, the possibilities of a less frontal approach were manifested when, after private negotiations, Washington, London, and Moscow simultaneously announced on April 20, 1964 their unilateral pledges to cut back production of fissionable materials.[11]

Moscow's growing concern over limited wars, possibly sparked by China's military and political ambitions, may have been reflected in two further proposals made by Khrushchev.[12] On December 31, 1963 he sent a letter to all heads of state proposing a treaty renouncing the use of force to settle disputes concerning "established" frontiers. Attempting to keep his kasha and eat it at the same time, Khrushchev qualified his statement by reaffirming the "sacred right" of oppressed peoples to resort to arms to obtain national independence from colonial rule. He spoke also of the just desire of China to regain Taiwan and of Indonesia's right to West Irian.[13] The extent to which these special cases might affect the generality of the Soviet proposal was not clear, but Moscow did not take up President Johnson's counterproposal in January 1964 to ban all use of force in frontier disputes without exception. And *Pravda* scored Chinese attempts to suggest that the Khrushchev proposal implied an end to national liberation wars.[14]

A second Khrushchev proposal that may have aimed at inhibiting violence in the emerging nations was his suggestion in July 1964 for the establishment of a United Nations peacekeeping force composed of contingents from non-permanent members of the Security Council but subject to that body (and hence to Moscow's veto).[15] Such a force could obviously be of use only against smaller states, but it might help to head off conflicts that could be provoked by China and that would bring in the United States. The Khrushchev proposal foundered, however, on the intransigence of both sides concerning payment for past U.N. peacekeeping operations and the refusal of Washington to submit all peacekeeping actions to the exclusive jurisdiction of the Security Council.[16]

The most urgent challenge to the vital interests of Russia and America, however, was not the elaboration of additional demonstrations to prove that the two superpowers acknowledged a common interest in stabilizing their military competition. As useful as such manifestations may have been, the more pressing task was to coordinate policies to keep China from acquiring a capability which, when developed, might drastically affect the stability of a more or less bipolar world. Such an objective, which would have been analogous to the earlier appeals that America intervene in time to quash the Axis threat or to pre-empt the Soviet atomic capability, may not have been feasible. A nonproliferation agreement would hardly have sufficed to stop the Chinese nuclear program unless it provided teeth to prevent by threat of force China's acquisition of atomic weapons by her own efforts. While the Chinese seem to have feared some such U.S.–Soviet action, there is no public evidence that either side gave serious consideration to such measures.[17]

The incentives in 1964 for Moscow to reach additional arms control agreements with the West were countervailed by a series of difficulties reinforcing one another to obstruct further movement toward détente. First, there were what might be called accidents of history—the assassination of President Kennedy and the resultant uncertainties for both sides (though President Johnson and Khrushchev agreed in April 1964 to slow down fissionable material production), the removal of Mr. Khrushchev from power, and the tensions inherent in a U.S. election campaign. Second, there was the increasing complexity of the matters under negotiation, such as the proposed "bomber bonfire," a measure that ran afoul of the gigantic disparities in the number and types possessed by each side. Progress toward a nonproliferation agreement was thwarted by the requirements for NATO cohesion (which Washington hoped would be braced by the MLF) and Moscow's opposition to a greater nuclear role for West Germany. Third, and perhaps most important, the intensive attacks by Communist China upon the Kremlin's revolutionary image began to take their toll, especially as the Vietnamese conflict wore on, thereby raising the political cost to Moscow of any deal with the West.

VI
The Struggle Within World Communism

As Moscow sought to stabilize its Western front, its left political flank became increasingly vulnerable to Chinese attacks. After mid-1963 it could no longer be doubted that Peking intended to challenge the Soviet Union's vanguard position in the communist movement, although the Chinese had probably decided on such a strategy as early as 1959 or 1960. Since Moscow had "sold out to imperialism" its leadership had to be supplanted—both at home and in the revolutionary movement. The withdrawal of Soviet military and technical aid in 1959–60 had left China with little incentive to abide Soviet policies which, given China's historical development, conflicted with her perceived interests and probably with her genuine convictions. Not only in spite of China's opposition but probably, to a large extent, because of troubles with Peking, the Soviet Government opted to signify dramatically its common political and military interests with the United States. The 1963 Moscow Treaty provided the last straw, and Peking threw down the gauntlet.

The struggle for power between the protagonists of international communism thus became more intense, dominating their relations with other communist parties, undermining what remained of the Sino-Soviet alliance, and eroding further the myth of communist unity. These aspects of the struggle are now considered one by one, as they evolved in the first several years following the Moscow Treaty.

INTRA-BLOC RELATIONS: AGAINST NONALIGNMENT

As has already been pointed out, numerous factors combined to wear down and break the bonds between Moscow and Peking. The role of the nuclear test ban, however, was unique. In the words of Morton H. Halperin and Dwight H. Perkins, the test ban may "turn out to be a landmark in the evolution of the international communist movement."[1] Not only did it help to signal and then to produce the open schism; but for almost two years it also became a major point of contention around which both parties tried to rally support and to "expose" their ideological adversary's errors.

Both the Soviets and the Chinese attempted in 1963–64 to exploit the Moscow Treaty to win support in the communist world. That the test ban agreement was even possible was hailed in Moscow as proof that the Soviet line was "correct" and Peking's "wrong." The Soviet line was that China's opposition to the treaty linked the Chinese leadership with "madmen" such as Adenauer, de Gaulle, and Goldwater. Peking, of course, held that Moscow's entente with the West allied the Russians with imperialism. The issue of the nuclear test ban generated pressures upon communist parties—like governments—to take sides for or against.

In the first six months or year following the Moscow Treaty, the West European and North American communist parties remained basically pro-Soviet, although some were extremist and others moderate. While splinter groups arose siding with Peking, only in Belgium did the pro-Chinese succeed in detaching a significant following. In Latin America, the struggle, in one sense, was more between Havana and Moscow than between Moscow and Peking. The old guard of most Latin parties adhered to the Soviet line, but Castro declared Cuba's neutrality in the Russo-Chinese dispute while at the same time refusing to sign the Moscow Treaty on the ground that it involved the United States. All the East European parties except the Albanian sided with Moscow, but managed to gain more autonomy in the process. The majority of the Australian party lined up with the Kremlin, although a strong splinter identified with Peking, as did the New Zealand party. The Malaysian, Thai, and Burmese parties remained fundamentally pro-Chinese.

Elsewhere in Asia only two parties stood fairly clearly with the Soviets—the Outer Mongolian, and the Ceylonese, joined by part of the Indian. Four parties that had attempted neutrality—the North Korean, Vietnamese, Indonesian, and Japanese—drew closer to Peking, as the test ban made more difficult the possibility of nonalignment in the Sino-Soviet rift.[2] The reduction of "neutral" parties, as Halperin and Perkins have pointed out, could make it more difficult at a later juncture to find middle men to mediate the Sino-Soviet rift,[3] although some Asian parties returned to a relatively neutral posture in 1965–68.

The embarrassment of having to choose between Russia and China was particularly acute in Japan, where popular sentiments against nuclear testing ran high. In part for that reason, a pro-Soviet faction later appeared in the Japanese party. When two of its deputies voted in the Diet for ratification of the Moscow Treaty, they were expelled by the pro-Peking majority, thus setting in motion an exchange of letters between the Soviet and Japanese Communist Parties exacerbating their already strained relationship.[4]

Whereas the Soviets had earlier sought to maintain a façade of unity, from the summer of 1963 until Khrushchev's ouster, they sought means to formalize the split in communist ranks, so as to halt if not reverse their losses within the movement.[5] In September and October 1963 they moved toward calling an international communist meeting for the purpose of excommunicating the Chinese. But even moderate, conditionally pro-Soviet parties such as the Rumanian and Italian opposed the Soviet plan, fearing that a formal split would limit their own freedom of action and, at least in the Italian case, add to internal factionalism. Soviet pressures for excommunication of China relaxed from November 1963 until the time of Suslov's speech in February 1964, which was not published, however, until April 1964, perhaps because of opposition within the CPSU leadership and also because of Rumania's attempts at mediation.[6] From April until Khrushchev's removal in October the Kremlin sought once again to organize a conference to expel the Chinese, though these efforts slackened somewhat after June 1964.

The Chinese, of course, were not idle. Behind the scenes they encouraged factionalism in pro-Soviet parties. Their official rationale was that no vanguard position was possible within the communist movement, since all parties are "independent and completely equal." The Soviet contention that majority rule is binding in the movement was rejected by Peking, which deemed the Soviet majority "false." An end to public polemics, advocated by Moscow from November 1963 to February 1964, was rejected.[7]

The result of Moscow's efforts to cut its losses, however, proved to be abortive. Not only did the CPSU fail in its attempt to excommunicate the Chinese, but—partly because of this failure—Moscow lost influence over the Eastern and Western European parties as well. By April 1964 Bucharest not only had sabotaged Moscow's plan for supranational planning within CMEA, but the Rumanian party issued a special "Statement" defending its autonomous course and criticizing both Peking and Moscow for their polemics and power struggle.[8] The Italian Communist Party also grew more independent, as dramatized most strikingly by its publication of the "Togliatti Testament" on September 5, 1964 over Brezhnev's objections.[9] Togliatti's last work postulated "unity in diversity" in the communist movement through "discussions," not personalized polemics.

Moreover, he indicated the "slowness and resistance" of the Soviet regime in cultural and political liberalization. In William Griffith's apt phrase, the fact that Moscow republished the Togliatti Testament "and took issue with it only very indirectly, made clear to the world that Moscow was increasingly becoming a paper tiger."[10] The Kremlin's declining fortunes in the ranks of international communism, coupled with Khrushchev's determination to mount an anti-Chinese conference, may have been one reason for his removal in October 1964.[11]

To be sure, the internal dynamism of most developments within the communist movement since Khrushchev's ouster has derived from sources other than Soviet and U.S. arms control policy—from factors so wideranging as China's Cultural Revolution; intra-bloc differences about tactics and strategy in Vietnam; the autonomous courses steered by Bucharest, Havana, and other communist capitals—coupled with Moscow's intermittent but dogged efforts to organize a "unity" conference. But these events would probably not have been so subversive to communist solidarity had they not been preceded by the polemics and maneuvers triggered by the Moscow Treaty and related events in 1963. Furthermore, though events of such magnitude as the Cultural Revolution were in themselves sufficient to exert a profoundly disruptive impact on intercommunist relations, their effect was reinforced by the movement toward Soviet–U.S. accord on a nonproliferation treaty. Not only for Peking but for Pankow and other communist capitals as well, treaty prospects raised the bogey of a Soviet "deal" with Washington at other communists' expense. For other communist capitals, however, though the nonproliferation treaty was itself not objectionable, it could be used to justify and facilitate a more independent course—with Rumania even threatening not to sign unless the superpowers agreed to her ostensibly constructive amendments.

END OF AN ALLIANCE

The role of the nuclear issue in the decline of the Sino-Soviet alliance was suggested by a Chinese statement in November 1965 charging that "the signing of the partial nuclear test ban treaty by the Soviet Union, the United States, and Britain was an important landmark in Khrushchev's alliance with the United States against China." The new Soviet leadership that succeeded Khrushchev was accused not only of having accepted his legacy, but of plotting new deals with the United States for the prevention of nuclear proliferation and other so-called disarmament measures to perpetuate the U.S.–Soviet nuclear monopoly "against China and all other independent countries."[12]

Given the bitterness of the Sino-Soviet polemics, it was no surprise that both sides called into question the validity—past and present—of their alliance signed on Valentine's Day, 1950.[13] Both the content and the tone of the polemics indicate that Moscow and Peking have in fact violated the formal provisions of the treaty on numerous occasions and that both sides consider it to be virtually a dead letter. In particular it appears that one or both parties have been unfaithful to the obligations stipulated by Articles I, III, IV, and V.

Article I obligated the two signatories, if one were attacked by Japan or states allied with her, to render immediately "military and other assistance with all means at its disposal." The major test of Soviet backing for China against possible attack by a state allied with Japan—the United States—came in the 1958 crisis in the Taiwan Straits. Though Moscow has consistently defended its reliability as an ally at that time, the Soviet contribution has since been belittled by the Chinese, as in Peking's statement of September 1, 1963.[14] The Soviet rebuttal on September 21, 1963 defended the Kremlin's position by reminding the Chinese leaders that they had publicly thanked the Soviet Government in September and October 1958 for support during the 1958 crisis. Moscow's statement then paraphrased the "cynical" Chinese view of 1963: "Well, Soviet leaders, protect us with your nuclear weapons, but we shall still criticize you." The Russian rejoinder recalled a proverb: "Don't foul the well; you may need its water." And while Moscow reaffirmed the "sufficiency" of the Soviet nuclear shield to defend the entire socialist camp, it posited that China's drive to obtain nuclear self-sufficiency could derive only from "special aims and interests . . . which cannot be supported by the military strength of the socialist camp." Moscow pointedly warned that if the Chinese leaders interpreted Soviet "good will wrongly" and continued their hostile actions, slandering, and factionalism, they would meet "the most vigorous rebuff . . . from the CPSU and from the Soviet people."[15]

A less qualified warning to Peking came in June 1964 when a Soviet propagandist hinted that Peking could not necessarily count on Moscow's support in any "terrible hour of trial."[16] Soviet spokesmen already had warned on several occasions, the first in August 1960, that Moscow would defend only the socialist states friendly to it.[17] And a major editorial in *Pravda* on May 6, 1965 was quite explicit:

> The Chinese leaders interpret proletarian internationalism to mean that the socialist countries and Communist Parties must support their every action, even if it is incompatible with the interests and line of the communist movement. . . . It should be emphatically stressed that the principles of proletarian internationalism do not at all imply that the socialist countries must support every action of another socialist country.

Thus, Peking has cast doubt on whether the Soviet side has fulfilled its obligations under Article I in the past, and the Russians have warned that their future support is conditional upon common aims and friendly relations with the Chinese.

It would appear that Article III—prohibiting either party from taking part in an alliance, coalition, or measures aimed against the other—has been violated also, at least in Chinese eyes. We have seen above how the signing of the Moscow Treaty led the Chinese to make repeated charges about a U.S.–Soviet conspiracy to dominate the world and, more specifically, to keep China from entering the atomic club. Peking has charged also that the Russians have teamed up with Washington and New Delhi against China. Thus, *People's Daily* published an article on November 2, 1963 entitled "The Truth about the Alliance the Leaders of the CPSU Have Concluded against China." Elucidating this theme, a major article in *People's Daily* and *Red Flag* charged on November 11, 1965:

> The new leaders of the CPSU are continuing and enlarging the business scraped together by the Khrushchevian firm of "Kennedy, Khrushchev & Nehru." They continue to tighten their union with Indian reaction, which is under the control of American imperialism, for the struggle against China. During Shastri's visit to the USSR the new Soviet leaders immediately promised India aid worth 900,000,000 American dollars, which exceeds the total credits Khrushchev extended to India over a nine-year period. They are intensively realizing their plan for military aid to India and they are working hand-in-hand with the U.S. in helping her expand her armaments, affording Indian reaction the opportunity to strike out with Soviet weapons against China and other neighboring countries. Recently, in the point of India's armed aggression against Pakistan, and in the point of the Indo-Chinese border, the new leaders of the CPSU fully revealed the abominable physiognomy of their alliance with the U.S. and India in their aggression against China.[18]

Article IV of the 1950 treaty provided for mutual consultation "in regard to all important problems" affecting one another. It is not clear to what extent the two sides consulted over their respective moves, e.g., in the 1958 crisis in the Formosan Straits. But on a number of other important issues (such as Soviet behavior in the Cuban missile crisis and the moves by Peking against New Delhi from 1959 through 1965) it appears that if consultation actually did take place, no accord was reached and both sides went their separate ways. We have the Chinese account of Sino-Soviet communication in 1962–63 over Moscow's plan to enter a nonproliferation agreement with Washington; but that exchange seemed to consist rather more of warnings than of consultation.[19] We have also Peking's word that the Chinese were told by the Kremlin on June 9, 1963—one day before President Kennedy announced that test ban negotiations would begin soon in Moscow—that "the Western powers' position on the halting of nuclear tests could not yet serve as a basis for agreement, and that whether negotiations could yield any results depended entirely on the Western powers."[20] Whether Moscow in fact was attempting to conceal its real intentions from Peking, the Chinese imply that this was the case.

Article V of the alliance stipulated "mutual respect for the state sovereignty and territorial integrity and non-interference in internal affairs" of the other party; it also committed the signatories "to develop and consolidate economic and cultural ties between the Soviet Union and China, to render each other every possible economic assistance, and to carry out the necessary economic cooperation." But the polemics hurled about during 1963–64 referred to events that contradicted all these provisions. The Chinese charged (and Moscow admitted) that the Soviets had given unsolicited advice against China's Great Leap Forward endeavor. Peking also claimed (and Moscow did not deny) that the Soviets sought military control of China in 1958 and had conspired with Defense Minister P'eng Teh-huai in 1959.[21]

The Chinese themselves had not been passive. From the summer of 1963 until Khrushchev's fall in October 1964, the Chinese openly attacked the Soviet Party leader, calling him an enemy of the Soviet people and appealing to the CPSU and the Soviet armed forces to overthrow him.[22] The Suslov speech of February 14, 1964 explicitly accused the Chinese of scheming "to isolate Comrade Khrushchev from the Central Committee. . . ."[23] In return, Soviet statements in the first half of 1964 explicitly attacked Mao's personality cult, comparing it with Stalin's. Moscow denounced also the Chinese Party's violation of its own statutes and its lack of party program.[24]

The territorial integrity of the Soviet Union was directly challenged in Mao Tse-tung's interview with a group of Japanese socialists on June 10, 1964, when he challenged the validity of Russia's territorial acquisitions under the Tsars as well as since World War II.[25] Appealing to German, Japanese, and East European irredentism and warning that China "had not presented its bill," Mao criticized Moscow's landgrabbing in Poland, East Germany (to compensate Poland), Finland, Rumania, and the Kurile Islands, as well as Russia's control over Outer Mongolia, and aggressive intentions along the Sinkiang and Amur River frontiers.[26] Moscow's reply indicated its sensitivity on such questions, but rejected the Chinese position as likely to "generate insoluble conflicts among countries of Europe and Asia. . . ."[27] Khrushchev himself replied also, threatening to exploit nationalist feelings in Sinkiang (from whence refugees had been fleeing into Soviet Central Asia for several years).[28]

As for the economic cooperation provided by the treaty's Article V, it had been clear since 1959–60, when Soviet technicians withdrew from

China, taking many blueprints with them, that Moscow was unwilling to go the limit in helping to accelerate China's economic growth. Soviet-Chinese trade continued on a businesslike basis, but on a scale far smaller than in the peak year 1959.

The Sino-Soviet alliance was shaken at another point when, on January 15, 1966, Moscow renewed its mutual defense arrangements with Outer Mongolia in terms that were on balance unfavorable to Chinese interests.[29] Earlier Soviet treaties with Ulan Bator had been directed first against the threat of Japanese aggression and second against Nationalist China.[30] The 1966 accord, like one signed by Outer Mongolia in 1960 with Communist China, aimed at the "maintenance of Asian and world peace." But Ulan Bator's new treaty with the Soviet Union also set itself the task of "constantly strengthening the defensive might of the socialist community." In addition, it affirmed both parties' intention to cooperate through the Soviet-dominated Council of Mutual Economic Assistance, a body to which China does not belong. And Article 6 of the new treaty pledged both signatories to strive for an ideal presently anathema to Peking—"the achievement of general and complete disarmament"—as well as the liquidation of colonialism and (according to Article 7) the "prevention and elimination of the threat of imperialist aggression in this part of the globe."

Defense Minister Malinovsky as well as party chief Brezhnev journeyed to Ulan Bator to sign the new pact with Outer Mongolia. Within a month, according to stories circulating in Moscow, large numbers of Soviet troops and armored units were moving into Outer Mongolia to take up positions along the Chinese frontier just 600 miles from Peking. Provision for the troop movements was believed to have been made in secret clauses of the January 1966 treaty. Estimates regarding the size of the Soviet forces varied from 2,000 to 10,000 or more, but the move appears to have been the first occasion when the Kremlin shifted its military forces in a show of strength obviously aimed at Peking.[31] "Not by acci-dent," a Russian might say, Soviet and East European party and govern-ment officials and radio broadcasts spoke in increasingly disparaging tones of border incidents allegedly provoked by China—over 150 re-ported in 1965—and of Chinese efforts to involve the Soviet Union in a European second front against the United States.[32]

The "whole course of events" (apparently from 1959 to 1963) as viewed from Peking would seem to have violated the essential provisions of the 1950 alliance. The Chinese assert:

> First the Soviet Government tried to subdue China and curry favor
> with U.S. imperialism by discontinuing assistance to China. Then it
> put forward all sorts of untenable arguments in an attempt to induce

China to abandon its solemn stand. Failing in all this, it has brazenly ganged up with imperialist bandits in exerting pressure on China.[33]

From Moscow's perspective, on the other hand, it appeared that China had sought to provoke a U.S.–Soviet conflict from which Peking would be the main beneficiary. Otto Kuusinen charged in August 1963:

> Inasmuch as China herself is not strong enough to fight the great imperialist powers, the Soviet Union, who is strong enough, is obligated, according to the Chinese leaders, to war against American imperialism and its allies if the Soviet Union does not want to gain the reputation of being "revisionist"—and China in the meantime would be able to achieve a decision regarding her own goals.[34]

Thus, for all practical purposes, the foundation of the alliance in the 1960s became fragile and rickety. Peking probably stated the conviction of both sides in saying: "We and the Khrushchevian revisionists occupy diametrically opposed positions on the fundamental questions of our time."[35] On the other hand, there were still a number of overlapping concerns based on ideology and national interest that could work to reactivate the alliance in altered circumstances. The unresolved outcome of the Vietnamese war left issues in doubt. The Soviets were showing increasing concern over their revolutionary image, at the same time that their conflict with Peking was growing more intense. Would they welcome, tolerate, or resist a U.S. attack upon China? Many Western analysts believed the Soviet leaders would not passively watch the replacement of a communist regime in China by one allied with the West (assuming such a contingency were at all possible). But what would be the Soviet response to a more limited action directed against Chinese territory? One that might include a surgical strike against China's nuclear plants? Only speculation was possible, but it seemed reasonable to believe that Moscow's behavior in the late 1960s would be guided by a calculation of Soviet interest, and not by any obligation deriving from the 1950 alliance or by abstract considerations of ideological fraternity. Peking vastly exaggerated the case, but its reaction to a proposed security arrangement for non-nuclear states proposed by Washington, Moscow, and London early in 1968 was summarized in the title of a *People's Daily* article on March 13: the proposal was "A Grave Step in Forming a U.S.–Soviet Counter-Revolutionary Nuclear-Military Alliance" against China.

END OF A MYTH: THE WITHERING OF IDEOLOGY

No matter which side gained or lost prestige and power in the international arena, the open schism that followed the Moscow Treaty hurt both the Chinese and Soviet regimes by demolishing, probably for all time, the myth of communist unity and the universal validity of the Marxist-Leninist ideology. True, communists had disagreed before, as witnessed by the history of the First, Second, and Third Internationals, by the Stalin-Tito split, by polycentrist movements in Eastern Europe, and by the Sino-Soviet maneuvers at communist meetings from 1957 to 1963. But since 1917 there had persisted the myth that there was a final repository of truth and wisdom, both for the direction of the Soviet state and for the communist movement as a whole. For many Russians this myth was shattered by Khrushchev's denunciation of Stalin.[36] But as late as 1958–59 many Russian intellectuals derided forecasts of an eventual power struggle with China on the ground that there was no "class basis" for such conflict, and because it was precluded by ideological solidarity. Those directly associated with Chinese affairs, such as the technicians withdrawn from China in 1960, knew differently.[37] Those familiar with the border incidents along the Central Asian and Siberian frontiers also knew differently.

But the average Russian must have been profoundly shocked by the dropping of the veil from Soviet charges about "some Comrades"—directed for a time against Albania—that occurred with the publication of the July 14, 1963 open letter in reply to the Chinese missive of June 14, and by the still more bitter and open exchanges that followed the Moscow Treaty. By their very vehemence, the indignant letters and public protests that poured from Soviet citizens about Chinese "ingratitude" suggested the depth of nationalist feeling that had been smothered by a blanket of doctrinaire unity. It would be surprising if these same citizens did not harbor some resentment also against their own government, which had so long kept from them the facts made public only in 1963. Readers of the Soviet press must again have been taken aback by *Pravda*'s publication of Togliatti's charges about the shortcomings of Soviet internal liberalization—a suggestion that even a West European party had the right to criticize CPSU policy.[38] Then, in October 1964, the man who had won public favor by reducing the excesses of Stalinist rule was suddenly removed for "hare-brained" subjectivism.

On another level, the Soviet leaders had for a long time been adjusting ideology to suit expediency. Usually they denied that Marxism-Leninist doctrine had been changed. Replying to Peking's ideological challenge in 1960, however, Khrushchev stated frankly: "We must not now repeat mechanically what Vladimir Il'ich Lenin said about imperialism many decades back, and again and again reiterate that imperialist wars are inevitable until socialism has won all over the world."[39] The July 14, 1963 open letter took another giant step toward the relativization of ideology. It proclaimed, again in response to Chinese criticism, that "the nuclear bomb does not adhere to the class principle." Granted this exception to the class principle, were there not others?[40] The competition between Russia and China in the third world led to still more desperate steps by both sides to broaden their definitions of acceptable allies. For example, whereas the November 1960 Moscow Declaration specified that "national democracy" required legalization of Communist Parties, Khrushchev stated in December 1963 that Marxist-Leninists would prefer to work with "national democratic" states, but that this "does not preclude other forms of development. . . ." Only one condition was prescribed: "Socialism cannot be built on positions of anticommunism, opposing the countries in which socialism has won the victory and persecuting the communists. . . ."[41] As William E. Griffith has stated, this meant that

to "build socialism" (and get Soviet support) a radical nationalist regime must ally itself with the Soviet Union and, although it may ban the existence of a communist party, it must not imprison or persecute individual communists, but rather allow them to participate in the ruling elite.[42]

The test ban was hailed by Soviet propaganda as proof of the validity of the peaceful coexistence line. It served as a kind of proof that it was possible to deal with "sober forces" in the West. Cooperation as well as collaboration was dictated "by life itself." True, "ideological coexistence" remained taboo, and Moscow rejected any suggestion of "convergence" of the Soviet system and Western capitalism.[43] But *Pravda* on April 12, 1964 published a hitherto unknown letter by Lenin urging Soviet diplomats at the 1922 Genoa Economic Conference to isolate and flatter the pacifist wing of the bourgeoisie and

to declare permissible and . . . desirable an agreement with them—not only on trade but also on policy (as one of the few chances for the *peaceful evolution* of capitalism to a new structure, [an event] that we, as communists have little faith in, but are willing to help test and consider it our duty to do so, as representatives of one power confronting others in a hostile majority).[44]

While Khrushchev's government sought legitimation for its moves toward coexistence with the "class" adversary, Moscow's deteriorating relationship with Peking made the concept of a fraternal bond based on common ideology vacuous and sterile.[45]

As for the Chinese, they had long been insinuating that Mao Tse-tung belonged in a trinity with Marx and Lenin. Since the summer of 1963 they had been seeking to take over or promote pro-Chinese factions in parties sympathetic to Moscow. They sought also to set up rival Asian-

African organizations to parallel the front movements controlled by Moscow, while simultaneously taking part in the Soviet-dominated groups. In October 1963 a speech by the deputy head of Chinese agitprop suggested an ideological basis, not only for factionalism, but for the virtual inevitability of political bifurcations:

> . . . Everything tends to divide itself in two. Theories are no exception, and they also tend to divide. Wherever there is a revolutionary, scientific doctrine, its antithesis, a counter-revolutionary, antiscientific doctrine, is bound to arise in the course of the development of that doctrine. . . .[46]

A subsequent article reiterated this formulation and held that true Marxist-Leninists must struggle against revisionists, even if the latter are in a "temporary" majority. But the guilt lay in Moscow—not in Peking:

> . . . The leaders of the CPSU headed by Khrushchev have become the chief representatives of modern revisionism as well as the greatest splitters in the international communist movement. . . .[47]

After Khrushchev's fall, Peking recalled that other "personages" such as Bakunin, Bernstein, Kautsky, and Trotsky had also been "relegated to the garbage-heap of history." It warned that Khrushchev's supporters—"the U.S. imperialists, the reactionaries, and the modern revisionists" would try to resurrect "Khrushchevism without Khrushchev." But history would nevertheless progress "in accordance with the laws discovered by Marxism-Leninism. . . ."[48]

This same article conceded that the "great Communist Party of the Soviet Union and the great Soviet people . . . are fully capable of making new contributions in safeguarding the great socialist achievements. . . ."[49] But it seemed more likely that Peking had different expectations from those expressed. From the Chinese communist standpoint—one not unaffected by the tradition of the Middle Kingdom, by power over the world's most populous nation, by victory in long years of civil war and more recent mastery of the atom—Peking probably saw itself as the successor to Moscow in the realm of orthodox Marxism. Moscow had become the "third Rome" in the fifteenth century, after Constantinople fell to the Turks, and Soviet Russia the "socialist fatherland" in 1917. But Peking now seemed to claim the vanguard position—even while Moscow enjoyed a "false majority"—after the Kremlin fell to revisionism, as demonstrated most clearly when it signed the Moscow Treaty with the Western powers.

Whatever the expectations of Moscow or Peking, it seemed altogether likely that the concept of one truth, one movement, devoid of basic internal conflicts, had itself been consigned to the "garbage-heap of history."

If so, the role played by the Moscow Treaty or even the more general schism within communism would not have been decisive, for Soviet and perhaps also Chinese society had been wrestling, even before 1963, with the challenges to ideology that seem to rise from the very process of modernization. From another perspective, that of *Realpolitik*, it was probably just a question of time before the two neighboring countries, each at different stages of development and with many historical controversies left unsettled, should come to blows. But if the test ban treaty had not directly produced an erosion of ideology (at least in Russia), it is probably safe to say, paraphrasing the poet Maiakovskii, that it had "hurried old history's horse."[50]

VII
Impact on the Third World

The Moscow Treaty occasioned a test of strength between Moscow and Peking not only in the communist world but also among the nonaligned nations of Asia and Africa. Since ideology offers one of the few spheres in which an underdeveloped land may challenge a superpower, Peking has sought to exploit to the hilt the propaganda grist afforded by the Moscow Treaty. Each side has defined the situation to enhance its own position. Moscow specifies the main contradiction in world politics as that between the socialist camp (which it still purports to lead) and Western imperialism. True, the national liberation struggle is a crucial element in the coming victory of socialism, but it must be subordinated to and integrated with the growing might of the socialist (Soviet-led) countries. Disarmament and peaceful coexistence will weaken the material and moral resistance of imperialism to national independence movements. A second alternative is stressed by Peking: the epicenter of world revolution is held to be the conflict between the underdeveloped nations (which China hopes to lead) and imperialism (with which it seeks to associate Soviet Russia).[1]

The summer of 1963 provided two key issues around which the Russians and Chinese could seek to mobilize support: the partial test ban treaty and the subsequent Chinese proposal for total *nuclear* disarmament and a meeting of all heads of state.[2] The extent of the pressures upon the Afro-Asian nations is evidenced by the fact that many of them responded favorably to both the Moscow Treaty and the Chinese counterproposal. (The latter, of course, could be dealt with more conditionally.) In the third world only Cambodia and Guinea refused to sign the partial test ban, for even Indonesia, Burma, the UAR, Laos, and Pakistan adhered.[3] But of sixteen African and Asian countries replying to Chou En-lai's call for an international conference in the period August 3–November 30, 1963, only Burma and Ghana appeared explicitly to reject the proposal, both of them stressing their belief in the utility of the partial nuclear test ban as a first step. (Ghana added that it would continue to seek the seating of Peking in the United Nations as a positive contribution to disarmament negotiations.) Afghanistan, Tanganyika, and Zanzibar also stated their support for the partial test ban, but expressed their interest in other measures that would facilitate disarmament. Indeed Tanganyika's message concluded:

> Much as we should like to see complete disarmament immediately, we believe that in the present state of world tensions progress can only come by taking every possible step aimed at the achievement of the goal of total disarmament. We have therefore welcomed the signing of the limited Nuclear Test Ban Treaty.

Similarly, Laos said she would "gladly attend" the conference, but reaffirmed her belief in the desirability of general as well as nuclear disarmament. Ceylon, Ethiopia, Kenya, Singapore, and Syria expressed cautious approval of Chou En-lai's conference proposal, but Ceylon, for example, warned that the meeting "will achieve effective results only if the major powers possessing nuclear powers participate in it, and are in general agreement with Your Excellency's proposals." The replies of Cambodia, Pakistan, and Sierra Leone, however, backed the Chinese proposal with little or no reservation, as did North Vietnam. But the most ardent enthusiast was North Korea, which—unlike Hanoi—went on to denounce the Moscow Treaty. Pakistan suggested that if the nuclear powers refused to attend such a conference, a second Asian-African Conference should then be convened to consider the Chinese proposals.[4]

The militant Chinese image resulting from Peking's opposition to the test ban generally undermined China's efforts to influence the already established governments of Africa and Asia, but the Soviet proclivity to put the cause of peace and disarmament above that of national liberation hurt Moscow's image with revolutionary movements and with radicals out of power. This situation was manifested by the results of Sino-Soviet competition within a number of international non-governmental organizations in 1963–64. On August 5, 1963, the very day the Moscow Treaty was signed, the Ninth World Conference against Atomic and Hydrogen Bombs opened in Hiroshima. A dispute ensued over the merits of the limited test ban that split not only the Soviet and Chinese delegations, with their followers, but also divided the Japanese Socialist and Communist Parties, and split the once powerful Japanese anti-atomic movement, Gensukyo. The final compromise resolution of the conference omitted any mention of the test ban treaty.[5]

A more clear-cut Soviet victory came at the Afro-Asian Peoples' Solidarity Organization meeting in Nicosia, Cyprus, from September 10 to

12, 1963. Peking tried to prevent the meeting from passing a resolution in favor of the test ban treaty, but the Chinese were so isolated that they abstained from voting against it.[6]

A convocation of more radical composition saw the Soviet Union lose points for its stress on the merits of the Moscow Treaty, disarmament, and peaceful coexistence.[7] The "Conference of Youth and Students for Disarmament, Peace, and National Independence" met in Florence, February 26 to 29, 1964, under the political and financial auspices of the Soviet-dominated World Federation of Democratic Youth and International Union of Students. The communist youth groups of China—followed by Albania, North Korea, North and South Vietnam—boycotted the meeting, on the grounds that it would not be "anti-imperialist" in orientation. Other states likely to take a militant line, such as Indonesia, also sent no delegation.

Nevertheless the Soviet position that progress toward disarmament was the condition for national independence encountered sharp criticism from many third world groups, e.g., from Senegal, Guatemala, and Cuba.[8] These cross-purposes were reflected in the contradictory final "Appeal" issued by the conference. The meeting

> considered the Moscow Treaty on the partial banning of nuclear tests recently signed by more than 100 countries to be a success for the forces of peace. World peace depends principally on the struggles of the people against aggressive imperialism and for the liquidation of colonialism.

As one observer put it: The Russian failure to sharpen the general tone of the Appeal in order to eliminate this contradiction "implied a willingness to antagonize and even be defeated by the floating vote from Asia, Africa, and Latin America for the sake of advancing the Soviet line."[9]

While Peking's line was popular among many rebels and youth out of power, however, Chou En-lai's African safari in December 1963–January 1964 appeared to aim in part at overcoming the bellicose reputation China had acquired through opposition to the nuclear test ban.[10] Repeatedly the Chinese Premier fell back on his earlier proposal for total nuclear disarmament and a meeting of all heads of state to show that Peking too shared the peaceful aspirations of other peoples. Not too much should be made of such declarations, but in all ten African countries he visited, Chou was able to find acceptable common language for a paragraph on disarmament in the final communiqué. When Chou interrupted his African trip to visit Albania, however, the resultant Sino-Albanian statement emphasized the necessity of "unremitting struggle" and condemned in strongest terms the Moscow Treaty. Chou En-lai also issued a number of calls for "revolution," but, as one scholar has noted:

Whatever others in China and Africa may have read into his remarks, on the surface he was talking about the prospects for revolutions of national liberation, rather than any social revolution which could be labeled a "communist take-over."[11]

To sum up, it appears that on balance the test ban's impact on the communist and third worlds in 1963–64 was to help Peking in the former and Moscow in the latter area. The rupture that the Moscow Treaty precipitated within the ranks of international communism strengthened Peking because it forced a number of Asian parties that had been attempting to walk a tight wire to come down on the side of the more proximate communist giant, China. The struggle for power within the communist camp hurt Moscow's position still more because Khrushchev's attempts (and failure) to oust China from the movement led to an upsurge of polycentrism and some pro-Chinese sentiment within European communism, weakening Soviet influence there. As for Africa and Asia, experience suggested that it was becoming increasingly difficult for any power—Soviet, Chinese, or Western—to "win" any decisive influence over the governments of the emerging nations. While some of these governments were sympathetic to Peking's revolutionary appeals, most of them probably found more to recommend Moscow's policies of détente and arms limitations, with the concomitant prospect of economic assistance by the great powers.

Part Three

ARMS CONTROL IN A NEW CONTEXT

VIII
China's First Atomic Tests and the World Response

CHINA JOINS THE CLUB

A double explosion took place in mid-October 1964, producing strong shock waves around the globe. Khrushchev fell from power on October 14, while on October 16 Communist China became the fifth nation to explode an atomic weapon. The first Chinese test (like the second and fourth that followed it in 1965–66) had a yield comparable to the Hiroshima bomb in 1945—about 20 kilotons. But, as Radio Prague noted soon after, a "small bomb" can do "great evil."

The long-range significance of China's first atomic test was underscored by the organ of the Slovak Communist Party:

> The first experimental atomic bomb has been exploded in the Chinese desert, and above it, a cloud of problems opened in its wings.[1]

These problems were manifold: Peking had to determine how to exploit its incipient nuclear power in foreign policy without provoking intervention from abroad. The United States and the Soviet Union had to consider whether they would seek a *modus vivendi* with a nuclear China or attempt—unilaterally or together—to remove the dragon's atomic claws. (The argument has been made that Khrushchev's ouster was precipitated by a hare-brained scheme on his part to destroy the Chinese test facility, but there is little evidence that he planned such decisive action. His removal appears rather to have been occasioned mainly by his personal style and certain domestic policies, although his plans for Germany and his failure either to force the Chinese to retreat or to mobilize collective action against them may also have contributed to his downfall.)[2]

The superpowers were forced to evaluate not only their own security, which might not be threatened directly by Peking for many years, but also the security of allies and nonaligned nations. Washington was particularly concerned over whether its commitments would continue to be trusted globally, while Moscow had to deal with a growing threat to its hegemonistic aspirations in the communist movement. China's neighbors—and potential nuclear powers over the world—had to reappraise their diplomatic, strategic, and general political situation. Should they move closer to or further from China? Should they rely on national, on allied, or on international means of defense?

Peking dealt with some of its problems by adopting a diplomatic posture designed to allay the fears of foreign observers, to disarm the proponents of a preventive strike on Lob Nor, and to undermine the arms control programs of the nations seeking to freeze the balance of nuclear power. The Chinese test on October 16 was accompanied by a statement reiterating Peking's support for nuclear disarmament. For the first time, however, the Chinese singled out a ban on the use of nuclear weapons as the most important and most desirable first step toward total nuclear disarmament. They pledged also "that China will never at any time under any circumstances be the first to use nuclear weapons."[3] Chou En-lai followed this statement with a letter to all heads of state calling for a summit conference to "reach agreement . . . that the nuclear powers *and those countries which may soon become nuclear powers* undertake not to use nuclear weapons, neither to use them against non-nuclear countries and nuclear-free zones, nor against each other."[4]

Peking's arms control position harmonized well with its incipient nuclear capacity. Chou En-lai's circular letter for a summit disarmament meeting was followed on November 22, 1964 by a major editorial in *People's Daily* discussing the alternative first-stage measures that had been proposed by different countries. The editorial considered and then rejected each of three measures: (a) a 3-environment test ban treaty; (b) a comprehensive test ban treaty; and (c) destruction of the means of delivery. Each of these, *People's Daily* reasoned, would freeze or change the balance of power to favor one side or another.[5] The panacea first-step, however, was China's own proposal: a no first-use agreement. Since no control would be necessary, *People's Daily* even suggested the possibility of a bilateral agreement between the United States and Communist China. Peking alleged also that its proposal would not conflict with one of the criteria for judging the usefulness of any first step: "It must serve to promote the struggle of the peace-loving people of the world over for the complete prohibition of nuclear weapons, and not lower their vigilance and pull the wool over their eyes."[6]

Thus, in putting forward its own scheme, Peking also managed to attack the partial and comprehensive test ban measures advocated, with differing degrees of enthusiasm, by Moscow and Washington. Throughout the first half of 1965—at Algiers, Accra, Helsinki and Tokyo—Peking continued its efforts to expose at international meetings the non-revolutionary character of Soviet foreign policy.[7] It did not succeed in wresting control of the World Peace Congress in Helsinki; but Chinese pressure was surely instrumental in obtaining a Resolution on Vietnam that was strongly anti-American, depicting all U.S. negotiation appeals "as sham concoctions designed to cover up the policy of the American imperialists."[8]

The Moscow Treaty was also assailed in 1965 by China's Albanian ally as Tirana spurned a bid by Poland (presumably in Moscow's behalf) to attend the January 19–20 Warsaw meeting of the Warsaw Pact Political Consultative Committee. Among the many conditions Tirana demanded before it would agree to attend was the immediate denunciation of the Moscow Treaty by the Soviet Union and all Warsaw Pact members. Further, if West Germany were admitted to the MLF or otherwise obtained nuclear arms, Albania demanded that all socialist countries also receive atomic weapons (presumably given by Moscow) as a "countermeasure."[9]

China's atomic tests and her accompanying proposal for a summit conference on nuclear disarmament brought forth a wide spectrum of response throughout the communist, nonaligned, and Western worlds. The reaction was on two main levels: first, in declaratory policy—diplomacy and propaganda; and second, in strategic planning. This chapter will deal primarily with the first level; military calculations will be considered in the following chapter.

THE DECLARATORY RESPONSE

Chou's 1964 summit appeal received a somewhat wider and more favorable reaction than had a similar proposal on July 31, 1963.[10] The Chinese Premier's 1964 letter elicited a response from about three quarters of the states that recognize the Peking regime and from almost half of the nations not recognizing Red China.[11] But most of the replies either opposed Chou's proposal or entered reservations. The Chinese leader claimed that the "great majority" of heads of state approved his suggestion, but believed it "cannot be realized for the time being." The reason, Chou averred, was opposition to the idea from the United States.[12]

All communist states except Yugoslavia endorsed the summit meeting idea, albeit with different degrees of enthusiasm. Moscow and its allies attempted to muffle the uniqueness of the Chinese proposal, reiterating their long-standing support for the banning and the destruction of nuclear weapons. Foreign Minister Gromyko in a speech at the United Nations granted that the Chinese proposal merited "positive consideration," but he mentioned the facilities afforded by the United Nations.[13] Other Soviet-bloc statements recalled that the Cairo Conference of Nonaligned Nations (earlier in October 1964) had already proposed a world disarmament parley.

All East European states except Rumania and Hungary specifically mentioned their support of past Soviet disarmament proposals. All but one claimed to advocate general and complete disarmament (and not merely nuclear disarmament); Bulgaria and Outer Mongolia specifically endorsed the Moscow Treaty on nuclear testing—a provocative act in these circumstances. Probably to emphasize that Soviet diplomacy had long endorsed a prohibition on the use of nuclear weapons, the Soviet delegation to the U.N. Disarmament Commission in the spring of 1965 raised the priority of such a ban in its list of desired measures of disarmament.[14]

Throughout 1965 and much of 1966, in a sharp departure from Khrushchev's practice, his successors seemed loathe to use disarmament propaganda as a means of proving the correctness of their position in the Sino-Soviet rivalry for influence in the communist and third worlds.[15] This trend was apparent as early as November 1964, when the slogans for the anniversary of the Bolshevik revolution failed to mention the nuclear test ban. The Kremlin did, however, continue to reaffirm its support of the Moscow Treaty, even though it was not played up in anti-Chinese polemics, and though Moscow did little constructive in 1965 to promote other forms of arms control. First Secretary Brezhnev, for example, specifically endorsed the Moscow Treaty in an important speech on November 6, 1964, reaffirming the validity of the Soviet line on peaceful coexistence as well as other policies classified as revisionist by Peking.[16] Only on occasion during 1966 did the Soviet Government begin again to suggest a positive association between a correct communist position and progress toward limitation of arms.

But Moscow's reluctance to take a stronger stand against China's nuclear tests and Peking's own disarmament proposals was part of a more general pattern in Soviet policy in 1965. The Kremlin seemed to prefer avoiding direct polemics with China, in part perhaps to lay the basis for a rapprochement, in part to legitimate a stronger posture later in case Chinese provocations should continue or intensify. The new management in Moscow, of course, needed to concentrate on putting its own house in order—clarifying who was to do what (and to whom), and proceeding with economic and administrative reforms. Further, even though they might have preferred better relations with the West, the new Soviet leaders were caught in a crossfire between Peking and Washington centering on the escalating conflict in Vietnam.[17]

Full support for Chou En-lai's proposal of October 1964 came from Albania, North Korea, and North Vietnam; and also from Cambodia, Indonesia, Congo (Brazzaville), Mali, and Senegal. Agreement in principle was registered by Algeria, Tanzania, and Yemen. Reservations were placed by Burundi, Kuwait, and Pakistan. Non-committal replies came from France, Burma, Denmark, Norway, The Netherlands, and Finland. Thus, General de Gaulle declared that France would take part in "serious negotiations." Helsinki referred Chou En-lai to its 1963 reply. At least three states argued the desirability of broadening disarmament negotiations to include China, but they proposed a forum different from that suggested by Peking. Ghana advocated a conference of nuclear powers, to be convened by certain non-nuclear powers. The Sudan contended that the best rostrum would be the United Nations. Afghanistan referred approvingly to the Cairo proposal for a world disarmament conference, but conceded that Chou En-lai's letter had merit. (The Sudan and Burma also expressed satisfaction at Peking's pledge not to be the first to use nuclear weapons.) A number of states replied to Chou En-lai's letter, condemning the Chinese nuclear test and taking a negative stance on the summit meeting: Britain, Japan, Yugoslavia, and Ceylon. Finally, several states, including West Germany and the United States, while not commenting directly on the summit proposal, did condemn the Chinese test.

More revealing than the responses to Chou's letter, perhaps, was the spectrum of comments regarding China's entry into the atomic club. The Soviet Government and its allies were reserved or negative to the Chinese test. Moscow announced the Chinese nuclear test and several days later called for a ban on all nuclear testing. Czechoslovakia, Hungary, East Germany, and Yugoslavia were critical also, as were most West European Communist Parties. Rumania, however, expressed her "understanding" of the sentiments that led China to test, a tactic employed also by Congo (Brazzaville) and Ghana.

Words of praise for the Chinese test came from the governments of Albania, Cuba, Cambodia, Indonesia, Mali, North Korea, and North Vietnam; from the Communist Parties of Japan, New Zealand, and South Vietnam; from the pro-Chinese faction of communist movements in various countries, such as the publishers of *Hammer and Steel* in the United States and the World Revolutionary Party in Uruguay; and from Chinese friendship societies in such countries as Mexico and Japan. A large number of African nationalists greeted the Chinese test—

representatives of the Pan-African Congress of South Africa; the South-West African National Union; the Rwanda National Union; the Mozambique National Democratic Union; the Zimbabwe African National Union; and even the Queen of Burundi.

By careful publicity of praise from abroad, Peking was able to emphasize the importance of its nuclear power without itself making sweeping claims, at least for the time being. Thus, Peking gave due attention to a joint communiqué from the Communist Parties of Indonesia and Australia ("Marxist-Leninist" faction) asserting that the Chinese bomb had altered the balance of forces in the world.[18] In the same vein, Peking announced the view of Malcolm X, who termed the Chinese explosion the "greatest event in 1964" and a "great contribution to the struggle of oppressed peoples."[19] After subsequent tests, Peking dutifully reported the news that Western authorities were upgrading their estimates of Chinese accomplishments, and indicating their belief that China was telescoping the schedule followed by the nuclear programs of other states.

The October 1964 Chinese test was condemned by the governments of Australia, India, Japan, Malaysia, Nationalist China, New Zealand, the Philippines, South Korea, South Vietnam, Thailand, Uganda, and—as noted above—by West Germany and the United States. Furthermore, whatever the position of governments, popular sentiment in many places opposed and feared additional testing, particularly because of radiation hazards. Nevertheless, despite the Declaration of the Cairo Conference in October 1964 against nuclear testing,[20] few nonaligned states censured the Chinese explosion later that month. Ceylon used the occasion to criticize U.S. China policy. Pakistan expressed the view on October 20 that the Chinese test made general and complete disarmament more urgent and suggested that a Second Afro-Asian Conference take up the matter.[21] At U.N. Disarmament Commission meetings in 1965 both Mali and Guinea joined Albania in statements attacking the atomic monopoly exercised by Moscow and the West.[22] And many delegations to the Commission expressed the opinion that the great powers should begin to disarm if non-nuclear nations were asked to desist from obtaining atomic weapons.

The relative silence after the first Chinese test strongly suggested, as Morton Halperin has written, that

> the underdeveloped countries have demonstrated that they are not prepared to let their general opposition to nuclear testing stand in the way of the possibility of improving relations with the Chinese and securing Chinese support for operations directed against Western countries. In addition, those countries which desire to play the

Russians and the Chinese off against each other recognize the desirability of remaining neutral on the nuclear question.[23]

Indeed, the number of states having diplomatic relations with Communist China increased sharply in the period just before and after Peking's first atomic test.[24]

THE SECOND TEST

China's second atomic explosion in May 1965 evoked a range of response similar to that to Peking's first test, but there were some important differences.[25] Some East European states became more explicit in expressing their negative sentiments; but Yugoslavia continued to be most critical, Belgrade's *Politika* warning on May 23 that Peking was "isolating itself." In the Soviet Union Premier Kosygin reportedly stated at a reception for India's Premier Shastri that there was "no nuclear blackmail" from China, but Shastri strongly denounced the Chinese tests during his Russian tour.

Representatives from a number of Asian governments in addition to India condemned the new test in severe terms—among them, Japan, Singapore, South Korea, and Thailand. In Japan the socialist left, the student group Zengakuren, and the pro-Russian wing of the Communist Party joined in protesting the May test.

On the affirmative side, Ho Chi Minh and Vo Nguyen Giap declared that the new Chinese test "enlivened the hearts of the Vietnamese people" at a time when the United States was increasing her aggression. North Korea termed the test a "blow to U.S. imperialism." The Pathet Lao broadcast its support. The pro-Chinese faction of Australia's Communist Party declared the test showed that China would "never retreat." Support continued to flow from the New Zealand Communist Party, from a wide range of nationalist groups in Africa, from the National Liberation Front in South Vietnam, and from friendship societies in Mexico and elsewhere. In Japan, interestingly enough, the Chinese test received strong support from the Council against Atomic and Hydrogen Bombs and from the National Council for Peace and against Nuclear Weapons. Further, the Mayor of Tokyo was quoted by Peking as saying that the test was beneficent insofar as it was for defensive purposes.

Cambodia's response seemed more qualified than after the first Chinese test. A Cambodian radio broadcast stressed that man must decide his own fate, implying that atomic weapons could be used for good or ill purposes. Some Cambodian leaders repeated the assertion that China's nuclear tests were for defense.

While Moscow continued to abstain from direct polemics with Peking, the Chinese exercised no comparable restraint. During the first six or seven months following their first atomic explosion the CPR leaders seemed increasingly confident about their position in world affairs (though this situation probably changed later in the year). China's archenemy had fallen in Moscow, even though his successors seem to have been equally misguided.

Peking's second atomic test, like its first, brought relatively little criticism of China and many acknowledgments of her world role, including a tie vote in the 1965 General Assembly on the question of seating Peking. Despite the costs of the atomic program and other problems, China's economy seemed to be on a gradual upswing from 1962 through 1965. And despite the increasing U.S. commitment to Vietnam, Peking seemed confident of the long-term outcome of that conflict, spurning all bids for negotiations in 1965.

The aggressive and confident Chinese mood after two years of open schism was aptly summed up in Peking's comment in 1965 on the second anniversary of the Soviet "open letter" of July 14, 1963. The same comment indicated also that Peking still intended to exploit the Moscow Treaty as a symbol of Russia's embrace of capitalist ways. Both *Red Flag* and *People's Daily* declared:

> Since the publication of the Open Letter, the Khrushchev revisionists committed a series of acts of treachery, the most glaring of which was the signing of a treaty on the partial halting of nuclear tests with the United States and Britain. . . . . Firmly grasping the opportunity provided by this treaty and by other acts of treachery, the Chinese Communist Party and the Marxist-Leninists of the world fully exposed the Khrushchev revisionists' alignment with the forces of war against the forces of peace, their alignment with the imperialist forces against the socialist forces, their alignment with the United States against China, and their alignment with the reactionaries everywhere against the people everywhere. The facts have proved that Soviet-U.S. co-operation for the domination of the world is the soul of the Khrushchev revisionist general line.[26]

A BIGGER YIELD AND LARGER CLAIMS

The third Chinese nuclear test came approximately one year after the second, on May 9, 1966, although some Western intelligence sources had expected it to occur as early as November or December 1965. The test coincided not only with Chou En-lai's visit to Bucharest, where it was expected to boost his influence, but also—to Moscow's chagrin—with the twenty-first anniversary of victory over Nazi Germany. The test further coincided with a major step in escalation of China's cultural revolution.

The newspaper *Liberation Army Daily* took the lead in attacking the editors of *Peking Daily*, organ of the party city committee, and two other papers of the committee, the magazine *Front Line* and the evening paper, *Peking Evening News*.

The bomb itself was over ten times as powerful as its predecessors. Whereas the first two tests had a yield of roughly 20 kilotons, the third test employed some thermonuclear material and achieved a yield of over 200 kilotons. The principle used, some experts believed, was the same as that which had enabled the Soviet Union to build her giant (and quite "dirty") warheads of over 50 megatons—the process of fission-fusion-fission.[27] Although relatively little radioactive fallout reached the United States, contamination over Japan was much greater—perhaps 100 to 200 times—than that produced by the first two tests.[28] The U.S. Atomic Energy Commission reported that the explosion had taken place above ground, a view that strengthened the general belief that the bomb had been dropped from a plane. Although one report out of Peking indicated the bomb had been carried by a missile, a high Chinese official, Liu Jen, to whom this report was attributed, immediately denied it.[29]

There was a new political ingredient in the Chinese justification for the third test. While the official Chinese statement employed many of the same justifications used in the past, it added a strikingly anti-Soviet element. The first purpose listed by Peking for its nuclear program was

> to oppose the nuclear blackmail and threats by United States imperialism and its collaborators and to oppose the United States-Soviet collusion for maintaining a nuclear monopoly and sabotaging the revolutionary struggles of all oppressed peoples and nations.[30]

Given these circumstances, it was not surprising that comment from certain foreign quarters became more hostile in 1966 than it had been in 1964 or 1965. East European and Soviet responses were considerably more negative than in the case of the first two Chinese tests.[31] India's Ambassador Trivedi in Geneva accused China of "anti-socialist arrogance."[32] India's Foreign Ministry seemed to demand either security guarantees or a national atomic arsenal. In one of the most radical changes since the second Chinese test—a development reflecting the massive liquidation of Indonesian communists—the military leader in Djakarta, General Suharto, declared that his country would build its own atomic bomb for defense. Virtually all members of the Eighteen-Nation Disarmament Committee condemned the new Chinese test. The protest note of the Swiss Movement Against Atomic Weapons was so stern that it was rejected by the Chinese Embassy in Berne.

The most significant new word of congratulation for the Chinese nuclear program came from Houari Boumédienne, leader of Algeria since Ben Bella's ouster in 1965, who, according to the *Peking Review* (May 22, 1966), "sent Chairman Liu Shao-chi a letter congratulating China on its nuclear explosion containing thermonuclear material." Praise for the May 1966 tests came also from Albania, from the New Zealand Communist Party, from the Australian Communist Party (Marxist-Leninist), from the People's Liberation Army of Laos, from the Thailand United Patriotic Front, from the Indonesian representative at the Permanent Secretariat of the Afro-Asian People's Solidarity Organization, from the Palestine Workers Federation, and from various African nationalist organizations such as the Cameroon General Confederation of Labour.

Cambodia sent a much less qualified note than the one that had followed the second Chinese test, but Prince Sihanouk seemed interested in increasing the moral and political inhibitions to any future atomic diplomacy by Peking. He declared:

> All peoples cherishing justice and peace and opposing the imperialist aggressors will draw from [the third Chinese test] added confidence in their future, and pay tribute to the wisdom of China, the only nuclear power which has solemnly declared that it will never be the first to use these weapons of mass destruction.[33]

After the May 1966 nuclear test, Peking's propaganda media intensified their efforts to make direct claims regarding the military and political significance of the Chinese nuclear program, in contrast to the earlier tendency to rely on the reporting of foreign assessments. Thus, a joint Albanian-Chinese statement signed in Peking on May 11 proclaimed that China's third test

> is a graphic evidence of the high level of science and technology and the relative power of the great Chinese people, a most important positive factor supporting all peoples opposing the nuclear monopoly, nuclear threats and joint schemes of the U.S. imperialists and the Khrushchevian revisionists, as well as a powerful factor conducive to international peace and security.[34]

In part, this new trend may have reflected a growing confidence based on actual performance, but it seemed keyed also to the mounting campaign to give personal credit to Mao Tse-tung for the nation's accomplishments in all spheres. Thus, a color documentary film recording China's first three nuclear tests began a country-wide showing in October 1966. Its title, "The Great Victory of Mao Tse-tung's Thought," indicated one of the motives behind the production. Its commentary was very outspoken in claims for the Chinese atomic program:

> The first nuclear test by our country surpassed the levels attained in the initial tests of the United States, Britain, and France! It took

China just over a year to carry out a nuclear explosion containing thermonuclear material after successfully exploding its first atomic bomb. This big-leap-forward speed fully proves that *the Chinese people, armed with the thought of Mao Tse-tung, dare to break a path none before has walked and dare to scale peaks others have not climbed.*[35]

Although the three tests provided "one triumphant song after another of Mao Tse-tung's thought," credit for their success was attributed also to "the great cooperation among commanders and fighters of the People's Liberation Army, the masses of workers, engineering and technical personnel, scientific workers, and all others concerned." The leadership of these people was provided, Peking declared, by the Party's Central Committee, Mao Tse-tung, Lin Piao, and Chou En-lai. In a claim that might be questioned on the basis of a reported anti-Maoist rebellion in Sinkiang in the winter of 1966–1967, Chinese propaganda declared that the "entire testing area was a great school of studying and applying Chairman Mao's works creatively. . . ."

Film shots of scientific activities in the testing area allegedly provided "material evidence" that "China's nuclear weapons are powerful and that it is entirely possible to build a defense against atomic weapons if great care is taken." The logic of this argument was not clear, however, unless "defense" was meant to convey "deterrence." But the next claim was even more confusing, for it held that the shots "forcefully smash the nuclear blackmail" efforts of Washington and Moscow, and belie their "nonsense that atomic bombs would 'destroy mankind and destroy everything'. . . ." China's propaganda, it seemed, was becoming more concerned with emphasizing certain conclusions and less constrained by their rationale.[36]

LATE 1966: TESTS OF NUCLEAR-MISSILE AND THERMONUCLEAR MATERIAL

These trends continued in Chinese media's commentary on the fourth test, held on October 27, 1966. Again, the element of timing was important—the test coincided with President Johnson's Asian tour. And again the test was said to aim at thwarting Soviet as well as U.S. policy. The fourth test was in one respect much more spectacular than its predecessors: the bomb was carried 400 miles on a missile (whether winged or ballistic was in dispute) before detonation. This event led Peking to proclaim:

Our country's successful launching of a guided missile-nuclear weapon is a great victory for Mao Tse-tung's thought and a magnificent achievement of the great proletariat revolution initiated by

Chairman Mao. As long as we are armed with Mao Tse-tung's thought, no miracle is impossible for us and we shall ever be invincible.[37]

To be sure, Peking continued also to emphasize foreign comments underlining the strategic and political importance of the Chinese nuclear program. Ho Chi Minh noted that the missile-bomb test proved "the speedy development of China's science and technology and the increasing might of her national defense forces to safeguard great China." Tirana's leaders declared that "missiles and nuclear weapons in the hands of the Chinese people are powerful weapons" for opposing the schemes of U.S. imperialism and Soviet revisionism for world domination. Prince Sihanouk sent his least qualified praise up to that time, stressing the contribution of the Chinese test to progress and to resistance against imperialism.[38]

Peking gave particular prominence to similar statements by Jacques Grippa, Secretary of the Central Committee of the Belgian Communist Party; Alphonse Massamba-Debat, President of the Congo (Brazzaville); Sekou Touré, President of Guinea; Nguyen Huu Tho, President of the Central Committee of the South Vietnamese National Liberation Front; and Souphanouvong, Chairman of the Central Committee, Neo Lao Haskat. It is no less interesting, however, that Peking quoted a number of individuals who, it appeared from their words, welcomed the fourth Chinese test and regarded it as a victory of Mao Tse-tung's thought. In this spirit Peking cited the views of certain persons in the Soviet orbit: a Rumanian and a Mongolian "worker"; a Polish "clerk"; and a Bulgarian "man in the armed forces." While these individuals were unnamed, Peking named a series of others who held the same view, but lived in countries outside the Soviet sphere—a Ceylonese "peace champion"; a student in Nepal and one in Mali; officials from certain organizations in Japan, Syria, India, Pakistan, Somalia, and elsewhere in Africa.[39]

Following upon the experiment in May with thermonuclear material, China's successful wedding of a warhead to a rocket seemed to place Peking's nuclear-rocket program ahead of General de Gaulle's, which had yet to explode an H-bomb or test-fire a nuclear bomb on a missile.

Intensifying this pace, Peking exploded still another bomb on December 28, 1966. This fifth successful test, like that of May 1966, utilized thermonuclear material, perhaps on the fission-fusion-fission principle. This approach produced China's biggest explosion to date—a yield of over 300 kilotons.[40]

The leitmotifs heard in Chinese propaganda since May also intensified. The fifth test was termed a blow to Soviet as well as to U.S. policy. The Chinese success was due first of all to the teachings of Mao. Among those contributing to the victory, the place of honor in the list went to the People's Liberation Army, after whom came "broad sections of workers and functionaries" and, lastly, "scientists and technicians." Once again, Peking expressed its interest in the elimination of nuclear weapons and declared that it would never be the first to use such arms.[41] A message from Ho Chi Minh proclaimed also that the Chinese nuclear advances were "the result of the correct leadership of the Chinese Communist Party headed by Chairman Mao Tse-tung." And the New China News Agency's year-end report declared confidently that "the torrential tide of revolution of the Asian people is surging forward to a new high."

1967: THERMONUCLEAR CHINA

What New China News Agency (NCNA), in a broadcast to Tokyo, called an entirely "new stage" in China's nuclear program commenced on June 17, 1967, when Chinese scientists detonated a thermonuclear bomb from a test tower in Lob Nor. Estimates of its yield ranged from three to seven megatons—from ten to over twenty-five times more powerful than China's previous tests and much larger than the Polaris or Minuteman warhead. Clearly, this was a bomb and not just a device. It was too heavy to be fitted to a rocket; but China had already made rapid progress in reducing yield-to-weight ratios, and a lighter H-bomb could be expected in one to two years.

Though China had entered the thermonuclear club, a step France had not anticipated until 1968, her propaganda approach continued to play up most themes heard after earlier tests. Man—not technology—was still "the factor that decides victory or defeat in war." China's nuclear arsenal was exclusively for defense and would never be used first. Its "ultimate" aim was "abolishing nuclear weapons."

Timing, as usual, played a role. The *Liberation Army Daily* revealed that the H-bomb test had come one month ahead of schedule—perhaps so that it would coincide to the day with Kosygin's arrival in the United States for the General Assembly and a possible summit meeting. Russia's failure to support the Arabs more strongly in the war with Israel was already being scored by Peking. The Chinese test implied that if the Soviets had no stomach to stand up to imperialism, Peking might do the job. In fact, rumors circulated by Soviet diplomats suggested that China might even send nuclear weapons to the Arab states. The test schedule may have been accelerated also in order to strengthen Maoist forces in a difficult period in their effort to consolidate power throughout China. According to the *Peking Review* (June 23, 1967), mass demonstrations all over China celebrated the thermonuclear test. In Peking "cheers, gongs, drums and firecrackers resounded throughout the night." "Red rebels of the Peking Bedsheets Mill . . . showered the crowd with handbills embossed with the character 'double happiness' in red." When the good news reached a Peking urban commune engaged in "fighting a night battle to harvest the wheat," they dispatched a team of 50 persons to salute Chairman Mao. At the Chinese Academy of Sciences 7,000 of the staff gathered together for a "flash demonstration." In Taiyuan, Shansi Province, the revolutionary masses pledged themselves to "a still fiercer general offensive against the handful of top Party persons in authority taking the capitalist road." High in the Pamirs "commanders and fighters at frontier outposts . . . jumped for joy." In the Awa mountain region, army units organized twenty-three "Mao Tse-tung's portrait" propaganda teams and carried the good news to every household, beating gongs and drums.

Credit for the success of the sixth Chinese test was attributed roughly to the same sources as for previous tests, but with subtle distinctions of possible significance. The NCNA communiqué began by recalling that Mao had said in June 1958: "I think it is entirely possible for some atom bombs and hydrogen bombs to be made in ten years' time." This "brilliant prediction," Peking now affirmed, "has been realized." The feat was termed a "great victory of Mao Tse-tung's thought" and of the Cultural Revolution. The leadership of the Party's Central Committee and of Lin Piao were also praised, though Chou En-lai's name was omitted this time.

As before, congratulations to the groups contributing to the effort went first to the People's Liberation Army more specifically, to all its "commanders and fighters." After the PLA were listed the "workers, engineers, technicians and scientists and the other personnel who have been engaged in the research, manufacture and testing of the nuclear weapons." For some reason, NCNA added a hope that these various groups would "guard against conceit and impetuosity, continue to exert themselves, and win new and still greater merit in accelerating the development of our country's national defense science and technology and the modernization of our national defense."

Continuing the pattern followed since May 1966, Peking added quite positive evaluations of its own work.

> China has got atom bombs and guided missiles, and she now has the hydrogen bomb. This greatly heightens the morale of the revolutionary people throughout the world and greatly deflates the arrogance of imperialism, modern revisionism and all reactionaries.

Peking noted also—a point emphasized by foreign analysts, too—that its H-bomb test had come just two years and eight months after China's first atomic test (compared with an eight-year interval for the United States, five years for Britain, and four years for the USSR). The new test allegedly dealt another blow to the attempts of Moscow and Washington to preserve a nuclear monopoly, and it gave great encouragement to the Vietnamese and Arabs in their struggles against imperialism.

Greetings on China's new achievement were reported from "friends in Britain," the "Syrian people," "Tunisian friends," and "African nationalists and progressives." North Vietnamese leaders declared that the Chinese test provided them with "a powerful inspiration in their own struggle against U.S. aggression," while *Zëri i Popullit* proclaimed that the Albanian people looked on "the explosion of China's first hydrogen bomb as their own achievement . . ." Warm messages came also from pro-Chinese communists of France, Belgium, Chile, Italy, Austria, Denmark, New Zealand, Portugal; from the Progressive Labor Party in the United States; from the June 14th Revolutionary Movement of the Dominican Republic; from the South Vietnamese Liberation Front; from President Touré of Guinea; and from Laotian Prince Souphanouvong. Samdech Sihanouk of Cambodia, in his own words, "once again" paid "tribute to the peaceful aspirations of China, which has renewed its assurances that it will never be the first to use its weapons of mass destruction." Rather ominously for China's neighbors with high hopes for prolonged peaceful coexistence, however, Peking after its sixth test gave special prominence to the greetings received from the Communist Parties of Burma, Thailand, and Malaya.

Abroad, as usual, U.S. intelligence sources expressed amazement not only at the magnitude of the Chinese achievement, but also at its timing, which had taken them by surprise. Increasingly the question was posed whether Peking had not perfected the gas centrifuge process for uranium separation, a technique the United States had attempted and then dropped. Nevertheless, the Defense Department continued to stick by its estimate, arrived at in 1965, that China would not possess a significant ICBM force until the mid-1970s. Various Congressmen, however, reacted differently; and pressures mounted for an initial deployment of antiballistic missile defenses in the United States. In other countries that felt themselves endangered by the Chinese tests, particularly Japan and India, political leaders continued to condemn the Chinese nuclear program. Over Japan, radiation increased to fifteen times the normal level, though health authorities did not consider this to constitute a great danger. Many Japanese viewed the Chinese tests as inevitable, but distasteful, thereby heightening the negative feelings engendered by the Cultural Revolution. Large numbers of Indians and Japanese felt increasingly the futility of protest, and many considered more seriously the need for their own countries to acquire an adequate defense against a thermonuclear China. Of the East European countries, Yugoslavia continued to discuss most critically the consequences of China's growing nuclear might. The act of mastering still another devastating weapon was sure to raise Peking's sense of "great power self-confidence," *Borba* warned on June 19, 1967. The paper cautioned that it remained to be seen whether this enhanced self-confidence would lead to efforts to implement some of the "extremely threatening concepts fostered by the Chinese leaders" or would result in a better understanding of the global responsibilities borne by great powers in the nuclear age. At the United Nations, U Thant expressed regret over "any explosion of an atomic or hydrogen bomb by any country anywhere . . ."

In December 1967 China detonated another nuclear device in a test that Western analysts judged a partial failure. Further, Peking failed in 1967 to carry out the space or long-range rocket test anticipated earlier in the year by U.S. experts. But technological difficulties in such an ambitious program are not surprising. What is perhaps more noteworthy is that so little impairment in the program could be traced to the political and economic dislocations effected by the Cultural Revolution, despite the fact that the party-military leader of Sinkiang province had to be put down by pro-Maoist forces. Apparently Peking tried to shield its nuclear scientists from the harassments inflicted on other intelligentsia by the Red Guard.* Indeed, a directive of the Central Committee of the Chinese Communist Party in August 1966 specified that scientists and technicians were to be treated gently. Western estimates about the number of scientists and engineers involved in China's nuclear and rocket programs ranged from 7.5 to 10 per cent of the country's highly trained personnel.

On the other hand, in a speech to a rally on October 9, 1967, Chou En-lai admitted that the Cultural Revolution had at least complicated the tasks of economic and nuclear development, even while giving "an impetus to . . . our country's construction." He continued:

It is already clear that there will be another bumper harvest in agriculture this year. Within the space of less than one year, we have conducted three more nuclear tests, including a guided missile nuclear weapon test and a hydrogen bomb test. Such a world-shaking revolutionary movement of course exacts a certain price in production in certain places and in certain departments. We took this into account in advance. Production is affected to a certain extent, especially in places where disturbances occur. But this is only a transient thing. As soon as disorder is turned into order, production can quickly pick up and rise. The revolutionization of the thinking of the people is bound to be transformed into a tremendous material

---

* See however p. 104 and the accompanying notes.

force. We believe that through this great Cultural Revolution, a new high tide in the development, by leaps and bounds, of our country's socialist construction will inevitably be brought about.

Further, as noted in Chapter I, an article "written collectively by the proletarian revolutionaries in departments directly under the Scientific and Technological Commission for National Defense" and published in *Peking Review* (November 3, 1967) stressed the extent of opposition dating from the 1950s on the part of Liu Shao-ch'i, P'eng Teh-huai, and others to the bootstrap nuclear program championed by Mao Tse-tung, Lin Piao, Chou En-lai and others (in good standing). While the article seemed to refer to events that transpired some years earlier, the fact of its publication, including the attack on current enemies of the Mao regime, suggests there might still be Chinese leaders who would opt to avoid the economic sacrifices entailed in building a national nuclear arsenal. If these leaders should ever obtain command of the country, particularly if they should also realign China with the USSR, might they not slow down the allocation of resources to defense—perhaps deciding in the manner of London that the superpower game is exorbitantly expensive? A slowdown, of course, would be much more likely than a shutdown, but China's great power aspirations seem unlikely to fade, and her leaders may well believe that the period of greatest economic dislocation from defense spending lies behind them.

TRENDS AND PORTENTS

A study of China's initial nuclear tests, of the accompanying diplomatic and propaganda campaigns, and of the world response point to several major conclusions. The overriding impression is that Mao Tsetung's dictum, "power grows out of the barrel of a gun," was substantiated on a number of levels.

First, few African or Asian nations condemned China's tests, although they had gone on record many times as opposing nuclear tests in principle and, in practice, by the United States, the Soviet Union, and France. The major exceptions to this pattern were India and Japan, both of which felt themselves directly threatened and which had the capacity themselves to "go nuclear." The majority of states condemning the tests were either in the Western or the Soviet alliance systems. Some nonaligned nations probably welcomed China's challenge to the U.S.–Soviet nuclear hegemony. Others, even though they may have regretted nuclear spread, were reluctant to antagonize China, in part because they wanted to play her off against the Soviet Union and the United States in the struggle for foreign aid; and in part because their strictures would add little to those already expressed by the great powers. Even in Japan, where public opinion has been passionately opposed to nuclear testing, many people found cause to rationalize acceptance of the Chinese bomb tests. Cambodia, among other lesser powers, ostensibly found solace in Peking's pledge never to be the first to use atomic weapons.

Second, whether from fear or from respect, many nations stepped up pressure for seating Red China in the United Nations. The 1965 ballot on this question in the General Assembly produced a tie vote (though a two-thirds majority would have been needed to carry)—the largest pro-Peking vote in the UN's history. In 1966 and 1967 China's supporters became less numerous in the General Assembly, but the shift was probably occasioned more by Mao's Cultural Revolution than by China's nuclear testing. When Communist China failed to gain a seat at the United Nations, many nonaligned states sought to bring Peking into the UN arena through arranging CPR participation in a World Disarmament Conference. Within the United States, China's nuclear program underlined the "realist" argument for recognizing the Mainland government, perhaps on a two-China basis. Washington placed a high premium on "keeping channels open" via the Warsaw Ambassadorial talks and other forums; the U.S. Arms Control and Disarmament Agency, among other government groups, became increasingly interested in Chinese affairs; and scholars wondered aloud "how to make China arms-control minded."

While China gained international bargaining power, her diplomacy—by emphasizing the defensive character of China's nuclear program—helped to weaken the case for a surgical blow to eliminate the danger of irresponsible Chinese atomic brinkmanship. Thus, Peking could enjoy much of two worlds—the benefits of power without its liabilities. This argument must be qualified, of course, by recognition of the inertial forces that would in any case work against a preventive strike; and second, by the fact that China suffered a number of foreign policy defeats in the third world in late 1965–66, the result perhaps of overplaying her hand.

China's diplomacy helped to justify her nuclear course on defensive grounds, but it seemed not to raise significant opposition to arms control efforts aimed at freezing the arms race. Those who objected to the existing distribution of power would have done so without Chinese goading. Similarly, those who called for great power disarmament as a condition for a nonproliferation accord had their own motives. The non-nuclear weapons states may have resisted such a treaty because they feared a nuclear China, but hardly because Chou En-lai had pointed out the inequities of a bipolar world.

A more disturbing trend, parallel with other developments in China, emerges from the pattern of Chinese communist propaganda. With each successful test since May 1966 Peking has become less cautious in appraising its nuclear program. While foreign praise is still rebroadcast, Peking has grown more willing to express directly its own estimate of the military and political significance of its weaponry. Some American analysts have taken comfort from the fact that Chinese statements about the nuclear tests have been "characterized on the one hand by pride and confidence, and on the other by restraint, if not defensiveness."[42] Thus, Peking has often declared that its nuclear tests are "undoubtedly a great encouragement for peoples who are fighting for their liberation."

But Peking has not explained in any specific terms how China's nuclear capability would be applied to assist national liberation movements. And she has constantly reiterated that her bombs are for defense only. This line of argument, however, fails to come to grips with the fact that we could hardly expect China to behave otherwise—at least in the present stage of her nuclear program. If Peking were to make more specific threats, the claim would hardly be credible, since nuclear weapons are difficult to employ in limited conflicts and their use would provoke U.S. retaliation. Even the threat of their application could tempt a U.S. strike against China. By not spelling out in more detail the strategic utility of her bombs, Peking helps generate an amorphous sense that a great power—and history as well—stands behind revolutionary struggles in Vietnam, Angola, and elsewhere.

Growing confidence in Peking regarding the significance of the Chinese weapons program coincided with the actual accomplishments of the program. It coincided also with other trends in 1966–67 that could point to a more forward foreign policy: provocations apparently aimed at breaking relations with Moscow; reiteration of the "blood debts" owed China by Russia, the United States, and even by African states which have dealt firmly with Chinese agents;[43] radical shifts in domestic policies, many of them ultra-left, and some of them related to a power struggle that has extended even to Sinkiang Province, where China's nuclear facility may have become a pawn.[44] None of these parallel trends provide a clear warning that China's external policies will become more aggressive in deed as they have been in word. But they do raise the specter that, given some combination of internal and external developments jeopardizing the vital interest of the existing regime, China's leaders may take a desperate step, even though it risked suicidal consequences. If this contingency seems remote for the present, owing mainly to the primitive state of China's nuclear weaponry, the probability may increase over time.

Pointing to related if broader problems, Stanley Hoffmann has cautioned that, as China's overall strength grows, "she may be tempted far more than the Soviet Union ever was to despise the enemy strategically" by exploiting uncertainties about commitments of the major powers in Asia "or by pursuing attempts at undermining American commitments —thus setting off, with limited moves (blackmail, threats, infiltration) or *faits accomplis* that misfire, a process of escalation to her own detriment." Conversely, Hoffmann continues,

> Americans might discount too easily the differences in "mental posture" between the Soviet Union then [during the height of the Cold War] and China now, give excessive weight to the handicaps under which China suffers (and which are indeed greater than the Soviet Union's then) and gradually push China into a *desperado* kind of misescalation [i.e., an embroilment that comes not from a wrong calculation, but from a process beyond calculation].

Considered together, he argues, the combination of haziness about commitments to the area, the communications abyss, and the uncertainty about this area of U.S.–Soviet rivalry gives the Asian sub-system "a far greater volatility than the Atlantic-Cold War system ever had."[45]

This volatility was increased by major uncertainties about China's military aims and capabilities. By 1968 many analysts believed Peking's rocket and nuclear development to be as much as a year behind schedule.* While little evidence had been gathered to indicate the possibly deleterious impact of the Cultural Revolution on China's military development, signs mounted in 1968 that top C.P.R. nuclear and rocket scientists had been under mounting political pressures since 1966.** Simultaneously, the Kremlin intensified its courtship of PLA commanders who wanted modern weaponry and not just a theory of people's war. Moscow had dangled this carrot in the 1950s, of course, and both sides might recall their earlier disillusion.

Within this context of large stakes and fluctuating probabilities, we shall examine the agonizing strategic reappraisals carried out around the world in view of China's impressive if uneven military growth.

---

* Besides the nuclear test failure of December 1967, another unsuccessful Chinese test near Wuhan on February 26, 1968, was reported by Radio Moscow to China on June 25, 1968. This broadcast also noted that Hong Kong sources believed China had produced only twenty IRBMs instead of the one hundred planned by June 1968.

** Radio Moscow also reported on June 25, 1968, that Nieh Jung-chen, Chairman of the Scientific and Technological Commission, had been denounced by Red Guard posters after the failure of the February nuclear test. Allegedly, Nieh had been under fire in August 1966, when he was saved by Mao's intervention. Since November 1966 the son of Liu Shao-chi, a rocket expert trained in Russia, had been under detention. Other experts trained in Russia were also being "persecuted."

IX
Agonizing Reappraisals

China's first steps toward becoming a nuclear power, although long predicted, produced consternation and even surprise in foreign ministries and defense establishments around the world. These reactions resulted not merely because the accomplished fact was perceived more vividly than the abstract prediction. Another aspect of the situation was that in both quantity and quality China's nuclear program had outpaced the expectations of intelligence sources, at least in the United States. To be sure, Peking had the advantage of learning from others' experience, but the same could be said of Paris. China, however, had advanced further in the space of two years than had any other nation including France, which apparently hoped to set off a thermonuclear blast late in 1966 during de Gaulle's Asian tour, but did not.[1] As a consequence, statesmen and strategic planners had to evaluate not only their declaratory policy regarding the Chinese tests but also the adequacy of their existing security system. The premises of long-held policies had to be reexamined, whether they focused on nonalignment, on good will, on nuclear deterrence, on collective security, or on some other foundation.

These agonizing reappraisals were complicated by a number of factors. First, analysis of the Chinese threat had to distinguish among a range of capabilities and hypothetical behavior patterns, aggressive and defensive. It was necessary to evaluate China's conventional armed forces not just in terms of gross size but also in relation to the task or tasks to which they might be put, the terrain, and logistic support. Similarly, an appraisal had to be made not only of China's nuclear stockpile but also of her present and future delivery systems. Each delivery system, in turn, had to be assessed against the defense capability (ASW, ABM, etc.) of potential foes.

Each nation was forced to decide whether—whatever China's past and present caution in foreign affairs—a more belligerent course might ensue in the future. Further, if some of China's neighbors were threatened, for example, Japan or India, did that mean eventual peril for the other states along her rimland? Would this mean a threat also to the Soviet Union and her Mongolian ally? If Russia were menaced, would the United States be left alone or also endangered? If America's security were challenged, what of Europe's?

Statesmen must guard against bias from two opposing directions: Westerners (and Russians) may be particularly prone to exaggerated fears based on the image of a yellow peril, but all governments must also resist the wishful thinking that denies unpleasant realities.

THE UNITED STATES

Washington, true to tradition, committed herself to many public estimates about the future size of China's nuclear program and strategic force. Often, however, Washington was compelled to upgrade earlier force. Regularly, however, Washington was compelled to upgrade earlier calculations. Thus, the Atomic Energy Commission several times revised upward its estimate of the third and fifth Chinese nuclear blasts. More generally, U.S. intelligence sources conceded in 1965–67 that the Chinese test program was proceeding on a faster schedule than had been expected, though in 1968 the opposite was true.

One possible sign that the Defense Department's estimates on China's rocket capability had been too low came in early 1967 when Secretary McNamara testified that China might "conduct either a space or long-range missile launching before the end of 1967." There was no manifest reevaluation at this time of earlier Defense Department calculations, and McNamara insisted that it was "unlikely" the Chinese could deploy a significant number of operational ICBM's before the mid-1970s.[2] In 1965, however, he had used other terms before a NATO ministers meeting in explaining the Chinese threat. At that time he had predicted (a) that China might deploy several launchers for medium-range missiles by 1969, with possibly "several dozen" by 1976; and (b) that she might make an initial deployment of ICBM's by 1975.[3] The implication of McNamara's 1967 testimony invalidated these estimates. If China should have a significant number of ICBM's by the mid-1970s, she could presumably have more than "several dozen" medium-range missiles and more than an initial deployment of ICBM's by that time. Indeed, several weeks after McNamara's January 1967 posture statement, intelligence sources indicated that China would have her first operational ICBMs in about three years, although it would be 1975 before she had a force of 50 to 100 such missiles.[4]

Thus, the estimate of 1965 seems to have been revised by that of 1967.

But even the later estimate appeared likely to fall short on the basis of China's past performance. If China could test an ICBM in 1967, would she need until the mid-1970s to deploy a significant number of these weapons? She had already demonstrated an ability to telescope the West's schedule for testing nuclear and thermonuclear bombs. China is known to have been working with Soviet and with domestically-produced rockets for years, and would seem to have gathered some momentum for dealing with the generational and other problems likely to occur in their development and procurement. If the Soviet Union and the United States had been able to deploy a fairly adequate if soft minimum deterrent in three to five years after their first test of an ICBM, why should China need seven to eight years to do the same? [5]

The Defense Department seemed to place the date for a significant Chinese ICBM capability rather far into the future, probably on technical military grounds rather than on international political ones. If China's ICBM force were to be judged truly significant only when it moved toward parity with the superpowers', a span longer than eight years would be needed. But if the question concerned the date when she would have an ICBM deployment useful in international bargaining or crisis situations, the estimate of 1975 might have to be moved forward by as much as five years. Secretary McNamara's testimony in January 1968 sometimes referred to China's likely ICBM capability in 1975 as "modest" and at other times as "significant"; in truth, a modest ICBM force could well prove significant.

Following China's H-bomb test in June 1967, *U.S. News and World Report* (July 3, 1967) posited the following timetable for the development of Peking's military potential: *1967.* Existing stockpile of perhaps 50 atomic warheads acquired since 1964 expanding at rate of over 20 per year. SDVs restricted to aging, limited-range bombers, capable of striking only a few totally undefended areas of Southeast Asia, India, and Soviet Siberia. As yet no deployment of even short-range missiles. A test firing of an ICBM likely in 1967—possibly over Indian territory into the Indian Ocean near Madagascar. *1968.* Modest production of reduced-weight H-bombs, able to be carried atop missiles. Four to eight missile launchers will be in place for rockets of 750-mile ranges. A new class of submarines with rockets for surface firing will appear. *1969.* Modern jet bombers and IRBMs will be in production, enabling Peking to strike at major targets in USSR, Okinawa, U.S. bases in the Philippines. *1970.* 80 to 100 IRBM sites operational. China will have perhaps 100 H-bombs. *1972–1975.* ICBMs in production—about 75 actually deployed, capable of striking most of the world.

These expectations were only slightly ahead of the Administration's, and experience to date suggests the official U.S. estimates could err by a large factor. On the other hand, deterministic extrapolations remain unprovable, for China might not decide to produce all that is within her capacity. Thus—like Khrushchev's Russia—she might produce many IRBMs and few ICBMs (at least of a first-generation type). Or Peking might decide to emphasize one kind of weapon to the virtual exclusion of another. Moreover, other variables could intrude to accelerate or hold back Chinese plans—factors so diverse as internal Chinese politics, technical difficulties or successes, and defense plans of other countries.

Although officials in Washington were obviously seeking to avoid either underestimating or overrating the Chinese potential, the United States seemed to be reliving some of her attitudes during the course of the Soviet Union's rise to world power. For many years, U.S. leaders had refused to recognize the Soviet regime, partly on the ground that it would be short-lived. Later, when the regime's at least temporary presence was admitted, its prospects for mobilizing economic, technological, and military growth were consistently minimized. This occurred between the wars as Stalin's five-year plans began; during World War II, even after Stalingrad; and then when Moscow detonated an atomic and a hydrogen bomb sooner than anticipated in the West.

Despite these experiences, the Soviet ICBM and Sputnik launchings in 1957 caught the United States unprepared. After this shock, however, the pendulum swung in the opposite direction, with American leaders exaggerating Soviet accomplishments in many spheres, and striving to emulate and outdo the Russian system across the board. This response, in turn, impacted not only on the U.S. elections in 1960 but also on the balance of power. Soon, improved reconnaissance revealed, the United States had created a strategic "gap in reverse'"—a four to one lead over Russia in intercontinental-range missiles as well as bombers. The possible dangers in this course were then manifested in a number of situations where Moscow sought desperately to improve its position—in Berlin, in the resumption of nuclear tests, and in the Cuban gambit.

This cycle has not had time to run its full course in U.S. attitudes to China. But some elements have been painfully present: first, in Washington's non-recognition policy; second, in its minimizing of the economic and social achievements of the new Chinese regime; third, in its underestimating of the military and political potential of the Chinese nuclear and rocket program. One wonders in what new sphere the Chinese communists will surpass Western expectations and, whether, in consequence, Peking's abilities may then be overrated. By late 1967–early 1968, the predicted testing by Peking of a space or long-range missile had not taken place, and Washington continued to stick by its estimate that a significant Chinese ICBM force would not be deployed before the mid-1970s. Nevertheless—as is discussed below in Chapter XII—in the fall of 1967 the U.S. Defense Department opted to proceed with plans for a "thin" ballistic-missile defense, ostensibly for use primarily against Chinese attack, although Secretary McNamara had argued just a half-year earlier that the contours of the Chinese threat were not sufficiently clear to justify such a decision.

WESTERN EUROPE

While the Defense and State Departments attempted during the first years after the Chinese detonation to reassure Congressmen and various Asian nations that the U.S. deterrent would restrain even a nuclear China, the approach to Europe was somewhat different. Washington sought to persuade its European allies that their new-found peace and prosperity could be disrupted by an expansionist China, and that they should lend a shoulder in erecting a bulwark to contain her. If only because Chinese ICBMs would be able to threaten Berlin as well as San Francisco by 1975, McNamara told the NATO ministers in 1965 that the more immediate Chinese pressures in Asia, Africa, and Latin America pose a threat to all NATO countries.[6]

Generalization is difficult, since different leaders and different governments had their own perspectives. On the whole, however, West Europeans did not share the U.S. concern regarding the threat posed by a nuclear China. Russia had mellowed; so—with time—would Communist China. In the interim, this was more a Pacific than an Atlantic problem, and hence beyond the immediate interest of Europe. Although some NATO members such as London and Bonn supported U.S. policy in Vietnam, many others thought that U.S. policy was indeed suffering from what Senator Fulbright termed the "arrogance of power." General de Gaulle led those who sought directly to reach some accommodation with Peking—Paris going so far as to attempt selling jet aircraft to Peking until it backed down under U.S. pressure.[7]

The divergencies in the German, French, and British approaches were suggested by editorial comments in leading newspapers following the Chinese nuclear test in May 1966. The *Frankfurter Allgemeine Zeitung* cautioned that Chinese nuclear armament was "something new" in the sense that "it is impossible to forecast how the new possessor will make use of her nuclear strength." *Le Monde*, in contrast, declared that realities must be accepted:

> The world must decidedly grow accustomed to include this new atomic power in its calculations. . . . All diplomatic effort, all the

weight of public opinion should now seek to resolve the conflicts between China and the Occident so that the barriers of hate and comprehension may be lowered.

Less optimistically, the *Manchester Guardian* observed that "we are back to the old arguments about proliferation, and about the need to bring China into disarmament talks that make no progress even without her."

Another view also current, however, saw Washington's increasing concern with China as a sign that Europe would have to fend for herself. And Russia's policy, even if mellowed, had not yet altered the deployment of over 700 missiles targeted on Western Europe nor taken any steps to alleviate the problems of a divided Germany. In the words of the German paper *Die Welt:*

> The Americans see Communist China as the chief enemy of today—and even more of tomorrow—while the Soviet Union, with her military divisions on German soil, will remain Germany's number one adversary so long as Moscow holds to its erstwhile European policy.[8]

This line of thinking led militant factions in West German political parties, both major and minor, to warn against steps that would sign away the country's birthright to nuclear arms.[9] On the whole, however, the nation's leaders and the largest part of public opinion showed little interest either in a shared or in a national nuclear arsenal.[10]

RUSSIA AND EASTERN EUROPE

While Western Europe did not generally share the U.S. concern with the threat from Peking, China's rise to power increasingly commanded the attention of the one "European" power whose territory extended far into Asia and faced the Chinese frontier for thousands of miles. The implications of the Chinese bomb for Russia had been foreshadowed in the Slovak paper *Pravda* as early as October 1964:

> The atom bomb is to be the crowning glory of China's position of power. Since this position of power was built without regard to the fact that the socialist camp has a sufficient nuclear and rocket shield in the hands of the Soviet Army, it is obvious that the Chinese atomic weapon was not created merely to balance American nuclear power as emphasized in the official Chinese declaration.[11]

The Soviet Union did not publish assessments of China's power and carry on public debate as was done in the United States. But mute testimony to Moscow's beliefs was provided by the beginning of an antimissile defense deployment in 1964–67; by the transfer of some troops from the European to the Asian frontier; and by a foreign policy aimed at maintaining quiet on the Western front.

Russia's allies in the Warsaw Pact, like Washington's partners in NATO, sought first of all to avoid involvement in Asia. To retain bargaining leverage many East European states had preferred to keep Sino-Soviet relations from the breaking point. This policy motive began to pale, however, when compared with the prospect that the Soviet Union might become militarily engaged with China, perhaps involving in some way the Warsaw Pact allies. These nations also feared lest the Vietnamese war escalate to the point where Hanoi would call upon the Pact nations to make good their 1966 and 1967 pledges to send volunteers if requested.

Frictions within the Warsaw Pact were probably heightened (again analogous to the situation within NATO) by the prospect that one ally but not others might soon find itself protected by at least a thin ballistic-missile defense system. While both superpowers sought to persuade their allies that a ballistic missile defense limited to the kingpin of the alliance would strengthen the nuclear shield, defense planners in Western and probably in Eastern Europe were not very much concerned about "deterring" China; what they feared was that a defense restricted to the superpowers would underline the have/have-not split, contribute to a go-it-alone attitude, and facilitate understandings between the superpowers prejudicial to the interests of their erstwhile associates.

In reply to such charges—and to critics in the U.S. arms control community—the Kremlin could reply that the Soviet Union would be more vulnerable to Chinese attack by medium- or intermediate-range delivery vehicles than any other Warsaw Pact (or NATO) territory. If only for the record, however, Soviet spokesmen did not distinguish between an anti-Chinese and an anti-U.S. ballistic-missile defense, stressing instead the ridiculously insignificant nature of the Chinese and the French nuclear threats. Nevertheless, Peking charged in 1967–68 that the Glassboro talks had led to a Kosygin-Johnson conspiracy to proceed on a parallel course of building missile defenses not threatening to each other but only to China.

Still another reflection of Soviet concern over the Chinese nuclear tests was discernible in the Kremlin's mounting interest in 1965–68 to obtain a nonproliferation treaty, in part out of fear that nations such as India, galvanized by Peking, might start a stampede to expand the atomic weapons club possibly to include even West Germany. Moscow's support for a treaty added to her troubles in Eastern Europe. The Ulbricht regime, for its part, probably disliked the treaty because it implied détente with the West and respectability for the alleged revanchists in Bonn, while at the same time allowing the nuclear sharing arrangements in

NATO to continue without any prospect of equivalent measures in the Warsaw Pact. The Rumanians, on the other hand, used the treaty proposal to boost their bargaining power on a range of issues.

ASIA

None of China's neighbors could ignore her climb to nuclear status. Most of the nations bordering on the erstwhile Middle Kingdom are small and economically underdeveloped, with no foreseeable prospect of producing their own nuclear arsenal. Among these states, two divergent responses to the Chinese threat took shape. First, some nonaligned states assumed that Peking would some day exercise hegemony in Asia. Since this was inevitable, they concluded that the Chinese giant should be appeased by kowtowing and other symbolic acts, hoping that Peking would remain true to its pledge not to employ its nuclear arsenal unless attacked by atomic weapons.

Other states, which did not share this fatalistic position, tried to retain their independence and security by some variant of balance of power politics. Some, such as Thailand and other SEATO members, placed themselves more directly behind the U.S. shield, allowing military bases to be built and used by American forces to contain Asian communism.[12] Still others, most notably Indonesia, sought a nonaligned course that brought support from Russia and America.

In the long run, many of these states might buy if not produce their own nuclear weapons. For the present, however, only two Asian powers had the technology, wealth, and other resources to become nuclear weapons countries within two or three years. Among all China's neighbors, therefore, her bomb had the most profound repercussions in Japan and India, for only these two countries had a real choice as to whether to go nuclear or seek their security by other means.

Japan

The Japanese Government[13] responded to the first Chinese test in October 1964 by attempting to downplay the military significance of the experiment,[14] though Tokyo soon expressed greater alarm after U.S. reports that the Chinese device was more sophisticated than had been expected.[15] The Ikeda government made clear its opposition to nuclear detonations by any and all countries, and lodged a strong protest with Communist China. One spokesman said that Peking's proposal for a summit meeting to ban nuclear weapons constituted mere propaganda and was unacceptable, for there were many difficult technical problems including inspection and control that had to be setteld prior to such a meeting.[16]

The replacement of Premier Ikeda by the regime of Premier Eisaku Sato on November 10, 1964 brought no alteration in this basic position. The new government stressed that it wanted to improve cultural and economic relations with China; but it condemned the Chinese test and called upon China to adhere to the nuclear test ban treaty, at the same time reaffirming confidence in the Japanese-United States Security Treaty.[17] Premier Sato later rejected, however, a suggestion that the treaty be extended until 1980 when the Sino-Soviet alliance would formally expire.[18] And the Japanese Government denied any plan to allow the United States docking rights for Polaris submarines.

Of Japanese political parties, only the communist specifically condoned the first Chinese test. A statement by its Central Executive Committee in mid-October 1964 declared that the Chinese bomb was needed "to prevent a nuclear war in Asia." Further: "The more important matter of today is not opposition to nuclear tests but how to realize an agreement for a total ban on nuclear weapons." For this reason, it was argued, Chou En-lai's summit meeting proposal should be supported. The ruling Liberal Democratic Party followed the government line outlined above. The powerful Socialist Party condemned the test but justified China's action in part as a consequence of United States pressure against Peking, and approved the idea of a summit meeting to ban nuclear weapons.[19] Socialists also censured China for testing, but omitted any justification for Peking's action. The Soka Gakkai Buddhists expressed regrets over the Chinese test and called for Peking's adherence to the limited test ban. All Japanese newspapers except the communist expressed displeasure at China's test.

The second Chinese test in May 1965 evoked a similar spectrum of response, but it strengthened the hand of those who called on Japan to revise her approach to national atomic armaments. Thus, a publication of the Current Problems Research Institute stated the following conclusion in June 1965:

> For the Japanese people who are the first victims of nuclear detonation, nuclear energy has for a long time been regarded as a symbol of fear. We, however, should not indulge in fear and sentimentalism; otherwise we may miss our future. In the nuclear age, all nations are required to be wise enough to make a right appraisal of the merits and demerits of whether they should have nuclear energy or not. In this case, Japan can hardly be an exception. If the Japanese should decide not to have nuclear energy, that is all right. If possible, it

would mean nothing worse than having no nuclear energy. But we should be aware of the fact that this course would be a thornier path than if we were equipped with nuclear energy.[20]

A similar view had been expressed by the columnist Tatsuji Hanami in the March 1965 issue of the monthly journal *The World and Japan.*

The Japanese Government, however, continued to assert its intention of pursuing national security without nuclear weapons. And a public opinion poll conducted in June 1965 by the Kyodo News Agency seems to support this policy, for only 2.6 percent of those interviewed favored arming Japan with nuclear weapons.[21] By the end of 1965, however, Premier Sato urged passage of a bill to raise Japanese defense spending from 1.3 percent of the gross national product to 2 percent. "The policy of Communist China denies peaceful coexistence," Sato declared. "It is a threat enough without being armed with nuclear weapons. With them, China's threat to Japanese security is real."[22]

As one observer described the psychological climate in 1966:

The Japanese are gripped by a curious fascination for China, a combination of attraction and repulsion, of guilt for the long war and atrocities inflicted on the Chinese and of nostalgia for China, born, in part, of roots in Chinese culture and, in part, in long years of residence during the Japanese occupation.[23]

While Ambassador Reischauer thought the Japanese did not fear China, another U.S. diplomat demurred, arguing that "two things have really shaken the Japanese": first, the Chinese nuclear test in May 1966; and second, the mounting crisis in China during 1966.[24]

But when Harrison E. Salisbury wrote in an analysis of the security problems of China's neighbors that Japan was "moving toward rearmament and almost certainly toward nuclear weapons," the Japanese Foreign Ministry replied that "it is not the intention of the Japanese Government to consider nuclear armaments."[25]

A Japanese scholar writing in 1966 reached a less black-and-white conclusion than either of those just mentioned:

It is probable that Japan for the time being will follow a firm policy of refusing to equip herself with any ability to become a nuclear power. This does not mean, however, that Japan will make no effort toward the development of potential nuclear capability. The more that nuclear energy is used for both peaceful and military purposes in the various countries of the world, the more Japan will have to exert herself to improve the level of her nuclear technology strictly for peaceful purposes. . . . The same can be said about her missile and satellite development. But equally this cannot fail to raise Japan's latent capability to become a nuclear power.[26]

India

In the other major non-nuclear power neighboring China, pressures within the Indian Government were also mounting for a decision to cross the nuclear threshold.[27] New Delhi had to face the possibility not only of Chinese nuclear attack, but of conventional aggression under a nuclear shield. Some Indian leaders said that the main problem was political rather than military—that India's lack of atomic weapons would symbolize her general inefficiency relative to her dictatorial neighbor. Some questioned whether India would not want (or need) to go nuclear in order to obtain a "spiritual bomb" that would energize the country. Others—observing the mounting demands for Peking's admission to the United Nations—asked whether an atomic arsenal was not a precondition for exercising a significant voice in world affairs. To give one small but revealing example, an Indian diplomat raised this precise question when he saw a Chinese calendar on the desk of an American subscriber to the *Peking Review*.

The fragmentation of the nonaligned world manifested in the decision not to hold the Afro-Asian Conference in 1965 added to speculation that India would take the nuclear route rather than rely on moral suasion.[28] And in the midst of the war over Pakistan (complicated by China's threats on the Himalayan frontier), eighty-six members of the Indian Parliament sent a memorandum to Premier Shastri demanding that India begin production of atomic weapons immediately.[29] Shastri, however, declared publicly and privately to high ranking visitors in 1965 that India would never build a nuclear weapon so long as he remained in power. And the chairman of India's Atomic Energy Commission stated that the Pakistan conflict would not affect India's atomic program. Homi Bhabha declared: "We are still eighteen months away from exploding either a bomb or a device for peaceful purposes and we are doing nothing to reduce that period."[30]

The deaths of Premier Shastri and Homi Bhabha in 1966 seemed to exert no perceptible impact on the Indian Government's attitude toward the nuclear issue. Mr. Bhabha's successor, however, was thought to be less interested than he in pursuing the nuclear weapons option.[31] A group of Americans who discussed India's future with members of the new government in 1966 came away with the belief that New Delhi did not intend to exercise its nuclear option, in part for economic reasons (especially the auxiliary costs such as radar, air defense, strategic delivery vehicles, etc). Rather, it appeared, New Delhi planned to maintain an ability to build nuclear weapons within a limited time period (which some experts placed at three years rather than eighteen months). Although Prime Minister Ghandi has been under pressure to authorize nuclear weapons development—to disarm her critics, and to mobilize public support—she remained firm throughout 1966 and 1967. When Pakistan charged in July 1966 that India was planning to circumvent the partial test ban treaty by exploding an underground test "for peaceful purposes," Mrs. Ghandi herself denied the charge. New Delhi also assured Canada that India was not diverting for weapons purposes plutonium from the joint Indian-Canadian reactor.[32]

To summarize the situation in these two crucial countries, there are a number of forces operating in both Japan and India to favor and to oppose the concept of a national nuclear arsenal. In both states the supporters of such an arsenal are in the minority, although they include many "Young Turks"—intellectuals, military officers, and civil servants. Against them are pitted older, more conservative leaders, allied with an indifferent or antibomb public opinion. Apart from the logic used by each side, the younger groups lean toward an activist, modernizing solution, while the older ones tend to rely upon the status quo and tradition. Their arguments pro and con on a national nuclear force deal with four main points:

Pro	Con
Security in face of the Chinese threat: need for assured deterrent and stabilizing counterweight in Asia	Insufficiency of autarkic posture; potential adequacy of a more developed system of collective security
Validity of U.S., Soviet, U.K., French, and Chinese nuclear strategy motives for all countries	Dangers if proliferation continues beyond Japan or India to Pakistan, U.A.R., etc.
National pride: nuclear status is essential for voice in world politics; need for a "spiritual bomb"	Attainment of national self-respect and international influence through (a) self-abnegation and (b) economic-technological development
Technological-economic feasibility of nuclear development; possible economic gain	Economic-technological gain through peaceful development of nuclear energy, space, etc., without wasting assets in arms

There are in addition a number of asymmetries that make India more likely than Japan to take the nuclear route in the foreseeable future, although if either takes this step, the other is likely to follow. Both countries enjoy good relations with the United States and the Soviet Union; but Japan has a security pact with Washington, while India—as of mid-1968—had only pledges from Moscow, Washington, and London that they would protect non-nuclear states from atomic threat or attack. India's situation is also more precarious than Japan's in that she has long borders with China that have been marked by intermittent warfare since 1959.

Moral sentiments among the élite and the masses have inhibited New Delhi and Tokyo from certain kinds of military buildup, but India's neutralism has waned faster and from an earlier date than has Japanese pacifism. India's nuclear program appears to have created a stronger base for a rapid development of atomic weapons production, although Japan is probably the third country after Russia and the United States in rocketry.

For the time being New Delhi and Tokyo, like other threshold powers, intend to keep their options open. The nonproliferation treaty, no matter how many states adhere to it, permits any signatory to withdraw if it believes its vital interests have become endangered. There is also the possibility the treaty might be denounced by several states at one of the periodic conferences which Japan, among others, has insisted be held to evaluate its operations.

The options before Japan, India, and other potential nuclear weapons states fall into five main categories:

1) Independent nuclear arsenal: "armed neutrality"
2) Independent nuclear arsenal within an alliance structure
3) Shared nuclear arsenal within an alliance structure
4) Foreign nuclear arsenal stationed on Japanese or Indian territory, but without sharing arrangements
5) Reliance upon non-nuclear arms, probably within framework of a nonproliferation treaty, linked with or followed by collateral obligations on at least some nuclear powers (security guarantees; general arms limitations, etc.)

The obstacles to this fifth solution and the progress toward its realization are discussed in the two following chapters. Suffice it here to point out the possible tension between what is good for the world and what is good for one's own country. Nuclear spread, many Indians and Japanese would probably agree, holds great dangers for the world. But why should their countries forswear what five nations already have and what most other states—at least for the present—either cannot produce or do not need for their security against a nuclear neighbor? The question is the more salient because, even if self-denial does not produce severe vulnerability to Chinese *diktat*, it could permit India and Japan to be frozen out of great power status through legitimizing "a reversion to the U.N. Charter," i.e., the rule of five particular policemen.

If, on the other hand, either New Delhi or Tokyo decides to build a national arsenal, whether within or outside an alliance framework, their action may well trigger a similar decision by other states in which the balance of forces pro and con nuclear weapons could be tilted by the example of India or Japan. While discussions of a nonproliferation treaty have been taking place, a number of threshold powers have kept their peaceful nuclear programs in a state of preparedness that preserves the option to move toward weapons testing and development if conditions warrant.[33] This has been Sweden's strategy since the late 1950s.[34] A similar course has been followed by Israel, which might some day decide that she needed atomic weapons to deter even a conventional Arab attack. In Latin America, to cite still other examples, although their present industrial development does not place them among the currently most eligible members of the atomic club, Brazil and Argentina have been reluctant to commit themselves to a nuclear free zone.[35] (The same has been true of Cuba, but for different reasons.)[36]

"The problem of new nuclear powers," as Leonard Beaton has written, "divides itself into two parts: the large industrial powers and the guerrillas." For certain large industrial powers, it is mainly a question of willingness to spend money and the general political context in which they find themselves. For very different reasons, the political context has discouraged Canada and Germany. Sweden and Japan find themselves in a less certain political position. Less endowed countries resemble more "guerrillas": they

> might spend their money to acquire something small and insecure. They present perhaps the most disturbing aspect of the problem of proliferation. The day might even come when these weapons would be available for a price and might conceivably be acquired for money by groups of people which could not claim to be states.[37]

Clearly, the governments of India and Japan have it in their power to shape profoundly the future of world politics.

Some analysts have sought to minimize the dangers of nuclear spread by arguing that it will create a quantitative—not a qualitative—problem. The nature of defense and deterrence, they argue, will not be affected by the mere addition of other nuclear powers to the international system. Arguing against complacency, however, the citizens committee headed by Jerome B. Wiesner in 1965 cited a series of quantitative and qualitative dangers that would be intensified by nuclear proliferation:

> . . . the number of nations now possessing nuclear weapons or seriously considering their construction is so large that the reciprocal expectations of mutual restraint, upon which efforts to halt the spread of nuclear weapons are ultimately based, are weakening. A

failure to surmount this crisis of confidence and to prevent the spread of nuclear weapons to additional countries promises to be at least as costly as some of the major failures of the last twenty years: in the time and attention of statesmen taken from more positive tasks; in expenditures; in the exacerbation of tense political relationships; and in increased risks of nuclear violence.[38]

X

The Impetus to Nuclear Spread

Given the impetus of the Chinese bomb, how likely was nuclear proliferation? One State Department official summed up the situation as it appeared early in 1965: "Last week no one believed that nuclear spread beyond China was possible; over the weekend people see it as inevitable." Indeed, spokesmen of the Western, Soviet, and nonaligned worlds expressed the opinion that if a nonproliferation treaty were not reached within the next year or two, the dikes would crumble, and many medium as well as large powers would proceed in time to obtain nuclear arsenals.

By late 1966–early 1967, however, although no treaty had been executed, none of the threshold states seemed to have edged significantly closer to a decision to go nuclear. Indeed, the necessity of examining this question seems to have made some governments more cognizant and fearful of the costs involved in building a nuclear arsenal, plus the delivery, defense, and communications systems needed to support it. Thus, predictions as to the "inevitability" of proliferation had to be reconsidered. On the other hand, even if the United States and Soviet Union could agree on the text of a nonproliferation treaty, there was no assurance that the relevant threshold powers would sign it. Still less was there any iron-clad guarantee that, even if they signed, they would abide by it indefinitely.

Unlike virtually all earlier arms control negotiations, the deliberations on nonproliferation in 1965–68 evoked deep concern on the part of a wide range of states—large and small; nuclear and non-nuclear; Communist, Western, and nonaligned. The reason was simple. In contrast to earlier arms control discussions, these would surely affect the vital interests of many nations, whether or not they led to an agreement. The limitations resulting from the nuclear test ban talks would directly concern only a few states, whereas the nonproliferation negotiations affected many groupings: those with nuclear weapons, the threshold powers, and the other medium and lesser powers. The security and national image of each state would be profoundly affected by the way the problem of nuclear spread was resolved.

Four major political-strategic problems thwarted progress toward a nonproliferation agreement in 1965–68: (1) the security and political needs of the threshold powers; (2) the conflicting interests of the great powers in Europe; (3) the war in Vietnam; and (4) the attitude and behavior of Communist China. These issues are analyzed in the present chapter, while the negotiations themselves—the alternative drafts discussed, the resolutions adopted by the General Assembly, etc.—are considered in the following chapter. (The impact of the Chinese bomb on the superpower arms race, the nature of which is also an important determinant of the struggle to halt "horizontal" proliferation of atomic weapons, is examined in Chapter XII.) Thus, the broad context is discussed first, and then the shifts in negotiating positions. As we shall see, the four problems in question constantly reappeared in the negotiations of 1965–68. At times it appeared that whenever one obstacle had been cleared away, another returned to take its place—albeit in a new form. Simultaneous with this pattern, however, there seemed to be a secular trend toward progress on a treaty, a narrowing of the gap between the points of view of the various nuclear and threshold powers.

THE POTENTIAL Nth COUNTRIES

The first problem concerned the potential nuclear nations—particularly those that stood on the threshold, such as India and Japan. Could their security and political needs be better met through a nonproliferation treaty (with possible collateral arrangements) or by development of a national or joint nuclear force, perhaps in the framework of a new alliance system?

New Delhi, Tokyo, Bonn, and other capitals expressed their opposition to discriminatory arrangements by the nuclear haves against the have-nots. India took the lead in demanding a "balance of obligations and responsibilities for the nuclear as well as the non-nuclear states." Thus, as conditions for a nonproliferation treaty, India and other states insisted upon a series of measures, sometimes combining them into a package:

  a) Security guarantees for the non-nuclear powers
  b) A comprehensive test ban (perhaps universally binding, i.e., restricting China as well)
  c) Steps toward disarmament by the nuclear powers
  d) The signature of all nuclear states, including China

e) A halt in all nuclear-weapons production

f) The right to carry out atomic explosions for peaceful purposes

g) Assurance that the spin-off from nuclear weapons technology would be shared with non-nuclear weapons states

h) Acceptance by the nuclear weapons states of the same inspection procedures by which they proposed to monitor reactors in the civilian nuclear states

i) A strong preference on the part of West European countries, particularly Germany, for inspection of atomic facilities by EURATOM rather than by the International Atomic Energy Agency

j) Assurances that the treaty would not impede but rather facilitate research and utilization of nuclear energy for peaceful purposes in all states, including those with civilian nuclear programs

k) The right to review, amend, and withdraw from the treaty under certain conditions[1]

Indeed, although some of these conditions originated in the special needs of a particular country, by early 1967 a British strategist noted that visitors to his office from Japan were using German objections to the proposed treaty, Germans were citing Indian arguments, Japanese were citing Indian demands, and so on. It was not surprising that the potential nuclear weapons states sought to raise the price for their forswearing atomic weapons. But the nature of their professed objections to a nonproliferation pact prompted a series of questions: First, were these governments not inserting jokers into the negotiating deck which they knew would create insurmountable obstacles to an accord, just as Paris and Peking had done before (and after) their first atomic explosions?[2] Second, was it not contradictory to call both for security guarantees and for nuclear disarmament by the very states whose power would be needed to deter China? Third, was there, in fact, a "sacrifice" involved in foregoing nuclear weapons for which some compensation should be provided? Fourth, why was China's signature essential, provided that in fact she did nothing to spread nuclear weapons? Fifth, what kind of guarantees were sought? India wanted both her nonalignment and guarantees at the same time. Assuming this dilemma were resolved, did she really believe in the efficacy of any verbal guarantees?

One Indian negotiator scoffed at a suggestion that the United States and Soviet Union guarantee all non-nuclear powers from atomic attack. "What is the worth of your promises," he asked in December 1965, "when Pakistan, contrary to President Eisenhower's assurances, is now using U.S. Patton tanks to invade our territory?" The only adequate insurance against China, he concluded, would be a knockout blow against her nuclear plants. The increasingly serious terms in which New Delhi viewed the atomic question were no doubt reflected in a policy statement by India's Ambassador to the ENDC recalling that pleading had achieved no results, and that the time had come to make the test ban treaty universally binding—apparently, it seemed, by coercion if need be.[3]

Considering the complications that such demands threw into the negotiations, the belief grew in 1966–67 that if a nonproliferation treaty were to be reached in the foreseeable future, it would have to be an uncomplicated one. It would have to state the minimum conditions—non-transfer and non-acquisition—and leave the remaining problems to be worked out over the next four or five years, after which the basic treaty might be formally reviewed. How these problems and the proposed solutions to them evolved in 1967–68 is discussed in Chapter XI.

CONFLICT IN EUROPE

A second major obstacle to a nonproliferation treaty arose from the conflicting interests of the great powers in Europe. Could a formula for nonproliferation be found that reconciled the U.S. interest in strengthening NATO and Moscow's objective in weakening it? More specifically, could an accord be reached that permitted West Germany a role in NATO strategy that satisfied the perceived military and political requirements of Bonn, Washington, and Moscow? Whereas the condition stipulated by certain threshold powers suggested that they put their national atomic programs above the goal of nonproliferation, the policies in Europe of the Soviet Union, the United States, and—neither last nor least—the Federal Republic implied that they too valued certain priorities more than a treaty against nuclear spread.

Probably the greatest political impediment to an East-West accord on arms control and related issues since Stalin's death has been the unsettled future of Central Europe. The problem became more sharply focused in the early 1960s as the United States attempted to keep her alliance from collapsing over the nuclear issue in the manner of the Sino-Soviet axis. Beginning in 1958 General de Gaulle had been provoked into his independent course in part as a consequence of U.S. refusal to give Paris a greater voice in the direction of Western nuclear strategy. Washington was determined to keep Germany from following the French (and Chinese) pattern. But the dilemma was more complex, for the United States sought to keep Bonn a satisfied member of the Western Alliance and still prevent her from having her own nuclear forces.

The basic means by which Washington sought to achieve these somewhat contradictory objectives was by promoting a multilateral nuclear

force (MLF) over which the United States retained a veto—thus halting
the de facto spread of independent control of atomic weapons.[4] But the
U.S. goals ran squarely athwart Moscow's long-standing interest in undermining the cohesiveness of NATO and Russia's historically-rooted
opposition to greater German access to *Blitzkrieg* weapons or increased
German influence over Western strategic planning.[5]

Toward the end of 1965, however, a solution came into sight for
reconciling the political-military aspirations of Bonn, the alliance strategy of Washington, and the European policy of Moscow. The formula
for this reconciliation had three parts. First, the West German and U.S.
governments tacitly agreed to bury their plan for a multilateral nuclear
force.[6] Second, although they denied that this was a substitute, a Consultative Committee of NATO ministers was created to give Germany
and other allies a greater voice in the strategic nuclear planning of the
Western alliance.[7] Third, despite initial reservations, Moscow suggested
that it might not regard the Consultative Committee as "indirect access"
to nuclear weapons for Germany—hence, not as incompatible with a
pact on nonproliferation.[8]

Despite this basis for reconciliation of divergent interests, no clear
accord was reached in 1966. Although the MLF seemed to have expired,
some Western officials sought to keep alive other options such as an
all-European nuclear force. Second, the NATO partners did not themselves reach any consensus on the composition and functions of the
Consultative Committee until late in 1966. Third, until the NATO powers
had clearly defined the nature of the Consultative Committee, Moscow
refused to commit itself on the compatibility of the committee and a pact
to halt nuclear spread.[9]

By late 1966–early 1967, however, it seemed clear that a three-way
understanding had been reached on the relationship between Germany
and nuclear proliferation. President Johnson had made it clear to Chancellor Erhard in September 1966 that the United States did not envision a
hardware solution for West Germany. Erhard's successors,[10] the Kiesin-
ger-Brandt coalition elected late in 1966, intensified Germany's own
program of peaceful engagement in Eastern Europe, leaving aside
Bonn's earlier anxieties about its role in Western nuclear strategy. That
role—Washington and Bonn now concurred—could be adequately realized through the Consultative Committee. Finally, Moscow agreed that
such consultation would not be excluded by a nonproliferation pact.

WAR IN ASIA: CONTAINMENT VS. DÉTENTE

The third major issue obstructing the negotiations derived from the
war in Southeast Asia. Could a means be found either to de-escalate the

Vietnamese conflict or to ignore it for purposes of arms control negotiations? The United States favored compartmentalization: the pursuit of nonproliferation without regard to the war.

The Kremlin apparently favored a similar view in 1955 when it simultaneously shipped arms to Cairo and promoted disarmament and the Geneva Spirit, while the Eisenhower Administration saw such policies as antithetical. A decade later the tables were reversed, and Moscow frequently declared—especially during the first half of 1965—that arms control negotiations could not move forward while a "sister socialist country" was being bombed by American planes. Whereas the United States in 1955 was primarily concerned with the substance of Soviet policies that could destabilize the Middle East, the Kremlin in 1965 seemed more agitated by considerations of its image. How could Moscow talk arms control with Washington without being branded as a traitor to revolution? How could it even encourage Hanoi to negotiate without exposing the Soviet Government to charges that it was collaborating with the White House to divide the world between them?

The policies of the superpowers toward Vietnam indicated that here, as in Europe, other political goals might take priority over pragmatic action to halt nuclear spread. There was a choice between immediate, relatively tangible goals and further range, somewhat uncertain ones. The engagement in Southeast Asia existed in the here and now; the dangers of nuclear spread and the possible benefits from avoiding it, if any, lay in the future. Some Westerners reasoned that the Soviets, if they sincerely wished to avoid nuclear spread, should comprehend the American predicament and sacrifice Russia's revolutionary image to the extent required to compartmentalize arms control from the upheavals in Asia. The Russians replied that the Americans should also understand their position; at a minimum, they argued, Washington should halt its bombing of North Vietnam.

The Kremlin's intransigence on these matters was particularly manifest in the first half of 1965. Moscow's refusal in February 1965 to resume ENDC negotiations in Geneva and its insistence on reconvening the entire U.N. Disarmament Commission in New York was a harbinger of propaganda tirades to come. When the Commission met in April 1965, Ambassador Fedorenko promptly initiated what became a series of attacks by Soviet and East European delegations on U.S. policies in Southeast Asia and elsewhere. As one African delegate put it, a major speech by Soviet Ambassador Fedorenko to the U.N. Disarmament Commission was "70 percent Vietnam and only 30 percent arms talk."[11] Even when Moscow agreed to resume negotiations in the relative intimacy of the ENDC forum in July 1965, and later during the General Assembly discussion of nonproliferation and other arms control matters, Soviet diplomats kept up their guard by frequent attacks upon U.S. imperialism.

By the summer of 1965, however, Moscow had adopted a less harsh position. Early in July, Moscow agreed to resume the ENDC meetings in Geneva. A Soviet diplomat was reported to have discussed carefully with William C. Foster his article on nonproliferation in order to understand fully its meaning.[12] W. Averell Harriman was received in Moscow for a series of private talks.[13] The Soviet direction of the World Peace Congress at Helsinki repeated the basic tactics of the 1964 Florence and other such meetings, attempting to fend off denunciations of U.S. imperialism—at least prior to the meeting—in order to obtain the widest popular support and unity in the cause of peace.[14] In the fall of 1965 some visitors to Moscow came away with the impression that if other roadblocks to a nonproliferation pact could be overcome, the Kremlin would not let Vietnam stand in the way of a treaty.[15] And on the eve of the resumption of talks at the ENDC in 1966, Soviet Ambassador Tsarapkin told newsmen that it would be difficult to negotiate against the background of the Vietnamese war, but that he did not want to make the arms control negotiations "interdependent" with the war. Rather, he said, that "difficult situation" made it all the more reason to "strengthen our efforts in the direction of disarmament."[16]

In 1966, as Moscow seemed more intent upon excommunication proceedings against Peking, and as China's image lost its luster as a result of the excesses of her cultural revolution, the Kremlin appeared less inhibited by Chinese accusations that Russia had joined forces with reactionary imperialism. A Soviet diplomat explicitly denied that arms control negotiations were hindered by the Vietnam war. On the contrary, Moscow began to emphasize, the existence of that conflict made it more imperative to reduce tensions and to contain the arms race.[17] A Soviet broadcast to Albania went so far as to argue the compatibility of working for wars of national liberation, as in Vietnam, and striving for a nonproliferation treaty in the ENDC. Although the logic was not entirely clear, Moscow's point was that the oppressed peoples were in no position to acquire nuclear weapons. Therefore any restriction on such weapons (even those that might be acquired by India?) or upon foreign bases could only redound to the benefit of anti-imperialist movements.[18] Nevertheless, the Kremlin kept a long spoon in its dealings with the devil. Brezhnev threw cold water on Johnson's invitation to visit the United States, saying it was a "strange and persistent illusion" that U.S. political leaders "make believe that the relations between the United States and the Soviet Union and other socialist countries can develop without hindrance, regardless of U.S. aggression against Vietnam and the Americans' interference in the affairs of other countries." Brezhnev qualified this statement, however, by declaring that

if the U.S.A. wants to develop mutually profitable relations with the
Soviet Union (and we would like this in principle), it is necessary to
remove the main obstacle: stop the piratic raids on a socialist state,
the Democratic Republic of Vietnam; stop the aggressive war
against the Vietnamese people; respect not in words but in deeds the
independence, sovereignty, and territorial integrity of other countries and peoples.[19]

CHINA AND NUCLEAR SPREAD

A fourth problem was the stand of Communist China: would she
hinder, countenance, or help efforts to halt nuclear spread? Unlike most
other nations that have acquired nuclear status, Communist China manifested little interest in shutting the door to the club behind her. It was, of
course, her military potential that provided a major incentive for states
such as India and Japan to obtain nuclear weapons. Beyond that, however, China talked at times as though she herself intended to contribute
actively to nuclear spread. And her general opposition to arms control
measures involving the superpowers might deter smaller states from
actively supporting a nonproliferation pact.

By the early 1960s Peking's declaratory policy came to advocate the
spread of nuclear weapons to socialist and, apparently, to other "peace-
loving" states as well.[20] The polemics following the Moscow Treaty
intensified this line. The Chinese argued in 1963 that "in fighting imperialist aggression and defending its security every socialist country has to
rely in the first place on its own defense capability, and then—and only
then—on assistance from fraternal countries and the peoples of the
world."[21] Furthermore, the possession of atomic weapons by additional
socialist states would add to the credibility of the deterrent capability of
the socialist camp as a whole.[22] As Peking put it on one occasion:

> Did the danger of nuclear war become greater or less when the
> number of nuclear powers increased from one to two? We say it
> became less, not greater.[23]

Finally, the Chinese argued that the spread of nuclear weapons would
enhance the prospects of worldwide nuclear disarmament.[24]

The immediate purpose of Chinese public statements on this subject
was to legitimate Peking's own determination to develop atomic weapons, and China's tune changed somewhat following her first nuclear test.
From October 1964 through April 1965 statements from Peking tended to
by-pass the issue of nuclear proliferation, stressing, however, that breaking the U.S. atomic monopoly would help to overcome nuclear blackmail
and to speed the road to nuclear disarmament. China's atomic shield, it
was frequently suggested, would protect the oppressed peoples.[25]

In June and July 1965, perhaps to take the sting from China's second atomic test, Peking returned to more explicit declaratory support for nuclear dissemination. Only when atomic weapons were shared by the opponents of imperialism, Peking now contended, would there be peace.[26]

Peking's ambivalent posture gave rise to speculation that she might give at least token assistance to putative allies such as Indonesia, or carry out a test on their territory for which both parties could claim some credit. In late January 1965 Vice-Premier Chen Yi had told the visiting Indonesian delegation that their negotiations would "definitely usher in a new, still higher phase in the comrade-in-arms relations of friendship, solidarity and mutual help between our two countries."[27] The final communiqué of their talks was reminiscent of the statements issued by Moscow and Peking in late 1957–early 1958. It affirmed that Chinese and Indonesian representatives had decided to strengthen their technical cooperation, expand their trade, develop maritime transportation between them, and strengthen their friendly contacts in the military field.[28] One analysis concluded from the evidence that "China also offered to extend technical and scientific aid to Indonesia, an important part of which could consist of the training of Indonesian specialists at Chinese nuclear installations."[29]

In the second half of 1965 the prospect that China might herself welcome the spread of atomic weapons seemed to diminish, for Peking began to encounter a series of foreign policy defeats in that period, culminating in the violent suppression of the Indonesian Communist Party (PKI). The net effect was probably to strengthen an awareness in Peking that putative allies could not be trusted indefinitely. (The Chinese may have recalled that the Russians, too, once had afterthoughts regarding nuclear aid.)

On the one hand, Peking was probably becoming less confident of its influence over other states; on the other, it may have felt less need to legitimate China's own nuclear program. Whatever the reason, in September 1965 Vice-Premier Chen Yi at a major press conference in Peking[30] declared flatly that China would not give nuclear military assistance to other countries. Asked by a *London Times* correspondent whether China were prepared to share her nuclear knowledge with any of the developing countries, Chen Yi first extolled the virtues of self-reliance, citing China's experience in sixteen years of construction. "So far," he declared, "there has not been any country in the world which can change its state of backwardness by merely relying on foreign aid." Once imperialist and colonialist controls were thrown off, Chen Yi predicted, "the people of Asia, Africa, Latin America will overtake the industrially advanced countries within a few decades." Zeroing in on the question asked him, the Chinese Vice-Premier declared:

There are two aspects to the question of nuclear cooperation. As for the peaceful use of atomic energy and the building of atomic reactors, China has already been approached by several countries, and China is ready to render them assistance; as for the request for China's help in the manufacture of atom bombs, this question is not realistic.

Chen Yi downplayed the need for atomic weapons and seemed instead to stress the need for political revolution and economic development. But he continued to pay lipservice to the theoretical ideal of a wider dissemination of nuclear weapons.

In my opinion, the most important task for the Afro-Asian countries today is to shake off imperialist control politically, economically and culturally and develop their own independent economy. This task is an acute struggle and its accomplishment will take quite a few years. Any country with a fair basis in industry and agriculture and in science and technology will be able to manufacture atom bombs, with or without China's assistance. China hopes that Afro-Asian countries will be able to make atom bombs themselves, and it would be better for a greater number of countries to come into possession of atom bombs.

He reiterated, however, that "the role of atom bombs should not be over-stressed," noting that twenty years of U.S. attempts at nuclear blackmail had accomplished nothing. Turning a phrase, Chen Yi declared that "the just struggle of Afro-Asian countries against imperialism and colonialism is the best atom bomb."[31]

When pressed further by Japanese correspondents about China's nuclear weapons development, Chen Yi said that a third bomb would be tested. "As to the time of its explosion, please wait for our communiqué. Atomic technology and delivery technology are, of course, rather complicated; but Chinese, Asians, and Africans certainly can all master them, if efforts are made."

He declared, however, that "China does not decide her foreign policies according to whether or not she has got atom bombs." She was "ready to enter into friendly cooperation with still more countries in order to oppose imperialism and colonialism, isolate U.S. imperialism and safeguard world peace." Chen Yi reaffirmed that China "is manufacturing atom bombs in order to liquidate them and for the purpose of self-defense," and had "pledged never to be the first to use atom bombs." He reiterated "that all countries, big and small, should come together and agree on the destruction of atom bombs and on the prohibition of the use, manufacture, stockpiling and testing of nuclear weapons."

Reviewing the negotiations at the ENDC and the United Nations in 1965 on nonproliferation, two Chinese statements attacked the principle of U.S.–Soviet collaboration on such matters, minimizing the differences between the U.S. and Soviet draft treaties. One article was skeptical about the U.S. treaty because it would permit nuclear sharing in Europe,[32] while the other noted that Moscow and Washington had supported the resolution cosponsored by the eight nonaligned members of the ENDC. Without clarifying to whom the pronoun "they" referred, Peking stated:

> It seems that they are in a great hurry to make an early deal on the "prevention of nuclear proliferation" in order to deprive the peace-loving nations of their right to possess the means of defense against U.S. imperialist nuclear blackmail.[33]

Neither statement suggested a great Chinese objection to halting nuclear spread to other countries.[34]

In 1966, however, China's objections to nonproliferation negotiations became more vehement. On numerous occasions Peking attacked the U.S.–Soviet collusion that sought to foist a legitimation of their atomic monopoly upon the rest of the world.[35] The Chinese Government even made a flat statement that

> We will never be party to the so-called nuclear nonproliferation treaty to deprive the non-nuclear countries of their rights and injure the interests of the people of the world.[36]

U.S. imperialism, the Chinese statement continued, would never agree to a ban on the use of nuclear weapons "when more or all countries possess them and when the U.S. nuclear monopoly is completely broken." Could "anything under the sun be more preposterous," China demanded, than a view that held it right for some nations but not for others to have nuclear weapons? Or for U.S. imperialism to back its aggression with nuclear weapons while other nations are deprived of the means of self-defense? The United States, Peking argued, is the world's "worst nuclear proliferator," stationing atomic weapons at bases and under oceans around the globe. By acquiescing in a Consultative Committee within NATO, the argument ran on, Moscow was contributing to the spread of nuclear weapons to West Germany.

"Rubbish!" was Peking's epithet for the notion that some nations might impoverish themselves by producing their own nuclear weapons, and hence should rely on a U.S.–Soviet nuclear "protection." "It is the business of every country in the world to decide for itself whether to develop nuclear weapons or not," China declared. Prior to general nuclear disarmament, "nobody is entitled to deprive another of the right to have nuclear weapons." To have U.S. "protection" would be to let "the wolf into the sheepfold"; to permit Soviet protection would be to put one's country "under the control of big-nation chauvinism."

The increased Soviet interest in achieving a deal with the United States while the latter expanded its aggression in Vietnam "further exposes . . . their sham support and real betrayal of the Vietnamese people." Both superpowers became more anxious to conclude a nonproliferation treaty after Peking's guided missile nuclear weapons test, but China's encouragement to and influence upon revolutionary struggles "cannot be checked."[37]

China rejected also a number of other arms control measures under discussion. Privately and publicly she turned down the idea of Chinese participation in a World Disarmament Conference, even though it would not formally be held under U.N. management.[38] She was cool to a U.S. query at the Warsaw Ambassadorial talks as to Peking's possible interest in linking its proposal for joint pledges for the non-first use of nuclear weapons with Chinese accession to the nuclear test ban treaty.[39] She refused even to approve a treaty declaring Latin America a nuclear free zone, arguing:

> Since the United Nations has ignored all the rights of the People's Republic of China in the world organization, China will have no part in its activities and therefore is in no position to support the Treaty on the Denuclearization of Latin America.[40]

An agreement whereby the U.S. Atomic Energy Commission would supply enriched uranium to India was also criticized. Peking noted: "The signing of the contract right after China's successful third nuclear test shows that the Johnson Administration wants to step up its collusion with Indian expansionists to oppose China." Further: "The new U.S. move once again exposes the hypocrisy of the U.S. Government in its loud clamors for the 'nonproliferation' of nuclear weapons."[41] As for the United Nations Organization, the Joint Albanian-Chinese Statement of May 1966 averred that it was "increasingly becoming a place for Soviet–U.S. political bargaining." Hence, the two sides declared that

> the domination of the United Nations by a few big powers must be ended and that the United Nations must rectify its errors and undergo a thorough reorganization.[42]

Signs of U.S.–Soviet rapprochement in other fields, as in the agreement for direct flights from Moscow to New York, were also denounced by Peking. President Johnson's October 7, 1966 address was labeled a "Confession of Worldwide U.S.–Soviet Collusion on a Big Scale." It was another indication that, in fact, "a U.S.–Soviet alliance is already in existence." Peking warned, however, that while Washington and Moscow might believe they shared "common interests" because of "the revolution of the peoples of the world and the Chinese people," they would also have a " 'common destiny'. . . for they are pitting themselves against the current historical trend."[43]

China's views in 1967–68 about the draft nonproliferation treaty and the proposed Security Council guarantee system were in line with previous utterances. The treaty, Peking noted, placed no obligation upon the nuclear powers to restrain their arms buildup, which the Chinese alleged was directed primarily against China. Whatever changes might be made in the draft treaty, *People's Daily* maintained on January 24, 1968, the counterrevolutionary aims of its sponsors would remain unaltered. The guarantee arrangement, *People's Daily* charged on March 13, 1968, was "A Grave Step in Forming a U.S.–Soviet Counter-Revolutionary Nuclear-Military Alliance." It was vainly aimed at raising the morale of "such anti-China flunkeys as the Indian reactionaries." "The height of impudence" was another way Peking summed up the U.S.–Soviet conspiracy.

> Making use of the so-called "nuclear protection," U.S. imperialism and Soviet revisionism arbitrarily want to drag all countries without nuclear weapons into joining the "treaty on the non-proliferation of nuclear weapons" which they have cooked up. This is a sinister conspiracy to control and enslave the countries without nuclear weapons and turn the peoples of these countries into their nuclear slaves. Banking on the nuclear weapons in their hands, they vainly hope to reduce the "non-nuclear countries" in the world to their "protectorates." If this conspiracy succeeds, any country without nuclear weapons subscribing to the "treaty on the non-proliferation of nuclear weapons" will never be able to possess nuclear weapons to resist the nuclear threat from U.S. imperialism and Soviet revisionism and will be deprived of its right to oppose the development, stockpiling and use of nuclear weapons by U.S. imperialism and Soviet revisionism. Such countries can only meekly submit their destiny to the whims of U.S. imperialism and Soviet revisionism.

> Countries, big or small and with or without nuclear weapons, should be treated as equals. The proposal for so-called "nuclear protection" is in itself an insult to the dignity of any country that has no nuclear weapons and an infringement on its sovereignty. Any country which cherishes its own independence and sovereignty will see through this plot hatched by U.S. imperialism and Soviet revisionism. The genuine peace-loving countries and people of the whole world firmly oppose the "nuclear protection" of U.S. imperialism and Soviet revisionism.

Our great leader Chairman Mao Tse-tung has pointed out: "Those who refuse to be enslaved will never be cowed by the atom bombs and hydrogen bombs in the hands of the U.S. imperialists."

The article ended by reiterating the defensive intentions of China's nuclear program; China's objective of defeating U.S. imperialism and Soviet revisionism; and her intention of pursuing to the end of the struggle the goal of "the complete prohibition and thorough destruction of nuclear weapons."

Thus, China's declaratory policy toward arms control (and also to the United Nations and its activities) seems to allow her little flexibility. True, she might be able to rationalize that a particular text on nonproliferation did not manifestly "deprive the non-nuclear countries of their rights" or that a change in the United Nations structure represented a step toward "rectification."

But China's actual view toward nonproliferation must be distinguished from her declaratory policy, since the latter is no doubt heavily influenced by various propaganda motives. Peking's real position on nuclear weapons spread will depend more on the political and military interests affected, both short- and long-term. The Chinese communists have a number of short-term, primarily political interests that could be served by the destabilizing effects on world politics and upon the social-political structure of her neighbors that might follow from the attempt of other states to join the nuclear club. In both Japan and India, for example, the decision would encounter severe internal opposition that could lead to domestic chaos which would weaken the regime generally and possibly strengthen the hand of the local Communist Party. Particularly in India such domestic strife would serve to reinforce centrifugal tendencies. And in Japan it would serve at a minimum to weaken the alliance with Washington. Finally, even if both India and Japan successfully developed their own nuclear programs, the consequence might merely be to produce a low-level balance of terror in Asia not different in kind from the higher-level one prevailing in Europe.[44]

Although Chen Yi's press interview in September 1965 seemed to exclude any chance that China would assist another country to manufacture nuclear weapons, the hypothetical possibility could not be ruled out that Peking might attempt to exploit its technology politically by some sharing arrangement. Rumors had it that Peking had planned to test an atomic device over Indonesian territory in 1965 and allow Sukarno partial credit. During the Middle Eastern crisis in 1967 Soviet diplomats expressed the fear that Peking might ship finished weapons to the Arab states. While such moves would depart from China's usual caution in foreign affairs, the potential gains for Peking might appear substantial, as against the rather intangible risks involved.

One of the most salient motives for China's actively seeking to prevent a nonproliferation treaty is that, if her tactics succeeded, they would strengthen her stature as leader of revolutionary forces. If the treaty were signed, Peking might still criticize it for propaganda reasons, even if welcoming it privately as useful to Chinese interests. In any case the ideological crusade Peking has waged against "imperialist-revisionist" duopoly would increase the risk of China's losing face if she decided to endorse openly an arms control measure supported by Moscow and Washington. Even though China's participation or acquiescence in the measure were justified on strategic grounds, Peking would have to weigh the cost to revolutionary élan abroad and to the sacrificial fervor of her own toiling masses. (Hence, it might be easier for Peking to enter an agreement with one superpower rather than both—quite possibly with the United States, with whom no doctrinal dispute has colored the relation.)

Long-range, predominantly strategic considerations, however, may dictate a rather different Chinese approach to arms control. Should any of China's neighbors go nuclear, she will lose whatever distinction accrues to being the only Asian atomic power. At best China is likely to run a treadmill, attempting to keep ahead of India and Japan, while trying to create a force capable of penetrating U.S. and Soviet defenses. A more cooperative Chinese approach to arms control would have the added advantage of reducing the motives and pretexts for a U.S. or Soviet strike against her nuclear plant. More generally, it would enhance the image of responsibility and caution which Peking has already sought to affix to its nuclear strategy. Finally, while the third world may not loudly protest Peking's atomic tests, China's influence among the established governments of Asia, Africa, and Latin America might well grow if her propaganda thrust aimed less at self-denial and upheaval and more toward peace and prosperity.

Is such a switch in China's line possible? One must ask first how much of a change would be needed merely to facilitate other governments' efforts to close the nuclear club membership at five. For this purpose China need sign on no dotted line, but she would have to refrain from military and political behavior that could deter others from signing or abiding by a non-dissemination pact. To go beyond non-interference in such arms controls to active support of them would be a much larger and more difficult step. It might depend upon the emergence of another generation, one less oriented to violent revolution and more pragmatically concerned with China's internal prosperity. It might also require the achievement by China of a minimum nuclear deterrent that would give her a greater confidence against outside attack and a more solid bargaining position in international negotiations. Thus, some of the immediate obstacles to Chinese participation in a nonproliferation agreement arise from the corollary measures possibly required to persuade the potential nth countries to join. A universally-binding test ban, for example, even if it did not prohibit underground tests, would severely limit the growth of China's nuclear program. And the guarantees New Delhi might demand from Washington and Moscow might seem to place a Damocles sword over China indefinitely while the test ban kept her from perfecting a deterrent force able to threaten the superpowers.

The limits to change should not be overestimated, however, if only because future contingencies are so difficult to predict. China's declaratory policy on arms control may already have a potential not only for attacks upon superpower collusion but for support of measures that strengthen peace and do not obviously contradict the needs of the emerging nations. The flexibility in China's theory has already been demonstrated, for example, by the innovation of the "second intermediate zone" to rationalize cooperation with Western Europe.

And the possibility of a rapid reversal in practice was shown in 1957–58 by the transition from the Bandung spirit. A totalitarian regime might move in the opposite direction with less trouble than expected—witness Russia from 1953 to 1955. In China, moreover, in contrast to the Soviet Union, shifts in the tack of external policy seem to be facilitated by the fact that the Peking leadership is much more engrossed in domestic than in foreign policy. For the outer world, at least, this ordering of priorities is fortunate, because it means that China is the less likely to pursue some external course regardless of its pragmatic consequences. And as noted at the end of the following chapter, Peking in Spring 1968 departed from a principled defense of unlimited proliferation to attack the prospect of nuclear spread in at least the case of Japan—even while Peking also railed against the draft nonproliferation treaty as a U.S.–Soviet plot. For several years Peking had criticized Moscow for blinking at West Germany's role in NATO's nuclear strategy in the course of negotiating the nonproliferation accord with Washington. Now, on April 5, 1968, *People's Daily* inveighed against the alleged nuclear ambitions of Japanese "militarists." Tomorrow it would hardly be surprising if China also berated India for wanting to maintain or exercise her nuclear option. Thus, Peking's principled position on nuclear spread seemed destined for qualification, even or perhaps especially in the Asian world, where principles would have to be looked on differently depending on whether they were applied to friends or adversaries.

XI
Toward a Nonproliferation Accord

Although the security and political obstacles to a treaty to halt nuclear spread varied in saliency through 1965–67, some basis existed for believing that the difficulties were not insurmountable. First, the non-nuclear weapons states might sign a treaty, with the caveat that they would withdraw if their security requirements were not satisfied over the years. Second, the Soviet Union indicated that she might not regard the present sharing arrangements in NATO, formalized through a Consultative Committee, as antithetical to such a treaty. Washington and Bonn, for their part, might agree to press for no more than such a committee as a means of institutionalizing the status quo. Third, the Kremlin also indicated that it might be willing to overlook the Vietnamese war while negotiating a ban on further atomic spread. Finally, while China would not sign the treaty, it appeared doubtful that she would take active steps to transfer atomic weapons or production facilities to other countries.

Against this backdrop—above this iceberg—negotiations continued at the Eighteen-Nation Disarmament Committee, at the United Nations, and privately—especially between Moscow and Washington. A similar pattern took shape both in 1965 and 1966. Negotiations during the early and middle part of each year moved at a sluggish pace, heightened occasionally by lapses into vitriol and self-righteousness. By September, however, whether to make amends, to make propaganda, or for other reasons, most parties to the negotiations cooperated in adopting at the United Nations disarmament resolutions that showed some willingness to compromise. In 1966, in particular, there was manifest a certain solidarity between, on the one hand, the nuclear weapons states and some non-nuclears; and on the other hand, those civilian nuclear powers hoping to raise the price for their participation in a nonproliferation accord. Even so, the technical debates during the early and middle months of 1965 and 1966 helped to clear the way for the limited progress achieved in the

General Assembly each year, and for the more substantial progress expected in 1967.

THE ENDC IN 1965: MOSCOW VS. NATO

Despite their declaratory support of nonproliferation, neither Washington nor Moscow came forward with a draft treaty on nuclear dissemination during the course of the U.N. Disarmament Commission meetings in April–June 1965. That body, however, urged the Eighteen-Nation Disarmament Committee (ENDC) to reconvene and to focus on the twin problems of extending the partial test ban to underground tests and of halting nuclear dissemination.[1] While Washington felt comfortable with these recommendations, Moscow refused initially to set a date for resumption of the ENDC meetings, perhaps because it wanted to see the outcome of the Second Asian-African Conference scheduled for Algiers late in June.

When "Bandung II" was cancelled, the Kremlin suddenly agreed that the ENDC should open on July 27, 1965. The conference began slowly, partly because the Western delegations had difficulty in finding support for a text on a nonproliferation treaty, and because Moscow persisted in propaganda attacks on U.S. policy in Vietnam. Further, instead of concentrating on the two priorities on the ENDC agenda, the Soviets dragged out the issues of abolishing foreign military bases and prohibiting the use of nuclear weapons.

Finally, on August 17, 1965, U.S. Ambassador Foster presented a draft treaty on nonproliferation, ostensibly in behalf of the Western allies. Article II provided what Moscow soon assailed as a crucial loophole:

> Each of the non-nuclear States party to this Treaty undertakes not to manufacture nuclear weapons; each undertakes not to seek or to receive the transfer of such weapons into its national control, either directly, or indirectly through a military alliance; and *each undertakes not to take any action which would cause an increase in the total number of States and other organizations having independent power to use nuclear weapons*[2] [emphasis added].

While the initial obligations specified seemed to go some distance toward meeting Soviet demands, the very last (italicized) undertaking would permit a multilateral force in which some existing nuclear power took part, even without a veto. London appeared to think that this provision left the door too far open, while Bonn objected in principle to any deal that might jeopardize its options for the future; and Moscow rejected the U.S. draft out of hand because it failed to prohibit institutions through which additional powers, Germany in particular, might gain access to nuclear weapons.[3] Editorially *The New York Times* termed the whole affair a "debacle," and added: "The melancholy conviction grows that neither in Moscow nor in Washington is there available the high statesmanship or the sense of history required to meet what may well be the greatest crisis humanity ever faced."[4]

Before the ENDC halted its meetings in September 1965, Italy submitted a draft of a unilateral non-acquisition declaration that would come into force if similar unilateral declarations were made by an agreed number of states. And the eight nonaligned members of the ENDC issued a closing joint memorandum, probably at India's instigation, indicating the desirability of linking steps toward nonproliferation with general disarmament.[5] It was not until the General Assembly reconvened that Soviet Foreign Minister Gromyko on September 24, 1965 tabled for the first time a Soviet draft on a nonproliferation treaty.[6]

If the U.S. draft treaty was somewhat open-ended, the Soviet project was the opposite, ruling out all forms of nuclear sharing. Articles I and II prohibited nuclear and non-nuclear powers from transferring or acquiring nuclear weapons or manufacturing information "directly or indirectly, through third States or groups of States." Non-nuclear powers were not to obtain "weapons in any form . . . for the purposes of ownership, control or use and shall not participate in the ownership, control or use of such weapons or in testing them."

Thus, the U.S. and Soviet positions stood diametrically opposed: one seeking to keep the options for nuclear sharing open, the other trying to close them. Each side justified its approach as a contribution to the containment of nuclear dissemination. Washington argued that without multilateral arrangements, Bonn would one day make her unilateral ones. Moscow contended that any step toward greater German participation in nuclear arrangements would only accelerate the movement toward Bonn's independent atomic force. Some in the West contended that the Kremlin was either short-sighted or cared more about sparking dissension in NATO than about halting proliferation.[7] Moscow, on the other hand, maintained that Washington and Bonn were concerned primarily with strengthening their military pact and only secondarily, if at all, with the dangers of nuclear spread.

THE UNITED NATIONS, NUCLEAR SPREAD, AND CHINA

Despite these disagreements throughout the first nine months of 1965, five resolutions dealing with nuclear spread and other arms control problems were adopted by the U.N. General Assembly in the closing months of the year.[8] Aside from one Soviet abstention (on a resolution dealing with nuclear testing),[9] the general pattern saw Washington and London, the key threshold powers, and the Soviet bloc (with occasional Rumanian defections in Peking's favor) vote affirmatively with the majority of the U.N. Assembly. France and Albania also maintained their customary postures, Paris always abstaining and Tirana usually opposing arms control resolutions.[10]

One of the most important resolutions adopted by the Twentieth General Assembly was designed to help span the gap between the U.S. and Soviet positions on nonproliferation, and was introduced in the First Committee in November 1965 by India, Sweden, Brazil, Mexico, the U.A.R. and the other three nonaligned states participating in the ENDC. The main principles of the resolution provided that:

a) The treaty should be void of any loopholes which might permit nuclear or non-nuclear powers to proliferate, directly or indirectly, nuclear weapons in any form;

b) The treaty should embody an acceptable balance of mutual responsibilities and obligations of the nuclear and non-nuclear Powers;

c) A treaty preventing the proliferation of nuclear weapons should be a step towards the achievement of general and complete disarmament and, more particularly, nuclear disarmament;

d) There should be acceptable and workable provisions to ensure the effectiveness of the treaty;

e) Nothing in the treaty should effect adversely the right of any group of States to conclude regional treaties in order to ensure the total absence of nuclear weapons in their respective territories. . . .[11]

The United States and the Soviet Union joined with the majority in voting for the resolution,[12] which was to be transmitted to the ENDC when it reconvened. The superpowers then announced that they would not press for a vote on their respective draft resolutions that sought endorsement for their own positions.[13] When the text was approved by the General Assembly on November 19, U Thant termed it "a good augury for the future negotiations," a statement of five principles that would focus and "provide the guide-lines for them."[14] Although the "no loophole" phrase was open to interpretation—specifically as to whether it permitted a system of nuclear sharing—a stronger basis for further narrowing of differences may have been created.

The resolution fell short of insisting on a comprehensive disarmament package to parallel the nonproliferation pact that India had frequently called for, but the resolution stated that such an accord should be a step toward general disarmament. Moscow had earlier recorded its view that a non-dissemination agreement should be "only a step toward the banning and destruction of nuclear weapons and not simply a method . . . of formalizing the nuclear monopoly of the present five great powers."[15] And Washington had made similar protestations, though usually with a clear indication that halting the spread of nuclear weapons should not be contingent upon other arms control agreements.

A Soviet statement issued toward the end of 1965 provided what could be a useful rationalization for limiting the nuclear club to its present five members—the nations designated by the U.N. Charter to hold permanent seats on the U.N. Security Council:

> The question as it now stands is whether new states will be in possession of nuclear weapons or [whether] it will be possible to check the process of proliferation and put it under control. If, apart from the Union of Soviet Socialist Republics, the United States of America, Great Britain, France, and the Chinese People's Republic who are already permanent members of the Security Council, other states embark on the road of producing their own nuclear weapons or gaining access to them, it will be too late, or even hardly possible to turn the tide of events.[16]

While the signing of a nonproliferation treaty did not depend juridically upon Communist China's participation, many states feared that the usefulness of General Assembly resolutions and subsequent ENDC talks would be profoundly undermined by the absence from these deliberations of the world's most populous nation and the fifth nuclear power. One means to bring China into arms control negotiations would be to convene a world disarmament conference—open to all nations whether or not they belonged to the United Nations. Such a conference would have the advantage of facilitating German and perhaps French participation, but it would provide also a possible route for bringing Peking into the United Nations arena, if by a side door. China herself had proposed a summit conference to discuss nuclear disarmament; perhaps she would not oppose the idea of a world conference even if below the summit level.

A world disarmament conference had been advocated also by the Second Conference of Nonaligned States meeting in Cairo in October 1964, which suggested that it be held "under the auspices of the United Nations." But this phrase was expected to alienate Peking, and was omitted from a recommendation of the U.N. Disarmament Commission in the spring of 1965 and from a resolution passed by the General Assembly on November 29, 1965.[17] By this resolution the General Assembly endorsed the Cairo proposal and called for the establishment of a preparatory committee that would arrange a world meeting to which all states would be invited, to convene no later than 1967. The preparatory committee, presumably, was to sound out Peking, Paris, and Bonn, and to carry out the other preparations needed to convene the conference. The resolution carried by a vote of 112 to 0 (France and Nationalist China abstaining). Washington reversed its earlier position and joined the majority, warning, however, that the United States might not attend the meeting if Peking took an obstructionist approach toward Taiwan and other issues.[18] The Soviet Union had, since Chou En-lai's summit proposal in 1964, reaffirmed its support for a world conference.[19]

Peking's reaction to the resolution provided mixed indicators as to the prospect of engaging Mainland China in any serious dialogue on arms control. Peking's Foreign Ministry declared on December 1, 1965 that China "will certainly not take part" in a conference organized by the United Nations or in any U.N. activities until her legitimate rights were restored and the Chiang Kai-shek "clique" expelled.[20] Since the operative paragraphs of the U.N. resolution did not mention the United Nations, however, the nonaligned nations backing the world conference proposal did not lose heart. Since the 1965 General Assembly had already rejected a motion to seat Peking, a conciliatory Chinese view was hardly expected.[21] And the failure of a long Chinese article dealing with the Twentieth Session of the General Assembly to condemn (or even mention) the world conference idea was seen as an encouraging sign.[22]

Another positive indicator may have been the fact that China's Albanian ally cast an affirmative vote for the world conference resolution. In the debate Tirana's Ambassador Budo asserted that disarmament could not be left "to the arbitrary whims of two great powers or to the result of compromise in a struggle of conflicting interests for hegemony." In any event, the preparatory committee was undaunted by China's initial reaction and began the field work needed to hold such a meeting. Vienna put in its bid as the site of the conference and February 1967 was mentioned as the earliest date on which such a meeting might be held. If Communist China had taken a seat in the United Nations in 1966, of course, most of the rationale for the conference would have disappeared. (As it turned out, Peking was not seated at the United Nations in 1966–67 nor was the World Disarmament Conference held—not only because of Peking's attitude but also owing to rising hopes that, left undisturbed, the ENDC might turn in a widely acceptable draft treaty to curb nuclear spread.)

In addition to the stand of the Twentieth General Assembly on nonproliferation and a world disarmament conference, the positions of Albania and other states friendly to China or interested in steering a neutral course may be analyzed with respect to the other three disarmament resolutions adopted by the Assembly. These three resolutions were adopted on one day—December 3—in an atmosphere of wide if yet unjustified optimism. One was the resolution on the urgent need for the suspension of nuclear and thermonuclear tests, on which the Soviet bloc abstained and Albania voted in the negative. Second, the General Assembly adopted with no negative votes a Declaration on Denuclearization of Africa that called on all states to refrain from testing, manufacturing, using or deploying nuclear weapons in Africa, and urged states neither to transfer nor to acquire weapons for use in Africa. While there were no negative votes, Albania and South Africa did not vote; Portugal and France abstained; Tanzania, Zambia, Yemen, Cambodia, Maldive Is-

TABLE 1

Voting Records of States Friendly to China, Twentieth Session, U.N. General Assembly (1965)

	Non-prol.	World Conf.	Test-Ban	Africa	ENDC[GCD]
Albania	Nv s	Ys	N	Nv	A
Cambodia	–	–	–	–	–
Congo (Brazzaville)	–	Yr	A	Yr	Y
Cuba	A	Y	A	Y	Y
Guinea	A	Yr	A	Yr	A
Mali	–s	Yrs	Ys	Yr	A
Rumania	A	Y	Y	Ys	Y
Tanzania	Ys	Yr	Y	Yrs	A

Key: Y, yes; N, no; A, abstain; –, absent; Nv, not voting; s, speech in the debate; r, cosponsored resolution.

lands, and three smaller Latin American states were absent. Both the U.S. and Soviet alliances, as well as Israel and the U.A.R., voted affirmatively.[23]

The third resolution was termed "The Question of General and Complete Disarmament." But its main significance was that it called upon the ENDC to resume its work as early as possible, and to consider the documents and records of the First Committee concerning arms control questions.[24] On this issue Albania, Algeria, Guinea, Mali, and Tanzania abstained; Cambodia was absent; but Congo (Brazzaville) voted affirmatively. (A compromise between Washington and Moscow set the date for resumption of the ENDC for January 27, 1966.)

As may be seen from Table 1, Albania provided loyal support for the Chinese position at the United Nations in 1965, voting against all resolutions except the world conference proposal. (Whether Tirana's position on this issue was approved by Peking is unknown.) Cambodia kept safe by absenting herself from all five votes. Congo (Brazzaville) and Guinea

TABLE 2

Votes and Activities of States on the Five Disarmament Resolutions,
Twentieth Session, U.N. General Assembly (1965)

State	Non-Prol.	World Conf.	Test-Ban	Africa	GCD
NONALIGNED STATES (36)*					
Afghanistan	— s	Y s	Y r	Y	Y
Algeria	Y	Y r s	A	Y	A
Burma	Y r s	Y r	Y r	Y	Y
Burundi	—	Y r	Y	Y r	Y
Cambodia	—	—	—	—	—
Ceylon	Y s	Y r	Y r	Y	Y
Congo, Dem. Rep.	Y s	Y s	Y	Y	Y
Cyprus	Y s	Y r s	Y r s	Y s	Y r s
Ethiopia	Y r s	Y r	Y	Y r s	Y
Ghana	Y s	Y r	Y r	Y r s	Y
Guinea	A	Y r	A	Y r	A
India	Y r s	Y r	Y r s	Y s	Y
Iraq	Y s	Y r s	Y r	Y	Y
Jordan	Y	Y r s	Y r	Y	Y
Kenya	— s	Y r s	Y r	Y r s	Y
Kuwait	Y	Y r s	Y	Y	Y
Laos	Y	Y	Y	Y	Y
Lebanon	Y	Y r s	Y r	Y	Y
Liberia	Y s	Y r s	Y r	Y r s	Y
Libya	Y s	Y r s	Y r s	Y r s	Y s
Malawi	—	Y r	Y	Y r	Y
Mali	— s	Y r s	Y s	Y r	A
Morocco	Y	Y r	Y r	Y r s	Y
Nepal	Y s	Y r s	Y r s	Y	Y s
Nigeria	Y r s	Y r s	Y r s	Y r s	Y s
Saudi Arabia	Y	Y s	Y	Y	Y s
Sierre Leone	Y	Y r	Y	Y	Y
Somalia	— s	Y r s	Y	Y r s	Y
Sudan	—	Y r	Y r	Y r s	Y
Syria	Y s	Y r	Y	Y	Y
Tunisia	Y s	Y r s	Y	Y r	Y
Uganda	Y s	Y r s	Y	Y r s	Y
U.A.R.	Y r s	Y r s	Y r s	Y r s	Y
U.R. of Tanzania	Y s	Y r	Y	Y r s	A
Yemen	—	Y r	—	—	—
Yugoslavia	Y s	Y r s	Y r	Y s	Y
Zambia	Y s	Y r	— r	— r	—

* This listing does not include Indonesia because she did not take part in the
Twentieth General Assembly.
CODE: Y – yes.
      N – no.
      A – abstain.
      — – absent.
      Nv – not-voting.
      r – co-sponsored resolution.
      s – speech in debate.
Source: Homer A. Jack, "Disarmament at the Twentieth U.N. General Assembly"
(Boston: Unitarian Universalist Association, 1966, mimeo.), pp. 17–19.

TABLE 2 (*Continued*)

	Non-Prol.	World Conf.	Test-Ban	Africa	GCD
NATO (14)					
Belgium	Y s	Y s	Y	Y	Y
Canada	Y s	Y	Y s	Y s	Y
Denmark	Y	Y	Y	Y	Y
France	A	A	A	A	A
Greece	Y	Y s	Y s	Y	Y
Iceland	Y	Y	Y	Y	Y
Italy	Y s	Y s	Y	Y	Y s
Luxembourg	Y	Y	Y	Y	Y
Netherlands	Y s	Y s	Y	Y	Y
Norway	Y s	Y	Y	Y	Y
Portugal	Y	Y	Y	A s	Y
Turkey	Y s	Y s	Y	Y	Y s
U.K.	Y s	Y s	Y s	Y s	Y
U.S.	Y s	Y s	Y s	Y s	Y s
COMMUNIST STATES (11)					
Albania	N v s	Y s	N	N v	A
Bulgaria	Y s	Y s	A s	Y	A
Byelorussian SSR	Y s	Y s	A s	Y	Y
Cuba	A	Y	A	Y	Y
Czechoslovakia	Y s	Y s	A s	Y s	Y s
Hungary	Y s	Y s	A	Y s	Y
Mongolia	Y s	Y s	A	Y	Y
Poland	Y s	Y s	A s	Y s	Y s
Rumania	A	Y	Y	Y s	Y
Ukrainian SSR	Y s	Y s	A	Y	Y
U.S.S.R.	Y s	Y s	A s	Y s	Y s
SEATO (5) *					
Australia	Y s	Y	Y s	Y s	Y
New Zealand	Y s	Y s	Y s	Y s	Y
Pakistan	A s	Y s	Y s	Y s	Y
Philippines	Y s	Y	Y	Y s	Y
Thailand	Y	Y s	Y	Y	Y
LATIN AMERICAN STATES (19) **					
Argentina	Y s	Y	Y r	Y	Y
Bolivia	Y	Y	Y r	Y	Y
Brazil	Y r s	Y s	Y r s	Y s	Y
Chile	Y s	Y s	Y r	Y	Y
Colombia	Y	Y s	Y r	Y	Y
Costa Rica	Y	Y	Y r	Y	Y
Dominican Republic	Y	Y	Y	Y	Y
Ecuador	Y s	Y	- r	-	-
El Salvador	Y	Y	Y	Y	Y
Guatemala	Y s	Y	Y	Y	Y
Haiti	Y	Y	-	-	-

* This listing does not include the U.S., U.K., and France.
** This listing does not include two new states: Jamaica and Trinidad & Tobago. Nor does it include Cuba.

TABLE 2 (*Concluded*)

	Non-Prol.	World Conf.	Test-Ban	Africa	GCD
Honduras	Y	Y	Y	Y	Y
Mexico	Y r s	Y s	Y r s	Y s	Y
Nicaragua	–	Y	–	–	–
Panama	Y	Y	Y	Y	Y
Paraguay	Y	–	Y	Y	Y
Peru	Y s	Y s	Y r s	Y s	Y s
Uruguay	Y	Y	Y	Y	Y
Venezuela	Y	Y s	Y	Y s	Y

INTER-AFRICAN & MALAGASY ORGANIZATION (OCAM) (14)

	Non-Prol.	World Conf.	Test-Ban	Africa	GCD
Cameroun*	–	Y r	Y r	Y r	Y
Central African Republic*	Y	Y r	Y	Y r	Y
Chad*	–	Y r	Y	Y r	Y
Congo (Brazzaville)*	–	Y r	A	Y r	Y
Dahomey*	Y	Y r	Y	Y r	Y
Gabon	–	Y	Y	Y r	Y
Ivory Coast	Y	Y r	Y	Y	Y
Madagascar	– s	Y	Y	Y	Y
Mauritania*	Y	Y r s	A	Y	Y
Niger	Y	Y	Y	Y r	Y
Rwanda	– s	Y r	Y	Y r	Y
Senegal*	Y	Y	Y r	Y r s	Y
Togo*	Y	Y r	Y	Y r	Y
Upper Volta	Y	Y	Y	Y	Y

MISCELLANEOUS (17)

	Non-Prol.	World Conf.	Test-Ban	Africa	GCD
Austria	Y s	Y s	Y	Y	Y
China	Y s	Nv s	Y s	Y	Y
Finland	Y s	Y	Y r	Y	Y
Gambia	–	–	–	–	–
Iran	Y s	Y s	Y	Y	Y s
Ireland	Y s	Y	Y	Y	Y
Israel	Y	Y s	Y	Y	Y s
Jamaica	Y s	Y	Y r	Y s	Y
Japan	Y s	Y s	Y r s	Y	Y
Malaysia	Y	Y	Y	Y	Y
Maldive Islands	Y	Y	–	–	–
Malta	Y s	Y s	Y	Y	Y r s
Singapore	–	Y	–	Y	Y
South Africa	Y	Y	–	Nv s	–
Spain	Y	Y s	Y	Y	Y
Sweden	Y r s	Y	Y r s	Y	Y
Trinidad and Tobago	Y s	Y r	Y	Y	Y

VOTING SUMMARY

	Non-Prol.	World Conf.	Test-Ban	Africa	GCD
Yes	93	112	92	105	102
No	0	0	1	0	0
Abstain	5	1	14	2	6
Non-Voting	1	1	0	2	0
Absent	18	3	10	8	9

* Also member of non-aligned grouping.

were either absent or abstained on the two issues most opposed by Peking; they voted (with Albania) for the world conference; and approved the denuclearization of Africa (proposed by their own Organization for African Unity) and the somewhat procedural matter of the ENDC. Mali followed a similar pattern, but deviated sharply to approve the test ban resolution. Cuba took a position midway between Moscow's and Peking's by abstaining on nonproliferation. By abstaining on the test ban, however, Cuba leagued herself with Moscow rather than with Peking. On the three other issues Havana joined the majority, which coincided with the Soviet vote.

Tanzania and Rumania voted with the majority on all issues, except that Bucharest abstained on the nonproliferation resolution. But in a speech approving the denuclearization of Africa, the Rumanian delegate used terms that might have been slightly more congenial to Peking than to Moscow: "Many delegations have insisted on the need to extend the ban on tests to the fourth environment, underground, but no such agreemen has yet been achieved. The Rumanian delegation is convinced that, in the field of disarmament, the essential measures are the general prohibition and destruction of nuclear weapons, the liquidation of military bases, and the withdrawal of foreign troops."[25] On the other hand, Rumania's support for nuclear free zones, in Latin America and elsewhere, harmonized more with the Soviet than with the Chinese position.

The broader picture of voting patterns on disarmament issues at the Twentieth General Assembly is indicated in Table 2.

THE KOSYGIN PROPOSAL AND A CHANGED U.S. TREATY DRAFT, 1966

The semblance of momentum generated at the Twentieth General Assembly waned perceptibly as ENDC negotiations resumed in January and continued in Geneva through the spring and summer of 1966.[26] For one thing, Peking's private as well as public comments made it clear that the Communist Chinese were basically negative to the idea of a world disarmament conference sponsored even indirectly by the United Nations. More immediate to the issue of a nonproliferation treaty, the negotiations in Geneva saw Moscow and then Washington alter their respective treaty drafts in ways which each claimed to be significant, but which the other believed of little avail in moving closer to agreement. The change in the Soviet position had to do with the problem of guarantees, while the U.S. draft treaty was amended with regard to loopholes permitting additional nations control over nuclear weapons.

A twofold solution for the security problems of non-nuclear powers had been proposed by the Wiesner Committee in 1965. It argued that

Non-nuclear states must be protected from the threat of such force as would persuade them that nuclear weapons were an easy, a necessary, an urgent counter.

The Committee therefore recommended

that the United States seek an agreement with the other nuclear powers pledging them (a) not to attack or threaten to attack with nuclear weapons a non-nuclear power and (b) if a non-nuclear power is thus threatened or attacked, to defend it with all necessary means.[27]

The United States Government did not go so far as suggested by the Wiesner Committee, but President Johnson did reaffirm to the ENDC in January 1966 virtually the same pledge he had made immediately following the first Chinese nuclear test in October 1964: "The nations that do not seek the nuclear path can be sure that they will have our strong support against threats of nuclear blackmail." He added that "the United Nations and other international security arrangements" should be strengthened for the sake of the non-nuclear states.[28]

The Soviet Government has shown great reluctance to make such commitments, particularly to non-socialist states. But in February 1966, perhaps in response to the U.S. assurances against nuclear blackmail, Premier Kosygin informed the ENDC that:

with the object of facilitating an understanding on the conclusion of a treaty [against the spread of nuclear weapons] the Soviet Government expresses its readiness to insert into the draft treaty an article forbidding the use of nuclear weapons against non-nuclear states, parties to the treaty, which have no nuclear weapons on their territory.[29]

Kosygin seemed in effect to endorse item (a) of the Wiesner recommendation—albeit with the important addition that the pledge was limited to non-nuclear powers without nuclear weapons on their soil. He was silent, however, on item (b), which proposed a sanction against nuclear attack upon non-nuclear powers.[30] The United States and West Germany objected to the discriminatory position toward non-nuclear states having foreign nuclear weapons on their territory.[31] Japan contended that the pledge of restraint was an inadequate assurance in the face of a possible attack by another nuclear power.[32] India and other states, however, welcomed the Kosygin proposal as a step in the right direction.[33]

Critics of the Soviet proposal could argue that a nonproliferation pact could be achieved without including any aspects of a package demanded by some threshold states, and that any kind of no first-use proposal would only create additional obstacles to U.S. ratification of the treaty. (Washington could also counter with a complicated inspection proposal to determine whether Warsaw Pact nations did or did not have nuclear weapons on their soil.) The Soviet proposal could inhibit U.S. use or the threatened use of atomic weapons in Vietnam and reinforce upon Bonn an awareness of the liabilities of having nuclear weapons on German territory. On the other hand, Washington did not seem to be contemplating the use of nuclear weapons in Southeast Asia (though it might consider them if a major conflict were to erupt in Korea). As for Germany, Bonn had long lived under the threat of Soviet MRBMs and was unlikely to be deflected by new Soviet threats from reliance upon the U.S. nuclear umbrella. A deeper objection to the Kosygin proposal may have been that, without its being paralleled by a nuclear guarantee like that advocated in the Wiesner report, its utility was quite limited. Further, it would not bind nuclear states (such as China) unless they signed the nonproliferation pact. Still it was implicit that if a relatively weak atomic power such as China used nuclear weapons against a non-nuclear state, the clause suggested by Kosygin would help to justify intervention by larger nuclear powers. Thus, although the proposal had disruptive value vis-à-vis NATO, if seen in conjunction with Kosygin's conciliation of India and Pakistan in Tashkent in January 1966, the Soviet initiative at the ENDC may have been another sign of Moscow's growing interest in stabilizing the third world.

While most Western governments expressed dissatisfaction with the Kosygin proposal, a Soviet negotiator stated that the major revision in the U.S. treaty language did not advance the negotiations by "one inch." The object of the U.S. draft treaty, as revised on March 22, 1966, was to bar any "increase, even by one, in the centers of nuclear power which have the right or ability to start a nuclear war."[34] The U.S. text continued to permit multilateral participation in the ownership of nuclear weapons by alliance arrangements, but restrictive language barred any new nation or association of non-nuclear states from the control, manufacture, or indirect acquisition of nuclear weapons. The key clause specified that "control" of nuclear weapons "means the right or ability to fire nuclear weapons without the concurrent decision of an existing nuclear-weapons state."

The American interest in keeping open the options for a NATO or a European form of multilateral nuclear force continued to be reflected in the U.S. draft treaty even after its revision in March 1966. The revised language would still permit an MLF via either of two possible routes. The first avenue resulted from the treaty's defining nuclear control so stringently that multilateral associations would not, so to speak, constitute new nuclear powers at all. Thus, an association including France, Britain, and Germany could be created in which each state would have a vote; where decisions were taken by majority rule so that neither London nor Paris had a veto. Since the association would not have "control" of nuclear weapons, it would be permitted under the U.S. treaty terms. Moreover, such an association could be assisted in the manufacture of nuclear weapons and it could receive such weapons from other parties.

A second, though more remote, route would hinge on the possibility that a nuclear weapons state might actually give up its own nuclear force. If, for example, Britain gave up her nuclear weapons, Belgium and Germany could obtain control of atomic arms if they persuaded France to join an association with them without a veto. If Paris joined, the association would not be one of non-nuclear states only—hence would not be covered by the obligation upon nuclear powers not to transfer nuclear weapons to the "control of any association of non-nuclear weapons states." In sum, as one analyst has written, the revised treaty would allow

> every kind of MLF ever considered to be superimposed on the existing nuclear status quo; in particular, it permits multilateral forces without any vetos to come into being without any changes in the present situation. Thus a French, British, West German force or a U.S., British, West German force with nations having one vote each and majority rule decisions, is quite clearly permitted. . . .[35]

HAVES VS. HAVE-NOTS: THE 1966 GENERAL ASSEMBLY

Not surprisingly, the Kremlin declared that the modified U.S. text still contained a "gaping loophole" by which West Germany could gain increased control over nuclear arms.[36] Only in the fall of 1966, when the General Assembly again convened, did there appear once again to be renewed movement toward a ban on nuclear spread. On this occasion, unlike the preceding autumn, manifestations of progress at the United Nations seemed to derive from important changes in the attitudes of the superpowers, particularly the Soviet Union.

A number of factors, the most important of which was probably strategic, underlay this shift. Moscow was coming to agree with Washington that nuclear spread—not just in Europe but also in the third world—would constitute a real danger. Additional supportive factors permitted the superpowers to take action to halt this spread. First, the White House and Bonn (particularly under Chancellor Erhard's successors) agreed to put aside hardware solutions and rely on a consultative role to achieve West German "sharing" in NATO nuclear strategy. Moscow, for its part, finally agreed that consultation was not tantamount to proliferation. Second, President Johnson attempted to show in word and in deed that the United States was ready to enter a long-range strategy of peaceful engagement with Eastern Europe and the Soviet Union. Third, Soviet readiness to cooperate with the United States in arms control and other areas was little inhibited by fear of Chinese criticism, for Peking's international prestige was at a new low. On the contrary, political and military developments within China and along the Sino-Soviet frontier inclined Moscow to mend fences on its Western front. Fourth, the internal solidarity of the Brezhnev-Kosygin leadership, coupled however with some economic difficulties, both facilitated and increased Moscow's interest in arms control. Fifth, as shown by Soviet policy in other domains, such as outer space, the Kremlin was willing to use arms control as a way of regulating the tensions growing out of the Vietnamese confrontation.

As in 1963, following President Kennedy's "Strategy of Peace" address at American University, the Soviet Government seemed to respond positively to a forthright declaration of U.S. willingness to seek accord in achieving peace and economic cooperation. To be sure, Soviet leaders continued to warn that improvement of U.S.–Soviet relations would be limited by the Vietnamese war, but four days after President Johnson's "peaceful engagement" address of October 7, 1966, Soviet Foreign Minister Gromyko told newsmen: "It looks like both countries, the United States and the Soviet Union, are striving to reach agreement to facilitate the conclusion of an international agreement" to halt nuclear spread. State Department spokesman McCloskey concurred, commenting "we agree" that both countries are "striving to reach agreement" on such a treaty.[37]

The closer accord between Moscow and Washington was based for the time on a change in spirit rather than in substance, and neither side ventured immediately to propose or negotiate specific treaty language. One official stated that the difference was in the way each side interpreted the other's proposals. Several years before—perhaps in August 1962—both governments had taken one another's proposals approximately at face value. With the emergence of the MLF issue, however, Moscow sought increasingly to assure that no hardware solution could be legitimized by a nonproliferation treaty, while the West sought to keep such alternatives open. As Moscow's campaign to prohibit an MLF intensified during 1963–65, the Soviet position gradually stiffened to the point where it demanded virtually a return to the status quo ante, i.e., the dismantling of the existing arrangements for nuclear sharing in NATO based on the two-key system. The United States, for her part, sought authorization to proceed beyond the status quo to develop additional forms of sharing.

In the winter of 1966–67, however, both Washington and Moscow again appeared ready to live with existing arrangements and to seek to prevent their elaboration. By late 1966 both sides seem to have regained a modicum of mutual trust. Their negotiations increasingly assumed that neither party sought actively to achieve more than the ostensible aim of the treaty: a halt to nuclear spread.

The apparent meeting of the minds during Gromyko's visit to the White House and State Department was soon reflected in what amounted to a common U.S.–Soviet stand at the United Nations on several key nuclear issues. Washington, together with a series of other states, joined in co-sponsoring a Soviet proposal urgently appealing to all states

(a) To take all necessary steps to facilitate and achieve at the earliest possible time the conclusion of a treaty on nonproliferation. . . . [and] (b) To refrain from any actions conducive to the proliferation of nuclear weapons or which might hamper the conclusion of an agreement on the nonproliferation of nuclear weapons.

Although all the major threshold powers voted for this resolution, none of them co-sponsored it.[38] Indeed, the potential weapons states made it clear that they would insist upon a "balance of mutual responsibilities"—arms limitations not only upon them but upon the nuclear weapons powers as well. Indian Ambassador Trivedi asserted that "a balancing provision will require that no country will produce nuclear weapons—the non-nuclear weapons countries will not produce them and the nuclear weapons countries will also not produce any more weapons." Several states suggested that a statement of future intent be incorporated into the treaty, as it was in the 1963 test ban treaty. Japan suggested that the treaty be of limited duration, "all countries having the opportunity to review the situation freely after a certain period of time."

After it had become clear that Washington and Moscow might soon agree on the terms of a nonproliferation treaty, the major question left unresolved by the negotiations in the winter of 1966–67 was whether the pact would be signed by India and other threshold powers. Two alternative approaches to a nonproliferation treaty were considered: (1) a relatively simple pact that put off to a later date any specification of the responsibilities to be observed by the existing nuclear powers; and (2) a more complex treaty dealing not only with nonproliferation but with the collateral steps to be taken by the nuclear powers to make it hold. The first alternative might well be the more feasible, but if the nuclear powers delayed on the collateral measures, would it endure? Would not one of the threshold powers—like Germany in 1933—decide that since other states had not disarmed, vital interests of the nation required it to build its own arsenal? The second alternative—at least by definition—was expected to be the more likely to survive, but would it ever be signed?

The threshold powers expressed in several ways their insistence upon a balance of obligations. First, a number of African, Asian, and Latin American states pushed through a resolution calling "upon all nuclear-weapons powers to refrain from the use, or the threat of use, of nuclear weapons against states" which conclude regional denuclearization treaties. The same resolution endorsed the Kosygin proposal of early 1966, recommending that the ENDC should "consider urgently the proposal that the nuclear weapons powers should give an assurance that they will not use, or threaten to use, nuclear weapons against non-nuclear weapons states without nuclear weapons on their territories. . . ." But this recommendation was qualified by an amendment proposed by the United States: that the ENDC also consider "any other proposals that have been or may be made for the solution of this problem. . . ."[39] The resolution as a whole was approved by the Soviet bloc and by the United States, but only reluctantly, because it raised the prospect that the nonproliferation treaty would have to be complex rather than simple.

Second, Pakistan and a number of other smaller powers not members of the ENDC initiated a resolution calling for a conference of non-nuclear weapons states to meet not later than July 1968 to consider how the security of the non-nuclear states can best be assured; how those states can cooperate to prevent nuclear proliferation; and how nuclear devices can be used exclusively for peaceful purposes. The resolution carried with only one negative vote—India's—but a large number of states abstained, including Israel, the USSR, the U.S.A., and Yugoslavia. Albania and many other states friendly to China were absent.[40] To some, especially New Delhi, the conference seemed to aim at raising the political cost in case a threshold power wanted to go nuclear. The original date proposed for the conference was "no later than July 1967," but when this deadline was changed to July 1968, many hoped that the meeting would follow the signing of a nonproliferation treaty rather than condition it. To other powers, notably the Soviet Union and the United States, the resolution was unwelcome since it too threatened to rock the boat, if not before, then subsequent to the signing of the nonproliferation pact.[41]

While Moscow and Washington stood together in opposing actions (or resolutions) that could obstruct the signing of a nonproliferation treaty in the near future, the Soviet bloc nevertheless attempted to manipulate other disarmament issues to embarrass the United States politically. In each of four instances, however, Washington managed to soften, defeat, or even reverse the thrust of the propaganda battle. First, Hungary submitted a resolution demanding compliance with the 1925 Geneva Protocol on gas and bacteriological warfare. But before its adoption, the resolution's text was amended three times in a sense favored by the United States and opposed by the Soviet Union.[42] Second, Poland and the Ukrainian S.S.R. proposed to call upon all states to refrain from sending aircraft carrying nuclear weapons beyond national frontiers. After some debate, however, the sponsors chose not to force a vote.[43]

Third, the Soviet Union submitted a resolution requesting states with foreign bases on the territory of African, Asian, and Latin American countries to eliminate them immediately. Moscow had to acquiesce, however, in an alternative resolution co-sponsored by India, the U.A.R., and Yugoslavia which declared only that the question was of "paramount importance" and should be considered by the ENDC.[44]

Fourth, and most interesting, the Soviet text of a declaration against intervention in the domestic affairs of other states was adopted, but not before it had been broadened to cover other forms of subversion. Moscow attempted to use the resolution as a propaganda vehicle to pillory U.S. intervention in the Dominican Republic, in Cuba, and in Vietnam. But representatives of many Latin American, African, and Asian states cited the indirect aggression mounted against them by various Communist states. Hence, with U.S. support, the resolution was broadened to condemn "armed intervention, or the promotion or organization of subversion, terrorism or other indirect forms of intervention undertaken for the purpose of changing by violence the existing system in another state or interfering in civil strife in another state."[45]

Another Soviet-bloc proposal had direct relevance to the proliferation issue, and was not opposed by the West. Poland, apparently acting upon the suggestion of the U.N. Secretariat, initiated a proposal requesting the "Secretary-General to prepare a concise report on the effects of the possible use of nuclear weapons and on the security and economic implications for States of the acquisition and further development of these weapons. . . ." This proposal was adopted, even France voting in the affirmative, although many delegates feared the study would be one-sided because of its motivation.[46]

The Communist Chinese opposition line to a nonproliferation treaty continued to be expressed by Albania, the only country to vote against the resolution on the need to desist from actions conducive to nuclear spread. Tirana's Ambassador Budo declared that the U.S. and Soviet draft treaties on nonproliferation "do not lead to general disarmament; on the contrary, they are designed to give a guarantee for the atomic monopoly of the great nuclear power." Albania was also the only country to vote against the call for a suspension of nuclear tests; and she was joined only by the Central African Republic in opposing the adoption of the Kosygin proposal or some other system of assurances for non-nuclear states. The other states friendly to China, such as Cambodia, Mali, and the Congo (Brazzaville), generally absented themselves or did not vote on disarmament resolutions at the Twenty-first General Assembly.

In 1966 as in 1965, a number of states attempted to orient the United Nations toward measures of interest to Communist China. Thus, Ethiopia, India, Nigeria, the U.A.R., and Yugoslavia introduced a resolution calling for the signing of a ban on the use of nuclear weapons. Such a prohibition, of course, is the first step in Peking's espoused disarmament program. The U.N. resolution went some distance also toward satisfying China's insistence on a summit meeting, except that the resolution called for the ban to be considered by "the forthcoming world disarmament conference."[47] No state opposed this resolution, although many abstained. But the unreality of the resolution—apart from its content—was deep-rooted: Peking was negatively disposed to the world disarmament conference project, and no one seriously expected the meeting to materialize.

On balance, however, the General Assembly closed in late 1966 on an optimistic note. The superpowers seem to have resolved major differences regarding a treaty on nonproliferation. What remained was to negotiate a treaty that would be signed by the threshold powers.

MOVEMENT TOWARD A TREATY, 1967-68

The specter of "discrimination" created serious dissension as negotiations to halt nuclear spread continued in 1967-68. While the negotiations pitted one major alliance system against another, the more profound conflict was one that divided the alliances themselves and engendered important realignments between nations of the third world and certain members of the Western and Soviet alliances. This conflict arose from the tension between the nuclear-weapon haves and the have-nots—particularly those have-nots who had the capability of entering the atomic club. (Even if they did not want to join, some participants believed they should be compensated for not doing so, while others wanted simply to keep their options open.)

Compromises were made between all these sets of actors, though some were left disgruntled by the limited extent to which their demands were met. Symptomatic of the trend toward superpower agreement was the extent to which the co-chairmen of the ENDC worked together, devising speeches and treaty drafts with identical language, and minimizing polemics against one another. Even at the General Assembly the usual Soviet disarmament proposals aimed at embarrassing the West (e.g. on the liquidation of foreign bases) appeared more *pro forma* in character than in past years.

The ENDC reconvened in Geneva on February 21, 1967, with high hopes that a draft treaty to halt nuclear spread would soon be concluded. The U.S. delegation hoped to present to the Conference those portions of the treaty text on which the U.S. and Soviet co-chairmen had reached agreement, but the Soviets were unwilling to put forward an incomplete draft and the Conference recessed on March 23. During the eight-week recess that followed, the United States carried out what the Arms Control and Disarmament Agency termed "an exhaustive program of negotiation, exposition and persuasion" designed to obtain an accord with her European and Asian allies and with other countries on the matter of "safeguards"—the main point on which Washington and Moscow had not been able to agree at Geneva.[48]

The safeguards issue lay close to the heart of the general problem of "discrimination." Given the present rate in the spread of civilian nuclear power reactors throughout the world, it seems likely that these reactors will produce enough plutonium to make twenty bombs a day by 1985. Uncontrolled, this material would be freely available on a worldwide basis for potential weapons use, thus making it all but impossible to prevent the further spread of nuclear weapons. Therefore it was necessary for the ENDC to arrive at a widely acceptable scheme for safeguards against the diversion of nuclear materials from peaceful to weapons uses. Agreement on such a scheme was complicated by the existence of two international safeguards systems—one administered by the International Atomic Energy Agency (IAEA) and the other set up earlier by the European Atomic Energy Agency (EURATOM) of the six Common Market countries. The European states, particularly West Germany, were reluctant to supplant or supplement EURATOM controls with those of the IAEA, partly because they believed this might have negative effects on European integration, and partly because they feared that IAEA inspectors (including those from the Soviet bloc) might commit industrial espionage. The United States found herself caught between the preferences of her allies and the intransigence of the Soviet Union, which opposed reliance on EURATOM on the ground that its safeguards amounted to self-inspection among six NATO partners, and also because Moscow would prefer to undermine Western integration. The search for a way out of this impasse focused on an arrangement that would preserve and utilize EURATOM safeguards while bringing these activities under the wing of the worldwide IAEA. This principle, suggested in March 1967 by Senator John O. Pastore, facilitated agreement the following year.[49]

When the ENDC reconvened on May 18, 1967, the Soviet delegation was not prepared to accept the formulations for the safeguards article which the United States had worked out with her allies, nor was it willing to submit an incomplete draft. The climate of the negotiations was troubled by the Arab-Israeli war and its aftermath, but on August 24, the United States and Soviet delegations tabled separate but identical texts for a draft treaty—Article III (on safeguards) being left blank.[50] Although Sweden came forward with a draft Article III,[51] the co-chairmen of the ENDC expressed the hope that members would concentrate on the other provisions of the August 24 draft and leave the safeguards article to the co-drafters to work out. The Committee then discussed detailed recommendations and amendments until the ENDC recessed again in December, having failed to produce a draft treaty which could be presented to the General Assembly for approval.

In order to counter the concern of many non-nuclear states that acceptance of IAEA safeguards would inflict commercial disadvantages on their civilian nuclear programs, Washington and London announced on December 2, 1967 that when safeguards were applied under the nonproliferation treaty, they could be applied to all nuclear activities in the United States and United Kingdom except to those with direct national security significance. The Atomic Energy Commission said that more than 80 nuclear reactors could be inspected under this offer, and that only military reactors, weapons laboratories, and some other classified activities—involving a total of six or eight U.S. atomic installations—would be exempted from IAEA inspection. The offer was not conditioned on any reciprocal action or concession by the USSR or any other country. For their part, the Soviets refused—at least for the time being—to accept any safeguards, arguing that safeguard provisions would not serve any useful purpose in a treaty designed to halt nuclear spread beyond the existing nuclear club. (Soviet disarmament specialists interviewed in Moscow in winter 1967–68 stressed [as did most U.S. arms control analysts at that time] that the benefits of the nonproliferation treaty to the potential nuclear powers justified their signing it, without any particular *quid pro quo* by the nuclear weapons powers.)

On December 7, 1967, the ENDC delivered an Interim Report to the General Assembly, stating that the Committee would remain in session in order to expedite work on the draft treaty.[52] The General Assembly responded on December 19 with a resolution calling on the ENDC "urgently to continue its work" and requesting "a full report" on the negotiations "on or before March 15, 1968"—a motion adopted by 112 votes to 1 (Albania was the lone dissenter), while Cuba, France, Gabon and Guinea abstained. Part B of the same resolution approved the recommendations of the Preparatory Committee for the Conference of the Non-Nuclear-Weapons States; specified that the conference would be held in Geneva from August 29 to September 28, 1968; and pointedly announced a decision "to invite to the Conference non-nuclear-weapon States Members of the United Nations and members of the specialized agencies and of the International Atomic Energy Agency." Partly because the timing implied that the meeting would be held *after* conclusion of the nonproliferation treaty, the USSR and United States joined with 110 other states in approving the resolution, on which no states voted negatively but 8 abstained (Afghanistan, Burma, Cuba, Cyprus, France, Gabon, Guinea, and India).[53]

The General Assembly also passed five resolutions dealing with other disarmament issues which many states saw as integral to efforts to attain a halt to nuclear spread, and which Secretary-General U Thant transmitted to the ENDC for its consideration in a letter dated January 11, 1968.[54] The first resolution hailed the Treaty for the Prohibition of Nuclear Weapons in Latin America of February 14, 1967, which had been signed by twenty-one Latin American states but had not yet entered into force.[55] This resolution called upon "all States to give their full cooperation to ensure that the regime laid down in the Treaty enjoys . . . universal observance." It also recommended the widest possible application of Additional Protocol I among the treaty's adherents, and invited nuclear-weapon powers to adhere to Additional Protocol II as soon as possible. The resolution was adopted December 5, 1967, by 82 votes (including the United States) to 0 with 28 abstentions (including the USSR).[56]

A second resolution urged all states to examine a prohibition on the use of nuclear weapons and the conclusion of an appropriate international convention, such as that proposed by the Soviet Union. This resolution, sponsored by the USSR, Czechoslovakia, Mongolia, Rumania and six non-aligned countries, was passed on December 8, by 77 votes to 0, with 29 abstentions (including the United States).[57]

A third resolution on the "Question of General and Complete Disarmament" combined two draft resolutions. Part A accepted as an authoritative statement on the effects of nuclear weapons and the implications of their acquisition and further development the report submitted by the Secretary-General in 1967—a motion accepted on December 19 by 113 votes to 0, with only Cuba abstaining. Part B requested that the ENDC reconvene at the earliest possible date to consider the question of GCD and report to the General Assembly in Fall 1968 on the progress achieved—a motion that passed by 113 to 0, with France, Gabon, and Cuba abstaining.[58]

A fourth resolution, on the "Urgent Need for Suspension of Nuclear and Thermonuclear Tests," urged all states to adhere to the limited test ban treaty, called for an end to nuclear weapons testing in all environments, hoped that states would contribute to international exchange of seismic data, and requested the ENDC to take up the subject of a comprehensive test ban treaty on an urgent basis and report to the General Assembly. The resolution was adopted on December 19 by 103 votes to 1, with 7 abstentions. China's ally Albania cast the only negative vote, while Algeria, Cuba, France, Gabon, Guinea, Mali, and Mauritania abstained. Both Washington and Moscow found aspects of the resolution which they could interpret to favor their respective positions.[59]

India, the U.A.R., and Yugoslavia submitted a draft resolution on "Elimination of Foreign Military Bases in the Countries of Asia, Africa, and Latin America," to which the Soviet bloc gave strong support. The resolution, which called on the ENDC to resume consideration of this question, was also adopted on December 19 by 105 votes to 0, with 13 abstentions including the United States.[60]

When the ENDC reconvened in Geneva on January 18, 1968, it had before it not only the resolutions trasmitted by U Thant, but a revised text of the draft nonproliferation treaty which U.S. and Soviet negotiators had worked out during the recess, complete with Article III, several amended articles and three new articles.[61] Three of the changes represented the conversion into treaty articles of what had been preambular statements in the identical treaty drafts of August 24, 1967. The conversions were employed to strengthen the nuclear powers' obligations: (in Article V) to ensure that potential benefits from any peaceful applications of nuclear explosions will be made available to other signatories on a non-discriminatory basis and at a low cost that excludes charges for research and development; (in Article VI) to negotiate in good faith on effective measures to end the nuclear arms race and move toward general disarmament under international control; and (in Article VII) to recognize the right of regional groups to conclude nuclear free zone treaties. In contrast to the August 24, 1967 drafts, the January 1968 text also stipulated that no signatory would be bound by any amendment it did not ratify; that the number of non-nuclear signatories (previously left blank) necessary to bring the treaty into force would be 40; and that the treaty would be of 25-year rather than unlimited duration.

Despite these concessions to them, the nuclear have-nots continued at the ENDC sessions in Geneva to press for further changes in the draft treaty. Some of these pressures, as indicated below, were reflected in a modified draft treaty submitted by Moscow and Washington on March 11, 1968.

As for Article III, the Soviet–U.S. draft treaty on January 18 obligated each non-nuclear signatory to meet IAEA requirements on safeguards "either individually or together with other States" within 180 days after the treaty entered into force. Thus, the IAEA could negotiate an agreement with EURATOM under which the administration of safeguards for members of EURATOM would be entrusted to that organization, with IAEA retaining the ultimate responsibility of assuring itself that the safeguards satisfy the requirements of the treaty. By agreeing to this formulation, the USSR made a fairly substantial concession to the preferences of West European states, one that Moscow apparently judged worthwhile in order to obtain Bonn's participation in the treaty. Throughout much of 1966 and 1967 the United States had favored a larger role for IAEA, and at most a transitional role for EURATOM, but Washington too found that its position—even when acceptable to Moscow—had to be modified to win acceptance by Bonn, Rome, and other NATO allies. Partly because of this situation, Soviet officials interviewed in the winter of 1967–68 expressed the view that it was West Germany—and appeasement of Bonn by Washington—that was holding up agreement on the draft treaty. The White House, on the other hand, became increasingly interested in achieving a "peace plank" in an election year. By mid-January, however, Moscow spared Washington the difficult decision of whether to override the objections of other key NATO powers by agreeing to a compromise formula under consideration since early November 1967, when it had been endorsed by the North Atlantic Council.[62]

A putative Soviet ally also raised major objections to the Soviet–U.S. entente, however. At the Sophia meeting of Warsaw Pact nations in early 1968 Rumania refused to sign a declaration favoring the agreement on nonproliferation—not because Bucharest opposed such a treaty in principle but, according to East European communist sources, on the ground that its conclusion at this particular time would dampen Vietnamese morale and give revolutionaries the world over the impression that Washington and Moscow were in collusion.[63]

While Bucharest apparently objected to the treaty on revolutionary grounds in inter-communist parleys, it utilized other justifications for proposing at Geneva a set of amendments to the superpower accords on nonproliferation. A Rumanian Working Paper dated October 19, 1967, had put forward a number of proposals,[64] some of which had been reflected in the Soviet–U.S. draft of January 18, 1968. But many of these suggestions had not been acted on, and Bucharest enunciated them again on March 8, 1968, with greater precision.[65] One apparent objective of the Rumanian amendments was to minimize IAEA interference in the peaceful nuclear activities of the non-nuclear weapon states by specifying limits to the organization's jurisdiction. Having appealed to the interests of the non-nuclear nations, Bucharest then included in its draft provisions for Article III what could only be an unacceptable joker: a demand that the U.N. Security Council establish "an appropriate control to ensure that non-nuclear-weapon States Party to the Treaty on whose territory there are foreign military bases shall not acquire in any form whatsoever access to nuclear weapons indirectly through such bases." By this amendment Bucharest would have reverted to the erstwhile Soviet insistence on dismantling the arrangements for nuclear sharing already existing among NATO powers.

Bucharest also put pressure on the superpowers. If nuclear disarmament had not taken place within five years after the nonproliferation treaty entered into force, Rumania proposed that the signatories "shall examine the situation thus created and decide on the measures to be taken." In that connection Bucharest also demanded that a review conference meet every five years on an obligatory basis, rather than the optional one preferred by Moscow and Washington. In the same vein, Rumania opposed any requirement that, when denouncing the treaty, a state need explain the "extraordinary events it regards as having jeopardized its supreme interests."

By the time of the Rumanian proposals, however, a Soviet–U.S. steamroller had already picked up considerable momentum and was determined not to be sidetracked. Having ironed out their own differences about the IAEA and EURATOM, the superpowers turned their attention to the problems of assuaging the security concerns of the non-nuclear-weapon states. On March 7, two days before the Rumanian suggestions, Moscow and Washington announced in almost identical speeches their support for a draft resolution of the U.N. Security Council on security assurances.[66] The resolution specified that "aggression with nuclear weapons or the threat of such aggression against a non-nuclear-weapon State would create a situation in which the Security Council, and above all its nuclear-weapon State permanent members, would have to act immediately in accordance with their obligations under the United Nations Charter." Second, the resolution welcomed "the intention expressed by certain States [i.e. by Moscow, Washington, and London and perhaps others] that they will provide or support immediate assistance . . . to any non-nuclear-weapon State Party [to the nonproliferation treaty] that is a victim of an act or an object of a threat of aggression in which nuclear weapons are used." Third, the resolution reaffirmed "the inherent right, recognized under Article 51 of the Charter, of individual and collective self-defense if an armed attack occurs against a member of the United Nations, until the Security Council has taken measures necessary to maintain international peace and security."

In agreeing to this formulation Moscow had laid aside its earlier "Kosygin proposal" with its discriminatory implications vis-à-vis West Germany, and also its long-standing support for a ban on the use of nuclear weapons, congenial to Peking but not to Washington. The commitment referred to in the draft Security Council resolution was quite similar to the main assurance suggested in 1965 by the Wiesner committee. It also followed the spirit of President Johnson's suggestion to the ENDC on January 27, 1966, "to strengthen United Nations and other international security arrangements" so as to protect the nations that forswear nuclear arms.

By providing a Soviet as well as a Western guarantee, reflected in the draft Security Council resolution, the superpowers hoped to meet India's concern lest her nonaligned status be jeopardized. In New Delhi, however, the question was raised whether any system of verbal assurances could be sufficient to assure the nation's defense under all circumstances. With regard to the particular guarantee proposed, India asked why it was not incorporated in the nonproliferation treaty directly, rather than via a Security Council resolution. Would the mechanism of the Security Council act with sufficient speed in a time of crisis? Could a veto (say, by China or France) not cripple its operations? To these questions Moscow and Washington replied that to make the guarantee part of the treaty could impede agreement on the main portions of the treaty and its ratification (not least of all in the United States); that debate in the Security Council would be regarded as procedural, and hence not subject to veto; that, in case of a delay in the Security Council, the residual right to action under Article 51 would become applicable whenever, in William C. Foster's phrase, "two or three nations" agreed to act collectively. (Other guarantees by the superpowers would in any case protect the security of NATO and Warsaw Pact members).[67] Whatever the weight of such reasoning, however, the weakness of Mrs. Gandhi's government and the growing strength of the pro-bomb lobby in India led the Indian correspondent of the *Economist* to predict, on March 16, 1968, that India's cabinet would take an "in-between position"—neither approving the treaty nor proceeding with steps to test and procure nuclear weapons.[68] At least the first part of this forecast was vindicated on May 14, 1968, when India's representative at the U.N. disarmament debate reiterated that "an acceptable and balanced" nonproliferation treaty would have to include Communist China and provide a "direct juridical and compulsive link with measures of nuclear disarmament." The erosive impact of such a stand had been indicated the previous day when Pakistan's delegate said that "the main purpose of the treaty would be defeated" unless it commanded "unqualified adherence" from potential nuclear-weapon states, such as India.

The General Assembly debate which began April 26, 1968, dealt with a revised Soviet–U.S. draft treaty on nonproliferation which the two powers had tabled at the ENDC on March 11, 1968. The revised draft incorporated comparatively minor amendments proposed by Sweden and other powers, but passed over those suggested by Rumania on March 8 as well as some others that had been submitted, e.g., by Brazil and by Italy.[69] One amendment authorized a conference of signatories every five years instead of only after the first five years, if a majority so request, for the purpose of reviewing the operation of the treaty. A second change added to the preamble a reiteration of the determination expressed in the 1963 Moscow Treaty to "seek to achieve the discontinuance of all test explosions of nuclear weapons for all time and to continue negotiations to this end. . . ." A third change strengthened the language of Article VI calling for negotiations on cessation of the nuclear arms race by adding the words "at an early date."

During the U.N. debate of the draft treaty a number of countries in addition to India registered various complaints. Japan wanted the nuclear-weapon states to promise not to use nuclear weapons against any signatory; Italy wanted assurances that non-nuclear-weapon states would have access to nuclear fuel for peaceful purposes; Yugoslavia (and—in the background—West Germany and also Rumania) sought assurances the nuclear powers would begin to disarm; Sweden wanted provisions that nuclear explosions for peaceful purposes would be carried on under international control; while Brazil continued to urge that non-nuclear-weapons countries be allowed to carry on such explosions themselves.

The USSR and the United States offered three additional if minor sets of changes in their draft treaty on May 31, 1968, after a debate in the Political and Security Committee of the General Assembly that had continued intermittently since April 26. (This text, on which the General Assembly later voted, is given as Appendix A below, with the final revisons italicized.) U.S. Ambassador Goldberg declared that these amendments would alter three categories of the treaty. First, by alterations made in Articles IV and V, they strengthened the provisions for sharing in the benefits of the peaceful uses of atomic energy. Article IV now stipulated that all signatories (including of course the nuclear-weapon countries) "undertake to facilitate" the fullest possible exchanges for the peaceful uses of nuclear energy. Article IV also specified that "equipment" and "materials"—as well as scientific and technological information—would be shared. In addition to emphasizing that nuclear sharing would be done "especially in the territories of non-nuclear-weapon States Party to the Treaty," there was also added the phrase, "with due consideration for the needs of the developing areas of the world." Article V, as modified, bound all signatories "to take appropriate measures to ensure that, in accordance with this Treaty, under appropriate international observation and through appropriate international procedures potential benefits from any peaceful applications of nuclear explosions will be made available to non-nuclear-weapon States Party to this Treaty." The language of Article V indicated an expectation that supplementary agreements would define the functions of the appropriate international body and the projects it would supervise. Negotiations on this subject, the article went on, "shall commence as soon as possible after the treaty enters into force."

The second category of changes cited by Goldberg strengthened the commitment of the nuclear-weapon powers to nuclear disarmament. The preamble declared their intention not only to halt the arms race at the earliest possible date but "to undertake effective measures in the direction of nuclear disarmament." Another change expressed the signatories' "hope for widest possible adherence to the treaty by both nuclear-weapon and non-nuclear states"—a plea for universality suggested by Japan, and perhaps addressed to New Delhi as well as to Peking.

A third category of revisions sought to strengthen the security of the non-nuclear-weapon states. The preamble now reiterated the obligations of the U.N. Charter on refraining from the threat or use of force. Further, Article IX was altered to provide that the treaty would enter into force only after ratification by the USSR, United Kingdom, and United States (as well as by forty other signatory states), so as to avoid the theoretical possibility that the treaty would be frustrated by a nuclear power that signed but did not ratify it. Goldberg stressed, however, that the security assurances to be offered by the three nuclear powers in the Security Council "constitute the most appropriate and effective solution that can be devised for this problem"—"a deterrent factor of the first magnitude."

Before and after the General Assembly vote on the draft nonproliferation treaty, two extraneous factors colored the prospects of its approval in the United Nations and subsequent signature and ratification. First, an Afro-Asian group of fifty-one countries introduced a resolution early in June recommending that the Security Council use force, if necessary, to evict South Africa so that South-West Africa could become an independent state. Further, thirty-nine of these countries favored delaying the vote on a nonproliferation treaty until wide support was obtained for the South-West Africa resolution. In the form offered, however, this resolution did not receive the backing of major Western, Latin American, or East European states—including the USSR. As a result, many African countries abstained on the nonproliferation vote.

A second exogenous complication resulted from the imposition by G.D.R. authorities of new controls and fees on West German travelers and transport to West Berlin. Even before this development, many West Germans objected to rushing into the nonproliferation agreement, although responsible officials did not want to hold out too long lest the nation's image and bargaining power diminish abroad.[70] Some Westerners speculated that Pankow's move aimed at thwarting conciliation between Bonn and other Warsaw Pact nations. In any event it led to increased reluctance in Bonn to sign the treaty under pressure and/or without receiving some *quid pro quo* from the East in return.

Finally, on June 10, the Political and Security Committee of the General Assembly endorsed the draft treaty by a vote of ninety-two to four, with twenty-two abstentions. By the time of the vote, forty-eight countries (the last being Liberia) had become co-sponsors of the draft. Among the affirmative votes were most of the nuclear capable countries to which Moscow and Washington had addressed revisions of their draft treaty: Italy, Israel, Japan, Pakistan, Rumania, South Africa, Sweden, Switzerland, and the U.A.R. All countries of Europe voted for it, except France, Portugal, and Spain, each of which abstained. (West Germany and East Germany, of course, do not hold seats in the United Nations and hence could not vote at this stage.) The four negative votes were cast by nations friendly to China—Albania, Tanzania, Zambia—and by ultra-revolutionary Cuba. The twenty-two nations abstaining included, besides the three European states noted above, Brazil and Argentina (which demanded the right to conduct nuclear explosions for peaceful purposes); Algeria, Burma, Saudi Arabia, and fourteen black African nations (some of them pro-Chinese, e.g., Mali, and most of them resentful at the weak measures taken by the United Nations in the dispute with South Africa over ending her control over South-West Africa).* But the most serious holdout was India, which insisted that she would not produce a bomb but would not surrender her right to do so.

---

* The fourteen black African nations included (besides Mali): Burundi, the Central African Republic, Chad, Congo (Brazzaville), Gabon, Guinea, Malawi, Mauritania, Nigeria, Rwanda, Sierra Leone, and Uganda. Six other countries did not attend the session: Cambodia, Cameroun, Costa Rica, and Gambia, as well as Haiti and the Dominican Republic—the latter two countries having been deprived of the right to vote because they were in arrears in their membership fees.

Still hopeful that the security concerns of India and other non-nuclear states could be met, the three nuclear powers formally offered their pledges in the Security Council on June 17 to defend non-nuclear-weapons countries, signatories of the nonproliferation treaty, from nuclear attack. On June 20 the resolution on defending non-nuclear nations (given in Appendix B) was adopted by a vote of ten affirmative votes in the Security Council and five abstentions—Algeria, Brazil, France, India, and Pakistan. Effectiveness and constitutionality were among the ostensible grounds for the abstentions. France declared that she did not want to block the resolution, but questioned whether any verbal guarantees could be effective. India's representative added the objection that "any linking of security assurances to the signature of a nonproliferation treaty would be contrary to the provisions of the Charter, which does not discriminate between those who might adhere to a particular treaty and those who might not do so." While it could be argued that the three nuclear powers were injecting new conditions for the fulfillment of their obligations as permanent members of the Security Council, it was nevertheless true that India was also being threatened with an absence or withdrawal of specific external guarantees in case of a Chinese attack. New Delhi may have reasoned, however, either that these assurances would still be operative—because of U.S. and Soviet vital interests— or that they would be in any case meaningless.

Peking seemed to be even more outraged over the security guarantees than by the nonproliferation treaty, and not suprisingly, since the guarantees could restrict Chinese actions far more than could the treaty. *People's Daily* charged in a June 13 editorial that the nonproliferation accord was a "thoroughly unequal treaty dished up by the U.S. imperialists and Soviet revisionists [which was] even more unscrupulous and outrageous than the 'tripartite [nuclear test ban] treaty' they cooked up five years ago." Peking also denounced the U.S.–Soviet attempt "to accelerate the rigging up of an anti-China encirclement by providing their 'nuclear umbrella' to India and other countries bordering China." The Chinese took solace, however, from the fact that many countries—even some "under U.S. control"—were "firmly opposed to this big fraud." The nuclear monopoly of the U.S. imperialists and Soviet revisionists, Peking declared, "was broken long ago and will certainly be broken again." The U.S. and Soviet weapons, *People's Daily* concluded, "will, in the end, be buried together with their possessors by the people of the world!"

The notion that Peking might somehow be drawn into a world disarmament conference was put down once more in late June when Peking refused to accept a telegram from U Thant inviting China to take part (like other "nuclear powers," without a vote) in the conference of non-nuclear weapons states planned for Geneva in August 1968. The Peking Telegraph Office observed curtly that the C.P.R. had "no relations what-soever" with the United Nations.

In West Germany, meanwhile, resentment mounted over the G.D.R. traffic controls and Soviet support for them. Thus, *Die Welt* (June 14) declared that "Bonn cannot, ought not and does not want to reject the ideal concept of nonproliferation," but it counseled against ratifying action by the Bundestag prior to the American presidential elections. The *Frankfurter Allgemeine* carried a statement on June 13 that Minister of Economics Schiller reportedly had suggested that Bonn's signature be tied to a guarantee of the routes to Berlin. Supporting this logic, the *Stuttgarter Zeitung* said on June 14 that:

> Ulbricht's visa requirement, established with the approval of the Soviet regime, and the weak American reaction, show that an ever so willing cooperation in making sacrifices on the part of the Federal Republic on behalf of Soviet-American general agreement, for example in such a matter as the nonproliferation treaty, would not bring in even the most modest honorarium.

The paper concluded that Bonn's signature should be made contingent upon "fulfillment of political conditions which will leave the door open for the declared main goal of its foreign policy." The *Frankfurter Rundschau* (June 15), on the other hand, argued against this course, partly because it doubted that the "United States would allow herself to be driven to tougher actions against the Soviet Union in return for a German signature." Nevertheless, Bonn indicated in July that it would not sign the treaty until "a whole series of problems" had been solved, including an end to "massive Soviet political pressure" and the provision of a special U.S. guarantee. Bonn argued that the NATO guarantee system (up for renewal in 1969) might expire before the nonproliferation treaty (set to run twenty-five years unless denounced), and that Security Council assurances might be ineffective.

Hesitation in Bonn and outright opposition in Peking were linked in Soviet propaganda aimed at rebutting Chinese charges about global collusion with the United States. *Literaturnaia gazeta* asserted that the real—not imaginary—collusion was in the identical stands against the nonproliferation treaty (and also on the Paris talks to end the Vietnamese war) taken by Peking and the reactionaries in the West ("American ultras" and "German revanchists"). Each of these groups, it charged, shared an "adventurist anti-Soviet line." Thus, Soviet media—as in 1963 when defending the Moscow Treaty—discriminated between various groups in the West and linked some of them with what Moscow termed the "nationalist" policies of Peking. To be sure, Moscow did not attack President Johnson, but neither did it praise him. Rather, his June 4 speech at Glassboro citing various agreements reached with the USSR was dismissed by *Pravda* on June 19 as, among other things, election talk. *Pravda*, like *Izvestiia* on June 13, countered the President's claims to improved U.S.-Soviet understanding with the assertion that the Vietnam war, Israeli aggression, the arms race, and the trade discrimination constituted major roadblocks to substantial improvements in relations between the two countries. On the other hand, Moscow also stressed that if U.S. deeds matched Washington oratory, the USSR would respond favorably. Further, some Soviet statements referred affirmatively to Ambassador Goldberg and to the cooperative position taken by the United States in the nonproliferation negotiations. Indeed, *Izvestiia* editorialized on June 20 that General Assembly approval of the nonproliferation pact shows that "it is quite possible to settle other disputed international questions." The article continued that the relaxation of tensions, which is attacked by reactionaries in the West and vociferous leftwingers—"above all in Peking"—"is not a utopia but quite a feasible thing which meets the interest of peace and progress." *Izvestiia* said that the treaty marked the first occasion when obligations were undertaken to press for realistic measures to achieve disarmament. Further, *Izvestiia* asserted that the pact "to a considerable extent ties the hands of all those who would like to upset peace and use mass terror weapons." The identity of these potential aggressors was not made clear, but a *Pravda* article on June 16 said that African and Arab countries were concerned about a nuclear threat from Israel and South Africa. The *Pravda* article plus, for example, a radio broadcast to Iran three days later, also implied that China might be a potential aggressor if she objected to security guarantees for non-nuclear powers. Of course West Germany was still highly suspect in official Russian eyes, but Soviet media seemed if anything to exceed the bounds of objectivity in stressing that the treaty "closes all paths and loopholes for the spread of nuclear weapons and guarantees the necessary international control over the fulfillment of pledges made by states for performing this control." Finally, Soviet media justified the pact as an example of an agreement with the capitalist world "to the advantage of progress and the cause of socialism"—the very type which, Moscow noted, Lenin himself had favored. That none of this meant reconciliation with capitalist imperialism, however, was manifest in the consistent and significant Soviet support to the Arab world and to Hanoi. At the same time, while Peking limited itself to hundreds of "serious warnings" issued publicly, it connived in secret with Washington to spare Chinese territory from involvements arising out of the Vietnamese war.*

---

* A tough line toward China (and the United States) was evident in messages to such different audiences as those addressed by *Pravda* (June 16); Radio Moscow to the United Kingdom (June 18); Radio Moscow to Iran (June 17 and 19); and a

The draft nonproliferation treaty which the General Assembly approved on June 10, 1968, was formally signed by many countries on July 1 at ceremonies in Moscow, London, and Washington, where it was also opened for signing by other countries. Premier Kosygin called the treaty a "major success for the cause of peace," while President Johnson termed it "the most important international agreement since the beginning of the nuclear age." The Soviet Government, as noted in the next chapter, took the occasion to put forward a series of measures to further limit the arms race, and the U.S. President announced that talks would begin with the Soviet Union "in the nearest future" on steps to limit and reduce both offensive nuclear weapons and defensive antimissile systems.

Only time would tell how many of the countries that voted for or against the treaty or abstained in the General Assembly would eventually sign and ratify it. Both Moscow and Washington seemed fairly hopeful that, once the bandwagon of signatures and ratifications began to roll, countries so reluctant as India and Brazil would feel strong incentives to jump aboard.* Surprisingly for some observers, the Kremlin did not leave to the White House the task of arm-twisting. First Deputy Soviet Foreign Minister Vasily V. Kuznetsov warned the United Nations on May 20 that the "iron logic of political struggle" placed all nations not signing the treaty in league with the enemies of the USSR. Earlier, on February 16, 1968, Soviet delegate to the ENDC Aleksei Roshchin read a list of communist and nonaligned nations whose peaceful nuclear programs had already been aided by the USSR. He then warned that future Soviet aid would be directed toward those countries that signed the nonproliferation treaty.** In private, both the U.S. and Soviet delegations warned that a refusal to sign the draft treaty would lead their governments to cut off

---

statement by Yuri Zhukov, Deputy Chairman of the Soviet Peace Committee in May 1968. Comments about the United States were most hostile in the broadcasts to Iran, which depicted the treaty as a Soviet initiative that triumphed over U.S. and U.K. opposition. Soviet audiences, however, heard a good word about Ambassador Goldberg and a negative one about U.S. Congressman Craig Hosmer, denounced for his statements about the possible advantage to the United States of limited proliferation. Broad indictments of Chinese policies since about 1954 appeared in a series of articles in April and May issues of *Kommunist* (Nos. 6–8).

* The German Democratic Republic, Rumania, and the U.A.R. were among the states that signed in Moscow on July 1, as was Chad, which abstained on the June 10 vote.

** One observer noted that the draft treaty failed to restrict ongoing research that could lead to the development of pure-fusion explosives which might be produced without fissionable materials and hence fall outside the treaty proscriptions. See William R. Van Cleave, "The Nonproliferation Treaty and Fission-free Explosive Research," *Orbis*, XI, 4 (Winter 1968), 1055–66.

access of non-nuclear-weapon countries to nuclear fuel, equipment, and technical information previously supplied. Asked early in 1968 what were the chances that India would sign the treaty, a Soviet diplomat quipped: "A hundred percent. You supply 50 per cent of the pressure and we apply the other 50 per cent."

Assuming that the treaty is ratified and enters effect—despite such hurdles as the planned conference of non-nuclear-weapon states, the negotiations to end hostilities in Vietnam, election campaigns, ferment in Eastern Europe, and continued power struggle in China—a series of major question marks will continue to darken the horizon. Because of these issues, a futurologist—although he might envisage some prospects conducive to world peace and stability—could easily produce a number of frightening but plausible scenarios pointing in the direction of unrest and conflict.

The main problem, of course, would be to make the treaty endure, despite the pressures likely to mount over time upon the signatories. Three kinds of issues illustrate the range of possible difficulties. First, how would the guarantee system function in practice? For example, if Peking used intensive nonmilitary or conventional military forces in pursuit of its territorial or other objectives, would this be treated as nuclear blackmail even though the Chinese continued to stick by their pledge not to be the first to use atomic weapons? If Peking and Moscow realigned, what would become of the common superpower front designed to protect nonaligned nations against nuclear threats? Would Washington continue to offer a unilateral guarantee on a global basis, as President Johnson did in October 1964? If Mainland China took a seat on the Security Council, she could not veto actions on pacific settlement of disputes (Chapter VI of the U.N. Charter) but her affirmative vote would be necessary on action with respect to threats to the peace (Chapter VII). Could the device of labelling debate on threats against the non-nuclear-weapon states as "procedural" effectively override a prospective Chinese veto? If U.S. and Soviet ABM systems were not highly adequate, would Washington and Moscow see it as "self-defense" to protect a third party from Chinese attack?

A second area of difficulty could develop in Europe, because the treaty drafted in 1967–68 permits of diverse interpretations regarding (a) nuclear sharing; (b) multilateral forces; and (c) a European defense force. Article I prohibited the "transfer" or "control" over nuclear weapons to "any recipient whatsoever," whether the transfer were accomplished "directly or indirectly." But the treaty did not define these concepts, and by implication seemed to tolerate the two-key sharing arrangments long established in NATO. Does the treaty then allow for the introduction of some form of nuclear sharing among the Warsaw Pact nations, even if residual Soviet controls are not identical with those of the U.S.? Or (a more likely contingency) could the United States not argue, if she wanted to revive some version of a multilateral force, that such a treaty arrangement would not surrender U.S. control over the weapons provided to this force? Moscow's view, on the other hand, has been that this type of "access" to nuclear weapons would constitute "proliferation." Looking further down the road to European unity, it also seems that Paris and/or London could put their atomic arms at the disposal of a European security force—even if the decisions of the force were taken by a majority vote—without violating the strict terms of the treaty. In all such cases, of course, Moscow and its allies could be expected to exert deterrent pressures and, if these failed, to consider denouncing the treaty if that would serve their purposes.

Third, the large-scale effectiveness of IAEA safeguards remains to be tested. The IAEA budget and staff must be drastically expanded. Workable arrangements with EURATOM must be perfected to the satisfaction of all parties. No matter how adequate these safeguards become, however, the problem will remain that the treaty drafted in 1967–68 does not prohibit the construction of uranium enrichment facilities or of plutonium separation plants. Facilities of this type have legitimate peaceful uses in supplying reactor fuel for power or for research purposes, but they also provide ready access to weapons-grade fissionable material. Given this state of preparation, the technical and industrial problems associated with constructing and detonating a nuclear bomb would not be a great hurdle. If a country wished to denounce the treaty, it need give only a three-month notice. No sanctions or enforcement provisions are provided in the treaty (although counteractions by other states might well make a government hesitate about withdrawing from the treaty). Presumably, such a government would also have to denounce the Moscow Treaty before carrying on nuclear tests in any environment except under ground.

Beyond these three problems, others could easily arise, which would certainly be discussed at the first conference held after five years to review the operations of the treaty. There is, for example, the underlying contradiction implicit in a commitment (a) to defend non-nuclear nations from nuclear attack, presumably by China and (b) to move toward a comprehensive nuclear test ban (which could inhibit ABM developments) and nuclear disarmament. For the present, the arms levels of the superpowers could be drastically reduced without affecting their ability to deter Mainland China. If Peking's nuclear arsenal grows, however, a kind of scissors crisis would eventually ensue.

Nevertheless, despite these possible difficulties, the nonproliferation

treaty and collateral security arrangements also have tremendous potential for improving the state of international security. These accords do
not create the best of conceivable worlds, but they promise better alternatives than many of those currently feasible. While no panacea, the accords
may afford an opportunity for less resource expenditure on arms competition and war and more on development—within the industrialized countries and in the third world. Hopes such as these may be more realistic
than those which underlay the founding of the United Nations in 1945.
The notion was probably naive that several "policemen" could maintain
international stability in an age when east-west distrust persisted and
when the United States enjoyed a qualitative asymmetry in the strategic
balance. Almost twenty-five years later, however, although diffidence and
tension continue in Soviet-Western relations, a semblance of strategic
parity has been achieved, making it increasingly obvious that the superpowers have important parallel interests as well as competitive ones. It
is possible, of course, that—just as they come close to understandings
based on parallel interests—extraneous forces will intervene to prevent or
unsettle such accords.

Much will depend on what some would call *fortuna* and others "uncontrolled variables." The nonproliferation treaty and security understandings may be able to sustain threats of one magnitude, but not of
another. China's behavior may or may not force the other nations into
painful decisions such as those outlined in the first set of scenarios above.
(In spring 1968, even while attacking the nonproliferation treaty and its
duopolistic implications, Peking broke precedent to attack possible nuclear spread to particular countries.[71]) As for Europe—and Germany—
where the second set of difficulties noted earlier might develop, present
trends could evolve in quite different ways. The peoples of Europe—
Eastern as well as Western—might direct their energies toward economic
and technological development, so that the loopholes of the treaty are
not tested, or they may revert to another recrudescence of explosive nationalism.[72] Among the non-nuclear-weapon states generally, interests may
evolve so that—despite an abundance of nuclear reactors and fuel—this
power is used for growth and prosperity rather than for stockpiling arms;
alternatively, once such resources are available, national autarky and
international anarchy may follow. As for the superpowers, their arms race
may spiral or it may come under control and, in time, even be reversed.
This last variable, of course, is important to the enduring quality of a
nonproliferation agreement. As the next chapter indicates, however, the
U.S.–Soviet strategic confrontation has not only an internal dynamism of
its own, but one that is highly responsive to one of the main forces conducive to horizontal proliferation: the prospect of a nuclear armed China.

XII
Impact on the Superpower Confrontation

China's entry into the atomic club brought new and profoundly disturbing dimensions to arms control and strategic planning in the governments of the atomic haves as well as in the nuclear-weapons have-nots. How the superpowers responded to the small but growing Chinese atomic threat would have vitally important consequences, not only with respect to the superpower confrontation and its attendant alliance problems, but also for the arms planning of the potential nuclear powers. Unless Washington and Moscow exercised restraint in their own arms build-up; unless they generated a sense that history is moving toward collective security and world law; unless there developed a sense that the security and prestige of states can be maintained by some means other than a national nuclear arsenal, the candidates for membership in the atomic club would be the more likely to seek their objectives in a strategy of nuclear autarky.

The United States and the Soviet Union have gone on record, to be sure, as supporting nonproliferation and other arms control measures.[1] But during the mid-1960s, perhaps despite the preferences of Soviet and U.S. leaders, powerful pressures—technological, strategic, and political—were pushing the governments in Moscow and Washington toward another round in the arms race. Since the early 1960s Western analysts had been wondering whether Moscow would resign itself to strategic inferiority vis-à-vis the West,[2] and whether both sides, regardless of the terrestrial balance of power, could resist the temptation to pursue further the military opportunities generated by space and other technology. The entry of a new factor—the prospect of a nuclear-armed China—gave a spurt to the accumulating arguments in the Kremlin and in Washington in favor of moving the arms race from the relative stability achieved in

1963. But countervailing forces were also at work, some of them becoming stronger during 1965–68. The cost of maximizing the military potential of technology imposed restraints on Washington as well as on Moscow, and in both capitals there were some signs of prudence and an unwillingness to push the arms race without regard for the consequences.

At the core of the U.S.–Soviet engagement in matters of arms and arms control in the mid-1960s lay four issues: the balance of defensive and offensive weapons, the production of fissionable materials for nuclear weapons, underground nuclear testing, and the militarization of outer space.

A DEFENSIVE-OFFENSIVE SPIRAL

The most obvious impact of China upon the superpowers' strategic calculations has been in the area of antiballistic missile (ABM) defenses. Soviet territory will probably be vulnerable at least by 1970 to Chinese medium-range rockets, and the continental United States by 1975 to long-range or submarine-based systems. While an ABM defense would be extremely expensive and of uncertain value against a superpower attack, a cheaper and less comprehensive system might be useful in protecting American (and Soviet) cities against a smaller-scale Chinese strike.

During 1965–66 there were indications that Russia was beginning to deploy ABMs and that the Pentagon wanted the United States to begin such deployment immediately.[3] While many U.S. arms control analysts argued that ABM defenses would escalate the offensive arms race and increase Russian fears of a U.S. first-strike,[4] Soviet theorists refused to link defense and offense in this manner.[5] They contended that "defense is defense," and that the Soviet Government would be irresponsible if it did not take all possible measures for the protection of the country. When a Soviet diplomat was asked whether his government did not foresee the likely impact on U.S. procurement plans of a Soviet ABM force, he replied, "How you plan your defense policy is your affair." The Soviet military press gave no hint that the Russian defense system was directed mainly against China. Rather, the rationale for the system as described in articles on strategy implied that the Soviets hoped to build a force useful against a large-scale as well as a limited attack.[6] The Soviet refusal to discriminate between different kinds of potential attack may have stemmed in part from the multiplicity of possible attackers—China, the United States, France, Britain, a NATO force, or—conceivably—some day, a West German force.

In the United States, on the other hand, both proponents and opponents of ABM generally distinguished between a hypothetical force intended to defend against a small-scale Chinese attack and a massive blow from the Soviet Union. Cost estimates for the former system ran from two to over five billion over five years. Some supporters of ABM deployment stressed the threat of a Chinese attack as a way to bolster their arguments about the need to defend against Soviet missiles and to reciprocate Russia's defensive buildup. First, if it were technologically and financially difficult to build a meaningful defense against Russia, it would be more feasible and cheaper to mount one against a smaller-scale Chinese attack. Second, a U.S. ABM force would strengthen the credibility of Washington's commitment to defend non-nuclear states from Peking's atomic blackmail. Third, evidence that the United States planned to remain basically invulnerable to Chinese attack might even deter Peking from attempting to build a force threatening to the United States.

Each of these arguments was challenged by U.S. opponents of a limited ABM deployment. First, it was not clear that it would be technically feasible to construct a limited defense against China. If the defense were spread thinly across the United States, Peking could punch through by concentrating a blow against several key cities. If the defense itself were concentrated, Peking might leapfrog across to other vital areas. In either event, missiles or nuclear-tipped torpedoes launched close to U.S. shores might well evade ABM systems designed to thwart ICBM attacks. Thus, the main deterrent would remain the U.S. offensive force, which would make a Chinese attack suicidal.[7] Second, the psychology involved in a U.S. defense effort could deepen the conviction of potential nuclear powers, such as India, that they should develop their own deterrent, rather than rely on the superpowers' hiding behind their modern Maginot lines. Threshold powers in Europe as well as in Asia might interpret ABM deployments by the superpowers to imply a greater likelihood of war and hence a greater need for the development and independent control of their own national arsenals. Third, the Chinese seemed intent on building their atomic forces regardless of foreign actions or foreign estimates of economic and strategic rationality.

But the most important impact of a U.S. decision to build even a limited AMB defense might well be on the superpower arms race. First, a light deployment to deal with China might readily develop into a medium- or large-scale system against Russia. Second, whether large or small, the development of such defenses would increase the incentives for the superpowers to step up the quantity and quality of their offensive systems. As Joseph I. Coffey has put it:

  Whatever the initial form of an ABM system designed for use against Communist China, it will ultimately become either largely ineffective or little different from that required to defend against Soviet forces. In the long run, therefore, ballistic missile defenses capable of coping with a Chinese attack are likely to increase markedly our capability to limit damage by Soviet strategic forces—a point which the USSR is not likely to miss.[8]

A third consideration was that, whether Moscow recognized this danger or not, superior U.S. resources might quickly enable the United States to create a "defense gap" that destabilized the balance of terror and made both sides more apprehensive over the possibility of a pre-emptive strike at some opportune moment. Significantly, even though the U.S. ABM had not been deployed in 1967, many experts considered the technical capability of the Nike-X superior to the Soviet system.[9]

Many of these arguments came to the fore in late 1965-early 1966 when Defense Secretary McNamara came out against a provision in the coming year's defense budget for the deployment of an ABM system, whether to deal with a large- or a small-scale attack. Despite the unanimous recommendation of the U.S. Joint Chiefs of Staff to begin deployment, McNamara argued that such a system would be of questionable value in opposing a Soviet strike, and that it was premature to deploy one against China.

Since each of the three types of Soviet strategic offensive systems (land-based missiles, submarine-launched missiles, and manned bombers) can, by itself, inflict severe damage on the United States, even a "very good" defense against only one type of system has only limited value. . . . At the other end of the spectrum, it now appears to be technically feasible to design a defense system which would have a reasonably high probability of precluding major damage to the United States from an Nth country nuclear threat, e.g., Communist China in the nineteen-seventies.

The Defense Secretary noted that even the best and most costly mix of damage-limiting measures, including ABM and civil defense, could hardly hope to reduce American fatalities from a Soviet surprise attack below fifty or more million lives. He observed that there was great uncertainty over how Moscow would respond to U.S. damage-limiting plans, and urged that U.S. choices "be responsive to projections based upon the observed development of the Soviet threat and our evolving knowledge of the technical capabilities of our own forces."

While McNamara contended there was no present need to decide on ABM deployment against a Chinese threat, he maintained also that "the development of the essential components should be pressed forward vigorously."[10]

The first public indication that McNamara would oppose the Joint Chiefs' recommendation on ABM deployment came on December 1,

1965[11]—immediately following the release of a report by a committee headed by Jerome B. Wiesner, former Special Assistant to the President for Science and Technology.[12] The Wiesner committee urged the White House to seek agreement—explicitly or tacitly—with the Soviet Union "to a moratorium of at least three years on new deployment (but not on the unverifiable research and development) of systems for ballistic-missile defense."[13]

The contents of the Wiesner committee report were not government-inspired. Indeed a number of Washington officials spoke out publicly against various elements of the report.[14] Most significantly, the timing of the December 1 announcement and the release several days earlier of the Wiesner report suggested that the Defense Department decision against ABM deployment was made independently of the citizens' committee, even though many of its members, such as Roswell Gilpatric, remained government consultants.

Nevertheless the moratorium suggestion received heavy editorial support from *The New York Times* and other papers,[15] and the arguments used by the committee and by Secretary McNamara were very similar—both of them citing technological difficulties, political risks, and the great costs of ABM deployment. (One writer, however, asserted that the Defense Department was far more constrained by the mounting costs of the Vietnamese war than by a fear that ABM deployment might spark a new round of offensive weapons competition.)[16]

Many nonaligned countries at the United Nations welcomed the Wiesner committee moratorium proposal, but communist delegations remained noncommital though not critical.[17] And an international affairs broadcast by Radio Moscow gave a favorable treatment to the conference for which the Wiesner report was prepared, but passed in silence the suggested moratorium.[18] Considering the delicacy of the matter in question, of course, Moscow could hardly take an affirmative stand on short notice; and the absence of a negative attitude itself was encouraging.

The position advocated by the Wiesner committee and top civilians in the Defense Department encountered mounting criticism later in 1966 and in 1967, due to a concatenation of political and technological developments. First, the rapid growth of China's rocket and nuclear program, discussed in chapters VIII and IX above, raised doubt as to the lead time available before Peking's arsenal would present a significant political if not military challenge to the United States and her allies. Particularly after China's H-bomb test in June 1967, Congressional critics such as Senators Henry M. Jackson and Richard B. Russell contended that, irrespective of Russia's behavior, the United States should move immediately to deploy an ABM because "the Chinese danger is so great." "This new threat from Red China," added Representative Robert L. F. Sikes, "would place the United States in double jeopardy if not recognized by us." Their anxieties were heightened further by reports that China might be two years ahead of U.S. expectations in developing a long-range carrier rocket.[19]

Second, the Soviet military posture—offensive as well as defensive, conventional as well as strategic—showed consistent improvement. Intelligence reports in late 1966 indicated that the Soviet Union had begun a potentially serious deployment of ABM defenses.[20] Western intelligence

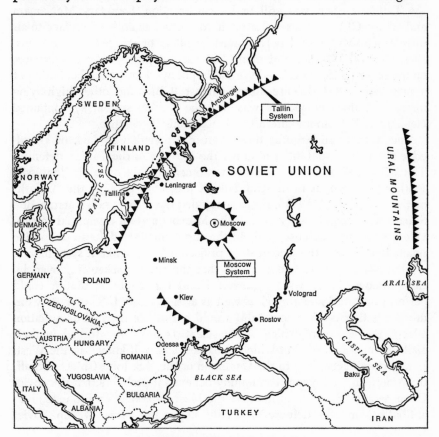

REPORTED SOVIET DEFENSE LINES

analysts differed over the magnitude and nature of the Soviet defenses, but aerial reconnaissance convinced observers that both a "Moscow" and "Tallinn" system were being developed. Most experts agreed that the Moscow installations included part of an ABM defense, and that some of its launch sites and radars had become operational at least by 1966, although other sites in the Moscow system would not be ready until 1968.

As for the Tallinn system, indications were that it had been deployed in at least three main areas: first, across the northern part of the USSR, where it formed an arc defending the path that would be taken by U.S. land-based missiles; second, in southern Russia where it could operate against an attack from Mediterranean bases; and third, in regions south of the Ural Mountains, where defenses might be useful against either Chinese or U.S. missiles (assuming the latter were launched over the Southern Hemisphere). But while most intelligence analysts agreed that the Tallinn system was still under construction, Secretary McNamara and many CIA analysts believed it to consist mainly of surface-to-air missiles (SAMs) useful only against bombers or winged (cruise) missiles. General Wheeler and many Defense Intelligence Agency experts, on the other hand, considered the Tallinn network to be the beginning of a new type ABM defense aimed against ICBM and other high-flying missiles. A third conjecture was that the Tallinn system(s) contained elements of both an antiaircraft and an antimissile defense.

Uncertainties so large as these were compounded by lack of knowledge about the capabilities of either the Moscow or the Tallinn defenses. The ABM defense around Moscow seemed to rely on a single-missile (rather than two, as in the U.S. Nike-X project)—possibly the "Galosh" or the "Griffon" (NATO designations) displayed in parades across Red Square. One hypothesis was that the Moscow system attempted to provide a wide area defense, without the supplementary defense of specific points intended by the second stage projected for the Nike-X system.

Alternatively, it was conceivable that the single rocket employed by the Moscow system was so powerful and fast climbing that it could perform both tasks—terminal as well as area defense. U.S. analysts wondered whether the Moscow ABM would not utilize thermal or radiation effects, the nature of which Soviet scientists probably studied in their 1961–62 nuclear tests, but which remained less well known in the West. In any event, according to the Chairman of the U.S. Joint Chiefs of Staff, the American intelligence community believed it probable that the Soviet Union would "continue to improve the Moscow system and to extend an antiballistic-missile defense over the important areas of the Soviet Union."[21]

Doubts about the nature of the Soviet defense system were further complicated by internal politics and economics in the United States. Thus, some observers on Capitol Hill charged that the Pentagon in 1966 had merely leaked information on Soviet ABM installations that had existed for several years on an experimental basis, in an attempt to generate domestic support for U.S. deployment of Nike-X. The White

House might not respond actively to a pilot ABM deployment in the Soviet Union, provided its existence remained known only in intelligence agencies. Whatever strategic arguments were most persuasive to the White House, the political hazards to opposing U.S. deployment of ABM systems were becoming increasingly formidable. As James Reston put it:

> The McNamara argument [against ABM deployment] would leave the U.S. vulnerable to intercontinental missiles, and the President would be left to face the charge that the Soviets were willing to provide an antimissile system for the Soviet people while President Johnson was not willing to do the same to protect the American people.[22]

The likelihood that economic pressures were also confronting the President was suggested by the interaction between news releases about the Soviet ABM and increases in the stock prices of companies expected to build Nike-X. The possibility that the press was inflating the dimensions of the Russians' defense system was suggested by the assertion of a Defense Department official in censored hearings that a major article on the Soviet ABM program by Hanson W. Baldwin contained "a number of errors."[23]

The political and strategic aspects of this controversy were heightened by the incontrovertible growth of Soviet offensive weaponry. The ratio of U.S. superiority in long-range bombers and missiles declined in 1965–66 from 4:1 to 3:1. By late 1966, the figures stood roughly as follows:[24]

	Soviet	United States
ICBMs	+340	934
Submarine-launched missiles	+130	624
Long-range bombers	up to 200	over 600
IRBMs, MRBMs	750	
Medium-range bombers	1,200	

Such figures suggested only a part of the strategic balance, of course, and had to be placed in a larger context. Thus, while the Kremlin enjoyed an asymmetry in terms of IRBMs, MRBMs and medium-range bombers, most of which were targeted against Europe, NATO forces maintained thousands of land- and carrier-based fighter bombers capable of carrying megaton weapons into the USSR. Problems of extraregional commitments, of alliance solidarity, and of quality vs. quantity also had to be considered. But four factors functioned to reduce the meaning of the 3:1 ratio of U.S. strategic superiority. First, Soviet missiles carried larger warheads than U.S., a point that some observers believed cut the American advantage to a 2:1 ratio. Second, Western population and industrial targets were more concentrated than Soviet. Third, Russia possessed more active defense and civilian defense facilities than the United States. Fourth, if only because a relatively closed society was more capable of mobilizing and mounting a surprise attack, Western planners believed they needed a larger number of strategic delivery vehicles (SDVs) than Russia in case some were eliminated by a first strike.

The Defense Department indicated in 1966 that present and programmed U.S. forces appeared adequate for the years to come, but conceded that U.S. intelligence had underestimated the dimensions of the Soviet strategic force as it would emerge in 1968–69.[25] But however the numbers in the various equations were evaluated, the fact remained that Soviet offensive strength was rapidly gaining, at a time when the United States looked forward to a leveling off in her deployment of SDVs. True, Washington planned to increase the striking power and penetration capabilities of its warheads, e.g., by converting thirty-one atomic-powered submarines so that they could fire Poseidon instead of the smaller Polaris missiles. Nor did Washington rule out the possible construction of new Poseidon submarines.

But Secretary McNamara in 1967 spoke of limiting the U.S. fleet of Polaris (or Poseidon) submarines to fewer than seventy vessels, in a total of one hundred and four attack submarines, while Russia already had an estimated fifty nuclear as well as three hundred and fifty conventionally powered submarines, and seemed intent on building more of the former.[26] Furthermore, the quantitative gains in Moscow's offensive weaponry were accompanied by hardening and dispersal of Soviet ICBM silos. Parallel with these changes, the Soviet Union showed signs also of trying to upgrade its capacity for conventional warfare, particularly by strengthening its air- and sea-lift abilities. Significantly, Soviet strategists in the mid-1960s argued the importance of preparing for limited war—a sharp departure from the earlier tendency to rule out such conflicts categorically on the ground that they would inevitably escalate.[27]

In late 1967–early 1968, however, the various elements in the U.S.–Soviet strategic balance presented a mixed and uncertain picture—for both the near and the intermediate future. Testimony by Defense Secretary McNamara in January 1968 gave the parameters of the strategic confrontation as they appeared in October 1967:*

	Soviet	United States
ICBMs	720	1054
Submarine-launched ballistic missiles	30	656
Long-range bombers	155	697

* Source: Statement of Secretary of Defense Robert S. McNamara before the Senate Armed Services Committee on the Fiscal Year 1969–73 Defense Program and 1969 Defense Budget, prepared by Department of Defense, January 22, 1968, pp. 53–73.

McNamara's estimates on the size of the Soviet submarine fleet differ from those given above in that his data include only SLBMs carried on nuclear-powered submarines, and exclude those on diesel-powered submarines whose primary targets are believed to be Eurasian. The Secretary conceded that the Soviet ICBM force had more than doubled in the past year, but expressed the belief that its growth over the next few years would be "at a considerably slower rate than in the recent past." He also took note of the fractional orbit bombardment system (FOBS) tested by the USSR in 1966–67, but reiterated the Department's belief that such a weapon would not be cost-effective for employment by the United States, although the Soviets might deem it useful in a surprise attack against U.S. bomber bases or as a penetration tactic against ABM systems. McNamara also announced that, although construction of the Soviet ABM defense around Moscow was proceeding at a "moderate pace," the Soviets had made "no effort . . . during the last year to expand that system or extend it to other cities." Further, the majority of the U.S. intelligence community held by 1968 that the so-called "Tallinn" system that was being deployed across the northwestern approaches to the USSR and in several other places was designed most likely against an aerodynamic rather than a ballistic missile threat.

The most important variable in the balance of power might, however, prove to be not the number of U.S. or Soviet rocket launchers, but rather the number of warheads that each carries. Partly to offset a possible gain in Soviet ABM capabilities, the United States was proceeding to deploy multiple, individually guided and targetable reentry vehicles (MIRVs) on its Poseidon and Minuteman III missiles. This meant that even if the USSR matched the United States in total number of ICBMs and SLBMs, Washington might still lead by a factor of five or ten—depending on the number of warheads attached to each missile. Whether the Soviets would also deploy MIRVs in this fashion was unclear early in 1968. Even if they were behind the United States in development of multiple warheads, however, it seemed doubtful that they would be prevented either by technological difficulties or costs from seeking parity in this as in other realms. Indeed, it was conceivable that the larger payload capacity of Soviet rockets would permit them to carry more warheads than U.S. missiles. One possible scenario, then, depicted the United States expanding her strategic lead in deliverable warheads for a period of several years, after which Soviet MIRV deployment would reestablish a more equal balance—assuming the development of no radical asymmetries due to other factors, such as massive ABM deployment by one side only.

Moscow's improved military posture in 1967 seemed to follow from a strategy that was accelerated if not adopted following the ouster of

Khrushchev in October 1964. The results of this "reconstruction" period may not have been entirely satisfactory to Moscow, since the United States still possessed a substantial lead in both strategic and conventional capabilities. The U.S. economic and technological base, furthermore, permitted Washington much more room for expansion of its defense expenditures than Kremlin planners enjoyed—provided they did not scrap entirely their commitment to improving Soviet living standards. Even within these restraints, however, the increases in unexplained residuals in portions of the Soviet budget suggested that Moscow's defense expenditures in 1965 may have risen by about fifteen per cent.[28]

Beneath the changes in Moscow's capabilities and the shift in doctrine, U.S. planners sought to understand Soviet objectives. Did the Kremliin seek superiority over the United States or only parity? Did it want to overthrow or merely redress the strategic balance? If the former objective prevailed, Moscow's ostensible arms control efforts might be designed to lull the West into a sense of complacency. If the latter aim dominated Soviet planning, however, negotiations might be sought to stabilize the strategic balance. In either case, as General Wheeler pointed out, the Kremlin appeared to have four subsidiary goals: (1) to reduce U.S. assured destruction capability; (2) to complicate the targeting problems of the U.S. strategic forces; (3) to reduce Washington's confidence in its ability to penetrate Soviet defenses, thereby reducing the chances of a U.S. pre-emptive attack; and (4) to achieve an exploitable capability, permitting Moscow freedom to pursue its objectives at conflict levels somewhat below general nuclear war.[29] A fifth goal, also consonant with either superiority or parity in the U.S.–Soviet balance, would be to deter a possible Chinese attack and to defend against it if it occurred.

In addition to the growth in Chinese and Soviet military capabilities, a third factor pushing for a reassessment in McNamara's position on ABM derived from improvements in defense technology. These changes, some strategists argued, made ABM defense much more cost-effective than it had been at earlier periods. Whereas the cost of upgrading defensive capabilities to match improvements in offensive forces had once ranged from about 100:1 to 10:1, the ratio had been altered to between 4:1 and 1:1—at least according to some scenarios. Thus, for example, the following figures indicate how a U.S. ABM system could increase the cost to Moscow of penetrating the U.S. defenses (assuming Soviet retaliation to a U.S. first strike):

Level of U.S. Fatalities Sought (millions)	Cost to USSR of Offsetting U.S. Cost to Deploy an ABM
40	$1 Soviet cost to $4 U.S. cost
60	$1 Soviet cost to $2 U.S. cost
90	$1 Soviet cost to $1 U.S. cost

Clearly, the greater proportion of its population a government seeks to protect, the higher the relative cost of defense in proportion to that of offense. Hence, as Donald G. Brennan has pointed out, a limited ABM defense "may thus seem relatively more valuable to planners [such as in Moscow] interested in saving thirty per cent of their population . . . than to strategists who would often have a 'who cares?' attitude toward such low survival levels, but who would be interested in saving higher percentages."[30]

The perfection in 1965–66 of new radar and rocket systems made it possible in 1967 to deploy special systems for both "area" as well as "point" defense. The Spartan missile would attempt to filter out missiles endangering a wide geographical area, while the Sprint missile would intercept those missiles that survived and which threatened key points, such as ICBM sites or certain cities. The Spartan might destroy a number of attacking missiles above the earth's atmosphere by means of high altitude explosions. Given this two-stage approach, it might also be worthwhile to station "Bambi"-type satellites hovering over enemy territory designed to intercept as many missiles as possible as they left their launching pads or in mid-course. Similarly, the Nike-X system could be deployed at sea to strike down enemy rockets well before they reached the airspace over the United States. Deployed under the North Polar icecap, for example, such defenses could intercept Soviet missiles before they could employ chaff or other penetration aids.[31] All these components were seen increasingly as building blocks from which a light, medium, or heavy ABM system could be constructed.

Given the political-military threats from China and the USSR, together with the emergence of a new ABM technology, the notion of a limited ABM deployment appeared increasingly attractive in Washington. If it were described as aimed primarily against China, it would mollify those who worried about another arms race with the Soviet Union. The fact that it would give some protection against a Soviet attack (and could in any case be expanded over time) would gratify proponents of ABM deployment.

Since the scope and future of the Soviet effort had still not become clear, the Defense Department and the White House wanted again to attempt persuading the Soviet Government to suspend further deployment. If the Kremlin persisted, many U.S. officials nevertheless argued that the appropriate U.S. response would be to increase the penetration capabilities and megatonnage of the U.S. strike force, rather than to respond in kind to the Russian defenses. This route, they believed, would be cheaper. It would avoid the necessity of building fallout shelters to accompany active defenses; and it would lead to just as much security in the long run, since an American decision to build ABM defenses would only trigger a still higher round of Soviet–U.S. competition in offensive systems. If Washington chose to respond to Soviet defenses mainly by increasing U.S. strategic systems, it could easily remain a large step ahead of Moscow. It appeared extremely doubtful that Russia's resources would permit the Kremlin to raise the level of its offensive and defensive weaponry in a competition where the United States sought to add only to her offensive forces.

If the United States deployed an ABM system and Moscow did *not* increase its offensive weaponry accordingly, casualties from both sides would still be extremely high in the event of an all-out strategic exchange. The following table[32] outlines the fatalities (in millions) that would occur given no ABM defense; a medium posture ("A") costing at least $12.2 billion; and a heavy deployment ("B") costing at least $21.7 billion (both estimates being subject to upward revision by as much as fifty to one hundred per cent):

	USSR Strikes First; U.S. Retaliates		*U.S. Strikes First; USSR Retaliates*	
	U.S. Fatalities	*Sov. Fatalities*	*U.S. Fatalities*	*Sov. Fatalities*
No ABM Defense	120	120+	100	70
Posture A	40	120+	30	70
Posture B	30	120+	20	70

If, however, Soviet offensive forces were increased to compensate for the U.S. ABM, the number of Americans killed would be the same as if no defense had ever been deployed:

	USSR Strikes First; U.S. Retaliates		*U.S. Strikes First; USSR Retaliates*	
	U.S. Fatalities	*Sov. Fatalities*	*U.S. Fatalities*	*Sov. Fatalities*
No ABM Defense (nor Soviet Response)	120	120+	100	70
Posture A	120	120+	90	70
Posture B	120	120+	90	70

While the Defense Department in early 1967 held it unwise to deploy an ABM system against the USSR, it contended that a light defense against China might offer a high degree of protection against a missile attack, at least through the 1970s. The total cost, including the nuclear warheads, might amount to roughly $3.5 billion. Nevertheless, Secretary

McNamara and the White House ruled out deploying even a token ABM force in fiscal year 1968 to defend against a Chinese force of unknown quantity or quality. They held that it was not "timely" to make a decision on how to cope with the Chinese threat, because "the length of time required to deploy such a [defense] system is less than the length of time required for the Chinese Communists to develop nuclear weapons that could conceivably threaten this nation."[33]

At the same time, the U.S. government continued research and development in ABM systems in 1967–68, if only to keep abreast of the technological possibilities governing its strategic relations with the USSR and Communist China. Washington's preference, however, was to work out an agreement with the Kremlin whereby both sides would refrain from further deployment of antimissile defenses. President Johnson set forth this aim in his state of the Union address on January 10, 1967. Ambassador Llewellyn Thompson carried with him to Moscow the same message, and discussed it with Premier Kosygin. But all signs indicated that a vigorous internal debate on the merits of ABM deployment was proceeding among and between both political and military leaders in Moscow.

Indeed, the spectacle presented by this debate provided the outside world with a fascinating indicator of the extent to which collective rather than monolithic leadership had come to characterize Soviet decision-making. One sign of internal disagreement in Moscow followed a question to Premier Kosygin at a press conference in London on February 10, regarding his views on the possibility of a moratorium on ABM deployment. The Soviet Premier, rather than answering the query directly, raised a question of his own: "What heightens military tension in the world more: an offensive or a defensive system?" His reply was that "a system that serves to ward off an attack does not heighten tension but serves to lessen the possibility of an attack that may kill large numbers of people." He added that it might be cheaper to build offensive than defensive systems, but argued that "this is not the criterion upon which one should base oneself in deciding this problem." His own choice for dealing with this problem, he went on, would be "an end to nuclear armaments and total destruction of nuclear stockpiles."

Kosygin's remarks were reproduced verbatim in *Pravda* on February 11, but they were given a quite different interpretation by the experienced journalist Fyodor Burlatskii in a *Pravda* article published on February 15, reporting that the Premier had "declared that the Soviet Government was ready to discuss the problem of averting a new arms race, both in offensive and defensive weapons." Just two days later, however, *Reuters* reported that the Soviet Foreign Ministry had indicated privately to Western officials that the Burlatskii commentary had misrepresented the position of the Soviet Government; that the author would be reprimanded; and that a correct treatment of the subject would be issued. Nevertheless, by February 21 U.S. officials reported that the Soviet Union had suggested that bilateral discussions take place, but with a broadened focus: the limitation of offensive as well as defensive weapons.[34] A letter from Kosygin making the same proposal was announced by President Johnson on March 3. As for Burlatskii, his pieces continued to appear in *Pravda*, and he led the Soviet journalists at Karlovy Vary in April.

Parallel with these manifestations of discord among Soviet political leaders, Russian marshals also were making claims and counterclaims. Thus, on February 20, 1967, General Pavel F. Batinsky, a Deputy Defense Minister, said that the antiaircraft troops (PVO) he led could "reliably protect the country's territory from an enemy attack by air." And General Pavel A. Kurochkin, head of the Frunze Military Academy, asserted that missiles fired at the Soviet Union would never reach their targets. "If missiles fly," he claimed, "they will never arrive in Moscow." "Detecting missiles in time and destroying them in flight are no problem today," Kurochkin stated at a press interview.[35]

These claims, of course, were not much more precise than Khrushchev's boast in 1962 that his missiles could hit a "fly in the sky." The 1967 claims, however, should be interpreted in a special context: they were issued on the eve of the forty-ninth anniversary of the Soviet Army and Navy. In any event, the broad assertions made by Batinsky and Kurochkin were followed by more modest statements by no less prestigious military leaders. Thus, Defense Minister Malinovsky, in an article in *Pravda* on February 23, made only the following claim:

> New and highly efficient antiaircraft rocket systems and aviation complexes for armament have been developed and accepted. The various means of combat available to our antiaircraft defense troops ensure the reliable destruction of *any aircraft and of many rockets* of the enemy [emphasis added].

The italicized phrase, including the qualification "many" rockets, had become a standard formula in Soviet writing in April 1966 and for months thereafter. Its use in 1967 by Marshal Malinovsky (shortly before his death) could only deflate any pretension that the Soviet ABM systems were impenetrable.

The same phrase was repeated in an *Izvestiia* article on February 23 by the man who soon succeeded Malinovsky as Defense Minister. Marshal A. Grechko wrote that the "country's modern means of antiaircraft defense ensure the reliable destruction of all the enemy's planes and many of its rockets."

On the previous day, February 22, in a broadcast over Moscow radio, Deputy Defense Minister Ivan K. Bagramian had even less to say about the capabilities of Russia's ABM defense. In a long speech extolling in superlative terms other aspects of the Soviet Armed Forces, he noted only that "in recent years a realistic possibility has arisen for us of effectively carrying out antirocket defense." As for the Soviet antiaircraft defense, however, its means ensured "the reliable repulsing of any aircraft." Similar claims were made the same day in an English-language broadcast of an address by Marshal Sokolovsky, who was quoted as saying that the Soviet "antiaircraft defenses have efficient missile intercepting systems." In the same vein, speaking on television on February 22, Marshal Chuikov, Commander of Civil Defense, called for an intensification of civil defense procedures, because "there are no means yet that would guarantee the complete security of our cities and most important objectives from the blows of the enemy's weapons of mass destruction." An article in Red Star on March 21 stressed the need for strategic defense measures along with the value of a powerful offensive posture. But as Thomas W. Wolfe noted in a statement before the Subcommittee on Military Applications, Joint Congressional Committee on Atomic Energy on November 7, 1967, "although Soviet military men may differ as to the present capabilities of the country's ABM defenses, none have questioned publicly the desirability of building such defenses."

An unsettled attitude toward the ABM question was also suggested by the contrasts in the debating postures taken by Soviet diplomats. In autumn 1966 their line was quite rigid, refusing to discuss the impact of ABM deployment on the arms race, a stance that implied their government's decision had been made and was irrevocable. By early 1967, however, one Soviet representative "doubted" that defensive technology could ever match the destructive power of offensive weaponry. Another argued that China's war potential would not threaten Russia in the foreseeable future, since Soviet strategic forces would remain much more powerful than Chinese. Still another Soviet spokesman denied that there was such massive ABM deployment in Russia as reported by U.S. intelligence agencies; their reports, he argued, served merely as a pretext for initiating defense expenditures to gratify the U.S. military industrial complex.[36] Several Soviet diplomats argued that an ABM moratorium might be reached, but only if the road were first smoothed by formalization of a nonproliferation treaty and other East-West accords.

When President Johnson and Prime Minister Kosygin met at Glassboro in 1967, Secretary McNamara lectured the Soviet leader on the disadvantages for both superpowers of deploying an ABM system. Throughout the rest of 1967 the Soviet government seemed to keep open the possibility that it might negotiate on the question of offensive as well as defensive force levels—perhaps after the nonproliferation treaty and its attendant problems were settled. On September 18, 1967, however, Secretary McNamara announced that the United States planned to proceed with deployment of an ABM system designed primarily against a Chinese attack—a move that led Peking to charge that a secret accord had been reached at Glassboro whereby each superpower would build an ABM defense aimed mainly at China. To be sure, Secretary McNamara went to great lengths to make clear his belief that this ABM system should not be expanded into one aimed at Soviet missiles, not because of the great cost, but because such an effort could easily be negated by an upgrading of the Soviet attack force. Nevertheless, he cited as "concurrent benefits" of the Chinese-oriented ABM "a further defense of our Minuteman sites against Soviet attack, which means that at modest cost we would in fact be adding even greater effectiveness to our offensive missile force and avoiding a much more costly expansion of that force." Finally, he noted that the ABM force would "add protection of our population against the improbable but possible accidental launch of an intercontinental missile by any one of the nuclear powers."

A number of paradoxes stood out in the Secretary's argumentation. First, since U.S. estimates about the timetable of Chinese weapons development had not altered, why did Washington favor a policy in September 1967 that it had seen as not "timely" in January? Second, if ABM defenses against the USSR were seen as futile, why cite their collateral utility for defending U.S. missiles and population centers against a Soviet attack? Did not the admission of this collateral value undermine the foundations of the case against a Soviet-oriented ballistic-missile defense? Perhaps because these questions loomed so forcefully, McNamara warned in his September 1967 speech against what he called a "psychological" danger. There is, he stated,

> a kind of mad momentum intrinsic to the development of all new weaponry. If a weapon system works—and works well—there is strong pressure from many directions to procure and deploy the weapon out of all proportion to the prudent level required.

It appeared the Secretary had made a good case against deploying any ABM system, but then used his powers of persuasion somewhat sophistically to justify a decision that he himself might not favor. A similar pattern prevailed in his arguments in favor of limited bombing of North Vietnam. In both instances the impression was strong that political considerations had prevailed over pure strategic reasoning.

As McNamara presented the evidence to the U.S. Senate in early 1968, the "austere" Chinese-oriented ABM defense would cost about $5 billion and could be "highly effective against the kind of threat a Chinese force might pose in the 1970s." The overall system would be designated "SEN-TINEL" and would consist of Perimeter Acquisition Radars, Missile Site Radars, long-range Spartan area defense missiles and, later, some Sprint local defense missiles. The effectiveness of this deployment in reducing U.S. fatalities from a Chinese first strike in the 1970s was expected to take the following contours:

	(Number of Chinese ICBMs)		
	X	2.5X	7.5X
U.S. *Fatalities* (in millions)			
Without SENTINEL	7	11	15
With SENTINEL	−1 to 0	−1 to 0	1

Thus, SENTINEL was expected to hold U.S. fatalities below one million, with "some probability of no deaths" in the event of a relatively primitive Chinese attack. For modest additional outlays the system could be improved so as to limit the Chinese damage potential to low levels into the mid-1980s. Although the SENTINEL system could serve as a foundation on which the United States could build a deployment to defend the Minuteman force, McNamara reiterated that even a fairly heavy ABM defense, including Sprint missiles to defend 52 cities, would still leave the United States highly vulnerable. If the USSR responded to such a defense by adding to her existing missile force multiple warheads and penetration aids, a Soviet first strike would kill 70 million Americans or a Soviet retaliatory blow against a U.S. first strike would kill 40 million Americans. If the Kremlin went on to add 550 mobile ICBMs to its force, U.S. fatalities would rise to levels of 100 million and 90 million assuming either a first or a second strike against the United States.

Given the objectives of arms control—less likelihood of war, less destruction if it occurs, and less military expenditure—even a small-scale ABM deployment would present large risks. The basic problem would remain that a defense useful against China's growing might would have to be expanded to the point where it downgraded the other superpower's deterrent capabilities, thereby impelling it to improve its offensive forces. While a limited ABM deployment might save U.S. lives if China struck in 1970 or 1975, it appeared doubtful that antimissile defenses would reduce the damage of war if their existence led Moscow or Peking to make its attacking force more numerous or more lethal to civilian targets. Certainly the cost of military competition would increase if the major antagonists embarked on a vicious cycle of defensive and offensive weapons building. Demands for similar protection by the European and Asian protégés of the superpowers would not only unsettle existing alliance systems but would lead to still more military expenditures—all of which could be rendered futile if offensive capabilities merely kept pace with defensive.

A freeze on offensive weapons, coupled with a deployment of defensive systems, might produce a more stable military situation than the balance of terror that relied only on offensive forces. This hypothetical situation, dubbed by some the "Russian freeze," might have theoretical advantages. First of all, however, it would be difficult to obtain such an accord, and still more difficult to maintain it—given the mounting Chinese threat, the uncertainty about the deterrent quality of one's own offensive forces, and the pressures to upgrade the penetration and destructive characteristics of weapons to exploit the latest technology. Second, even a high performance ABM system would save only a fraction of the population from an ICBM attack; and it would leave the country vulnerable to submarine-launched or "suitcase" weapons that could evade the ABM defense. Finally, its "success" might result in lethal side-effects thrown back in the face of the defended nation.

Hence, from the standpoint of arms control, the most hopeful outcome would be that both superpowers limit ABM deployment and curtail expansion of their offensive weapons. On the other hand, if one or both superpowers decided to build a wide network of active defenses, it would be important to improve their dialogue so as to minimize the multiplier effect of ABM systems on the arms race. If Moscow and Washington intended their defenses primarily against China, there would still be some time to gauge the system to fit the nature of the Chinese delivery force as it emerged. Whether or not the defense were intended to be a limited one, it would be desirable for Washington and Moscow to seek an understanding whereby—even though defenses increased—offensive systems would be limited, frozen,[37] or even reduced.

STRATEGIC FORCES AND CONTROL OF FISSIONABLE MATERIALS

The possible groundwork for such an entente had been strengthened in September 1965 by a change in the U.S. position on the reduction and inspection of nuclear delivery systems, making the U.S. proposals more negotiable for Moscow. Since January 1964 the United States had advocated a verified freeze on the number and characteristics of strategic nuclear offensive and defensive vehicles; a verified "bonfire" of U.S. B-47 and Soviet TU-16 bombers; and a verified cutoff in the production of fissionable materials for use in weapons and a transfer of such materials to peaceful uses—for example, a quantity such as 60,000 kilograms to be transferred by the United States and 40,000 kilograms by the Soviet Union.[38]

The tendency of such measures to freeze Soviet forces at levels inferior to those of the United States plus their emphasis on verification made these steps unacceptable to Moscow. The Soviets, for their part, suggested the phased elimination of all bombers by a specified deadline and the elimination of all missile forces except for a specified number retained by the U.S.S.R. and the U.S.A. until the end of the third stage of general disarmament.[39]

The change in U.S. policy in autumn 1965 was not dramatic, but it provided an opening for compromise between the U.S. and Soviet approaches. Ambassador Goldberg renewed the U.S. proposal for a freeze on offensive and defensive systems, but did not take up the bomber bonfire issue. Second, he again proposed a verified halt in the production of fissionable materials and their transfer to peaceful uses. He went on:

> In connection with such a halt in fissionable material production, we now propose the demonstrated destruction by the United States and the Soviet Union of a substantial number of nuclear weapons from their respective stocks.

Repeating the U.S. offer to transfer 60,000 kilograms to nonweapons uses if Moscow transferred 40,000 kilograms, Goldberg broadened the latitude open to each party: "If the U.S.S.R. accepts this proposal, each of us would destroy nuclear weapons of our own choice so as to make available for peaceful purposes such amount of fissionable material."[40]

The movement of the U.S. proposals away from the earlier emphasis on inspection of armaments and toward verification of disarmament brought the U.S. position closer to some aspects of the Soviet. Furthermore, the U.S. Arms Control and Disarmament Agency indicated that the number of weapons that would have to be destroyed to provide such a transfer of fissionable material would involve "several thousand" weapons of up to megaton range.[41] While Washington was not prepared to reduce to the same size strategic nuclear force as Moscow's, some U.S. officials showed a readiness to consider seriously the elimination of large numbers of U.S. and Soviet missiles and bombers.[42] Indeed, while some Washington officials criticized many aspects of the Wiesner committee report on December 1965, they did not seem to object to its recommendations on strategic delivery vehicles: first, that the United States redouble her efforts to achieve a balanced freeze on "specified weapons levels" (if necessary omitting a freeze on their characteristics); and second, that

Washington seek "a reduction in total numbers of strategic delivery vehicles amounting to . . . one-third of [U.S. and Soviet] medium- and long-range vehicles, beginning with the destruction of obsolete stocks."[43]

Finally, the proposals introduced by Ambassador Goldberg, if implemented, held considerable promise for assistance to the developing nations. The U.S. Mission to the United Nations indicated that 100,000 kilograms of fissionable material would suffice to produce energy equivalent to several years' power output by all the countries of Africa, Asia, and Latin America combined. Alternatively, it would equal about two-thirds of the combined U.S. and Soviet annual output of electricity.[44]

Inherent in the U.S. proposals was the premise that American strategic forces had reached a level adequate for dealing with the security problems of the near- and intermediate- if not the long-range future. Washington seemed to hope the Kremlin would feel that Soviet forces were likewise reaching a level where further increases would be superfluous. The formula proposing a larger U.S. than Soviet transfer of fissionable materials (the 60:40 ratio) implied that Washington could more easily afford such measures. But if Moscow declined such an offer, the Soviet propaganda image would be the more difficult to maintain.

The Kremlin did in fact turn down the U.S. proposals in 1966, arguing that they still had little to do with real disarmament. This argument was rather sophistic, for—given the Kremlin's apparently ambitious program in offensive as well as defensive weaponry—it was not surprising that Moscow showed little interest in proposals for a cut-off in fissionable material production. Indeed, Western analysts questioned whether the Kremlin was abiding by its pledge of April 1964 to slow the pace of such production.

On the other hand, some U.S. officials believed in 1966 that the Soviet bloc was taking a more positive view toward extending the principle of international inspection to reactors engaged in production for peaceful purposes. In September 1966 Poland and Czechoslovakia offered to open their reactors to inspection by the International Atomic Energy Agency, provided West Germany did the same. This offer, some East Europeans indicated, stemmed from the original conceptions in the Rapacki Plan for disengagement and a nuclear-free Central Europe.

There was some suspicion that the Polish-Czech move was just another device to embarrass West Germany by underlining her potential as a nuclear power. Why, from Bonn's perspective, such special attention to the Federal Republic? Further, some Westerners noted, why should Germany open her many and sizable reactors to inspection in a trade-off vis-à-vis the much less significant reactor capabilities of the two East European states?[45] Finally, was this not a communist device to undermine West European unity, since Germany's reactors were already subject to Euratom inspection?

Because the United States took an increasingly firm position on the need for IAEA inspection, the East European states may have felt a material incentive as well as political and strategic ones for accepting IAEA inspection. The Polish-Czech proposal of September 1966 seemed to derive from earlier negotiations for the sale of U.S. and British reactors to East European countries, conditioned in part on the establishment of IAEA safeguards.[46] Bucharest, Prague, Budapest, and Warsaw showed a serious interest in such arrangements.

Some Western officials, however, found the Polish-Czech proposal worth exploring. It could open the door to the principle of inspection so that its practice could be later expanded. The United States had for several years been inviting international inspection tours of certain U.S. reactors and seemed willing to enlarge this operation in order to gain wider support for a nonproliferation treaty.[47] There was no necessary conflict between IAEA and Euratom inspection in Germany; in any case it seemed desirable to develop the IAEA for worldwide inspection purposes.[48] Some West German officials saw the Czech-Polish initiative as a response to Bonn's note of March 25, 1966, on peace and disarmament although this move had been negatively received at the time both by Prague and Warsaw. Finally, of some political interest was the fact that the Polish and Czech delegations seemed displeased when East Germany sought to co-sponsor the inspection proposal two days after it had been made—a suggestion that Warsaw and Prague were serious and did not want their proposal complicated by Bonn's refusal to recognize Pankow.

As with the original Rapacki Plan, there was again speculation over the extent of Soviet support for the Polish-Czech proposal. But the Kremlin seemed to support the initiative and, indeed, to favor a broadening of IAEA controls generally so as to facilitate nonproliferation efforts.[49] As of mid-1968, however, Moscow frowned on the idea of IAEA inspection of reactors for peaceful uses in Soviet territory. The Kremlin did not accept the U.S. argument that the nuclear powers should also permit inspection so as to minimize the discrimination against non-nuclear powers implicit in a treaty to halt nuclear spread.

Some change in the Soviet attitude, however, was not entirely excluded. The Soviet Union no less than the other nuclear powers was confronted with a world in which the progress of nuclear technology made it ever cheaper and easier for additional states to enter the atomic club, if only with a "primitive" device. In addition, the problem of accounting for fissionable materials produced by "peaceful purposes" reactors was sharply mounting. At the same time, the degree of intrusion required to police nuclear materials production was dropping. A study for the U.S. Arms Control and Disarmament Agency in 1966 indicated that a production cutoff would be considerably easier to verify than Washington and London had earlier presumed. This change would obviate one of the main objections, particularly for Moscow, to extending IAEA inspection: "the assumption that such a proposal would require a system of verification calling for intrusion all out of proportion to the benefits to be gained. . . ."[50]

Not long after publication of the ACDA study, the United States introduced a new proposal in the Geneva negotiations calling for an international system for monitoring nuclear activities as a check against clandestine weapons development.[51] The U.S. proposal could probably be adapted so that IAEA controls were extended (a) to all reactors in civilian nuclear power states; (b) to some reactors in the military nuclear states; or (c) to all reactors in the civilian and the military nuclear states. Thus, *if* the Soviet Union or other countries did not wish to continue or to initiate weapons-grade production, an agreement on international inspection should have been easier to reach, since less intrusion by the inspectorate would be needed to verify the accord. To formulate more precisely the ways in which destruction of nuclear weapons could be demonstrated without revealing sensitive information on weapons design and fabrication, the United States carried out field tests at four Atomic Energy Commission facilities in 1967. To maximize the sense of realism, actual weapons of mixed types and complexity were used, and teams of "inspectors" conducted the tests under specified circumstances contrived to reflect varying degrees of access and other variables, and thus to provide a broad range of data on possible procedures.

UNDERGROUND NUCLEAR TESTING

A third factor complicating U.S. and Soviet arms control efforts generally and impeding movement toward a nonproliferation treaty has been the failure of Washington and Moscow to come to terms on an agreement to end underground nuclear tests. India and other states had suggested in 1965 that the preconditions for their renunciation of a military atomic program might include the extension of the partial test ban to prohibit all nuclear testing. Since 1963, however, Moscow as well as Washington had found it useful to conduct such tests, and might find them virtually indispensable for perfecting the warheads for antiballistic missile defenses.

Whatever the ulterior motivation, both the superpowers remained at loggerheads in 1965–67 over the technical requirements for distinguishing certain man-made from natural seismic disturbances. The United States contended that further refinement of national detection systems or the provision of on-site inspection procedures was necessary to identify a certain number of seismic events, while Moscow continued to maintain that existing scientific apparatus was already sufficient for this purpose.

The sensitivity of the Soviet Union to any suggestion that national detection systems were inadequate was manifested in the absention of almost the entire Soviet bloc [52] on a General Assembly resolution in 1965 calling first, for the suspension of nuclear testing, and second, for all countries "to respect the spirit and provisions of the Moscow Test Ban Treaty." The third paragraph of the resolution provoked Soviet opposition, for it called on the ENDC to work on a comprehensive treaty "taking into account the improved possibilities for international cooperation in the field of seismic detection. . . ." [53] This clause, according to Ambassador Tsarapkin, was superfluous and might allow the West to "drown this whole question of banning underground tests in a morass of endless, completely fruitless technical discussions. . . ." [54]

For her part the United States continued to invest great resources in efforts to test and improve the reliability of national detection systems for detecting and identifying seismic disturbances. In October 1965 Washington announced the completion in Billings, Montana, of a Large Aperture Seismic Array (LASA) five to twenty times more sensitive than the best seismic station previously built in the United States. The array consisted of 525 seismometers spread over an area with a diameter of 150 miles. Since this installation made it possible to eliminate almost all recorded disturbances produced by earthquakes, the total number of unidentified events remaining was expected to include all detectable underground nuclear tests.

On October 8, 1965, before its capabilities were in complete working order, the array identified in Soviet Central Asia a low to low-intermediate yield underground nuclear explosion the equivalent of about 20,000 tons of TNT. The array was expected to reduce from 75 to 30–45 the annual number of unidentified seismic events in the Soviet Union. Some observers speculated that the United States could therefore reduce her demands for on-site inspections from seven to three or four annually, but they added that such action would hinge on confirmation of estimates by the Montana station and a Soviet willingness to enter into serious discussions of the inspection issue. [55]

William C. Foster told the United Nations First Commitee:

> If a system of ten to twenty such large arrays were to be established on a worldwide basis, then it would be possible to detect events which produce signals equivalent to nuclear detonations in the

range of only hundreds of tons. Yet after an event has been detected it is still necessary that we attempt to identify its cause. . . . If the scientists of the Soviet Union, or of any other country, could demonstrate to us any satisfactory techniques for identifying these events without on-site inspection, they would be making a great contribution to our objective.

Foster concluded, however, by reaffirming that the United States was "prepared to take current scientific capabilities fully into account in discussing the numbers and modalities of on-site inspections for verification of a comprehensive test ban." [56]

While Moscow did not accept the U.S. invitation to supply technical data that proved the sufficiency of national identification systems, many states were apparently impressed with the U.S. effort in Montana and gave overwhelming support to the resolution authorizing the ENDC to work out a comprehensive test ban "taking into account the improved possibilities for international cooperation in the field of seismic detection"—a phrase that led most of the Soviet bloc to abstain on the resolution.[57] Even the Secretary-General seemed to chide the Soviets for their attitude:

Nations must not ask only what is already possible by way of detection and identification techniques to sustain confidence in a test ban treaty, but also—and perhaps more immediately—what they can do together to develop still better means so as to facilitate a treaty acceptable to all.[58]

It was uncertain whether, in the words of President Johnson on October 12, 1965, the Montana array would in fact constitute "another giant step toward a comprehensive test ban." Some observers contended that the gap between the United States and the Soviet Union over the inspection issue was basically political rather than technical; that some technical requirement for on-site inspection could always be found, even though the threshold below which certain seismic events were unidentifiable could be progressively lowered. Hence, they concluded, no agreement would be reached until either Moscow or Washington developed the political will to make concessions in principle. On the other hand, improvements in the technical foundations for monitoring underground disturbances could facilitate a reduction by the United States of her requirements for on-site inspection and generate pressure upon Moscow to budge from its dogmatic intransigence.

Two compromise solutions were proposed in 1965–66 to skirt the differences between the U.S. and the Soviet positions. Both proposals took advantage of present or potential improvements in the mechanisms for studying seismic events. The first method was suggested by the

U.A.R. and received Soviet but not U.S. support; the other approach, put forward by Sweden, was at least considered by Washington but seemed in 1966–67 to have been refused by Moscow.

Cairo advocated a treaty barring underground tests above a seismic magnitude of 4.75, with a moratorium on those below this threshold.[59] Although the United States held that existing technology made it "possible to identify about 80 percent of the natural earthquakes which produce seismic signals that correspond to yields above a few kilotons," Washington opposed "an unverified moratorium" because Moscow had broken a previous one and because "a moratorium might diminish pressure for the stable and permanent comprehensive test ban we all seek." [60]

Sweden's proposal envisioned a comprehensive test ban based on a "challenge" system of inspection in which the ultimate sanction was the threat of withdrawal. Thus, if country X suspected country Y of conducting an underground test, and Y failed to disprove this contention— perhaps by inviting international inspection—country X could withdraw from the treaty. The initial U.S. response to this suggestion was cool; but in June 1966 both American and Soviet representatives, acting "privately," were reported to be taking a positive attitude toward such a system.[61] In the winter of 1966–67, however, Soviet officials made clear that Moscow would not accept any system that implied a need for on-site inspection.

As it became clear that neither the threshold nor the challenge approach would bridge U.S. and Soviet differences, another Swedish suggestion gained support and was endorsed by the General Assembly in late 1966: the proposal for a nuclear detection club. The Assembly called upon states to "contribute to an effective exchange of seismic data." The assumption was that the pooling of resources would make it possible for national detection systems to be coordinated to provide highly reliable information for the identification of seismic disturbances. Moscow endorsed the proposal, since it implied no need for on-site inspection. Washington also voted affirmatively, in part because no obligation was entailed and because the resolution recognized "the importance of seismology in the verification of the observance of a treaty banning underground nuclear weapons tests. . . ." [62]

Shortly after the General Assembly resolution, however, a report on an experiment carried out in an underground salt dome in Mississippi struck hard at hopes that the United States would ever rely exclusively on national systems of identification. The experiment showed that an underground nuclear blast could be muffled by a very large factor if set off in a cavity that cut off (de-coupled) its shock waves from the surrounding earth by the presence of a dampening air barrier.[63]

Hence, although a ban on underground testing would serve as a kind of nonproliferation treaty for those states that signed, in 1967 it began to appear that the goals of curbing nuclear spread and promoting détente could be more easily achieved through other, more direct routes. All three approaches to circumvent U.S.–Soviet differences—the threshold, the challenge, and nuclear club methods—would at best produce a treaty with a considerable capacity for stirring up domestic and international political complications and suspicions within and between the two superpowers and other states.[64] Further, if the superpowers embarked on ABM deployment, they would want to be free to continue underground testing of warheads. These problems, plus the cost in time and good will involved in such negotiations, struck many observers as not worth the possible gain for arms control in making a test ban treaty more comprehensive. Ostensibly preoccupied with the nonproliferation problem, the ENDC did not discuss a ban on underground tests in 1967, and efforts to organize a nuclear detection club did not deviate from dead center, due in large part to Soviet reluctance to admit the insufficiency of national detection systems. Despite or because of these trends, the General Assembly passed a resolution on December 19, 1967, which reaffirmed the urgent need for the suspension of nuclear and thermonuclear tests; expressed the hope that all states would contribute to international exchange of seismic data; and requested that the ENDC take up the subject of a comprehensive test ban on an urgent basis. Only Albania voted against the resolution, while Algeria, Cuba, France, Gabon, Guinea, Mali, and Mauritania abstained.

OUTER SPACE

It may be significant that the domain in which Moscow and Washington made the most specific progress in arms control in 1965–67 was one far removed from the Chinese question—a treaty on the peaceful uses of outer space. More precisely, it was a "Treaty on Principles Governing the Activities of States in the Exploration and Use of Outer Space, Including the Moon and Other Celestial Bodies." Even in this area, however, there were important implications for U.S.–Soviet–Chinese relations and for arms control generally.

First, the treaty underlined the measure of military bipolarity extant even after the expansion of the nuclear club to include China. There were only two superpowers, and their decisions about whether to militarize outer space were taken mainly on the basis of bilateral expectations, with little reference to third powers. To be sure, both Moscow and

Washington had an interest in economizing resources so as to develop their terrestrial and sea-based forces; but this principle would hold even if China had no atomic potential. Second, for China herself, the treaty had relevance as another sign of U.S.–Soviet collusion. Anticipating Chinese charges of a sellout of revolution, Moscow argued that the very intensity of the Vietnamese war made it useful to control tensions through the outer space treaty. And finally, the treaty had two possible effects on negotiations to halt nuclear spread: (1) it improved the climate for U.S.–Soviet efforts toward nonproliferation; and (2) it could serve as at least a partial sign that the superpowers were willing to contain their own arsenals at a time when they called on potential "haves" to forgo nuclear weapons.

Some observers argued that the outer space treaty was virtually meaningless, because neither the White House nor the Kremlin wanted to put bombs (as distinguished from military support systems)[65] into orbit. But this criticism underestimated certain signs in 1965 that one or both superpowers might lead its opposite number into a military space race. More generally, this argument ignored the usefulness of "preventive" arms control for the formalizing of an entente that neither party would embark on military procurements primarily out of fear lest the foe carve out a hegemonistic position while one's own program remains peacefully idle.

In October 1963 both Moscow and Washington reached what one Soviet diplomat called a "gentleman's agreement" not to orbit weapons of mass destruction in space. This accord was noted and approved in a General Assembly resolution calling upon all nations to desist from stationing such weapons in space.[66] But the U.N. resolution had only moral force.[67] And the danger persisted that the Soviet Union and the United States might willy-nilly extend the arms race into outer space as each side drove to exploit to the utmost the military potential of technology, stimulating an interaction chain that functioned as a self-fulfilling prophecy, provoking each side to match or exceed what it expected the adversary to do.

The Kremlin, like the White House, seemed to conclude that land- or sea-based weapons were more efficient and less costly than any that could be orbited in space.[68] But offensive weapons were only part of the story, for the 1963 understanding left the way clear for other military uses of space—whether by manned or unmanned space ships. And strict considerations of cost-effectiveness might not guide either superpower indefinitely, for the possible gains from military exploitation of space could not be foreseen. The hope of such gains might have special appeal for the Kremlin, long interested in psychologically compelling quick-fixes to redress the terrestrial military balance. Indeed, the Kremlin displayed on May 9 and November 7, 1965 a liquid-fueled, three-stage rocket which *Tass* described as an "orbital missile" capable of delivering "a surprise blow on the first or any other orbit around the earth."[69]

United States as well as Soviet actions raised fears that the 1963 understanding on bombs in orbit would not endure the strains of the arms race. Soviet (and many Western) observers took as an ominous portent of U.S. ambitions in space President Johnson's announcement on August 25, 1965 that the Air Force was being authorized to proceed with development of a Manned Orbiting Laboratory (MOL) to determine the strategic utility of man in space. Isolated Soviet statements could not have been taken as a firm indication of Moscow's position, but one of the first Soviet responses to release of U.S. plans for a MOL implied a wish to guide Soviet policy-makers as well as to rebuke Western.

The Deputy Commander-in-Chief of Soviet strategic rocket troops contended that the Pentagon intended to develop a platform from which to bombard the earth with nuclear bombs—which, he added, "does not tally with Johnson's hypocritical announcement about extending the reign of law to outer space." Furthermore, in a viewpoint that Moscow later overruled, the same author suggested that the very development of the MOL "leads to a definite breach of the agreement on non-orbiting of weapons of mass destruction," because "the concept of nuclear weapons covers both carriers and the warheads proper."[70]

That this line might not prevail was suggested to some observers at the United Nations when Soviet representatives to a meeting of the Legal Subcommittee of the U.N. Committee on the Peaceful Uses of Outer Space failed in September 1965 to denounce the MOL. Later that month as a matter of fact, Moscow disclosed that it too would put up a similar vehicle. Cosmonaut Aleksei Leonov told the 16th International Aeronautical Congress meeting in Athens that a permanent manned space platform was the next major project in the Soviet space program.[71] Unlike Washington, Moscow did not specify that its platform would be for experimental military purposes. It was subsequently reported, however, that one of the reasons President Johnson ordered the Air Force to proceed with the MOL was that intelligence indications suggested the Soviet Union was already well advanced in developing such a spaceship.[72]

That Moscow was indeed moving in this direction was suggested by an article in *Red Star* early in 1966, entitled "Now—To An Orbiting Station." While the article did not specify that such a station would have military applications, this semed to be implicit—not only because of the author's position,[73] and the vehicle of publication, but also because of the article's contents. It discussed in a matter-of-fact way, for example, the problems involved in extra-vehicular activities, one of which involved armed satellites:

. . . imagine that two enemy ships are flying parallel courses and are shooting at each other. In this case the shells will not fall on the target. They will come back and it is not impossible that they could hit the ship from which they are shot. There is a paradox for you.

The author did not explicitly recommend the arming of satellites, but he concluded on the note that "cosmonautics of our days had already solved a series of problems connected with maneuvers in space." Hence, the agenda for cosmonauts in the twentieth century would include a series of steps in succession:

The meeting of ships in space, assembling in orbit large inhabited stations, and the building of cosmic "railway stations" from which will go into deep space "interplanetary long distance trains". . . .[74]

A subsequent article in *Red Star* again assailed what it viewed as a contradiction between the President's assurances that the United States intended to adhere to the 1963 understanding on weapons in space and his transfer of authority over the MOL to the Pentagon. Citing many Western periodicals,[75] *Red Star* concluded that the Western press viewed this shift of responsibility from NASA to the Defense Department as "the birth of the era of military cosmonautics." The Soviet article declared that "the strategists from the Pentagon must realize that they are making a step toward madness." *Red Star* concluded:

We notice that the further the development goes on American cosmic apparatuses, the more the dividing line between their "peaceful" and "military" designation is erased.[76]

Thus, during 1964–66 both Moscow and Washington did much to encourage mutual suspicions that arms control in space was a utopian chimera. Repeated Soviet claims of an "orbital missile," even if it were only in limited production—combined with signs that both sides would soon test the military uses of manned orbiting laboratories—suggested that the 1963 "intention" not to station weapons of mass destruction in space might soon be revised.

Parallel with these portents, however, other developments occurred in the East-West dialogue, indicating that the declarations of intent might not only be observed for some time but might even be converted into a bilateral or multilateral treaty. Despite the parading of so-called orbital missiles across Red Square and the announced plans of both superpowers to orbit manned stations, the future of outer space remained open-ended. Options were not yet closed. Although both Moscow and Washington sought to exploit outer space for certain propaganda and strategic values, neither seemed anxious to convert this domain into the locus of a full-fledged arms race. If only implicitly, each superpower seemed to recognize the wisdom of maintaining or extending the principle of preventive arms control in outer space.

Following the Soviets' November display of an orbital missile, the State Department demanded whether the Soviet Government intended to abide by its 1963 declaration of intent. Considering the seriousness of the American inquiry and the complexity of the problem, Moscow reacted with impressive dispatch. Soviet Ambassador Dobrynin visited the State Department on December 8, 1965 to reaffirm his government's 1963 position.

Dobrynin's clarification, it was reported, followed the lines of an article published the next day in *Pravda* under the authoritative signature of "Observer." This article, entitled "False Doubts," noted that the 1963 General Assembly resolution did "not apply to the production of orbital rockets, or, for that matter, to any other rockets launched into space." The Soviet Government, *Pravda* stated, was fulfilling the terms of the resolution and would do so "in the future, having in view that other governments will act in the same way." "Observer" asserted that the United States knew of Moscow's peaceful intentions, but sought by protesting the Soviet orbital rocket to divert attention from the U.S. space program—the military goals of which were said to be manifest in the recent Presidential announcement of U.S. plans for a manned orbiting laboratory (MOL). This clarification was apparently acceptable to the State Department, which had consistently held that the 1963 understanding related only to deployment of certain weapons and not to their production; further, U.S. analysts seemed to discount the military significance of the "orbital" missiles paraded in Red Square.

As for U.S. intentions, President Johnson, in announcing the MOL program declared:

> We intend to live up to our agreement not to orbit weapons of mass destruction and we will continue to hold out to all nations, including the Soviet Union, the hand of cooperation in the exciting years of space exploration which lie ahead for all of us.

To demonstrate further the U.S. desire for cooperation in space, the President announced that top-ranking Soviet scientists were being invited to the next Gemini launching in October, 1965.[77] Probably in response to widespread concern over the implications of the MOL, Ambassador Goldberg reassured the General Assembly that U.S. "space activities have been, and will continue to be, non-aggressive, and peaceful and beneficial in character."[78]

These storms weathered, negotiations toward a space treaty received a strong impetus in May 1966 when President Johnson announced that the United States would seek a treaty prohibiting the stationing of weapons of mass destruction on a celestial body.[79] The Kremlin responded with a broader counterproposal: one that would ban the orbiting as well as the stationing on celestial bodies of weapons of mass destruction.[80] The United States soon accepted this broader position (which already existed in the 1963 understanding); and both sides made concessions in the summer and fall during meetings of the U.N. Legal Subcommittee of the U.N. Committee on the Peaceful Uses of Outer Space.[81] Bilateral accord was finally reached in private negotiations and a treaty was placed before the First Committee and the General Assembly for approval with little opportunity for debate by the other powers.[82] It was endorsed by acclamation on December 19, 1966; signed at Washington, London, and Moscow on January 27, 1967; and ratified later in the year by the necessary states, entering into force on October 10.[83]

The treaty forbids the orbiting or deployment in any manner in outer space or on celestial bodies of nuclear and other weapons of mass destruction. It prohibits also "the establishment of military bases, installations and fortifications, the testing of any type of weapons and the conduct of military maneuvers on celestial bodies. . . ." These restrictions, together with other principles in the treaty, such as the provision that celestial bodies shall not be subject to national appropriation, represent a large step toward establishing a legal regime for outer space.

But the permissive nature of the treaty must also be recognized. Article IV does not attempt to restrict the existing and planned deployment on land and in the sea of missiles which, if fired, would pass through outer space en route to their target. The testing in peacetime of such weapons, as well as their use in war, is permitted under the treaty. The accord does not proscribe the deployment in outer space of weapons not capable of mass destruction, e.g., anti-satellite weapons, anti-missile weapons (unless they involve nuclear warheads), certain weather modifiers, etc. Nor does it prohibit military support activities in outer space, provided they do not take place upon celestial bodies. Thus, a wide range of existing and planned military activity may continue, e.g., reconnaissance satellites, command and control stations, manned orbiting laboratories, weather and geodetic satellites.

Many questions of interpretation remain to be clarified: What, for example, is a weapon of mass destruction? Both superpowers seem to regard biological, chemical, and radiation weapons as instruments of mass destruction. Both seem clear that the treaty does not forbid the building of orbital weapons; it even permits the orbiting of rocket launchers—provided no warhead is on board. But may it not become difficult at some point to determine with assurance whether certain weapons systems have in fact become instruments for mass destruction, e.g., weather modifiers, lasers, anti-satellite weapons, etc. which may be placed in space either in manned or unmanned vehicles? Because of questions such as these and, equally important, because of ambiguities in other parts of the treaty,[84] one Soviet official declared: "We decided first to sign the treaty and interpret it later." This approach has been shared also by the U.S. Government, which showed great interest in expediting the signing and ratification of the treaty.

The Soviet Union, by testing reentry vehicles for fractional orbit bombardment systems (FOBS) in 1966–67, demonstrated the wide limits of the treaty, even before it went into force. While it was clear that the testing or launching of an unarmed FOBS would not violate the treaty, Secretary of Defense McNamara went still farther in providing a liberal interpretation of the pact. At a moment when a debate was proceeding within the U.S. government over whether a missile placed in partial orbit would violate the treaty, McNamara volunteered at a press conference that a state could launch an armed FOBS and bring it down (presumably without exploding and presumably on friendly territory) without breaking the pact. His apparent premise was that a fractional orbit is not an orbit or even a "deployment" in outer space. In part because the Defense Secretary did not consider the FOBS an effective addition to the U.S. arsenal, he may have wanted to deflate possible Soviet claims (on the eve of the fiftieth anniversary of the Bolshevik Revolution) so as to minimize their impact internationally and in the United States.

A series of military, technological, political, and economic factors have led both superpowers to an interest in a treaty governing exploration of outer space. Strategically, both seem reasonably content with existing threat systems for purposes of international bargaining, although the prospect cannot be ruled out that the Soviets—who have experimented not only with the FOBS but with multiple orbit space ships from which rockets could be launched to earth—might decide to break the treaty. On balance, however, it seems Moscow would be unlikely to "deploy" either a fractional or a multiple orbit system for bombarding the earth until the eve of a major war. The Soviet tests may amount merely to research and development as part of a larger strategy of contingency planning. Soviet officials interviewed have taken a line similar to that of the United States: there would be little gain and some loss for security through extension of the arms race into another dimension—outer space.

A number of technological considerations strongly favored the treaty.

First, it would not be easy or cost-effective to put major weapons into space due to limitations of existing fuels, striking power, and control; and because of the actual or potential capabilities of sea- and land-based weaponry. Second, technology has helped to lessen the need for the on-site inspection of missile launchers, demanded until the fall of 1962 by the United States as a precondition for a ban on bombs in orbit. Third, Russia's lack of overseas tracking stations deepened her interest in a treaty that would facilitate acquisition of such posts.[85]

The role of economic factors is implicit in most of the foregoing argumentation. Neither superpower wanted to stretch its resources— already taut as a result of activities connected with defense, with the civilian space program, and with its own internal economic problems— for arms that did not significantly bolster security.

While military, technological, and economic factors conditioned and facilitated both the U.S. and Soviet interest in the treaty, the prime motivation for each superpower probably lay in the area of foreign policy. Both Washington and Moscow saw the treaty as a way to improve relations and to reduce tensions in the face of the Vietnamese war. The experience of 1963 indicated how even limited arms control measures could have a salubrious effect on the whole range of East-West problems. The test ban treaty also showed how damaging such measures could be to Sino-Soviet relations.

It may be significant that Moscow edged toward a renewed interest in arms control at a time when the Soviet Communist Party was again attempting to organize an international communist meeting. The political inhibitions to arms control and to such mobilization reached a low point as a result of widespread disdain for the excesses of Chairman Mao and the Chinese "cultural revolution."

Many U.N. observers believed that the content and style of the U.S.– Soviet accord on outer space reflected the concern of the superpowers regarding China as a political and military problem. One diplomat from a nonaligned country went so far as to call the space treaty an "anti-Chinese" move by Moscow and Washington. While this view is probably an exaggeration, it seems likely that both countries were anxious to get U.N. approval for a treaty that dealt basically with their bilateral affairs. This approval would minimize for Moscow the expected Chinese denunciations of Soviet collusion with the United States. An arms control move approved by United Nations would also emphasize the isolation of Communist China in her opposition to steps to freeze the military status quo.

The fact that the treaty was multilateral rather than bilateral meant also that it could be more plausibly defended as being universal international law, and hence binding on any future space powers. Even China's

Albanian ally had difficulty opposing the steamroller diplomacy employed by Moscow and Washington. Tirana's representative was not present in the First Committee when the treaty was reported, and the vote in the General Assembly was by acclamation, which meant that Albania would have to do more than press a button to register dissent or abstention.[86]

The timeliness of the U.S.–Soviet space accord was underlined by the fact that China would soon become a space-faring power, one that might soon have the capacity to unnerve the superpowers in their attempt to regulate the space race, just as their efforts in other areas of arms control had been complicated by the emergence of an incipient Chinese nuclear capacity. During the late 1950s both the Soviet Union and Communist China had frequently predicted that China would soon become a space nation, but these predictions ceased with the ending of Soviet technological assistance in 1960. By early 1967, however, Western and Chinese sources alike were again asserting that China had the capability to orbit a satellite lifted by the missiles designed for Peking's nuclear warheads. On January 21 the organ of the Red Guard of the Peking Aeronautical Institute reported that China in 1967 would carry out "the launching of a space vessel and a new experiment involving a missile with a nuclear warhead."[87] While such tests were not in fact carried out in 1967, China's technological ability to make experiments of this kind in the future remained widely accepted abroad.

*   *   *   *

In summary, China's impact on the superpower arms race had mixed effects and competing prospects. It made both the Soviet Union and the United States increasingly aware of certain parallel interests, but it also complicated their relationship. A game theorist might comment that both states had just become aware that they were engaged in a two-player, non-zero sum game—only to find that a third major actor had joined the competition, undermining the common interests and relative simplicity of the earlier confrontation. If the Kremlin—its anxieties heightened by proximity to China—proceeded with ABM deployment, the general stabilty of the Soviet–U.S. arms competition would probably be shattered, thus destroying all hope for an accord on underground testing, on the control of fissionable materials, and on a halt to nuclear spread. On the other hand, if this challenge were mastered, it might open the door to progress in domains that would otherwise be shut off by the need to perfect and accumulate the means for a new round of defensive-offensive competition.

The General Assembly vote on the nonproliferation treaty in June 1968 marked a kind of transition from one stage to another in the postwar efforts to control the arms race. On the one hand, assuming the treaty were ratified by West Germany and other key threshold powers, the Kremlin and the White House could take it as a given that the nuclear club would be fixed at five members, at least for the time being. If one complex task of multilateral bargaining were resolved (more or less), time and energy could be devoted to another. On the other hand, if the superpowers did not succeed in limiting their own arms buildup, the chances would increase that some key threshold power might decide to go nuclear. The preamble to the treaty recorded the nuclear powers' "intention to achieve at the earliest possible date the cessation of the nuclear arms race and to undertake effective measures in the direction of nuclear disarmament." Whatever the legal significance of this commitment, failure to fulfill it could help justify denunciation of the treaty by a non-nuclear-weapon state.

A major shift in Soviet negotiating posture on arms control was suggested on May 22, 1968, when First Deputy Foreign Minister Vasily V. Kuznetsov addressed the Political and Security Affairs Committee of the U.N. General Assembly. Although the main thrust of his speech dealt with the draft nonproliferation treaty, Kuznetsov also singled out "strategic means of delivery" and assigned new importance to this item. He declared: "We deem it necessary to make a special point of the fact that the Soviet Union is prepared to agree on concrete steps aimed at limiting and, subsequently, reducing strategic means of delivery of nuclear weapons." Kuznetsov indicated that, once the nonproliferation treaty was concluded, Moscow assigned a priority to an accord on delivery vehicles second only to a ban on underground nuclear tests. This ranking differed considerably from that offered in an April 26 speech by the Soviet official, who mentioned delivery vehicles far down on the list of disarmament goals. Another reordering of possible significance concerned a convention to ban the use of nuclear weapons, which Kuznetsov had put forward as the "foremost" requirement after the nonproliferation treaty in his May 22 speech.

Soviet media, as indicated in the previous chapter, declared that conclusion of the nonproliferation treaty would open the door to progress across the board on various measures of disarmament. In private talks Soviet diplomats had indicated in 1966–67 that serious negotiations on limiting ABM defenses could not begin until the nonproliferation treaty was achieved. Consonant with these various assurances, Soviet Foreign Minister Gromyko announced on June 27 that his government was prepared to open talks on limiting and reducing both offensive and defensive strategic weapons.

On July 1, 1968, at the same time that he signed the nonproliferation treaty, President Johnson announced that the United States and USSR had agreed to open talks "in the nearest future" on what U.S. officials indicated both sides accepted as a two-stage approach: first, a limitation, and second, a reduction in the missile launchers possessed by each superpower. Such talks had been actively sought by the United States since January 1967, although the idea of a freeze on offensive and defensive systems had been proposed by President Johnson as early as January 1964. The principle of the limitation, however, seemed similar to the Soviet proposal (made in 1962 and 1963) for a "nuclear umbrella" —a notion that in turn could be traced back to suggestions made by U.S. scientists at Pugwash Conferences on Science and World Affairs, especially to that held in Moscow in 1960.

For its part, Moscow used the occasion of the signing of the non-proliferation treaty on July 1 to propose to the world a nine-point program of "urgent measures on an end to the arms race and on disarmament in the near future." No priorities were affixed, but a limitation and reduction of SDVs came third in the list, while a ban on the use of nuclear weapons (omitted by Kuznetsov on May 22) returned to the top of the list. The second item was an end to the manufacture of nuclear weapons, the reduction of stockpiles, and the subsequent total ban on and liquidation of nuclear weapons under appropriate international control. If some progress were made toward limiting SDVs, perhaps a cutoff of fissionable material production—such as that proposed by Ambassador Goldberg in 1965— would also be negotiable, although an end to the manufacture of weapons would be less feasible, if only because each side would seek to replace if not improve existing missiles.

The fourth item was a ban on flights of bombers carrying nuclear weapons beyond national frontiers and an end to the patrolling by missile-carrying submarines within striking range of the borders of the contracting sides. Fifth, Moscow proposed an immediate understanding on the banning of underground nuclear tests "on the basis of using national means of detection to control this ban"; sixth, a ban on the use of chemical and bacteriological weapons; seventh, the liquidation of foreign military bases; eighth, regional disarmament—including nuclear-free zones and controls on arms races, as in the Middle East (dependent, however, on evacuation of Israeli forces from Arab territory); ninth, steps to ensure use of the sea bed beyond the limits of territorial waters exclusively for peaceful purposes.

Clearly, some of the measures proposed by Moscow on July 1 were more negotiable and some more significant than others. The outcome of this new round of negotiations could not be foreseen with any assurance, but a number of important factors bearing on Soviet policy had shifted in 1967–68 to incline the Kremlin leadership toward a more positive attitude toward arms controls of various kinds, including curbs on strategic weaponry. Some of these factors have been mentioned above as they functioned in 1966 to strengthen Moscow's interest in a treaty to ban weapons of mass destruction in outer space. By 1968, however, many of these conditions became more salient, their trends more discernible, and their import for stabilizing the arms race more general.

The most important trend bearing on Soviet interests in arms control was probably the shifting nature of the balance of strategic power. In 1968–69 the USSR was expected to equal or even exceed the number of land-based ICBMs possessed by the United States. It could be debated which superpower held the advantage in other aspects of military competition, though the overall balance still seemed to favor the United States. What was clear, however, was that if Washington chose to do so, U.S. industrial and technological power could probably outstrip Soviet military accomplishments or—at a minimum—make the cost of maintaining strategic parity more painful for the Soviet economy than it was for the American. Many observers believed, in fact, that Soviet resources were becoming quite strained as the Kremlin leadership tried to upgrade Soviet living standards while maintaining superpower standards in outer space and in strategic and conventional weaponry.

Moscow's concern about the implications of an unbridled strategic arms race were probably prompted in part by Washington's decision in 1967–68 to proceed with deployment of the Sentinel ABM system. Statements by Defense Department officials and some U.S. Senators in spring and early summer 1968 indicated that the Sentinel system would have value against a Soviet as well as a C.P.R. attack and that it might well be expanded into a massive ABM deployment. The Kremlin may have reckoned, nevertheless, that it could still forestall or at least limit the U.S. defense system deployment by timely negotiations.

Technological as well as economic considerations may have affected Soviet thinking about antimissile defenses. Signs multiplied in late 1967–68 that the Soviet Government had strong doubts about the efficacy of ABM defenses and that it planned to give much more attention to civil defense activity. The Atomic Publishing House, for example, planned to publish at least six brochures in one hundred thousand copies each on civil defense.* Indeed, the head of Soviet defenses (PVO)** Marshal

---

* One was entitled: *From MPVO* [apparently Ministry of Antiair Defense]—*to Civil Defense.* Other titles: *Civil Defense in a Rocket-Nuclear War; The CPSU on the Necessity of Perfecting Civil Defense; To School Children—On Civil Defense; Civil Defense Is a Task for All the People; Conversations with the Population on Civil Defense.* See *Novye knigi,* No. 42 (1967), items 35–40.

** A Soviet dictionary explained in 1965–66 that PVO is defense against aerial attack whether from airplanes, rockets (PRO) or from outer space (PKO). PVO forces included those which defend the country in general, the armed forces, and the navy. See *Tolkovyi slovar' voennykh terminov* (Moscow: Voenizdat, 1966), pp. 347–48.

Chuikov, wrote in *Pravda* on February 21, 1968, that "it is now difficult to give a full guarantee" that part of an enemy ballistic missile strike against the Soviet Union would not reach its target. In contrast to statements he had made as late as autumn 1967, Chuikov did not so much as mention ABM defenses in his February 1968 article, but gave much attention instead to the need for civil defense measures. Similarly, an article in *Sovetskaia Rossiia* on June 5, 1968 by Lt. Gen. G. Malinin noted that modern weapons had revolutionized military affairs since the Great Patriotic War, with the result that "it now became possible for any large populated area or industrial unit to be demolished, regardless of its distance from the country's frontiers." Malinin then outlined plans for disseminating civil defense knowledge through the press, radio, television, cinema, the Znanie (Knowledge) Society, other clubs, DOSAAF, the union of Red Cross and Red Crescent societies. Relevant "games" would be held, he said, in every Pioneer camp in 1968.

Looking at U.S. domestic politics, Moscow may also have considered in summer 1968 that the next occupant of the White House might be less interested in arms control than President Johnson, particularly if Mr. Nixon won the 1968 election. Further, if the Johnson Administration could show some progress toward peace and arms control, the Democratic Party candidate would presumably run stronger in the election, an outcome that Moscow would see at least as the lesser of two evils.

From the standpoint of international politics, the limitations placed on U.S. bombing of North Vietnam in 1968 and the fact of the Paris peace talks helped Moscow to justify in revolutionary circles the opening of bilateral arms control negotiations with the United States. The Kremlin in any case seemed prepared to disregard as worthless any ideological utterance that might issue from Peking—at least so long as Maoist forces remained dominant there. Moscow also seemed increasingly peeved by Cuba's independent course, documented in sources so diverse as Che Guevara's diary, published in Havana one day before the signing of the nonproliferation pact, and Cuba's vote at the United Nations against the treaty.

Finally, political trends within the Soviet power structure also seemed conducive to a positive approach to arms control. A number of younger, apparently more hawkish leaders had been removed from key power centers in the aftermath of the 1967 Arab-Israeli war. Although Moscow acted promptly to rebuild the U.A.R. armed forces, the Kremlin seemed to aim at inducing Cairo to accept a *modus vivendi* with Israel. In another test of wills within the Soviet hierarchy, the challenge of Czechoslovakia's independent course after January 1968 did not produce armed Soviet intervention (as some hard-liners in Moscow reportedly sought) but a combination of non-violent pressures aimed at keeping Prague within certain limits.

The outcome of the arms control negotiations commencing in mid-1968 would not depend exclusively on Moscow, of course, nor would the wishes of the White House necessarily prevail. The success of the non-proliferation treaty, developments in Southeast Asia, the internal and external thrust of Peking's policy—these were but a few of the political variables over which the superpowers could exercise only partial control. Further, technological successes or failures would affect the respective interests of the U.S. and Soviet governments in limiting their competition in arms. With these diverse factors in view we turn, in Part Four, to the underlying forces—ideological, national, and other—that have shaped and will continue to condition the approaches of Soviet Chinese decision makers to vital issues of strategy and arms control.

Part Four

THE OUTLOOK

XIII
World Views in Conflict

The imponderables in China's future course combine with other technical and political factors to make the prospects for arms control in the mid-1960s most uncertain. The very forces making it desirable to halt the vertical and horizontal extension of the arms race also complicate the effort to do so. And while the tide has seemed to shift toward arms control, the current could be reversed. Lasting progress is not assured. The incentives to the great powers to explore and exploit the military usefulness of antiballistic missile systems, of outer space, and of further refinements in weaponry through underground testing may in the long run seem to outweigh the economic and political costs inherent in such moves. And before the major participants agree to a nonproliferation accord, the conditions of each will need satisfaction. Among the communist powers, the Soviet Union will need assurances that the pact excludes independent German access to nuclear weapons. And the Kremlin, like Peking, will need to be persuaded that the stabilizing military consequences of the treaty outweigh the risks it poses for the communist revolutionary image.

But the most profound obstacle to arms control is probably psychological rather than technical, and lies in the widespread failure of political will to place security upon a basis other than strategic autarky. The governments of the West and the nonaligned nations have been guilty of myopia, inertia, and chauvinism. But the reluctance of the non-communist nations to rely more upon collective security and world law may in the main be a reaction to the drive of communist powers to transform the world scene to their own likeness by whatever means may prove expedient. Already, however, one of the major communist states is slackening in ideological fervor, at least in its dogmatic zeal to revolutionize the world by any means. The more that national interest rather than ideology guides the policies of both communist protagonists, the greater the prospect of a recognition that politics need not be a zero-sum game, and that adversaries may benefit from agreed limits on their competition.

To obtain a deeper insight into the dynamics of communist policy we turn now to an analysis of the theoretical positions taken by Moscow and Peking on matters of war, peace, and disarmament; to the hard-core interests shaping these world views; and to the problems and prospects for the future emerging from this interaction of ideology and traditional power factors.

The two power centers of world communism have come openly to verbal blows over peace, disarmament, and other questions of ideology. Each side has quoted scripture—mainly Lenin's works—to justify its position. Both Moscow and Peking agree that "Leninism" should guide communist policy today, but they disagree radically over interpretation. The Chinese understanding of Leninism derives primarily from Lenin's works written before the Bolshevik *coup d'état*, while Soviet ideologists rely more on the ideas developed by Lenin during the formative stages of the New Economic Policy. Further, while Mao would apply Lenin's ideas mechanically and literally to the present era, Moscow purports to relate them "creatively," mindful of the changes wrought in the "balance of forces" and in military technology.[1]

Moscow has been accused of revisionism or reformism and Peking of dogmatism. The doctrinal controversies preceding and following the open schism in 1963 provide an essential if only partial source of information concerning the general nature of the Soviet and Chinese strategies. Because the disputants have distorted and exaggerated the theses of one another, the areas of agreement and discord are somewhat blurred. Nevertheless it is clear that, despite ostensible agreement on certain basic principles, Moscow and Peking have drawn highly divergent conclusions on the correct views to be taken toward matters of war and peace and, in consequence, toward questions of arms control policy and limited collaboration with the capitalist camp. While Soviet and Chinese doctrine did undergo some change after Khrushchev's ouster and during the "great proletarian revolution" in China, the ideas expressed by the two sides in the mid-60s on matters of war, peace, and arms control indicated a basic continuity with those of the early 1960s.[2]

Of all the areas of ideological discord between Moscow and Peking, probably none—even Khrushchev's attack on the personality cult—has stirred more discord or reflected such divergent interests as the war-peace issue. The most bitter pill for "dogmatists" to swallow has been the "revisionist" downgrading of the necessity and desirability of violence, and the concomitant emphasis on peaceful competition as the best means of furthering the interests of world communism. Four aspects of the problem are considered in detail: the inevitability of war, the morality and consequences of violence, the road to revolution, and disarmament as a tactic and as a strategy.

THE INEVITABILITY OF WAR

Lenin argued the inevitability of war between capitalist states on grounds of economic determinism, but his later assertions about the inevitability of conflict between the capitalist and socialist camps were more in the nature of political exhortations during the years of foreign intervention. Stalin's doctrine of "socialism in one country" in 1924 implied that violence would be needed to break the "capitalist encirclement." The need to prepare for war was stressed by the Sixth Comintern Congress in 1928 as the Soviet Union embarked on its first Five-Year Plan. In 1935, however, when the Third International pursued a "popular front" against fascism, Dimitrov, General Secretary of the Comintern, downgraded the necessity of either type of war—inter-capitalist or capitalist-socialist. The post Second World War era saw some ambiguities in Soviet doctrine, but Stalin's *Economic Questions of Socialism* in 1952 was silent on the likelihood of capitalist-socialist conflict, while specifically stressing the inevitability of inter-capitalist war.[3]

Political Economy: A Textbook, published in 1954, the authoritative guide to Soviet doctrine before 1956, agreed with Stalin that war between capitalist states was inevitable, but it affirmed that war between the socialist and capitalist camps could be averted if the "people" exerted sufficient pressure. This point, an echo of Dimitrov in 1935, was incorporated into Chairman Khrushchev's line at the Twentieth Party Congress in 1956, since which time Moscow has stressed the avoidability of all kinds of war—inter-capitalist, capitalist-socialist, and domestic civil war—but not wars of national liberation, which are said to be unavoidable.[4]

Moscow since 1956 has held that wars between the capitalist and communist states are "not fatalistically inevitable," and Peking has conceded that they "can be prevented." Both communist capitals agree that this is so because the balance of power has shifted in favor of the socialist camp and because nuclear weapons have become unprecedentedly destructive. The capitalist powers are still by nature aggressive, but they know that if they unleashed a war they would be destroyed in it. While the capitalists' self-interest therefore dictates restraint, the "struggle" of all peoples united for peace is also required in order to "force" the imperialists to refrain from war. Despite allegations from followers of Moscow, the Chinese Government, like the Soviet, is pledged never to attack the capitalist states.[5]

Moscow concludes that while the danger of capitalist aggression persists, socialist-capitalist wars can be avoided entirely, even though socialism has not yet triumphed on a global scale. Peking agrees with this proposition, but almost contradicts it with qualifying references to Lenin's speeches during the First World War to the effect that peace can be assured only by the global victory of socialism and an end to the class struggle. As a resolution of a People's Liberation Army Political Conference put it in 1966: ". . . the root cause of war will remain until imperialism is overthrown and capitalism is eliminated."[6] This stress by Peking on the probability of capitalist-socialist war is, however, contradicted by Chinese assurances that local wars will not escalate.

Moscow and Peking agree that inter-capitalist wars are still possible. The degree of probability, however, is disputed. As noted above, Lenin's theory of imperialism provided a logical basis for arguing the inevitability of war *between* or *among* capitalist states. It was the inevitability of inter-capitalist war that Stalin reaffirmed in 1952. It is this aspect of communist ideology that post-Stalin ideological revisions challenge most directly, because Lenin and Stalin enunciated no clear-cut doctrine on the probability of capitalist-socialist war. Soviet ideologues have tended to lump together all wars involving capitalism and to say they are avoidable (except for wars of national liberation). Perhaps because Moscow was prodded by the Chinese statements in 1960 stressing the likelihood of inter-capitalist war, Khrushchev's address of January 6, 1961, affirmed the *unlikelihood* of such war, on the ground that "the imperialists are compelled to heed the Soviet Union and the entire socialist camp."

Moscow and Peking agree that wars of national liberation are "unavoidable" because the colonial powers will not surrender their rule peacefully. Khrushchev enunciated this doctrinal position again with particular force on January 6, 1961, due in part no doubt to Chinese propaganda attacks in 1960.[7] Moscow claims that it has fulfilled its obligations to assist wars of national liberation "in every way," and points to the extent of Soviet assistance to Cuba, Vietnam, Egypt, and other states that have received weapons from Moscow. But Moscow warns repeatedly that such wars could escalate, and therefore concerns itself more than Peking with limiting the scope and intensity of such conflict. Moscow's hesitations are ridiculed by the Chinese, who point out that none of the many wars of national liberation since 1945 has yet brought on a major war involving the great powers.[8] Such wars are rather included by Peking among the major means of achieving "peace." The upshot is that Peking would encourage such wars, while Moscow has preferred to give them only limited support, as in Algeria.[9]

A typical case of "cognitive dissonance" developed for Moscow at the First Afro-Asian-Latin American Solidarity Conference meeting in Havana in early 1966. In Peking's phrase, Moscow's strategy was "sham anti-imperialism but real capitulation." The Soviet delegation felt compelled to sign revolutionary proclamations that later in the year led Latin American governments at the United Nations to amend a Soviet-sponsored resolution against interference in internal affairs so that it condemned indirect as well as direct actions. But the Soviet delegation in Havana refused to approve a proposal of the Cambodian delegation urging all states to refuse to engage in any political, diplomatic, economic or cultural cooperation with the United States, even though all other delegates in the subcommittee approved this motion. Similarly, Moscow refused a proposal from the Dominican Republic delegation condemning the United Nations as an instrument of colonialism and neocolonialism. Soviet delegates fought also against a motion urging states to break all relations with Israel. On the positive side, the Soviets in Havana insisted on inserting a passage on peaceful coexistence in a draft resolution to the effect that "all nations, big and small, should take peaceful coexistence as the foundation for their international relations." When this motion was defeated by Chinese and other delegations, it finally carried as an extraordinary resolution of the conference.[10]

Divergent attitudes of the Chinese and the Soviets respecting violence in the third world were particularly manifest in the responses of Peking and Moscow to the prospect of negotiations to halt the Vietnamese war. While the Soviets refused to take decisive steps to encourage Hanoi to negotiate and in fact helped to stiffen resistance through large doses of military and economic aid, the Kremlin apparently welcomed Hanoi's decision in 1968 to meet with U.S. representatives after President Johnson reduced the scope of bombing attacks on North Vietnam. Peking, on the other hand, seemed to oppose negotiations to settle the conflict. (Hanoi, for its part, claimed to act without consulting either Moscow or Peking.)

Moscow's future attitudes and behavior toward flash points in the third world constitute one of the major question marks on the international horizon. Soviet doctrine in the mid-1960s has moved toward greater emphasis on the need for readiness to combat imperialism in local conflict situations—the implication being that these will not necessarily escalate, as Soviet strategic writers earlier argued. Moreover, the Kremlin's military forces have demonstrated a growing ability to establish a Soviet presence in trouble spots and to deliver men and goods to such areas by sea or air.

Although the Kremlin may prefer to avoid dangerous confrontations with the United States, such engagements may come about as the "general purpose" forces of the two superpowers overlap around the globe. If such a pattern emerges, Peking's recent course of extending mainly moral support to other people's wars may come to appear tame indeed.

THE MORALITY AND CONSEQUENCES OF VIOLENCE

Peking and Moscow agree that some wars are just, others unjust. The first category includes defensive wars to repel aggression, wars of national liberation, and civil wars "of the oppressed against the oppressors." Both capitals maintain that it is the duty of all communists to assist just wars and to resist unjust ones (those waged by capitalist regimes). Although revolution may be assisted in various ways, it cannot be artificially transplanted, Moscow and Peking aver, asserting that "the principle of non-interference in domestic affairs must be observed."[11] In September 1965 the Chinese Defense Minister put it this way:

> Of course, every revolution in a country stems from the demands of its own people. The people's role cannot be replaced or taken over by any people from outside. In this sense, revolution cannot be imported. But this does not exclude mutual sympathy and support on the part of revolutionary peoples in their struggles against the imperialists and their lackeys. Our support and aid to other revolutionary peoples serves precisely to develop their self-reliant struggle.[12]

Related to the moral problems of violence is the question of the destruction likely to result from violence. The Kremlin leadership has come to sanction the view, alluded to by Malenkov in 1954, that nuclear war would be self-defeating for all countries. Soviet strategists have assigned greater weight to the role of surprise attack and have downgraded the "permanently operating factors" that were supposed to protect Russia against a Nazi *Blitzkrieg* or America's nuclear monopoly at an earlier period.[13] Moscow holds that nuclear war would be catastrophic for all countries; that the atomic bomb is oblivious to class distinctions. Peking has conceded that nuclear weapons are "unprecedentedly dangerous." But the Chinese bravely contend that if nuclear war broke out, a new and great civilization would rise from the ashes of imperialism.[14]

In part, no doubt, to spur on the North Vietnamese and to bolster the Chinese people if war came to them, Lin Piao laid great stress on these principles in his September 1965 remarks. War can be a great school, he declared, because the "sacrifice of a small number of people in revolutionary wars is repaid by security for whole nations; whole countries and even the whole of mankind; temporary suffering is repaid by lasting or even perpetual peace and happiness. War can temper the people and push history forward. . . ." In "diametrical opposition to the Khrushchev revisionists," he went on, "the Marxist-Leninists and revolutionary people never take a gloomy view of war."[15]

Chinese spokesmen ridicule what they term Soviet "fetishism" about nuclear armaments, and affirm that man—not technology—is the decisive factor in history. This somewhat un-Marxian view is supported by references to Lenin's dictum (uttered in 1920 during the Civil War) that "morale" is the decisive factor in war.[16] For obvious reasons[17] Peking finds further solace in Stalin's assurances (while Moscow was trying to break the American nuclear monopoly) that nuclear technology is not decisive in war. The Chinese refer favorably also to Stalin's further remarks that the imperialists will not long enjoy their nuclear monopoly.[18]

Even after China's first atomic tests, Peking continued to downgrade the potential role of nuclear weapons. The major statement by China's Defense Minister in September 1965 made three key points: that atomic weapons could afford no guarantee for the security of U.S. imperialism, that they constituted no absolute threat to world revolution, and that they were no excuse for Soviet cowardice. His remarks warrant careful reading:

> U.S. imperialism relies solely on its nuclear weapons to intimidate people. But these weapons cannot save U.S. imperialism from its doom. Nuclear weapons cannot be used lightly. U.S. imperialism has been condemned by the people of the whole world for its towering crime of dropping two atom bombs on Japan. If it uses nuclear weapons again, it will become isolated in the extreme. Moreover, the U.S. monopoly of nuclear weapons has long been broken; U.S. imperialism has these weapons, but others have them too. If it threatens other countries with nuclear weapons, U.S. imperialism will expose its own country to the same threat. For this reason, it will meet with strong opposition not only from the people everywhere but also inevitably from the people in its own country. Even if U.S. imperialism brazenly uses nuclear weapons, it cannot conquer the people, who are indomitable.

Lin drew a caricature of Soviet strategic views, and tore it down:

> The Khrushchev revisionists insist that a nation without nuclear weapons is incapable of defeating an enemy with nuclear weapons, whatever methods of fighting it may adopt. . . . Isn't this helping the imperialists in their nuclear blackmail? . . .

The Khrushchev revisionists assert that nuclear weapons and strategic rocket units are decisive while conventional forces are insignificant and that a militia is just a heap of human flesh. . . . Their
line in army building is the bourgeois line which ignores the human
factor and sees only the material factor and which regards technique
as everything and politics as nothing.

Again to cast aspersions on Moscow's revolutionary image, Lin declared:

The fundamental reason why the Khrushchev revisionists are opposed to people's war is that they have no faith in the masses and are
afraid of U.S. imperialism, of war, and revolution. They submit to
the nuclear blackmail of the U.S. imperialists and are afraid that, if
the oppressed peoples and nations rise up to fight people's wars or if
the people of socialist countries repulse U.S. imperialist aggression,
U.S. imperialism will be incensed, they themselves will become
involved and their fond dream of Soviet–U.S. cooperation to dominate the world will be spoiled.[19]

The wisdom of putting politics first and putting man above technique
was frequently reiterated during 1966.[20] At the same time, as noted in
Chapter VIII, Peking's statements about the significance of its nuclear
and missile technology were growing more strident, making some of
Lin's dogmas look the more anachronistic. Although Chinese statements,
at least implicitly, paid greater respect to technology, even this source of
power was traced back to a human (or demigod) factor: the thought of
Mao Tse-tung.[21] After China successfully tested a hydrogen bomb in
1967, Peking continued to emphasize that the "imperialists and modern
revisionists can manufacture atom bombs, but . . . no class enemy can
ever create such an invincible army as the Chinese People's Liberation
Army"; and that Soviet revisionists were wrong in trying to intimidate
African people with the notion that "weapons decide everything" and a
modern war cannot be fought without the atomic bomb. "By mastering
Mao Tse-tung's thought, the most powerful spiritual atom bomb," *People's
Daily* asserted on October 16, 1967, "the revolutionary people of the
world will be able to wipe out all ghosts and monsters, smash the dark
old world and create a red new one."

In the wake of rebuffs around the world for Chinese foreign policy and
in the turmoil accompanying the Cultural Revolution, Chinese statements related to the morality of violence began to take on a much more
nationalistic flavor in 1966. Peking's declarations noted the "blood debts"
owed China by a series of foreign devils—the reactionary Indonesians
who not only killed local communists but persecuted overseas Chinese;
the various African regimes breaking relations with China; the United

States aggressors who, among other crimes, strafed and killed Chinese fishermen; and the Japanese who, earlier had occupied Taiwan and later recognized the Kuomintang regime.[22] Wall posters called for the "burning" or "skinning" of Soviet revisionists, although offenses against the person of Soviet diplomats seemed limited to spitting and noise-making. Peking's Ambassador to Warsaw told his U.S. counterpart that "the great Chinese people are not to be trifled with. The debt of blood incurred by the U.S. Government must be cleared and repaid."[23] While such comments could be regarded merely as a blustering warning to an outside foe, Chinese citizens were being indoctrinated in the importance of struggling without quarter. Thus, Lu Hsun, father of an earlier cultural revolution, was praised because "he never forgave the enemies of the people." He

> summed up many lessons learned at the cost of blood, and pointed out that "preaching not to 'beat a mad dog in the water' is very harmful." If those "mad dogs in the water" are not beaten thoroughly, once they crawl back onto the bank, they will bite to death many revolutionaries. This will cost more blood.

The moral of the story, a Chinese leader asserted in 1966, was that appeasement or pity will simply "cost a lot more energy and lives" of future revolutionaries.[24] Indeed, the result of Moscow's peddling the opium of revisionism and selling out revolutionary struggle, Lin Piao declared on November 6, 1967, was that "Communists and revolutionary fighters have been massacred [presumably in Indonesia but perhaps elsewhere, such as Vietnam] in their tens of thousands by imperialism and its lackeys." The Soviet renegades, he declared, had committed heinous crimes against their own people and the people throughout the world, for which they would be tried in the dock of history by Marxist-Leninists and true revolutionaries all over the world. And early in 1968 following massacres of Chinese nationals, Peking reiterated that "The Indonesian Reactionaries Owe the Chinese People a New Blood Debt" (*Peking Review,* February 9).

An outsider could hardly judge whether the more violent inflection in Chinese declaratory policy ought to be interpreted figuratively or literally. At least some China experts in the West believed that the message intended was allegorical and, moreover, mainly for domestic consumption rather than foreign policy application. But few would deny that the Chinese have historical grounds for offended sensibilities, and that with their rising power base they might like to even past scores, although they may ultimately be deterred by the discrepancy between themselves and the superpowers. If the Chinese people are not being prepared to attack, they are at least being readied to defend their land in depth;[25] if they are not being trained to export revolution, they are being attuned to appreciate social change without fear of violent consequences.

THE ROAD TO REVOLUTION[26]

The triumph of socialism is both desirable and inevitable in every country of the world, according to Moscow and Peking, both of which pledge themselves to assist the forces of revolution in every way possible. Although socialist governments may compromise and coexist peacefully with capitalist governments, the oppressed masses within capitalist states are to make no such arrangements with the ruling classes. The duty of the masses is to overthrow the capitalist class and to establish a dictatorship of the proletariat.[27]

Moscow, however, differs with Peking as to whether the socialist revolution may be accomplished by non-violent means. Moscow quotes Lenin to the effect that a socialist should have an unlimited array of means in his arsenal. He should use violent means when the capitalist class resorts to force to defend itself. A peaceful transition to socialism, however, is said to offer great advantages, because it permits a "radical reorganization of social life with the least sacrifices on the part of the workers and minimal destruction of the productive forces of society."[28] Peking concedes that peaceful means might be hypothetically preferable, but argues that the transition to socialism must always be accomplished by an armed uprising, for the capitalists will always use force to defend their rule. This view was underlined in 1966 when, during a moment when the cultural revolution seemed destined to produce "commune" style governments in China, *Red Flag* summed up certain lessons to be considered on the 95th anniversary of the Paris Commune. *Red Flag* concluded that the proletariat could emancipate itself only by seizing arms, and by adopting revolutionary methods to seize state power and establish a dictatorship of the proletariat. To suggest the possibility of a "peaceful transition," the journal argued, is to cooperate with reaction. Once power has been seized, revolutionaries should be on guard against phony peace negotiations with the enemy, for his peace talk must be exposed and his plans for counterrevolution must be crushed.[29] Again, in the course of an attack on "China's Khrushchev" late in 1967, an article by Yen Chang-kwei entitled "Bourgeois Counter-revolutionary Strategy and Tactics" (*Peking Review*, December 25) argued that "violent revolution is the only correct road to be taken by the proletariat in seizing political power; this is a universal law governing the proletarian revolution."

The practical implication of all the foregoing arguments is that the doctrinal underpinning of Moscow's foreign policy places less reliance on force than does that of Peking. Violence, in the Soviet view, may be counterproductive and unnecessary while in the Chinese view it is useful and essential. Moscow considers peaceful coexistence the "highest form" of class struggle; Peking sees it as a means, but not the only means, of policy. The Chinese, in fact, purport to fear that primary reliance on peaceful coexistence will give rise to false hope on the part of the masses and that, eventually, it will prove ineffective in furthering the communist cause. Therefore, Peking declares, peaceful coexistence should "never be described as the main content of the transition from capitalism to social-ism, still less should it be asserted that peaceful coexistence is mankind's road to socialism."[30]

DISARMAMENT AS A TACTIC AND AS A STRATEGY

Both Peking and Moscow purport to subscribe to Lenin's position on questions of disarmament as well as on related questions of conflict and collaboration with the adversary. Both sides can in fact find scriptural support, because Lenin's attitude toward disarmament passed through two distinct and somewhat contradictory stages.[31] In its first stage, his approach to disarmament negotiations was entirely negative. He argued that such negotiations could not be fruitful; therefore they should not be attempted. Espousing the slogan of disarmament could merely distract the masses from the only real means for eliminating war—a communist revolution that would end the class struggle. Not surprisingly, Lenin argued in this way at times when revolution was ripe—in 1905 and during the First World War, that is, before his party had come to power.

After the October 1917 Revolution, however, Lenin's tactics began to change. His government advocated an end to the First World War and to foreign intervention in Russia. Once hostilities along the Russian frontier had ended in 1920–21, the Soviet Government urged that the peace treaties should embody measures of what the West now calls "arms control," for example, demilitarized zones. The Soviet proposals aimed in part at demonstrating the peaceful nature of the first socialist govern-ment; at inciting the masses of other countries to overthrow their own belligerent governments; and at safeguarding the military security of the Soviet Republic. These policies culminated in a new stage in Lenin's view of disarmament, which led to the Soviet regime's posing itself as the only government generally interested in and able to promote disarma-ment. Throughout 1921–23 this posture was assumed during the course of four international conferences: the Washington Naval, the Genoa Economic, the Moscow Disarmament, and the Lausanne Conference on the Near East.

Although the Bolsheviks came in the early 1920s to advocate disarmament negotiations, the Soviet leadership appears to have retained Lenin's earlier disbelief in the possibility of a disarmament agreement so long as capitalism existed. Furthermore, while Russia's weaknesses gave the Kremlin material grounds for favoring reciprocal disarmament agreements, the Bolsheviks seem to have considered such agreements as undesirable, since they would impede the dialectic of revolution. In short, they saw disarmament neither as possible nor as desirable.

Thus, the Soviet campaign for disarmament that began in 1921–22 did not seek negotiated agreements with the West. Instead the new Soviet policy strove to put the capitalist governments on the diplomatic defensive, and to cultivate pro-Soviet and even pro-revolutionary sentiments among the masses and "pacifist bourgeoisie" outside Russia. This second stage of Lenin's attitude toward disarmament appears to have characterized Soviet policy under Stalin, both in the era of the League of Nations and later during the negotiations at the United Nations. Soviet proposals then aimed not at a disarmament treaty but at borrowing time and embarrassing Western governments.

Moscow's attitude toward arms control and disarmament since Stalin's death in 1953 seems to have fluctuated between Stage II Leninism—using disarmament negotiations primarily as a propaganda tactic—and a new stage that views arms control (though probably not general disarmament) as a feasible and useful object of Soviet strategy. Moscow has contended that a test ban and other measures of disarmament can be agreed to by the capitalist and the socialist countries, thanks to the imperialists' survival instinct and to popular pressure. Further, proposals for general and complete disarmament are useful as agitational means for "exposing" the imperialists and limiting their machinations for war.

To rebut Chinese attacks on the Soviet position, the Khrushchev government brought to light previously unpublished correspondence between Lenin and his Foreign Minister Chicherin that laid the basis for the Soviet campaign for disarmament begun in 1922.[32] Ignoring the fact that Lenin saw disarmament negotiations primarily as an instrument to divide the enemy, Soviet apologists now assert that the Kremlin's present approach to disarmament—like that in 1922—has been no mere "tactical" expedient. "We sincerely want disarmament," the July 14, 1963 Soviet letter affirmed, citing Engels' words that disarmament was "possible" and would be a "guarantee of peace."[33]

Moscow, in Peking's view, goes too far. The Chinese repeatedly cite Lenin's warnings from 1916 that disarmament is a dangerous slogan even as a tactic, because it can spread the illusion that peace and disarmament may come without the triumph of communism. The Chinese letter of June 14, 1963 quotes Lenin's *War Programme of the Proletarian Revolution,* written in 1916:

> Only *after* the proletariat has disarmed the bourgeoisie will it be able, without betraying its world-historical mission, to throw all armaments on the scrap heap; and the proletariat will undoubtedly do this, but *only when this condition has been fulfilled, certainly not before.*[34]

The kernel of the June 14 letter had been expressed three years earlier in the reply which the mainland magazine *China Youth* gave to a reader who inquired about the way to achieve a "warless world." The editor, in language strikingly similar to Lenin's phraseology of 1905 and 1916, declared:

> The so-called "warless world"—if it is not a childish fantasy—can only be a world where there is no imperialism . . . where there is no class. To realize this ideal, the human race must necessarily undergo a long-term, sinuous, complicated and violent struggle so as to eliminate imperialism and class. At a time when the imperialists not only still exist but are even armed to the teeth, any thought that there is a short cut to realizing a "warless world" will only disarm the people's vigilance against the imperialists. . . .[35]

The same spirit ran through the editorial entitled "Long Live Leninism!" published in the Chinese theoretical journal *Red Flag* in April 1960. "Marxist-Leninists," the journal warned, "absolutely must not sink into the mire of bourgeois pacifism." Citing Lenin's endorsement of the principle that war is only the continuation of politics, *Red Flag* denied that Lenin's teachings on imperialism, on proletarian revolution and dictatorship, on war and peace are obsolete. Although the world situation has changed drastically since Lenin's lifetime, these changes were said to "have more clearly confirmed the truths uncovered by Lenin and all the theories he advanced during the struggle to defend revolutionary Marxism and develop Marxism."[36]

Statements of this kind were not long without challenge. Despite President Eisenhower's refusal to apologize for the U-2 incident in May 1960, at the June Bucharest Conference of Communist Parties Khrushchev defended against Chinese criticism the foundations of his coexistence strategy. To ascertain the nature of the mounting dispute, however, it was still necessary to read between the lines of Soviet, Chinese, and other communist pronouncements. One of the earliest direct rebuttals to the Chinese interpretation of "what Lenin really meant" appeared in the *World Marxist Review* of May 1962[37]—two months before the Moscow

Congress on World Peace and General Disarmament, but during the time when China was not yet being explicitly attacked in public. The *Review* article, written by a French communist, censured "dogmatists of the type of the Albanian leaders," because they failed to see the urgency of "the demand for *general and complete disarmament* now resounding throughout the world." The dogmatists' fallacy, according to the *Review,* is that they regard the struggle for disarmament as futile, on the grounds that "it is aimed against the *means* of waging war and not against the cause and *source* of war—imperialism." To justify this view the dogmatists twist and distort theses such as "war is the continuation of politics by other means." Thus the dogmatists identify politics with war, and thereby vilify the communist movement. But the article continued:

> To regard the destruction of imperialism as the only road to peace would mean renouncing the policy of peaceful coexistence, which, far from implying rejection by the socialist camp of the struggle against the system of exploitation and violence, presupposes prosecution of the struggle in the conditions of peace; it would mean substituting for this policy the export of revolution by force of arms, which is utterly alien to Marxism-Leninism.

May Lenin's works on disarmament in 1916 be cited now to justify opposition to the Soviet struggle for disarmament? The *World Marxist Review* replied in the negative, arguing that Lenin's remarks were made in an entirely different context, when world war was being transformed into civil war, and that it was on Lenin's personal instructions that the Soviet Delegation proposed disarmament at the 1922 Genoa Conference.[38]

The *World Marxist Review* article charged essentially that the dogmatists were opposed to disarmament—certainly as a strategy and perhaps even as a tactic: "For all their hypocritical protestations to the contrary, they [the dogmatists] are opposed to the struggle conducted by the socialist camp and all peace supporters for general and complete disarmament."

The charge of hypocrisy was partially substantiated in the summer and fall of 1963. China had long paid lip-service to the possibility and usefulness of East-West disarmament agreements. Once the test ban treaty was signed, however, Peking denounced it as a betrayal of the revolutionary struggle and an alliance with capitalism against China and the other emerging forces. On the other hand, it must be conceded that Peking had long opposed not only the concept of a partial test ban, but also—especially in private Sino-Soviet parleys—a comprehensive test ban treaty taken as an isolated measure. China's position had long been to view the test ban as a step to be taken parallel with total nuclear disarmament, if at all. While such a linkage—especially without conventional disarmament—would disadvantage the nuclear powers, it was clear that a test ban treaty on the eve of China's joining the atomic club put unwelcome pressure on her to desist from her chosen course.

Apart from these strategic inequities, of course, Peking objected to the Moscow Treaty on political grounds also, particularly with regard to the treaty's potential for eroding revolutionary élan within and without the communist camp.

To sum up, the Chinese seem to be hovering between the first and second stages of Lenin's thinking on disarmament. Just as Lenin condemned as illusory and counter-revolutionary the disarmament talk of Karl Kautsky, so Peking has denounced the peace and disarmament efforts of Soviet leaders, comparing them with the "revisionists" Kautsky and Bernstein.[39] If the Chinese pay homage to the ideals of peace and disarmament, they oppose the raising of false hopes that the class struggle may be resolved without resort to international and civil violence. If they go so far as to countenance disarmament negotiations, they appear nevertheless to be opposed to conducting negotiations in a spirit of conciliation and compromise directed toward achieving an agreement.

On the other hand, the post-Stalin Soviet leadership seems to have vacillated between Lenin's second stage and the new stage that has emerged since 1953. The Kremlin now employs disarmament as a tactic, as Lenin did, to divide and isolate the foe and win support for the communist cause.[40] In addition to using disarmament as a political weapon against capitalism, however, both Moscow and Peking have wielded it against one another in their struggle for power within world communism. But Moscow seems to regard certain forms of arms control as strategically useful, and not just those that one-sidedly favor Soviet rather than Western interests. The Kremlin rejects the view, championed in Peking, that arms control and disarmament are dangerous as a tactic and harmful as a strategy. The Kremlin's course has led Peking to exclaim in the bitter words of its June 14, 1963, letter to Moscow, that "to make no distinction between enemies, friends and ourselves and to entrust the fate of the people and of mankind to collaboration with U.S. imperialism is to lead people astray."

To be sure, the Soviet leaders must harbor many doubts about Western intentions. And Moscow continues to look for soft spots in the West or the third world which can be exploited by propaganda and diplomatic devices. Nevertheless, the Russians appear to believe that modern political and military realities make it imperative—for communist and non-communist interests alike—to moderate the arms race; to reduce the threat of accidental war; and to stop the spread of nuclear weapons.

Moscow seems confident that, free of the heavy burden of armaments expenditures, the Soviet Union could decisively advance its interests by economic and political competition with the West. Peace, like goulash, is expected to win support for the communist system.

In 1963–64 Moscow attempted to prove the correctness of its general policy by pointing to successes in the field of arms limitation. In 1965 this type of propaganda logic was conspicuously missing in Soviet media. The years 1966–68 saw signs that the Kremlin again sought to stabilize its overall confrontation with the West, including the issue of the arms race; but political conditions seemed to impede a full return to the propaganda theme that disarmament agreements demonstrate the validity of Soviet-style communism. If Moscow again chooses to sound this chord, the prospects for arms control will probably have gained. But Moscow's decision on this score will be an effect—not the cause—of deeper reasons again facilitating and militating against East-West accords.

XIV
Underlying Factors in Soviet and Chinese Policy

Communist statements on war and peace, like other ideological pronouncements, have been subjected to two extreme interpretations. One stresses the apparent importance of the role played by ideology in communist politics; the second reverses the proposition and terms the verbal battle a fig leaf to cover a struggle for power.

The first view argues that the dispute over the correct line is proof of the seriousness with which the communist leadership takes its doctrine. Were the ideas at issue not of great intrinsic importance, the communist governments would not allow mere verbiage to become the basis for a profound rift within the alliance. The opposite interpretation holds that ideology is merely an instrument in the game of power politics. China, disgruntled with the meagerness of Soviet military and economic support, has decided to vie for hegemony in the communist bloc. She seized upon the *pretext* of a certain softening in Moscow's policy and now forces the Kremlin into a rigid defense of its doctrinal position. Even Stalin, not known for his theoretical commitment to pacifism, would have had to defend strongly the Litvinov proposals of 1927–32 had they been challenged then by another communist regime, if one had existed (say, in China). Accusations that Moscow is deviating from orthodoxy are one of the easiest means by which a relatively weak power such as China can exert its claim for leadership, since little material strength is needed to claim the mantle of ideological purity—a fact long demonstrated by Albania.

Both interpretations have some validity, but they need to be broadened and seen in conjunction with other factors. By limiting the range of possible forces to "national interest" and "ideology" the analyst leaves out such other relevant determinants as culture, language, personal interest, personality, perception, external threat, and even nationalism.

A major purpose of the present chapter is to analyze the material interests conditioning Soviet and Chinese doctrinal statements discussed in the preceding chapter. In order to do that, however, we must place them in the wider array of forces influencing the decisions of Peking and Moscow (and by extension, any governing body), as shown in Fig. 5.

Although the outline focuses on the factors that condition foreign policy decisions, it provides only a skeleton of the relevant forces.[1] A more detailed outline would show the origins of components that are merely suggested here, such as the structure of the decision-making process, the communication of decisions, the interaction between decisions by one government and another. Further, the flow suggested in the outline is mainly a movement toward a decision; missing is an explanation of the (a) interdependence among the various factors and (b) the repercussions of each decision—the feedback—upon its conditioning factors. In reality, all the variables listed would tend to affect one another, either reinforcing or obstructing some existing trend. At best the outline provides an enumeration of the relevant factors; it does not attempt to weight them. The beginnings of any systematic inquiry, of course, require classification as a first step toward deeper analysis.

Each of the components in the outline is in itself a complex topic, but some brief description will be suggested. "Culture," the heritage and products of a society, is the primary matrix conditioning the other domestic inputs integral to a foreign policy decision. Understood in a broad sense, it means the way of life, the total life style of a people, reflecting and embracing its history and its language.[2] Thus, culture is the underlying influence shaping sentiments about group identity and group interests. It is also the substratum upon which ideologies build in order to systematize values or create new ones. Culture, in short, is imbibed with mother's milk, profoundly affecting the receptivity of decision-makers to influences they encounter later in life. It shapes not only the way leaders express themselves, but also how they think and perceive. Thus, it has both a positive and negative impact, generating but also blocking out trains of thought and feeling.

Arising from the country's way of life come both personal and extra-personal factors conditioning policy decisions. The distinction is somewhat artificial, in that many leaders may tend to identify their personal good with that of the group or vice versa. But some separation of this nature is necessary, for—particularly in communist studies—arguments about the dichotomy "national interest vs. ideology" often tend to overlook the fact that these forces operate, to the extent they do, through

FIGURE 5

Outline of Factors Conditioning Foreign Policy Decisions

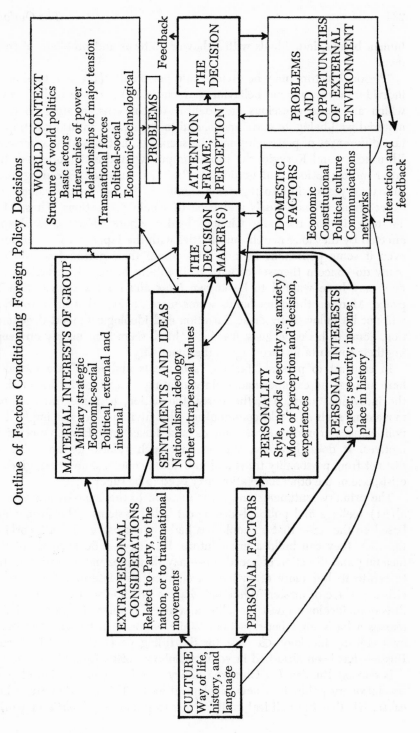

human beings, individuals with behavior patterns and problems of their own.

"Personal factors" may be divided into personality (the sum total of an individual's learning and behavior characteristics) and personal interests, which are more conscious and deliberate concerns, relating to one's material well-being, to one's image, and to one's place in history.[3] Important differences of personality may be seen, e.g., in the contrasts between Khrushchev and Kosygin, the former impulsive and action-oriented, the latter more cautious and gradualist. Profound experiences during one's formative years will also register a significant impact on the values and expectations of individuals and even of whole generations. Thus, Mao Tse-tung is not the only Chinese leader whose views were deeply affected by the "long march" and battles with the Japanese. Furthermore, even if some politicians do not think about their personal well-being, many do concern themselves with their role in history. Khrushchev, for one, may have wanted to be known *inter alia* for his contribution to peace; Mao, on the other hand, seems more anxious that his revolution will not be followed by de-stalinization and ideological-moral degeneration. Some of his colleagues, less far-sighted, seem bent mainly on keeping their comfortable dwellings in the Inner City.

In contrast to personal factors, "sentiments and ideas" are included here among the extrapersonal values relating to an identity larger than the individual actor, e.g., the Party, the nation, or some transnational movement such as world communism. This division does not imply that politicians affirm certain sentiments and ideas only from hypocritical motives. It does, however, suggest that such values are an influence distinct from personality traits and individual concerns; and that, given a crisis, one or the other motivation may need to be subordinated.

The primary sentiments and ideas relevant to this analysis are national(ist) feelings and political-ideological belief systems.[4] The former are based on the sense that a people has had a great past and that, working together, they can build a great future. Ideology—a doctrine about the meaning and direction of social life—may denounce nationalism and try to refute it, but more often has succumbed and intermingled with it, either as slave or master. While nationalism provides a kind of tradition-direction, ideology gives the élite a source of inner-direction and the masses a basis for other-direction. While nationalism has roots in one's own culture, ideology—at least for the ruling generation in China and Russia—has been absorbed in young manhood, often from alien sources.

Is current Russian (or Chinese) policy merely a continuation of pre-revolutionary policy in a new ideological garb? This question arises because, whether the political entity wants to pursue *Realpolitik* or world revolution—or both—it must proceed from a base of material power. Thus, the material interests of the group for which a leader works are another influence on decision-making. The qualification "material" is noted merely to distinguish tangible factors such as military and economic power from sentiments (e.g., pride) or skills (e.g., management), although these intangibles may depend in part on the material base. The "group" for which a leader is ultimately concerned may be an entity larger or smaller than the nation-state, such as the Party or the alliance-system. A half decade of history since the Bolshevik revolution, however, has shown that, even in communist practice, "material interests of the group" corresponds roughly to the concept "raison d'état." A fundamental distinction must be made, however, between a material interest as perceived by the decision-maker and one seen by an outside observer. Thus, what Mao deems good for China may diverge widely from the estimate of a Martian. Even granting that the latter accepted the goals of Chairman Mao, he might suggest other tactics.

From these four sources—cultural, personal, sentimental, and material—derive the main ingredients *internal* to a decision-maker's actions. But his decisions—even his so-called initiatives—take place in response to an external environment as it intrudes upon his attention frame and as it is perceived by him. This environment, in addition to casting up the problems and opportunities that stimulate decisions, provides also the international and domestic context which further conditions the political actor's thoughts and deeds. There is both a cause and effect relationship, an interdependence, between the military position and national sentiment of one state and the broader structure of world politics, with its hierarchies of power and transnational forces. The domestic context— economic, constitutional, etc.—will also condition the final decision as well as the inputs such as personal interest and national sentiments.[5] There is, of course, a continuous interaction between all the elements outlined, and feedback from each decision impacting on all factors in the chain.

Given the complexity of this system, it is hardly surprising that some decisions will reflect more the logic of the situation while others will suggest more traditional response patterns or even random behavior.[6] As Stanley Hoffmann has suggested, the increasing number of important variables that policy-makers should take into account makes it more likely that there will be a "communications overload." Given an increase in the number of nuclear powers and/or more intense competition, there may be times "when calculation—rational or unreasonable—becomes impossible."[7]

How do these forces condition the arms and arms control policies of

Moscow and Peking? Generalizations are difficult for many reasons. First, the weight of elements in the mix will change with time, place, the particular problem, and the leaders in command. Second, detailed comparative studies are lacking. Third, because scientific methods to weight the role of the various forces are also lacking, the analyst must rely to a heavy degree on speculation and intuition.[8]

Having entered these caveats, we nevertheless suggest that a qualified materialist interpretation offers the most adequate explanation for the manner in which Moscow and Peking have formulated their policies, particularly with respect to war, peace, and arms control. The hypothesis is that material factors—particularly strategic-military considerations—seem to have been most frequently the decisive element in leading the Soviet and Chinese communists to adopt one foreign policy posture or another. The argument concedes that some decisions may be better explained by cultural, sentimental, or personal factors; but that—quantitatively and qualitatively—the most significant forces in their decisions have usually been military-strategic considerations.

This interpretation is consonant with Mao's opinion that "power grows out of the barrel of a gun."[9] It has roots in Marx's view that the material base determines the political superstructure; in Tolstoi's concept that historical forces transcend the role of the individual;[10] in "political realism," as propounded in Morgenthau's *Politics Among Nations;*[11] and, in some respects, in Rostow's theory on the stages of economic growth.[12] Closer to the point, this interpretation derives from agreement with the historical schools that stress the continuities over the changes in Soviet and Chinese policies since the revolutions of October 1917 and October 1949.[13]

More immediately, it is the conclusion reached after empirical investigation of the arms control policies of communist regimes in Russia, Eastern Europe, and China. It is a dreary, unpleasant conclusion in that it underscores the Machiavellian-Hobbesian view of man and government, particularly in that anarchical arena of world politics. But it is also a moderately hopeful view insofar as it suggests there is a handle by which to order international relations, appealing to the self-interest of states, even while important ideological differences may remain.[14] This view does not accept, for example, the fatalism of the radical "gamesmanship" thesis which holds that disarmament negotiations are bound to fail, since each participant deliberately includes among its proposals a joker the adversary cannot accept.[15] Rather, the record shows that while some proposals have been advanced mainly for propaganda reasons, and some have been unacceptable due to strategic asymmetries, others have led (or could have led) to agreement because they advanced the interests of both sides.

The factor that shapes national policy most immediately is the strategic balance of power, for this element both limits and facilitates the nation's ability to intervene in world affairs, whether to support or to overthrow the status quo. The most pervasive and profound influence, however, is economic development. Viewed objectively, it is the prime determinant of the country's military capability; viewed subjectively, it is the main force shaping the people's attachment to the existing order. Thus, material factors condition the objective state of the nation's military and economic capabilities and problems, and its attitude toward the desirability of radical change, effected perhaps by violence.[16]

To be sure, culture in its broadest sense constitutes the womb in which the components internal to a decision-maker are nurtured. Cultural differences also intensify communication problems, as seen in the way that many Americans have misunderstood such terms as "we'll bury you" or "peaceful competition," while Russians have often misinterpreted such notions as "arms control," "deterrence," and even "containment." Quite conceivably, "blood debt" has different connotation in Chinese than in English. But tensions between nations arise from deeper sources than misunderstandings. In any event, cultural influences—like parental—may be sharply modified, even completely disregarded. One might expect, surveying Russian and Chinese culture, that Moscow would favor apocalyptic foreign policies and Peking gradualist ones.[17] At least in arms control, however, the Soviets in recent years have championed the value of partial measures while the Chinese have called for quite radical ones. In both cases, hardly by coincidence, the policies proposed accorded with the strategic interests and problems of each party.

The personality and personal interests of individual leaders will also stamp a heavy imprint on any government decision. After all, no matter how important material forces are, they operate on history only through the decisions of human beings. Had Stalin remained in power for several more years, would not the new tack adopted by Moscow's arms control policy in 1954–55 have been delayed? Granting the validity of such arguments, it is still contended that differences between leaders (particularly those of the same generation and background) recede in importance as these men take office and confront the awesome problems of the external environment, pitted against the resources and values of the nation. Thus, for example, once Malenkov had been demoted (and Molotov after him), his foreign policy was pursued again by Khrush-

chev. Similar cases abound, where, despite some embarrassment, the
victor has adopted the policy of the vanquished, e.g., Trotsky-Stalin,
Djilas-Tito, Khrushchev-Kosygin and Brezhnev.

National sentiments and ideology are also vital ingredients to decision-making, but they too are limited and conditioned by the material
capabilities and problems of the nation-state. It turns out that the dichotomy "raison d'état vs. ideology" is somewhat artificial, because of the
intimate synthesis joining the two. Ideology is no mere fig leaf, cynically
manipulated and adjusted to serve the interests of the ruling group and
the state. As a world view, providing a systemic scheme about the
direction and meaning of social life, ideology naturally (if subcon-
sciously) reflects the imperatives of military, economic, political, and
even personal expediency. Even so, it exerts both a significant subjective
and objective influence on policy. Subjectively, ideology provides a way
of looking at the world, a set of premises and categories that function to
determine the range of alternatives and values considered by decision-
makers. The ideology in which men are schooled and to which they pay
homage becomes a part of their basic frame of reference, stimulating but
also restricting their responses. Objectively, ideology provides a doctrine
that must be revered and followed, at least ostensibly, in government
action. Within the country, it offers a means for communicating with
Party workers. In the world communist movement it serves also to
communicate policy and to defend the correctness of one's tactics and
strategy.[18]

Seen in this context, ideology is neither an all-unifying doctrine nor a
mere rationalization after the fact. As Daniel Bell has noted, the purpose
of an official creed is to make intellectually coherent and rationally
defensible its mobilization of the people for war, for economic development, and for other major goals.[19] If only because ideology is among
other things an "action program," it must take into account the material
problems facing a regime.[20] Given the different interests of states such as
the U.S.S.R. and China, it is hardly surprising that their polemics reveal
"a core of *real* issues which divide the communist world—problems
which are not contrived but genuine, not insignificant but profound."[21]

Some ideological sparring is dishonest or insincere, designed mainly to
win propaganda points even if this means distorting the opponent's
position—Peking calling the Russians "bourgeois pacifists" and Moscow
accusing the Chinese of seeking global nuclear war. But the doctrinal
conflicts between the Soviet and Chinese leaders are probably, for the
most part, sincere in that they represent divergent perceptions of reality,
based on different levels of material attainment and satisfaction. These
contrasts in perception and satisfaction, in turn, give rise to different

values which color attitudes toward risk-taking and even estimates of risk, summed up doctrinally in abstract debate about the "strength of the imperialist camp."[22] Such is probably the substructure beneath ideological formulations favoring a "forward" or a moderate foreign policy.

Thus, there are different cultural backgrounds distinguishing one country's communism from another's. There are divergent personalities and personal interests inclining different leaders to seek variations on given policy positions. And there are nationalistic and doctrinal assumptions that exert both a subjective and objective impact on foreign policy decisions. Nevertheless, it is argued, behind the apparent ideological disagreements between Moscow and Peking over arms limitation and collaboration with the capitalist adversary, there is a bedrock of raison d'état, of expediency, of divergent material interests.

If we survey the period since 1917, it seems clear that Soviet arms control policy, particularly in its early years, has reflected Bolshevik doctrine in a number of ways, e.g., in its proclivity for all-out solutions and in its underlying suspicion of capitalist schemes for arms control and inspection.[23] These tendencies, however, have reflected also certain historical and cultural influences that may be considered Russian rather than communist. Moreover, these proclivities in Soviet arms control policy coincided with power-political interests arising from the Soviet Union's weak military position vis-à-vis the outer world.

As this material foundation changed, so did communist ideology with respect to disarmament: first in 1921–22, as the inevitability of an imminent war between communism and capitalism receded; on other occasions such as the late 1920s and in the era of the Baruch Plan; but most radically in the mid-1950s—coinciding with Russia's acquisition of an effective minimum deterrent and the passing of Stalin. In short, communist disarmament doctrine has changed profoundly over the years, most of the alterations corresponding to national interest as conditioned by changes in the material base.

STRATEGIC FACTORS

Granted that no one factor or constellation of factors will always determine a nation's foreign policy decisions, it seems clear that military-strategic considerations effectively account for many of the conflicts in Sino-Soviet relations, particularly in arms control and related matters. Indeed, one detailed study of the Khrushchev era has concluded that military-strategic factors most consistently explained both the constants and the variables in Moscow's arms control policies from 1954 to 1964 both on its Western and on its Eastern front.[24]

Because the Soviet Union enjoys a credible deterrent to inhibit any foreign foe, she can contemplate freezing the existing military balance far more readily than can Peking.

Several examples of Sino-Soviet discord on arms control show the strategic underpinning of each side's attitude. One case in point provides a comparative look at the Soviet and Chinese positions at different stages in the development of each country. Moscow in 1963 supported an arrangement to freeze the military balance, which was opposed by Peking, whereas in 1922 the Kremlin denounced such provisions when they were enacted at the Washington Naval Conference.[25] Even though its limitations on capital ships and aircraft carriers did not directly affect Russia, the Kremlin accused the great powers of misleading the people: they planned to limit only the arms that were obsolete, while stepping up competition in lighter ships, submarines, and airplanes.[26] Peking's response to the 1963 test ban treaty followed closely the lines of Moscow's reaction to the Washington Treaty. Peking in 1963, like Moscow in 1922, was not invited to the great power negotiations. She was in a position of general military inferiority to the great powers and denounced the agreements reached as schemes to freeze the status quo to the advantage of the great powers. She pointed out what military forces were *not* included in the agreements (everything except certain ships in 1922, everything but certain nuclear tests in 1963). She predicted that the arms race and the danger of war would increase, and offered counterproposals devised to appeal to world opinion, namely, *general* disarmament of all types of weapons and a genuinely international conference to reflect the interests of all states.[27]

The strategic motive in Peking's policy toward the nuclear test ban was noted both by Western and Soviet officials. The Soviet Government, commenting on Peking's displeasure that Moscow had not provided a sample atomic bomb, declared: "The Chinese leaders abuse the Soviet Union in every way because it has nuclear arms while the CPR does not have them."[28]

Similarly, Soviet strategic interests might well be served by enactment of the schemes for general and complete disarmament (GCD) that Moscow has espoused since 1959, but particularly by the variant the Kremlin has advocated since September 21, 1962.[29] The Soviet Government accepted in 1962 and expanded in 1963 the principle that the two superpowers should retain a nuclear umbrella until the process of general and complete disarmament had been completed. While Soviet diplomats have been vague about the details of this proposal, they seem to have in mind a relatively small missile force to be retained by both Moscow and Washington. United States forces would thus be reduced by a much greater factor than Soviet, while nuclear-rocket forces for other states (such as China) would be prohibited or severely limited.[30]

The Soviet GCD proposals introduced since 1959 have also envisioned drastic cuts in the conventional forces that would compel the withdrawal of U.S. forces from Europe and neutralize the manpower advantages of states like China vis-à-vis the nuclear umbrella retained by Moscow. Moscow's proposals specify that military training of civilians should be prohibited as well, a measure aimed perhaps in part at destroying China's militia system rooted in the farm and factory.[31]

Not surprisingly the Chinese response to such Soviet proposals has been negative. Peking refuses any measure that would foreclose its hopes of overcoming present strategic inferiority. The prohibition and destruction of all nuclear weapons would be acceptable, the Chinese have stated, but not a test ban or any other agreement that would freeze the strategic balance in China's disfavor.[32] (London and Paris responded in similar fashion to proposals that would have kept the former from testing hydrogen bombs in 1956 and the latter from testing atomic weapons in 1960.[33] Furthermore, the de Gaulle government, like Peking, has for its own reasons refused to sign the 1963 "Moscow Treaty.") Not surprisingly, although Peking campaigns for complete nuclear disarmament, its proposals since 1963 have shown little enthusiasm for limits on conventional arms which, in a non-nuclear world, would make China's population a formidable source of military power.

ECONOMIC AND SOCIAL FACTORS

At the basis of Moscow's general interest in stabilizing the existing order is the fact that the Soviet Union has already become an industrialized power on the threshold of an age of consumer abundance. Soviet economic might has built the minimum nuclear deterrent that guarantees Russian security. This economic power has finally reached the stage where, after a half decade of sacrifice, the foundations have been laid for a rapid march into a relatively affluent "goulash" or even "gastronome" communism. The ability of the Soviet economy to perform this march, however, depends in an absolute sense on the maintenance of peace, and the rate of progress hinges in part on a limitation and reduction of allocations to defense.[34] All these considerations heighten the Soviet interest in the reduction of East-West tensions and some tempering of the arms race.

Modern Soviet society, in sharp contrast to that of Lenin's day, possesses a sense of having arrived, of being accepted as a leading and respected great power, of having built the foundations of a way of life that will consistently improve.[35] The only contingency that may interrupt this progress, Soviet leaders feel, is another war. Soviet society, therefore, has a greater stake in international stability than in world revolution—revolution that may produce rival communist regimes and/or trigger violence that could escalate precariously. Increasing Soviet interest in disarmament parallels other major trends dating from Stalin's death. These trends—though interrupted by some sharp exceptions—have moved toward less reliance on violence in Soviet domestic and foreign policy, and toward greater promise and production of improved living standards for the Soviet people, with some liberalization in politics, economics, and culture.[36]

Before classifying any state as "have" or "have-not," of course, we must determine what sort of possession is at issue—the quantity or quality of population, raw materials, agriculture, industry, or armaments (nuclear and conventional). Clearly, governments and peoples derive varying degrees of satisfaction from their material environment. Each will have a subjective image of "what is" and "what ought to be."[37] The lesser the perceived gap between the two, the more satisfied the state will be and the less anxious for change. As Robert A. Scalapino has pointed out, "the Soviet Union has become a 'have' nation psychologically, not in terms of being satisfied with the status quo, but in terms of being relatively satisfied with the rate and direction of change."[38]

Communist China, by contrast, has little cause to be satisfied with the basic structure of world politics, the state of her internal development, or the apparent thrust of economic and social change. Paradoxically, despite Mao's dicta on the priority of man over technology, one of China's greatest sources of satisfaction so far may be her mastery of the atom, albeit on a small scale so far. This achievement, unfortunately, was purchased by diverting skilled human and valuable industrial resources from other areas of potential economic-technological development.

There is some evidence to suggest also that economic development in the Soviet Union and the West is proceeding in somewhat similar directions. Both capitalism and communism may be seen as attempts at mastering the challenges of the industrial revolution. As these challenges are met, the similarities between the two countries will probably increase, even though some differences remain—including the prohibition against private means of production in the U.S.S.R. The West is coming to appreciate the need for economic planning and welfare programs, state or private, while Russia and the Eastern European countries are recognizing increasingly the inefficiency of excessive centralization with its attendant suppression of initiative and its low standards of living.

This sort of economic convergence may be expected to enhance the prospects for peace, for it would undercut at least one cause for international tension—dogmatic assertions on both sides that coexistence between "opposite" systems cannot endure.[39] The growth of free enterprise and private property in the East should inhibit the totalitarian rule conducive to aggression, while the growth of planning and welfare programs in the West should contribute to stable economic growth and temper egotistic drives. Economic convergence, of course, does not ensure a similar political development, although it may be conducive to it.[40]

Communist China, by contrast, has a lean and hungry look that portends at a minimum a strong desire for change and probably a willingness to gamble to bring about such change. The Chinese economy, which is just beginning to industrialize, offers the rapidly growing population little imminent prospect of improved living standards. The mellowing process known as *embourgeoisement* may already have vitiated revolutionary thrust in Russia but has little base for a similar result in China. Despite or because of the Great Leap Forward, China remains a basically agrarian and underdeveloped country with less in common with Russia than Russia has with the West. Mao's Government—as did Lenin's—feels itself insecure, unable at times even to feed its army, confronted with Herculean tasks of construction, harassed by counterrevolutionary forces along its borders, and ostracized by the broader community of nations. Because of its burgeoning population and recurrent climatic catastrophes, among other reasons, China's problems are in some respects more acute than those of the Soviet regime under Lenin.

POLITICAL INTERESTS

As Mao Tse-tung's interview with Japanese Socialists in 1964 made clear,[41] the Soviet Union's territorial gains during and after World War II leave her highly vulnerable to irredentist and revisionist pressures all around her periphery—from the Far East to East Germany. While Moscow tends on the whole to prefer the preservation of existing frontiers, Peking wants to change them, to move again toward a grand design of a Middle Kingdom, and is calling for the overthrow of existing governments all over the world. Hence the Soviet interest in the kind of proposal for the renunciation of force in the settlement of frontier disputes suggested by Khrushchev on December 31, 1963—even with its possible exclusion of wars of national liberation.[42] Moscow is not unmindful of Peking's displeasure with the territorial provisions of treaties imposed on China by the Tsars (as well as by Stalin), and has already observed China's willingness to use force to revise her Indian boundary.

Moscow, in sharp contrast to Peking, seems to value the preservation of world peace over revolutionary considerations that might be undermined by accommodation with the adversary. One factor in this calculation is that, since about 1961, Moscow seems to have grown pessimistic over the possibility of winning over nonaligned nations and putting them on the road toward Soviet-style socialism. The Cuban case has shown the liabilities and uncertainties that can result from adopting such regimes in a client relationship. The fall of Ben Bella in 1965 made the same point. Kosygin's efforts in January 1966 at conciliating Indian-Pakistani differences over Kashmir may have constituted a landmark in a new course in Soviet policy toward the developing countries, one that sought to reduce Chinese and U.S. influence in these lands, but which also ran parallel to Washington's interest in reducing instabilities that Peking might exploit to accelerate internal and international conflicts.[43]

The Kremlin's policy toward the Vietnamese conflict does not really contradict the foregoing thesis: Kosygin's presence in Hanoi in February 1965 probably indicated a Soviet assumption that the United States would soon withdraw, and that Moscow could gain influence in the area without a high risk of confrontation with U.S. forces. From 1965 to early 1968, the Soviet government was put in an awkward position by the bombing of North Vietnam, but continued to avoid direct engagement with the United States and showed some signs of trying to mediate the conflict. As Peking has pointed out, Russia has done nothing to divert Washington by reopening some European flashpoint.

Elements in Moscow's Middle Eastern strategy have been more adventurist than Soviet foreign policy in other areas. Beginning in 1955, the USSR and her allies have been pumping arms into the Arab states valued at well over $2 billion. Even if it is true, as Soviet diplomats have claimed, that Nasser surprised the Russians in 1967 by ordering the U.N. Emergency Force withdrawn and by closing the Strait of Tiran, Soviet declaratory policy continued to fan Arab passions at a time when the brink of war was quickly approaching. Despite the precipitous nature of Kremlin policy in the area, however, it was Moscow that initiated the use of the hot line to assure the other superpower that it did not intend to become involved in the war. The very intransigence of Moscow's public posture after the Israeli victory implied that the Kremlin's contribution to the Arab cause would be moral and material, but would not risk Soviet intervention. On the other hand, before and after the Arab-Israeli war in 1967, Moscow certainly seemed willing to make large investments of prestige and rubles to gain (or at least try to maintain) Soviet influence in this part of the third world.

There is, of course, no guarantee that Soviet policy may not become more bellicose in some particular part of the globe at some moment when pressures, strengths, and opportunities seem optimal. Nevertheless, the general picture, at least since Stalin's demise, has been that Moscow has usually opted to put priority on maintenance of security on its western front, while doing what it can to promote Soviet interests on the eastern and southern fronts. To this end Moscow has generally endeavored to create a virtue out of necessity—avoidance of war—by arguing, *contra* Peking, that peaceful coexistence is the policy best suited to bring revolution as well as peace and prosperity to the third world. It is not a betrayal of revolutionary interests, as Peking says, but the best and most necessary vehicle for their realization. At the same time, Soviet spokesmen have refused to rule out "non-peaceful" measures as the appropriate means of struggle within other countries, and they have continued to hold that wars of national liberation are necessary to oust colonial occupation regimes. Moreover, as noted earlier, the Kremlin's role in the third world may become more activist with its increased preparation and capability for far-flung military interventions.

Moscow and Peking slant their propaganda line to the emerging nations in different terms. China argues that the main revolutionary front lies in the struggle of the oppressed against the imperialist nations. Being a have-not nation in most senses of the term, China aspires to lead this struggle, appealing to accumulated anti-white and anti-imperialist sentiments and identifying them with Russia. The Soviet Union, in contrast, argues that the main contradiction in present-day politics is between the socialist camp (led by Moscow) and the capitalist. The outcome of this conflict, according to the Kremlin, will be settled by the growing economic might of socialism, a victory that will automatically redound to the political and economic benefit of the emerging nations.[44]

The internal political requirements of the Soviet and the Chinese governments account also for their conflicting views on the utility of moving toward accommodation with the West. Mao's government—like Stalin's at the outset of the Five-Year Plans—magnifies the image of hostile external foes, partly to justify great sacrifices at home. The Kremlin since the death of Stalin apparently has felt that its domestic support will be strongest if it proves the feasibility of the co-existence line. Khrushchev staked the success of his foreign policy upon the possibility and desirability of coming to terms with moderate groups in the West. Khrushchev and his successors have promised the Soviet people peace as well as prosperity, while Mao Tse-tung has called for a struggle against imperialism and for self-abnegation in communist labor. The Soviet regime has seen that limited and gradually increasing contacts with "bourgeois" culture are not necessarily disastrous to political stability but may serve as a useful release valve for mounting internal pressure.

The Chinese Government, however, is much more xenophobic when dealing with Westerners or, for that matter, with the Soviets. If liberalizing movements in Eastern Europe proceed to a certain threshold, of course, the Soviet leaders may behave very conservatively to attempt thwarting alien penetration.

Thus, internal and external political restraints upon China, much more than in the Soviet Union, join with strategic and economic considerations to militate against relaxation of East-West tensions and steps toward arms control. The policy implications of this situation are considered in the following chapter.

XV
Implications for Policy

We have seen that many basic differences between the Soviet and Chinese outlooks arise from the fact that Russia has become a have nation—militarily, politically, economically, and, perhaps most important, psychologically. China, on the other hand, although she now has the prestige of having made several atomic tests, remains a have-not in almost every sense except demographic. This stark reality means that the Soviet regime has a much greater stake in preserving the present order than does China, while Peking has more reason to pursue revolutionary policies involving high risks to bring about the great changes needed to satisfy its interests.

The point is not that the present or any future Soviet Government is absolutely committed to a policy of non-violence and progress toward a disarmed world, but that Russia's interest in stabilizing the international environment is much greater than Peking's—if less than Washington's. If an opportunity were to emerge for Moscow to seek and obtain a commanding power position vis-à-vis the West, the Kremlin might well engage in high-risk policies to attain such a goal. But the present constellation of internal and external conditions facing the Kremlin seems to be conducive to a somewhat cautious and gradualist policy, whereas Peking has been impelled toward a more radical course.

It would be foolhardy, however, to attempt drawing a simple correlation between have or have-not status and general foreign policy orientation. The forces that shape an aggressive or moderate approach to external affairs are complex and variegated, as seen by the shifts in Soviet policy before and after the Cuban missile crisis. Moscow's decision to emplace missiles close to U.S. shores probably aimed chiefly at altering the military balance through a quick fix, economical and dramatic.

If we survey the conditions facing the Kremlin after the showdown in the Caribbean, we find an array of factors apparently characterized by their continuity with the pre-crisis situation, but modified in subtle yet decisive ways. First, Soviet strategic inferiority continued, but now without any foreseeable prospect of sudden improvement. Second, although the same persons continued to hold power in Washington, their resolve as well as their restraint could no longer be doubted. Third, while Chinese-Soviet relations had since 1959 been virtually irreparable, the events of September–October 1962 added a deeper bitterness that seemed to impel both sides more inexorably toward an open break. Fourth, while Khrushchev's domestic opposition remained strong, its back seems to have been broken when Frol Kozlov became ill in April 1963. A fifth condition—the economic scarcities that forced a decision between guns and butter—was still present, but became more decisive in the mood of relaxed tensions between Moscow and the West as 1963 progressed.

Yet, while many of these altered conditions continued in 1964–65 after Khrushchev's fall, his successors showed less interest in arms control agreements with the West. Why? Again, many elements were at work, including new administrations in Washington and Moscow. But one in particular seemed sufficient to account for the retrenchment in Soviet policy: Increased U.S. military activity from Santo Domingo to Vietnam—especially the bombing of a "sister socialist state"—made it extremely difficult for Moscow to retain its preferred revolutionary image while negotiating with Washington to stabilize the military environment.

The following outline, based on study of Soviet policy 1954–68, lists—tentatively—some indicators of a Soviet interest in arms control agreements to stabilize the military environment, as opposed to propaganda gestures designed merely to affect the political climate. The outline does not mean to imply that, should all the indicators be present, Moscow will inexorably search for arms control agreements. But it does suggest the configuration of military, political, and economic conditions likely to attract the Kremlin to move toward such a policy. The list, however, deals mainly with relatively objective factors, the impact of which could vary significantly with the subjective composition of a particular leadership.

SOME INDICATORS OF SOVIET INTEREST IN ARMS CONTROL, 1954–68

A. *Sine Qua Non Requirements*

    1. Soviet possession of a credible deterrent

    2. Arms control arrangements that balance security interests of the signatories

3. Manifest interest in partial measures as opposed to general disarmament
4. A perceived interest in agreements on the part of Western governments' signs in Soviet propaganda that there are "sober forces" in the West

B. *Probably Necessary Requirements*

1. No prospect of radical shift in balance of power to Soviet advantage resulting from technological or political change
2. Arms control arrangements not requiring intensive physical intrusion by foreign inspectors
3. Some fear of increased threat by accretions to U.S., NATO, or F.R.G. forces unless restraints are established by arms control accords
4. Sufficient collective backing in the Soviet Government to permit the regime to commit itself to international agreements with far-reaching consequences
5. Ability and willingness to defend arms control agreements within the international communist movement even if challenged by Peking

C. *Helpful but Not Essential Requirements*

1. "Creative" Marxist-Leninism: emphasis on victory through peaceful competition; talk of collaboration as well as conflict with capitalism
2. Concern for domestic economic development, especially in the consumer sector
3. Use of private negotiating channels as well as public (Intransigence in public forums can be superseded by radical changes in actual negotiating posture while a conciliatory tone in public need not indicate a strong desire for agreement)
4. Approval of the third world for arms control agreements
5. A crisis prior to or during the negotiations which both superpowers want to tranquilize
6. Mutual interests in trade

Arms control, of course, is but one of many goals Moscow has pursued with varying intensity over the years. It has often been used by the Soviets as an instrument for gaining other priority objectives. The following list outlines a number of the policy instruments theoretically available to the Kremlin. The list is arranged to suggest a syndrome of peace, stability, and pragmatism at one end (the top) of the spectrum, and with aggression, revolutionary activism, and dogmatism at the other. Thus, Soviet use of instrument no. 3 (entente with the West) implies more commitment to stability than does instrument no. 8 (technical cooperation), which could well be useful from Moscow's perspective even if the main thrust of Soviet policy were toward revolutionary activism. It is also conceivable that Moscow might pursue arms control proposals in tandem with some more belligerent course, such as military threats (witness the coupling of the second set of the Rapacki Plan proposals and the Berlin "ultimatum" in November 1958), although such a combination might well reduce the prospects of arms control accord. There can be no consistent connection between any of these instruments and a particular "syndrome," however, because each lends itself to diverse uses. Depending on their precise nature, arms control proposals and agreements may be seen as revolutionary or as status quo, offensive or defensive, pragmatic or ideological. The same is true of such aims as "world government," which could be the apotheosis of ideology if understood as the culmination of global communist revolution. Similarly, war might be waged for pragmatic reasons (*Realpolitik*) or for ideological ones (e.g., fear that capitalism might strike first rather than yield without a fight).

Clearly the role of each instrument has fluctuated greatly since 1917 in response to a host of variables, and some—such as world government (in the status quo sense)—have probably received little serious attention. It is also clear that each item on the spectrum could be unfolded to several other categories (e.g., heavy industry development could be useful as a base for propaganda as well as for military power). Finally, as suggested above, the logical position of any item along the spectrum could be altered depending on its mode of implementation (e.g., foreign aid for revolutionary or for stability purposes).

In sum, the main purpose of the listing is not to describe the saliency of one instrument or another in Soviet policy, but to underscore the point that arms control is only one tool in a large armory.

PARTIAL SPECTRUM OF INSTRUMENTS AVAILABLE TO SOVIET FOREIGN POLICY

1. World government
2. Comprehensive arms control agreements
3. Entente with the West and intensive political cooperation
4. Limited arms control agreements
5. Détente and limited political cooperation
6. Foreign economic aid
7. Peace and disarmament propaganda

8. Technical cooperation and foreign trade
9. Developing Soviet consumer good capabilities
10. Developing Soviet technology and heavy industry
11. Strengthening Soviet influence in the communist movement
12. Promoting revolution in the third world
13. Psychologically compelling feats of prowess and force
14. Military-strategic threats for limited purposes (as in Berlin, November 1958)
15. Promoting revolution in the West by non-violent means
16. Military-strategic threats to change internal institutions of other countries
17. Armed intervention abroad
18. Armed attack (following Herman Kahn's "escalation ladder") *

Chinese policy, like Soviet, has also undergone transformations accounted for only in part by Peking's subjective estimate of what is and what ought to be. Peking may lean toward a forward strategy in part because China is basically a have-not nation, but this tendency may not lead to action unless circumstances abroad appear favorable. From 1954 to late 1957 China followed a moderate line, hoping to gain influence among the emerging Asian-African states, though she was then as much a have-not as in late 1957–58 when a tougher line took shape. True, the decision to launch the Great Leap Forward domestically was due in part to disappointing grain deliveries; but China's harsher approach to foreign policy probably stemmed largely from Mao's estimate that the "east wind was now prevailing over the west wind," conveying his judgment that the balance of forces had shifted in favor of the communist camp.

Peking's world view was later buoyed by its 1962 feats in the Himalayas, by China's mastery of the atom, and by the fall of Khrushchev and the dissipation of Soviet influence in international communism, coupled with China's increasing stature in the third world and Asian communism.[1] But if foreign opportunities collapse and alternatives narrow, as happened in mid- to late 1965[2] when Peking's prospects suddenly if temporarily became much dimmer, China might turn inward to concentrate on building her forces for a later attempt at external siege.[3] The rationale might be for Peking, as it was for Russia in the 1920s, that since the time was unripe for revolution abroad, the seeds should be cultivated more tentatively while the main effort is concentrated on developing the base of revolution at home.[4]

Indeed, China's Cultural Revolution in 1966–68 resembled in many

* See Herman Kahn, On Escalation: Metaphors and Scenarios (New York: Praeger, 1965).

respects Stalin's Russia in 1927–28. In each case an internal power struggle was in process; a series of foreign policy defeats had occurred on many fronts; domestic propaganda promoted a war scare even though economic and military planning remained geared to the long run, indicating little real fear of imminent attack from abroad. Meanwhile the psychological and political levers of power in both cases mobilized the population for the sacrifices inherent in an intensive round of industrialization. Neither in China nor in Russia did "turning inward" exclude a high level of verbal hostility, even though actions abroad were somewhat restrained. Curiously, at the same time that Comintern propaganda shifted leftward in 1927–28, Moscow began to take part in League of Nations economic and disarmament conferences.

Here, however, the analogy seems to break down, since Peking has spurned proposals in 1966, –67 and –68 for a world disarmament conference. Nevertheless, it is not excluded that the excesses of the cultural revolution may be followed by a Chinese effort to mend fences, somewhat in the spirit of Bandung, as practiced in the mid-1950s by Chou En-lai.

Historical analogies are of course hazardous in the extreme, and declaratory policy too may be misleading. This latter point is illustrated by the various interpretations made of Chinese Defense Minister Lin Piao's 1965 article, written to commemorate the 20th anniversary of the Chinese triumph over Japan, and entitled "Long Live the Victory of the People's War."[5] Lin Piao appealed for a united front on the part of Asia, Africa, and Latin America—the "rural areas of the world"—to encircle and defeat in protracted conflict the "cities of the world"—North America and Europe. Was Lin's speech just a replay of an old tune or did it have special significance for present policy?[6] Was it a tocsin calling confidently for an intensified struggle or a warning (perhaps to Hanoi) that, although the revolutionary tide was ebbing, morale should not flag?[7]

The fact that Lin's statement amounted to a projection to the international arena of lessons successfully applied in civil war suggests still another reason for the difficulty in assessing China's external objectives and tactics: the tendency of the Chinese communists to draw no sharp distinction between two spheres of conflict—domestic and international. This trait probably reflects a historical tradition of the Middle Kingdom holding a vague suzerainty over its periphery, the long isolation of the Chinese leadership from foreign intercourse, and the success of Mao's protracted conflict with the Japanese on Chinese territory. The attempt to project Mao's strategy abroad may help to account also for the discrepancy between Peking's statements that revolution cannot be exported and its support for "national liberation movements" everywhere.[8]

Faced with such uncertainties, the student of Chinese (and Soviet) politics may do well to heed the admonition of Winston Churchill and seek the explanation of apparent "riddles" and "enigmas" in the "key" of national interest,[9] as the government conceives it. The problems most likely to touch on the vital interests, of course, are the military and economic issues close to issues of national survival. But the observer of communist politics, while he studies ideological programs for indications of the compelling problems agitating the regime, will seek to understand these problems in the perspective of the cultural and political traditions of the regime.

If conditions facing the Chinese regime change in the course of time in the same way that the environment confronting the Kremlin has altered, thus facilitating a mellowing in Soviet doctrine, will Peking's policy be modified as has Moscow's over the years? The Soviet state, like China, was once isolated and insecure. It had few allies and many foes who worked within and outside the country. Russia stood brooding, excluded by her own choice and by the League of Nations and Washington, from the community of nations. As the Soviet government developed a greater stake in the existing order, its concern with security became greater than that with revolution.

Will the same transformation overtake China?[10] It is possible, of course, that China's views toward disarmament may evolve as has Soviet theory, quoting Lenin from 1922 instead of 1916, and even going beyond the limits he saw to collaboration with the adversary. But history does not repeat itself mechanically and the number of variables is legion. In the first place, because China's economic-demographic problems are not likely to be solved in this century, a constant source of frustration, aggressive feeling, and expansionist tendencies will exist. Furthermore, even if China masters her material problems, she could follow the jingoist route taken by many nations, including the United States in 1898.[11] Defense Minister Lin Piao has asserted, in fact, that China will never lose her "fighting will," even though her economy is forging ahead. The Defense Minister may, of course, protest too much, as he contends that to assume any such mellowing process would be "sheer day-dreaming."[12]

Despite the admonitions of the aging rebel generations, most revolutionary movements do seem to lose their momentum in time; and the reduction of internal problems and external threats removes at least some causes of a bellicose foreign policy.[13] The economic cost of attempting to overtake the other nuclear powers militarily may well provide a sharp incentive for China to limit her military investment and concentrate on developing the non-military factors of power in which she, as the world's most populous nation, is potentially very strong. Assuming that China becomes, as Russia now appears, relatively content with the pace and direction of internal and external change, Peking could use issues other than war and peace to challenge the Kremlin's position among the communist and emerging nations. The model of Chinese economic development, for example, might be stressed rather than Peking's defiance of revisionism and paper tigers in order to appeal to Asians, Africans, and Latin Americans.

For the foreseeable future, however, political and economic conditions seem likely to ensure that Peking's views on peace and disarmament will resemble those that prevailed in Russia fifty years ago under Lenin. The cost of procuring and maintaining even a small nuclear arsenal may seem a trifling price to pay for acquiring a kind of symbolic parity with the world's military giants. And, unfortunately, if a greater measure of détente should develop between Moscow and the West, Peking may find it all the harder to concede that her policies need amending.

Notes

CHAPTER I

1. J. Malcolm Mackintosh, "The Soviet Attitude," in Morton H. Halperin, ed., *Sino-Soviet Relations and Arms Control* (Cambridge, Mass.: The M.I.T. Press, 1967), p. 209.

2. Lincoln P. Bloomfield, Walter C. Clemens, Jr., Franklyn Griffiths, *Khrushchev and the Arms Race: Soviet Interests in Arms Control and Disarmament, 1954–1964* (Cambridge, Mass.: The M.I.T. Press, 1966).

3. Alexander George, *Propaganda Analysis: A Study of Inferences Made from Nazi Propaganda in World War II* (Evanston, Ill.: Row, Peterson, 1959), pp. 58–61.

4. Harold Hinton has suggested that Peking made a bid to receive Soviet nuclear weapons immediately after Stalin's death, but was rebuffed. Hinton bases this view on the strongly military composition of the Chinese delegation to Stalin's funeral (March 9, 1953), and the presence in the delegation of Lo Jui-ch'ing, Minister of Public Security, whose opposite number Beria was then in charge of the Soviet nuclear weapons program. A scientific delegation headed by Ch'ien San-ch'iang, Communist China's leading nuclear physicist, had arrived in Moscow on February 25. "By about mid-March it became clear to the Chinese that they would receive no effective support from Stalin's successors, and they accordingly had no choice but to sign a disadvantageous Korean armistice on July 27" (Harold C. Hinton, "The Chinese Attitude," in *Sino-Soviet Relations and Arms Control*, p. 184). By pointing out the connection between the Chinese visit and the Korean War, of course, the author raises the possibility that Peking could have been interested in negotiations on a whole range of issues other than nuclear weapons.

5. The last Chinese scientists left Dubna only in late June 1965. (NCNA [New China News Agency] in English, Peking, June 23, 1965; *SCMP* [Survey of the Chinese Mainland Press], 3486, June 28, 1965). As late as January 1964, however, *Pravda* announced that a new group of staff workers from China had arrived in Dubna to work in the neutron physics laboratory. The Soviet paper added that the Chinese contingent at Dubna "is now larger than any other group of staff members from the countries of people's democracy" (*Pravda*, January 22, 1964, p. 6). Perhaps the Vietnamese crisis in 1965, even more than the polemics of 1963–64, had undermined Sino-Soviet relations to the point where the Chinese scientists either were asked or decided to leave Dubna. In any event North Vietnamese scientists remained at Dubna even after the Chinese departure (Radio Moscow in Vietnamese to Vietnam, September 18, 1965, 1030 GMT).

6. See George A. Modelski, *Atomic Energy in the Communist Bloc* (Melbourne: Melbourne University Press, 1956); SCMP, 1038, April 30–May 2, 1955, p. 16; A. Doak Barnett, "The Inclusion of Communist China in an Arms-Control Program," in Donald G. Brennan, ed., *Arms Control, Disarmament, and National Security* (New York: George Braziller, 1961), pp. 284–91; Anne M. Jonas, "The Soviet Union and the Atom: Peaceful Sharing, 1954–1958" (Santa Monica, Cal.: RAND Corporation, RM-2290, November 20, 1958), p. 88; Lewis A. Frank, "Nuclear Weapons Development in China," *Bulletin of the Atomic Scientists*, XXII, No. 1 (January 1966), pp. 12–14, plus references in the February 1966 issue, p. 28. For a list of monographs and periodical and newspaper articles in the English language on atomic energy research and technology in Mainland China, see "Nuclear Research and Technology in Communist China," External Research Paper 39, U.S. Department of State, July 1963. 7 pp.

7. Document 7 in William E. Griffith, *The Sino-Soviet Rift* (Cambridge, Mass.: The M.I.T. Press, 1964), pp. 340–53, at p. 351.

8. Soviet statement of August 21, 1963, Document 8 in Griffith, *op. cit.*, pp. 354–70, at p. 365.

9. See Robert Guillain's article, "Ten Years of Secrecy," written for *Le Monde*, but appearing also in *Bulletin of the Atomic Scientists*, February 1965, p. 24.

10. There remains a question as to who signed the pact and when. The date of October 15, 1957 specified by Peking preceded by three days the arrival of a Chinese scientific delegation in Moscow. A delegation of the Supreme Soviet was in Peking at the time of the alleged agreement, but was probably too low-ranking to have signed an obligation of this nature. (See Alice L. Hsieh, "The Sino-Soviet Nuclear Dialogue: 1963," *The Journal of Conflict Resolution*, VIII, No. 2 (June 1964), p. 111.) A Chinese military delegation and Mao Tse-tung himself arrived in Moscow in early November. Perhaps secret negotiations by plenipotentiaries, either in Moscow or in Peking, had paved the way for subsequent negotiations to clarify and elaborate an understanding reached on October 15.

11. Alice L. Hsieh, *Communist China's Strategy in the Nuclear Era* (Englewood Cliffs, N.J.: Prentice-Hall, Inc., 1962), pp. 100–101.

12. *Ibid.*, p. 102.

13. *Ibid.*, Chapter II.

14. Harold P. Ford, "Modern Weapons and the Sino-Soviet Estrangement," *The China Quarterly*, No. 18 (April–June 1964), pp. 161–65; see also Ralph L. Powell, "Everyone a Soldier: The Communist Chinese Militia," *Foreign Affairs*, Vol. 39, No. 1 (October 1960), pp. 100–11. Peking's continued infatuation with the militia is suggested by the publication in China's leading newspapers on January 4, 1964 of a new poem by Mao Tse-tung, entitled "Inscription for the Portrait of a Militia Woman," *Peking Review*, VIII, No. 2 (January 10, 1964), p. 3.

15. Klaus Mehnert, *Peking and Moscow* (New York: Putnam's, 1963), p. 436; Ciro E. Zoppo, "The Test Ban: A Study in Arms Control Negotiation" (unpub. Ph.D. dissertation, Columbia University, 1963), pp. 379–80.

16. Arnold Kramish, "The Chinese People's Republic and the Bomb" (Santa Monica, Cal.: RAND Corporation, P-1950, March 23, 1960), p. 5.

17. See Chinese statement of September 6, 1963, Document 10 in Griffith, *op. cit.*, pp. 388–420 at p. 399.

18. Halperin, "Sino-Soviet Nuclear Relations, 1957–1960," in *Sino-Soviet Relations and Arms Control*, p .124.

19. Speech of October 18, 1964, text in *The New York Times*, October 19, 1964, p. 14.

20. See Dwight D. Eisenhower, *Waging Peace* (New York: Doubleday, 1965), pp. 405–408.

21. The abrogation occurred in June 1959; the "unreasonable demands" between February and April 1958, as discussed in Chapter II.

22. Arnold Kramish, "The Great Chinese Bomb Puzzle and a Solution," *Fortune*, LXXIII, No. 6 (June 1966), pp. 157 ff. See also Morton H. Halperin, *China and the Bomb* (New York: Praeger, 1965), pp. 75–80; David R. Inglis, "The Chinese Bombshell," *Bulletin of the Atomic Scientists*, February 1965, pp. 19–21. Similarly, in May 1965, following the second Chinese nuclear explosion, the U.S. Atomic Energy Commission expressed the judgment that the first two Chinese atomic devices had utilized uranium derived from a gaseous diffusion plant or other separation process and not, as some had supposed they would be, from enriched uranium or a reactor handed over by the Russians before 1960. See *The New York Times*, May 21, 1965, p. 7. For the view that the Chinese gaseous diffusion plant was built without Soviet aid, see Frank, *loc. cit.*

23. Zoppo, *op. cit.*, pp. 18–21; Bloomfield, Clemens, Griffiths, *op. cit.*, pp. 244–50, 266.

24. Chinese statement of August 15, 1963, in Griffith, *op. cit.*, p. 352.

25. See Halperin, *loc. cit.*, in *Sino-Soviet Relations and Arms Control*, pp. 134–40.

26. *Ibid.*, pp. 141–42.

27. Even this gap seemed to be reduced by late 1962 to the difference between three and seven on-site inspections. For an account of what appeared to have been Khrushchev's sense that Washington upped its ante after Moscow's concession of three on-site inspections, see Norman Cousins, "Notes on a 1963 Visit with Khrushchev," *Saturday Review*, November 7, 1964, pp. 20–21, 58.

28. Bloomfield, Clemens, Griffiths, *op. cit.*, pp. 152–57.

29. Moscow's statement of August 21, 1963, announced that it could not divulge the results of the Soviet tests during 1961–62, but referred Chinese readers to testimony several days earlier before the U.S. Congress and to statements by the U.S. Joint Chiefs of Staff. (See document in Griffith, *op. cit.*, p. 361.) For more specific Soviet claims, see the editorials in *Krasnaia Zvezda*, September 21, 1963, and in *Pravda*, September 26, 1963, cited in Thomas W. Wolfe, *Soviet Strategy at the Crossroads* (Cambridge, Mass.: Harvard University Press, 1965), p. 323.

30. Halperin, *loc. cit.*, pp. 134–39.

31. A. L. Hsieh, "The Chinese Genie: Peking's Role in the Nuclear Test Ban Negotiations" (Santa Monica, California: RAND Corporation, P-2022, June 20, 1960), pp. 1–2.

32. Radio Moscow, International Service, June 14, 1959, cited in Hsieh, *China's Nuclear Strategy*, p. 165.

33. This summary of Chinese views is based largely on *ibid.*, pp. 103–108, 154–66; see also Eugene Hinterhoff, *Disengagement* (London: Stevens and Sons, 1959).

34. China had deferred comment on the original Rapacki proposals of October 2, 1957 until December 19, 1957, i.e., until after the signing of the defense technology pact, when Peking announced its support of the Soviet Union's recent peace proposals including a nuclear-free zone in Central Europe. In addition, the Chinese welcomed the TASS proposal of January 21, 1958 that the Middle East be turned into an area free of nuclear and rocket bases. Throughout 1958 there were conflicting indicators regarding Peking's view toward a nuclear-free zone in Asia. The president of the Chinese Academy of Sciences stated that he would welcome a conference to (a) establish de-atomized zones; (b) stop flights with nuclear bomb loads; (c) stop nuclear testing; and (d) ban the manufacture, stockpiling, and use of such weapons. This fourth condition, of course, almost negated any semblance of Chinese desire to acquiesce in a de-nuclearized Far East. At other moments in 1958 China approved a nuclear-free zone for Asia and Africa but showed no anxiety over the nth-country problem; rather, there were hints that China planned to become a nuclear power.

35. *Pravda*, January 28, 1959.

36. Hsieh, *op. cit.*, pp. 159–60.

37. Rumania had made a similar proposal in 1957.

38. To round out this picture we should note that in Riga on June 11, 1959 Khrushchev proposed a nuclear and missile-free zone in the Scandinavian peninsula and Baltic area. Either as a result of or despite Khrushchev's suggestion, the governments of Norway and Denmark opted against installing U.S. missile bases on their territories.

In the one contemporary example of formally agreed demilitarization of a significant territory, the Soviet Union, the United States, and ten other countries with interest in Antarctica on December 1, 1959 signed an agreement to use that territory "for peaceful purposes only." The parties obligated themselves not to build military bases there, nor to carry out maneuvers, nor to test weapons, nor to carry out nuclear explosions.

39. Davis A. Charles, "The Dismissal of Marshal P'eng Teh-huai," *The China Quarterly*, No. 8 (October–December 1961), pp. 63–76.

40. See the Chinese statement of August 21, 1963, Document 9, in Griffith, *op. cit.*, p. 382.

41. Griffith, *op. cit.*, pp. 233–34. Moscow's niggardly attitude toward helping China economically was no doubt one reason why Peking decided finally to go it alone. From 1950 to 1957 the Soviet Union gave China about $790 million in grant aid, and extended Peking about $1.3 billion in credits, which China began to repay in 1956. Contrary to the implications of the 1957 Moscow Declaration, as one author has put it, "the relatively well-to-do Communist West failed to carry out [its] fraternal socialist obligations toward the Communist East. This was fateful. It brought about the division of the Marxist world into a Communist West ruled by Russia, and a disillusioned, dissenting, bellicose, needy, Communist East ruled by China." Through 1962 China had received only 13 percent of Russian aid to the bloc and 8 percent of total Soviet economic aid credits. In terms of overall economic assistance, China has received less aid from Moscow than East Germany, Poland, or India. (Frank O'Brien, *Crisis in World Communism: Marxism in Search of Efficiency* [New York: The Free Press, 1965], pp. 119–20.) In contrast to the 1957 Moscow statement, the CPSU Party Program adopted in 1961 noted that the different economic and cultural levels from which the socialist countries began their development "predetermines the non-simultaneous completion of socialist construction in these countries and their

non-simultaneous entry into the fullscale construction of communism. . . . (*The New York Times*, August 1, 1961.) The Soviets have put the blame for the radical decline in material and cultural transactions between China and the CMEA partners on the "nationalist" leadership in Peking. The Russians have also observed that, by 1966, 57 per cent of China's foreign trade was with capitalist countries. See *Kommunist*, No. 8 (May 31, 1968), pp. 95–108.

42. NCNA English, Moscow, February 4, 1960 (*SCMP* 2194, February 11, 1960, pp. 42–46, at p. 44).

43. For text, see G. F. Hudson, Richard Lowenthal, and Roderick MacFarquhar, *The Sino-Soviet Dispute* (New York: Praeger, 1961), pp. 82–112. The Kremlin replied almost immediately, when Otto Kuusinen told a Lenin anniversary meeting at the Moscow sports palace that those who opposed the CPSU's "creative development" of Leninism with respect to matters of war and peace were adopting a "dogmatic" position. He rejected the argument that minimized the significance of nuclear weapons on the ground that man, not technique, determined history. (*Ibid.*, pp. 116–22.)

44. Resolution of the National People's Congress, January 21, 1960, reported in NCNA, January 21, 1960, in *SCMP*, 2185, p. 4.

CHAPTER II

1. Variants of this view have been advanced, e.g., by a number of British analysts, including J. Malcolm Mackintosh. See his "The Soviet Attitude," in Morton H. Halperin, ed., *Sino-Soviet Relations and Arms Control* (Cambridge, Mass.: The M.I.T. Press, 1967), pp. 203–13.

2. Chinese statement of September 6, 1963, Document 10 in William E. Griffith, *The Sino-Soviet Rift* (Cambridge, Mass.: The M.I.T. Press, 1964), pp. 388–420 at p. 399.

3. BBC Summary of World Broadcasts, Part 3, FE/1488, as reported in *The China Quarterly*, No. 18 (April–June 1964), p. 238. A participant in the Moscow Conference in 1960 heard reports that Peking had earlier refused "the Soviet government permission to build a joint early warning radar station that would be used to defend Pacific waters, Chinese and Soviet, for mutual protection." (Elizabeth Gurley Flynn, "Recollections of the 1960 Conferences," *Political Affairs* [New York], Vol. XLII, No. 11 [November 1963], p. 30.)

4. Edward Crankshaw, "Sino-Soviet Rift Held Very Deep," *The Washington Post*, February 12, 1961; Raymond L. Garthoff, "Sino-Soviet Military Relations," *Annals of the American Academy of Political and Social Science*, Vol. 349 (September 1963), p. 87. Alice L. Hsieh, "The Sino-Soviet Nuclear Dialogue," *Journal of Conflict Resolution*, VIII, No. 2 (June 1964), p. 111.

5. See Mackintosh, *loc. cit.*, pp. 206–10 and note 22.

6. Harold P. Ford, "Modern Weapons and the Sino-Soviet Estrangement," *The China Quarterly*, No. 18 (April–June 1964), pp. 162 ff. See also Donald Zagoria, *The Sino-Soviet Conflict, 1956–1961* (Princeton, N.J.: Princeton University Press, 1962), pp. 189–94.

7. Chinese statement of September 6, 1963, *loc. cit.*

8. *Life*, Vol. 47, No. 2, July 13, 1959, p. 36. In 1959 the Vietnamese Communist leader Ho Chi-minh had been quoted as saying, "In the not distant future the Chinese as well will have atomic bombs" (*L'Unita* [Rome], July 1, 1959). In July–August

1958 Moscow appears to have planted rumors in East European capitals that it was giving or had already given atomic weapons and ballistic missiles to China. Whether the purpose was to inhibit the U.S. response to Peking's subsequent probing in the Taiwan Straits, to prod the U.S. into a nuclear test ban, or some other motive, is a matter for speculation. For additional information on Soviet aid to China's missile program, based on Chinese sources, see Alice L. Hsieh, "China's Secret Military Papers: Military Doctrine and Strategy," *China Quarterly*, No. 18 (April–June 1964), p. 122.

9. Interview with Cyrus Sulzberger, *The New York Times*, September 8, 1961.

10. See Morton H. Halperin, "Sino-Soviet Nuclear Relations, 1957–1960," in *Sino-Soviet Relations and Arms Control, op. cit.*, pp. 117–44; and, in the same volume, Harold C. Hinton, "The Chinese Attitude," p. 176.

11. For a listing of China's reactions to Soviet proposals on general disarmament, a nuclear test ban, nuclear free zones and other arms control measures—skewed, however, so as to exaggerate the extent of Sino-Soviet solidarity prior to late 1962—see the article by the Nationalist Chinese law professor Hungdah Chiu, "Communist China's Attitude Towards Nuclear Tests," *The China Quarterly*, No. 21 (January–March 1965), pp. 96–104.

12. On selective perception in foreign policy-making, see, e.g., Ithiel de Sola Pool and Allan Kessler, "The Kaiser, the Tsar, and the Computer: Information Processing in a Crisis," *American Behaviorial Scientist*, VIII, No. 91 (May 1965), pp. 31–38.

13. See Halperin, *loc. cit.*, p. 134.

14. *People's Daily*, November 1, 1958, in *ibid.*, p. 139.

15. Statement of August 15, 1963, Document 7 in Griffith, *op. cit.*, pp. 340–53 at p. 352.

16. This view was first developed in the author's "The Test Ban and Sino-Soviet Relations," Cambridge, Mass.: Harvard University Center for International Affairs, 1965, mimeo., prepared for the Conference on Sino-Soviet Relations and Arms Control, August 30–September 4, 1965, pp. 5–6.

17. See the "Resolution of the Plenary Session of the Party Central Committee—On the Anti-Party Group of B. M. Molotov, L. M. Kaganovich and V. M. Molotov," *Pravda*, July 4, 1957, pp. 1–2; *CDSP*, Vol. IX, No. 23 (July 17, 1957), pp. 5–7; see also, "For a Leninist Peace Policy," *International Affairs*, No. 7, 1957, pp. 5–10.

18. For the November 1957 Moscow meeting, see Griffith, *op. cit.*, pp. 17, 396–98, 415–17, 445, and, more recently, Suslov in *Pravda*, April 3, 1964, and "The Proletarian Revolution and Khrushchev's Revisionism—Comment on the Open Letter of the CPSU (VIII)," *People's Daily* and *Red Flag*, March 31, 1964, and *Peking Review*, Vol. VII, No. 14 (April 3, 1964), pp. 5–23.

19. The author wishes to acknowledge the suggestions of Zbigniew Brzezinski in developing these alternative scenarios.

20. See the previous chapter.

21. This view is maintained by Hsieh, "The Sino-Soviet Nuclear Dialogue," *loc. cit.*, pp. 111–12. On the other hand, Robert Guillain probably gives a too narrow estimate of Soviet aid when saying that the 1957 "agreement was probably implemented, at the very most, only by some scientific documentation and the residence of Chinese scientists in Russian atomic establishments" (Guillain, "Ten Years of Secrecy," *Bulletin of the Atomic Scientists*, February 1965, p. 24).

22. Such an interpretation has been offered by several students of decision-making with whom the various aspects of the puzzle have been discussed. None of them, however, were specialists in Soviet or Chinese affairs. But one variant of this thesis has been suggested by Morton H. Halperin: "Khrushchev undoubtedly was interested in securing at least the neutrality, and if possible the support, of the Chinese Communist Party in his effort to deal with opposition in the Soviet Union. His willingness to grant nuclear aid to China might have been part of his effort to insure Chinese neutrality and possibly to convince the Peking leadership that their own security would be enhanced if Khrushchev emerged the dominant figure in the Soviet hierarchy" (Halperin, *loc. cit.*, p. 122). See also *The New York Times*, May 21, 1965, which reports that Soviet diplomats told Western officials about the existence of a pro-Chinese faction before 1960.

23. See, e.g., Wolfgang Leonhard, *The Kremlin Since Stalin* (New York: Frederick A. Praeger, 1962), pp. 242 ff.

24. He was in Yugoslavia and Albania from early to late October—during the time when the defense technology pact was allegedly signed.

25. Molotov had a reputation, dating from the Stalin era, of taking a consistently hard line toward China.

26. See Chapter I.

27. Edward Crankshaw, *Khrushchev: A Career* (New York: The Viking Press, Inc., 1966), pp. 235–36; see also p. 270.

28. A hope that a test ban might be useful in halting nuclear proliferation was suggested in the answer by Mikoyan to a question by a Norwegian student in February 1960. Asked what effects the recent French atomic explosion would have on "peaceful coexistence," and whether it would lead Communist China to desire possession of atomic bombs, Mikoyan replied: "We wish to forbid all atomic tests." He reportedly went on: "If there will be no agreement on this, China may have atomic weapons. The sooner we get an agreement the greater are the chances that there will be no more explosions." (*Arbeiderbladet* [Oslo], February 15, 1960, cited in A. Doak Barnett, "The Inclusion of Communist China in an Arms-Control Program," in Donald G. Brennan, ed., *Arms Control, Disarmament, and National Strategy* [New York: George Braziller, 1961], pp. 294–95.)

29. The failure of the U.N. Disarmament Subcommittee to reach an agreement on a nuclear test ban in spring and summer 1957 may have led Moscow to believe that such a treaty was infeasible, possibly because certain U.S. officials—especially Secretary of State Dulles—would scuttle any agreement. (On the possible connection between the denigration of Harold Stassen, the President's Special Assistant for Disarmament, by Dulles, and the breakup of the Disarmament Subcommittee by the Russians in August 1957, see Bernhard G. Bechhoefer, *Postwar Negotiations for Arms Control* [Washington: The Brookings Institution, 1961], pp. 399–408.) A pessimistic Soviet estimate of this nature could have helped to lower the Kremlin's resistance to Chinese requests for nuclear assistance in October 1957. In 1958, however, the prospects of Soviet-Western nuclear test ban agreement seemed to improve, perhaps adding to the Kremlin's afterthoughts about aiding China.

30. The research reactors given to China and Yugoslavia by Moscow utilized fuel uranium enriched with only 2 per cent U-235, while the reactors in the satellites, where Russia exercised firmer control, were standard Soviet models using fuel enriched with 10 per cent U-235 (a grade which, if diverted, could be reprocessed far more easily to weapons grade than can 2 per cent material). Furthermore, despite

Chinese claims as early as 1956 that "atomic power stations" would be built in China with Soviet assistance, in late 1959 Peking was still quite vague on how it would acquire such reactors. See Barnett, *loc. cit.*, p. 293. On the apparent reluctance of Moscow to proceed with full speed in assisting China's nuclear program, see Zagoria, *op. cit.*, pp. 170–71; Leonard Beaton and John Maddox, *The Spread of Nuclear Weapons* (New York: Praeger, 1962), pp. 121–35. Moscow may also have over-extended its commitments in Eastern Europe, perhaps intentionally so as to obtain temporary bargaining power. Soviet pledges to aid various CMEA countries, made in 1955–56, have been only partially fulfilled or not at all, or long delayed. See Jaroslav G. Polach, "Nuclear Power in East Europe," *East Europe*, XVII, No. 5 (May 1968), pp. 3–12.

31. To be sure, Moscow's pressure for a German peace treaty initiated in November 1958 reflected an increased confidence in Russia's bargaining position. But Soviet military force—conventional and nuclear—was much stronger in Europe than in Asia, and tensions over Berlin could be managed from Moscow much more readily than those which Peking might provoke in the Far East.

32. Zagoria, *op. cit.*, p. 168; Ford, *loc. cit.*, pp. 161–62.

33. In addition to its probable anxieties regarding China, the Kremlin showed increasing concern over Western plans to defend Europe with "tactical" nuclear weapons.

34. "On the Struggle of the CPSU for the Solidarity of the International Communist Movement," Report by M. A. Suslov on February 14, 1964, at the Plenum of the CPSU Central Committee, *Pravda*, April 3, 1964.

35. The Kremlin may have judged in 1957 that additional nuclear powers would appear sooner and in greater numbers in the West than in the communist bloc. A study of the "Nth" country problem undertaken in 1958 listed the following countries as *able* to embark on a successful nuclear weapons program in the near future: Belgium, Canada, Communist China, Czechoslovakia, France, West Germany, East Germany, India, Italy, Japan, Sweden, and Switzerland. Countries that were economically and technically capable but which were more limited in scientific manpower were Australia, Austria, Denmark, Finland, Hungary, The Netherlands, Poland, and Yugoslavia. See *The Nth Country Problem and Arms Control*, Planning Pamphlet No. 108 (Washington: National Association, 1960), pp. 27–28. In retrospect it may appear that Moscow's opposition to the M.L.F. was also short-sighted, for the Soviet position may have helped thwart a plan for nuclear sharing within NATO, only to have contributed to a German desire for unilateral acquisition of nuclear weapons. Or, to take a different tack, Washington's concern to appease its allies' nuclear desires by such measures as the M.L.F. may only have stimulated these ambitions and rendered them less quenchable.

36. A participant in many official and private conferences with Soviet representatives has written that a major political reason for Moscow's reluctance to accept international inspection is the "pressure from the Russian equivalent of the American military-industrial clique. . . ." This pressure is cited by "many Russian officials and advocates of disarmament . . . as the main cause of Soviet intransigence on the inspection issue." See Jerome B. Wiesner, *Where Science and Politics Meet* (New York: McGraw-Hill Book Company, 1965), pp. 170–71.

CHAPTER III

1. Chinese Government statement of August 15, 1963, given in William E. Griffith, *The Sino-Soviet Rift* (Cambridge, Mass.: The M.I.T. Press, 1964), p. 352.

2. *Ibid.*, p. 351.

3. *Ibid.*, p. 351.

4. See appendices to *People of the World, Unite, for the Complete, Thorough, Total and Resolute Prohibition and Destruction of Nuclear Weapons!* (Peking: Foreign Languages Press, 1963), pp. 127–35.

5. ENDC/PV.76, August 29, 1962, pp. 14–23; ENDC/PV.79, September 3, 1962, pp. 72 and 78–80. See also Verbatim Records of September 5, 1962.

6. (Russian Edition), September 8, 1962.

7. *Pravda*, October 2, 1962.

8. NCNA English, Peking, September 12, 1962. (*SCMP* 2820, September 18, 1962, pp. 30–31.) This policy statement crowned a series of declarations on disarmament in which nuclear test cessation was generally made dependent on the banning of nuclear weapons. See Ciro E. Zoppo, "The Test Ban: A Study in Arms Control Negotiation," unpublished Ph.D. dissertation, Columbia University, 1963, p. 385.

9. Chinese Government statement of August 15, 1963, in Griffith, *op. cit.*, at pp. 351–52.

10. The Chinese statement hinted that Moscow's views had been criticized many times before 1962, at least by silence. According to Peking the Soviet leaders after 1956 "were wrong on certain (disarmament) issues and correct on others, and we supported them in all their correct views." Text in Griffith, *op. cit.*, at 352.

11. See the materials in Alexander Dallin, ed., *Diversity in International Communism: A Documentary Record, 1961–1963* (New York: Columbia University, 1963), pp. 664–829. For discussion of the Bulgarian, Hungarian, Czechoslovak, Italian and East German Party Congresses, and the Sino-Soviet ideological exchanges of December–January and February–March, 1963, see Griffith, *op. cit.*, pp. 67–104.

12. Griffith, *op. cit.*, p. 162.

13. As early as February 1963, however, *People's Daily* charged that Khrushchev's unilateral abrogation (at some unspecified time) of "hundreds" of agreements and contracts concluded with China constituted an extension of "ideological differences to state relations . . ." (*The New York Times*, February 27, 1963, p. 1).

The major exchanges over the test ban treaty were attributed to the Soviet and Chinese "governments" rather than to the respective "parties." See the Chinese statements of July 31, August 2 and 15, and September 1, 1963. (Texts in *People of the World, Unite for the Complete, Thorough, Total and Resolute Prohibition and Destruction of Nuclear Weapons!* [Peking: Foreign Languages Press, 1963].) Of course Party newspapers and mass meetings in both the USSR and China parroted the lines of their "governments."

The flavor of the controversy may be seen from the title of Peking's communication of August 15, 1963: "Statement by the Spokesman of the Chinese Government—A Comment on the Soviet Government's Statement of August 3." The CPR note was characterized by the Soviet Government as "slanderous and hostile." (*The New York Times*, August 22, 1963, p. 15.)

In contrast to the *People of the World* volume cited above, two other books published by Peking's Foreign Languages Press include primarily "party" statements: *Workers of All Countries, Unite, Oppose our Common Enemy!* (1963); and *The Polemic of the General Line of the International Communist Movement* (1965). The latter work gives the June 14, 1963 letter, the nine replies made by the Chinese Party to the CPSU letter of July 14, 1963, and the November 21, 1964 statement, "Why Khrushchev Fell." The Soviet Party letters of March 30 and July 14, 1963 are given as appendices. One difference between the 1965 and the 1963 documentary collections was that the former used surrogates (e.g., Italy or Yugoslavia) instead of naming names.

14. On September 21, 1962, Foreign Minister Gromyko modified the soviet GCD proposal (to China's disfavor) by allowing for a limited nuclear umbrella to be retained by the two superpowers in Stage I instead of insisting upon the complete destruction of all such weapons at the very outset of the disarmament process (United Nations Document A/PV.1127, September 25, 1962, pp. 38–40).

Moscow's concessions in the arms control negotiations still left the Soviet Union and the United States far from agreement, even on a test ban. Perhaps the concessions were to parallel other moves designed to tranquilize official Washington before it woke up to the fait accompli of Soviet missiles emplaced in Cuba. Alternatively, Moscow may have conceived a complementarity: compromise arms control agreements in exchange for U.S. acquiescence in a more credible parity resulting from Russian MRBMs along the coast of Cuba. In any event we are left with this puzzling situation: that Moscow chose to alienate Peking further by the message concerning nonproliferation at the very time the Kremlin most needed to bolster its alliance prior to the Cuban showdown. A partial answer may lie in internal contradictions within the Kremlin that precluded any completely logical strategy toward either the East or the West.

15. The announcement came on December 19, 1962 (*Documents on Disarmament, 1962* [2 vols; Washington, D.C.: U.S. Arms Control and Disarmament Agency, 1963] II, 1239–42). It was preceded on December 3 and 10 by Moscow's public espousal of the idea of utilizing automatic seismic stations—"two or three" on the territory of the states possessing nuclear weapons, particularly in areas prone to earthquakes (ENDC/PV. 90, December 10, 1962, pp. 23–25).

16. Peking may well have inferred from President Kennedy's announcement on June 10, 1963, to the effect that test ban negotiations would commence soon in Moscow, that the Soviets had decided to sign a treaty with the West. However, the Chinese claim to have been informed by Moscow "as late as June 9, 1963 . . . that the Western powers' position on the halting of nuclear tests could not yet serve as a basis for agreement, and that whether negotiations could yield any results depended entirely on the Western powers." A similar statement by Khrushchev in a press conference on June 15, 1963, is cited also in the same Chinese document; but its mention suggests that the Soviet communication of June 9 was merely intended to inform Peking before the announcement by President Kennedy of the impending negotiations, and implied no particular Soviet commitment to China (Chinese Government Statement of August 15, 1963, in Griffith, *op. cit.*, p. 341). While Peking later referred to the American University speech as "Kennedy's Big Conspiracy" (*Peking Review*, VI, No. 26 [June 28, 1963], pp. 12–14), the first Chinese report on the address was neutral. The Peking Home Service toward the end of its bulletin on international news at 1500 GMT, June 11, 1963, reported briefly that, according to TASS, Khrushchev, Kennedy, and Macmillan had agreed to a meeting in Moscow in mid-July with representatives of their three countries to resume talks on banning nuclear tests. NCNA also carried a similar report (BBC FE/1273/i, June 30, 1963).

17. Emphasis added. The divergent expectations of both sides and the general uncertainties were reflected in the fact that seismologists in the U.S. delegation to the Moscow negotiations were reportedly unable to find their Russian counterparts in town.

For discussion of W. Averell Harriman's role in encouraging the President to make an effort toward détente and a test ban, see Robert F. Kennedy, "Foreword," in Walter C. Clemens, Jr., ed., *Toward a Strategy of Peace* (Chicago: Rand McNally & Co., 1965), pp. xiii–xiv. For analysis of the speech and the Soviet response, see the editor's Introduction, especially pp. 10–11.

18. But Moscow's representative had declared already on April 5 that his government agreed to this U.S. proposal "immediately without waiting for general and complete disarmament" (ENDC/PV. 118, April 5, 1963, p. 52).

The Chinese reaction to the hot line agreement was not especially hostile. On June 21, 1963 NCNA at 1530 GMT and the Peking Home Service at 1600 GMT both reported the agreement without comment (BBC FE/1282/i, June 24, 1963).

CHAPTER IV

1. Emphasis added. Also in *Izvestiia*, August 22, 1963. For a similar reaction by officials in Washington, see *The New York Times*, August 16, 1963, p. 1. Interviews with leading communists from Italy and Yugoslavia in 1961 and 1962 specified disarmament as a fundamental area of disagreement between Moscow and Peking. See interview with Velio Spano in *L'Unita* (Rome), December 23, 1961, quoted in William E. Griffith, *Albania and the Sino-Soviet Rift* (Cambridge: The M.I.T. Press, 1963), and interview with Marshal Tito by Drew Pearson in *Review of International Affairs* (Belgrade), September 1962, p. 32.

2. *New Times*, No. 35 (September 4, 1963), p. 1.

3. See, e.g., Max Beloff, *The Foreign Policy of Soviet Russia* (2 vols; London: Oxford University Press, 1949), Vol. I, pp. 249–70; also, Vladimir Petrov, "A Missing Page in Soviet Historiography: The Nazi-Soviet Partnership," *Orbis*, XI, No. 4 (Winter 1968), pp. 1113–38.

4. As described in the article, "Concerning Mao Tse-tung's Talk with a Group of Japanese Socialists," *Pravda*, September 2, 1964, p. 2. Conflicts along the Central Asian frontier, though rumored earlier, were not admitted publicly by Peking or Moscow until 1963 after the Moscow Treaty signing. But already on March 7, 1963, *People's Daily* declared that Khrushchev's taunts about China's allowing "imperialists" to remain in Hong Kong and Macao were opening the subject of all the old treaties imposed upon China in the nineteenth century by Russia as well as by the Western countries. Peking stated it hoped to settle these "outstanding issues" with Russia by negotiation (*The New York Times*, March 9, 1963, p. 1).

5. To be sure, the cessation or prohibition of nuclear testing would have to be on terms acceptable to Moscow, with little or no on-site inspection, if only because of Khrushchev's internal opposition. See Bloomfield, Clemens, Griffith, *op. cit.;* also Jerome B. Wiesner, *Where Science and Politics Meet* (New York: McGraw-Hill, 1965), pp. 170–71. That Moscow broke the nuclear test moratorium in September 1961 does not contradict the foregoing argument, for that decision probably stemmed from a situation unexpected as late as 1959 or 1960, i.e., that U.S. ICBM production would far outstrip Soviet, thereby encouraging Soviet tests of warheads much larger than those of the U.S. in order to offset Washington's numerical advantage. This line of thinking was reinforced by the Berlin crisis in the summer of 1961.

6. Among the other considerations are: the lack of any prospect after the Cuban debacle to alter radically the balance of strategic weapons: Kennedy's apparent resistance to domestic pressures to exploit further the Soviet retreat; the mounting economic troubles facing the Soviet leadership; Khrushchev's need to have a tangible

victory for his coexistence line, coupled with the incapacitating illness in mid-April 1963 of one of its major opponents, Frol Kozlov.

The partial test ban treaty Moscow agreed to in July 1963 was quite similar to one of two alternative proposals the United States offered on August 27, 1962. As noted earlier, Moscow's counterproposal on August 29, 1962 called for a partial test ban with an unpoliced, indefinite moratorium on underground testing, a proviso unacceptable to the United States. Even though the August 29, 1962 Soviet proposal was rejected by the West, however, Soviet propaganda treated it as a major concession; and Peking claims it was informed on August 25, 1962 of Moscow's intention to sign a nonproliferation treaty.

7. For a comparative analysis and documents, see Walter C. Clemens, Jr., ed., *World Perspectives on International Politics* (Boston: Little, Brown and Company, 1965), pp. 41–47, 57–155.

8. The Soviet action was likened to "another Munich." *Peking Review*, V, No. 45 (November 9, 1962), pp. 12–13.

9. *Peking Review*, VI, No. 1 (January 4, 1963), VI, No. 9 (March 1, 1963); VI, No. 10/11 (March 15, 1963).

10. See articles on the congress in *Pravda*, June 24, 25, 27, 29, 30 and July 1, 2, 1963; *Izvestiia*, June 24 and 28, 1963; *Peking Review*, July 5, 19, 26, 1963.

11. The Chinese delegation received a hero's welcome when it returned to Peking. *People's Daily* of July 22, 1963 pictured Mao Tse-tung himself at the airport, and listed the names of many other officials who attended the reception, some of them having been in semi-exile theretofore. However, the jet aircraft pictured in the background bore the conspicuous marking "CCCP [USSR]."

12. *The New York Times*, May 13, 1964.

13. Griffith, *The Sino-Soviet Rift*, p. 101.

14. *People's Daily*, July 29, 1963, p. 3.

15. Bloomfield, Clemens, Griffiths, *op. cit.* See especially Part III.

CHAPTER V

1. Document 8 in Griffith, *op. cit.*, p. 361.

2. See Chapter VIII.

3. Some of the same statements containing these arguments, however, also cast doubt on the continued validity of the Sino-Soviet alliance. Because China had revealed military secrets, its assurances could no longer be trusted; and the Soviet Government stated it would "draw its own conclusions" (statement of August 21, 1963, in Griffith, *op. cit.*, p. 365).

4. Peking claimed the CPR "always stands for general disarmament and resolutely stands for the complete prohibition and destruction of nuclear weapons" (statement of July 31, 1963, in Griffith, *op. cit.*, p. 328). On the need for struggle, see the CPR Statement of August 15, 1963, in Griffith, *op. cit.*, p. 350.

5. See Chapter I, note 29.

6. Moscow in Italian to Italy, October 12, 1963, 1900 GMT. Soviet news agencies were earlier directed not to publish a statement by J. D. Bernal, President of the World Peace Council, charging that the U.S. resumption of underground testing was "an affront to humanity" and "a direct blow against the spirit of the agreement." See Bloomfield, Clemens, Griffiths, *op. cit.*, p. 155.

7. Mandarin upsmanship is keenly demonstrated by three appendices to the booklet *People of the World, op. cit.*: "Excerpts from Previous Statements of Khrushchev on the Question of Banning Nuclear Tests"; "Excerpts from Previous Statements and Memorandums of the Soviet Government on the Question of Banning Nuclear Tests"; and "From Concession to Capitulation—the Record of the Soviet Government in the Negotiations for Halting Nuclear Tests" (*ibid.*, pp. 136–62).

8. See Walter C. Clemens, Jr., *Outer Space and Arms Control* (Cambridge, Mass.: The M.I.T. Center for Space Research, 1966) [processed], pp. 41–69.

9. Interview with Harry Shapiro, United Press International, text in *Pravda* and *Izvestiia*, December 31, 1963, p. 1.

10. *Izvestiia*, December 15, 1963; *Pravda*, December 16, 1963. The published outlay for defense in 1963 was 13.9 billion rubles, that is, 10 per cent more than in 1962. This sum, according to Khrushchev's announcement in mid-December 1963, would be reduced to 13.3 billion rubles, a reduction of about 5 per cent. In 1965 the official Soviet military budget declined to 12.8 billion rubles. According to the annual reports of the Institute for Strategic Studies, London, the total size of Soviet forces remained at 3,300,000 men in 1964, but dropped to about 3,150,000 men in 1965. See *The Military Balance, 1964–1965* (1964), p. 3, and *The Military Balance, 1965–1966* (1965), p. 2.

11. Texts in *Toward a Strategy of Peace, op. cit.*, pp. 214–18.

12. The Kremlin's alarm at Mao Tse-tung's attitude toward revision of frontiers was clearly demonstrated in the Soviet response to Mao's interview with Japanese Socialists (cf. *Pravda*, September 2, 1964), as discussed in Chapter XIV. But speeches by Khrushchev (December 22, 1963) and Suslov (February 14, 1964) showed concern also over violence between emerging nations and between them and Western powers. One observer suggests that Moscow "apparently regarded prevention of local wars, in return for Soviet aid, as part of a package deal." The countries which Khrushchev and Suslov cited as examples of Russian support—Algeria, Indonesia, Yemen, Panama, Cyprus, Vietnam, Zanzibar, and East Africa—were instances where "arms had been utilized only for purposes of political demonstration, guerrilla infiltration, or 'domestic' conflict, but never for full war between two nations." (Uri Ra'anan, "Tactics in the Third World: Contradictions and Dangers," *Survey*, No. 57 [October 1965], pp. 32–33.) For an interpretation arguing that Moscow hoped to win influence in the third world through its apparent escape clause for national liberation wars, see Helmut Sonnenfeldt, "International Consequences of the Sino-Soviet Dispute," in *International Communism After Khrushchev*, ed. L. Labedz (Cambridge, Mass.: The M.I.T. Press, 1965), pp. 205–16 at p. 208.

13. Published in *Izvestiia*, January 4, 1964, pp. 1–2.

14. "Why Mislead?" *Pravda*, January 30, 1964.

15. *The New York Times*, July 5, 1964, section IV, p. 9; for U.S. and British comment, see *ibid.*, July 8, August 7, and August 30, 1964. For a reaffirmation of Moscow's interest in this measure, see N. Pitersky, "On the Establishment of International United Nations Forces," *Disarmament* (Paris), No. 5 (March 1965), pp. 5–8. Foreign Minister Gromyko reiterated on September 24, 1965, Moscow's insistence that all U.N. peacekeeping actions be subjected to Security Council approval, including the affirmative votes of the permanent members (U.N. Doc. A/PV.1335, September 24, 1965, p. 32).

16. For a review of the manner in which Western interests would be helped or

hindered by implementation of the Soviet proposal, see Walter C. Clemens, Jr., "Implications for United States Policy," in *Toward a Strategy of Peace*, pp. 195–97.

17. Following the Moscow Treaty, however, it was rumored that the United States proposed and Russia rejected a nonproliferation agreement that would in some way deter or eliminate China's nuclear capacity. For a suggestion that the Administration intended to use the test ban as a step toward the broader objective of stopping China's nuclear program, see Stewart Alsop, "Affairs of State: The Real Meaning of the Test Ban," *Saturday Evening Post*, September 28, 1963, p. 20. See also the *Washington Post* report, October 2, 1964, p. A21. It seems highly unlikely, however, that Moscow ever seriously considered a pre-emptive strike either with the United States or unilaterally, although it may have welcomed unilateral U.S. action in 1963–64. But it is also doubtful whether Harriman did more than to raise with Khrushchev in 1963 the possible impact of a future Chinese bomb or the durability of the Moscow Treaty. See also Arthur M. Schlesinger, Jr., *A Thousand Days* (Boston: Houghton Mifflin Co., 1965), pp. 904, 906, 908.

CHAPTER VI

1. *Communist China and Arms Control* (New York: Praeger, 1965), p. 170.

2. See Griffith, *The Sino-Soviet Rift*, pp. 177–202; for a comprehensive listing of parties with their respective allegiances and factions as of late 1964, see "International Communism: The End of an Epoch," *Survey*, No. 54 (January 1965), pp. 190–96.

3. Halperin and Perkins, *op. cit.*, pp. 269–70.

4. The expulsion is reported in *Akahata*, May 23, 1964, translated in *Peking Review*, VII, No. 22 (May 29, 1964), pp. 17–21. For the exchange of correspondence, see *Partiinaia Zhizn'*, No. 14, July 1964, pp. 8–9 and *Akahata*, August 8, 1964 and September 2, 1964 in *Peking Review*, VII, No. 37 (September 11, 1964), pp. 27–28 and VII, No. 38 (September 18, 1964), pp. 12–19. For a sample of the Japanese Communist Party's intransigent position vis-à-vis the CPSU, see Kenji Miyamoto's report to the Ninth Congress of the J.P.C., in *Akahata*, November 25, 1964. For a more general discussion of Japanese attitudes toward China's first atomic tests, see Chapters VIII and IX.

5. The analysis that follows draws mainly on William E. Griffith, *Sino-Soviet Relations, 1964–1965* (Cambridge, Mass.: The M.I.T. Press, 1967).

6. *Pravda*, April 3, 1964.

7. See Peking's seventh "Comment" entitled "The Leaders of the CPSU Are the Greatest Splitters of Our Times," *Peking Review*, VIII, No. 6 (February 6, 1964), pp. 5–21.

8. "Statement on the Stand of the Rumanian Workers' Party Concerning the Problems of the World Communist and Working-Class Movement," Bucharest: Meridiane, 1964.

9. Text in *The New York Times*, September 5, 1964.

10. Griffith, *Sino-Soviet Relations*, p. 36.

11. Peking's interpretation as to "Why Khrushchev Fell," cited as one of his errors his call on July 30, 1964 for an "illegal international meeting" to split the communist movement. But Peking also cautioned (and probably believed) that "Khrushchevism without Khrushchev" might prevail (Editorial, *Red Flag*, November 21, 1964).

12. *People's Daily* and *Red Flag* editorial translated in *Peking Review*, VIII, No. 46 (November 12, 1965), pp. 13–14.

13. "Treaty of Friendship, Alliance, and Mutual Assistance between the Government of the U.S.S.R. and the Government of the People's Republic of China, Moscow, February 14, 1950," in *Disarmament and Security: A Collection of Documents, 1919-1955* (Washington: D.C., Government Printing Office, 1956), pp. 594–95. For commentary on this and other Soviet mutual assistance pacts, see Jan F. Triska and Robert M. Slusser, *The Theory, Law, and Policy of Soviet Treaties* (Stanford, Cal.: Stanford University Press, 1962), pp. 231–40. For a series of relevant essays, see Raymond L. Garthoff, ed., *Sino-Soviet Military Relations* (New York: Praeger, 1966).

14. Peking contended that the Soviet statements of support for China on September 7 and 19, 1958 came only when "there was no possibility that a nuclear war would break out and no need for the Soviet Union to support China with its nuclear weapons (*Peking Review*, VI, No. 36, September 6, 1963, p. 1). The Chinese evaluation of the 1958 case purported to respond to a claim by *Krasnaia zvezda* on August 25, 1963, that "the nuclear might of the Soviet Union, the very country which has now been abused by the slanderers of Peking, had saved millions of Chinese from nuclear death and defended the sovereignty, security and independence of their country." For a criticism of the commonly held view by Western scholars favoring the above Chinese interpretation, see Morton H. Halperin and Tang Tsou, "The 1958 Taiwan Straits Crisis," in *Sino-Soviet Relations and Arms Control*, ed. Morton H. Halperin (Cambridge, Mass.: The M.I.T. Press, 1967), pp. 265–303.

15. Document 12 in Griffith, *The Sino-Soviet Rift*, at pp. 434, 440, 460.

16. *Partiinaia zhizn'*, No. 11, June 1964, pp. 8–20, quoted from *CDSP*, XVI, 22 (June 24, 1964), pp. 3–8 at p. 8.

17. In August 1960 Soviet spokesman Titarenko mentioned China directly in a statement on the economic and military vulnerability of an "isolated" socialist state (see Donald S. Zagoria, *The Sino-Soviet Conflict, 1956–61* [Princeton, N.J.: Princeton University Press, 1961], pp. 335–36). Marshal Malinovsky noted in January 1962 that Soviet strength would defend "those socialist states friendly to us" (*Tass*, January 24, 1962). An editorial in *Pravda*, January 7, 1963, complained that those criticizing the Soviet Union for the Cuban venture could not defend themselves without Soviet aid.

18. On the basis of talks with government officials, Stewart Alsop wrote in early 1966 that the Chinese appeared to expect a tri-pronged attack in the next six to nine months: a U.S. attack on south China; a Soviet move into Sinkiang; and an Indian invasion of Tibet. He contended further that Peking had been preoccupied with this idea since late 1962 ("The Mind of Mao," *Saturday Evening Post*, January 15, 1966, p. 14). The difficulty in separating real expectations from propaganda on such questions was manifested as Foreign Minister Chen Yi held a four-hour press conference in Peking on September 29, 1965. He invited an attack on China by U.S. "aggression," Indian "reaction," British "imperialism" and Japanese "militarism." He added: "Let the modern revisionists act in coordination with them from the north. We will still win in the end. The great Soviet people and the Communist Party of the Soviet Union will not allow their leaders to take such a criminal action." Chen Yi went on to say that Peking had been awaiting a U.S. attack for 16 years; that he might not have the "luck" to see it; but that his children might, and they would be ready (text from NCNA in *Survival*, VII, No. 9 [December 1965], pp. 326–27).

19. See chapter III.

20. Chinese government statement of August 15, 1963 in Griffith, *The Sino-Soviet Rift*, p. 341; see also Chapter III.

21. Chinese statement of September 6, 1963, in Griffith, *The Sino-Soviet Rift, op. cit.*, pp. 388–420, esp. at p. 399; also "The Leaders of the CPSU Are the Greatest Splitters of Our Times," *Peking Review*, VII, No. 6 (February 6, 1964), pp. 5–21.

22. See the interview with Foreign Minister Chen-Yi reported in *The New York Times*, October 29, 1963; see also *People's Daily*, November 19, 1963; also "The Leaders of the CPSU Are the Greatest Splitters of Our Times," *loc. cit.* At the end of May 1964 Hoxha added that Khrushchev and his associates were criminals who had conspired to kill Stalin, and that "terror, murder, imprisonment, and concentration camps prevail in the Soviet Union" (*Zëri i Popullit*, May 27, 1964).

23. Published in *Pravda* only on April 3, 1964. The fact that Chou En-lai promptly came to Moscow after Khrushchev's fall, apparently with high hopes of major Soviet concessions to Peking, again suggested the large role the Chinese attributed to Nikita Sergeivich, though Peking's expectations were also buoyed no doubt by China's recent atomic test. By Marxist logic, however, all this attention to one man seemed misplaced, for Chinese statements attributed Khrushchev's revisionism to the "lush growth of the bourgeois elements in the Soviet Union" ("The Leaders of the CPSU Are the Greatest Splitters of Our Times," *loc. cit.*).

24. See the Suslov speech, *Pravda*, April 3, 1964; *Kommunist*, No. 7, May 1964; *Pravda*, April 28 and 29, 1964; May 10, 11, and 12, 1964.

25. For documents and analysis, see Dennis J. Doolin, *Territorial Claims in the Sino-Soviet Conflict* (Stanford, Calif.: The Hoover Institution, 1965).

26. Published initially in Japan and then in *Pravda*, September 2, 1964.

27. On September 2, 1964, *Pravda* reprinted Mao's interview, which had previously appeared only in Japan, appending a vigorous Soviet rebuttal.

28. *Pravda*, September 20, 1964. The Chinese statement of September 6, 1963, accused the Russians of carrying out "large-scale subversion" in Sinkiang in 1962 to entice and coerce "several tens of thousands of Chinese citizens into going to the Soviet Union." Document 10 in Griffith, *The Sino-Soviet Rift*, p. 410.

29. Text of the January 15 treaty transmitted by Moscow Radio on January 16, 1966, International Service in English. For commentary, see Paul Wohl in *The Christian Science Monitor*, January 20, 1966, p. 4. Ulan Bator's relations with China had been relatively comfortable until April 1964, when the Mongolian government ordered about 6,000 Chinese workers to leave the country and accused Peking of "interference in internal affairs" of Mongolia. Three months later Mao Tse-tung charged that the Soviets had "placed Mongolia under their domination." In January 1965 Soviet sources reported that the Mongolian party was purging pro-Chinese elements. Throughout 1965 there were reports of infiltration and agitation by Peking agents along the Sino-Mongolian border (*New York Times*, March 16, 1966, pp. 1, 10).

30. The Soviet friendship pact with Outer Mongolia concluded on November 5, 1921, was modified by a defense protocol on March 12, 1936, and converted into a more elaborate ten-year, mutual assistance treaty on February 27, 1946. It could have been renewed automatically in 1966 as it had been in 1956.

31. *New York Times*, March 16, 1966, pp. 1, 10. Many of the reports were traced to the CPR Embassy in Moscow.

32. *Ibid.*, February 1, 1966, p. 14. The text of a long report circulated in Soviet party circles was reproduced in *Die Welt*, March 21, 1966, and then in the *New York Times*, March 24, 1966, p. 14.

33. Statement of August 15, 1963, pp. 351–52.

34. "To the People—Happiness, To the Worshippers of War—Disappointment," *Pravda*, August 12, 1963. The same accusation was repeated in the CPSU report cited above in footnote 32.

35. *People's Daily* and *Red Flag*, November 11, 1965.

36. Schoolchildren had been taught to believe in Stalin's omnipotence and some began to question all they had been taught. Grown men who had dedicated their lives to the communist cause became disillusioned, some becoming alcoholics.

37. See Mikhail A. Klochko, *Soviet Scientist in Red China* (New York: Praeger, 1964). Some specialists on Chinese affairs gave up writing in that field as early as 1958 and turned to other research.

38. *Pravda*, September 10, 1964.

39. *Pravda*, June 22, 1960.

40. See also Raymond Aron, "Coexistence and the Class Struggle," *The New Republic*, CXLIX, No. 13 (September 28, 1963), pp. 10–11.

41. *Pravda* and *Izvestiia*, December 22, 1963.

42. *Sino-Soviet Relations*, p. 53.

43. See, for example, G. Frantsov, "What Lies Behind the Slogan 'Ideological Disarmament,'" *Kommunist*, No. 13 (September 1962), pp. 110–19; also Ven. Motylev, "The Prevention of War and Contemporary Reformism," *Mirovaia Ekonomika i Mezhdunarodnye Otnosheniia*, No. 12 (1963), pp. 127–39. The Motylev article explicitly criticizes John Strachey's *On the Prevention of War* (London, 1962) for offering as an ideological justification for disarmament the convergence of capitalism and socialism.

44. See Walter C. Clemens, Jr., "Lenin on Disarmament," *Slavic Review*, XXIII, No. 3 (September 1964) at p. 512. Emphasis added. The "pacifist wing," according to Lenin, consisted of "petty bourgeois, pacifist and semi-pacifist democracy, of the type of the Second International or the Two-and-one half International, and then of the Keynes type, and so on. . . ."

45. Even for domestic audiences Soviet propagandists portrayed Chinese strategy as a kind of yellow peril menacing all civilization. *Cf.* Radio Moscow's Domestic Service, August 2, 1963; also the TASS statement broadcast in English to Europe on August 5, 1963, reporting on the Sino-Soviet disputations in Hiroshima at the Ninth International Conference for Outlawing Atomic and Hydrogen Weapons.

46. Chou Yang, "The Fighting Task Confronting Workers in Philosophy and the Social Sciences," *People's Daily*, December 27, 1963, quoted from *Peking Review*, VII, No. 1 (January 3, 1964), pp. 10–27 at p. 12.

47. "The Leaders of the CPSU Are the Greatest Splitters of Our Times," *loc. cit.*

48. "Why Khrushchev Fell," *Red Flag*, November 21, 1964, in *The Polemic on the General Line of the International Communist Movement*, at pp. 490–92.

49. *Ibid.*, p. 492.

50. Daniel Bell has argued that ideology is losing its coercive and persuasive power in the Soviet Union as well as in Eastern Europe. To that extent, an "end of ideology" in the communist world is in sight. Not only the specific formulations of communist theory are questioned, but the very claim of the Party to direct all fields of activity. (Daniel Bell, "Marxism-Leninism: A Doctrine on the Defensive; the 'End of Ideology' in the Soviet Union?" in Milorad M. Drachkovitch, ed., *The Appeals and*

Paradoxes of Contemporary Marxism [New York: Frederick A. Praeger, for the Hoover Institution, 1966].) Robert C. Tucker and Richard Lowenthal, among others, have also argued that the changes in Soviet doctrine may be of a long-term rather than temporary, tactical character. Tucker has suggested studying the deradicalization of the German Social Democratic movement at the end of the nineteenth century in order to develop criteria to evaluate such trends. And Lowenthal has concluded, after Khrushchev's fall, that: "The formal continuity of the party regime remains unbroken, but the erosion of its ideological dynamism is far advanced. The new men are objectively and subjectively unable to continue the revolution; they will have to be content with administering its results. . . . As the revolution withers away, its heirs are reduced to the conservative role of stabilizing its institutions and defending their oligarchic privileges" ("The Revolution Withers Away," *Problems of Communism,* January–February 1965).

CHAPTER VII

1. See especially the Chinese statement of June 14, 1963 (Document 2 in Griffith, *The Sino-Soviet Rift*); also Robert A. Scalapino, "The Sino-Soviet Conflict in Perspective," *The Annals of the American Academy of Political and Social Science* (January 1964), p. 10.

2. See "The Statement of the Chinese Government Advocating the Complete, Thorough, Total and Resolute Prohibition and Destruction of Nuclear Weapons and Proposing a Conference of the Government Heads of All Countries of the World," July 31, 1963, and Premier Chou En-lai's "Letter to All Government Heads," August 2, 1963, in *People of the World, op. cit.,* p. 1–8.

3. Other accessions of interest included the Republic of China, India, Austria, Switzerland, and the Federal Republic of Germany. As was implicit in the previous discussion of Communist party responses, the German Democratic Republic and the other Eastern European governments (except Albania) signed, as did Outer Mongolia. But North Korea and North Vietnam joined China in opposing the treaty. For a list of countries ratifying the treaty as of December 31, 1963, see *Documents on Disarmament, 1963* (Washington, D.C.: U.S. Arms Control and Disarmament Agency, 1964), pp. 291, 693–94.

4. Finland also replied, declaring her readiness to "support all practicable measures . . . to further . . . total disarmament . . . and peace."

The dates and source for each country's reply are as follows:

Country	Date (1963)	Source	Date (1963)	
Ethiopia	8/3	NCNA—English, Peking	9/4	
		SCMP No. 3056	9/10	p. 6
Ghana	8/7	NCNA—English, Peking	9/14	
		SCMP No. 3062	9/18	
North Korea	8/13	SCMP No. 3043	8/20	p. 38
Kenya	8/16	NCNA—English, Peking	9/10	
		SCMP No. 3059	9/13	
North Vietnam	8/19	SCMP No. 3046	8/23	p. 19
Sierra Leone	8/20	SCMP No. 3057	9/11	p. 38
Cambodia	8/21	NCNA—English, Peking	8/25	
Laos	8/24	SCMP No. 3035		

Tanganyika	8/28	SCMP No. 3086	10/24	p. 40
Zanzibar	8/28	SCMP No. 3064	9/20	
Burma	8/28	SCMP No. 3058	9/12	pp. 39–40
Pakistan	9/1	SCMP No. 3067	9/25	pp. 43–44
Finland	9/6	SCMP No. 3080	10/15	pp. 24
Afghanistan	9/21	NCNA—English, Peking	11/21	
Ceylon	10/9	NCNA—English, Peking	10/31	
Syria	11/9	SCMP No. 3112	12/4	pp. 30–31
Singapore	11/30	SCMP No. 3124	12/20	p. 22

5. For analysis and bibliography, see Griffith, *The Sino-Soviet Rift,* pp. 202–203.

6. *Ibid.,* pp. 203–204.

7. The analysis that follows is based on Franklyn Griffiths, "Soviet Difficulties at Communist Peace Conference, February 1964" (Cambridge: M.I.T. Center for International Studies, 1964, ditto, 23 pp.).

8. Zengakuren from Japan poured scorn on the houses of Moscow and Peking as well as on Washington for playing power politics at the expense of the peoples. But the Italian Communist Party Youth group attempted to exaggerate the extent of "anti-imperialism" expressed at the conference. Even before it met, the Italians added the phrase "National Independence" to the conference title, while the Soviets preferred it to mention only "Disarmament and Peace."

9. *Ibid.,* pp. 14–15. Griffiths points out that Soviet successes in "disarmament," especially in reduction of overseas bases, as contrasted to the mere curbing of nuclear testing, would bolster Moscow's propaganda line in the third world. As indicated below, in Chapter XII, note 39, the Kremlin's line did in fact shift in this direction during the spring 1965 debates in the U.N. Disarmament Commission.

10. However, one indication of China's continuing effectiveness in the third world was Peking's ability to prevent acceptance of Moscow as a full member at the Djakarta preparatory meeting in April 1964 for the Second Afro-Asian Conference ("Second Bandung") and to keep uncertain till the meeting's postponement in June 1965 the question of whether the Soviet Union would be seated.

11. W. A. C. Adie, "Chou En-lai on Safari," in Roderick MacFarquar, ed., *China under Mao: Politics Takes Command* (Cambridge, Mass.: The M.I.T. Press, 1967), p. 463. See also Halperin and Perkins, *op. cit.,* pp. 184–90; and Robert A. Scalapino, "Sino-Soviet Competition in Africa," *Foreign Affairs,* Vol. 42 (July 1964), pp. 640–54.

CHAPTER VIII

1. *Pravda* (Bratislava), October 24, 1964, p. 5.

2. The psychological premise of this argument is quite plausible: that Khrushchev regretted his previous aid program to China and sought to undo its effects. But there is no firm evidence for this line of speculation, as is seen from consideration of three arguments adduced by Harold C. Hinton, a major proponent of the preventive strike hypothesis (*Communist China and World Politics* [Boston: Houghton Mifflin Company, 1966], Chapter XVII).

One factor is the timing of Khrushchev's fall: Hinton suggests that the First Secretary wanted to strike immediately after the Chinese test; hence, Peking delayed its test until two days after Khrushchev's ouster. The Chinese test, however, was probably intended to occur on October 1—the fifteenth anniversary of the regime—but took place on October 14, due to technical problems. (See statement by Secretary of State Rusk, *The New York Times,* September 30, 1964, p. C-16; Ralph L. Powell, "China's Bomb: Exploitation and Reactions," *Foreign Affairs,* Vol. 43, No. 4 [July 1965], p. 616.) Hence, if his opponents in the Kremlin wished to prevent his hare-brained project, Khrushchev should have been ousted before October 1. A second argument by Hinton illustrates further the implausibility of the first. He suggests that Khrushchev left Moscow for the Crimea because he was sure that his preventive strike plan would surely be carried out. But the opposite seems more likely: he was away because he had no plan to act against China. A third argument is based on actions after Khrushchev's removal: The country most vulnerable to a retaliatory Chinese blow—Outer Mongolia—was the promptest and most enthusiastic in commenting on the ouster. But this behavior could also be accounted for by Ulan Bator's general dependence upon Russia's good graces.

Two other bits of evidence may be cited for the preventive war thesis. One is that the Chinese themselves gave signs of thinking that a new era had entered after Khrushchev's removal, as seen by Chou En-lai's trip to Moscow to explore the new situation. But Peking's hopes may be explained by reasons other than relief that Khrushchev's plan had been pre-empted.

Perhaps the most direct evidence—and it is hardly persuasive—of Soviet interest in stopping the Chinese test is found in reports from the 13th Pugwash Conference meeting in Karlovy Vary, Czechoslovakia, September 13–19, 1964. Soviet participants in the panel dealing with nonproliferation are said to have argued for a comprehensive ban on nuclear testing, with sanctions provided against any state that tested—whether or not it adhered to the treaty. However, the formal statement issued by the Conference Continuing Committee did not go that far. It called for extension of the partial test ban treaty to cover underground testing, if necessary by a moratorium, affirming that technical problems of control "should not now be an obstacle." The report added: "It is very important that ways and means be found to convince the governments and the people concerned of the inadvisability of *any further atmospheric testing* [italics added]."

Thus, the evidence that Khrushchev sought a surgical strike is not very compelling. And it would appear basically implausible that Moscow, either alone or in coordination with the West, would initiate such a radical move. On the one occasion when a Western statesman is known to have inquired of Khrushchev what to do about the Chinese nuclear threat—during the Test Ban signing in 1963—the Soviet leader dismissed the problem with a shrug. (See also *The New York Times,* July 30, 1963 and October 2, 1964; *The Washington Post,* October 2 and November 15, 1964.)

3. Text in the *Peking Review,* VII, No. 42 (October 16, 1964). For the first steps that Peking suggested toward total nuclear disarmament in its initial attack on the Moscow Treaty, see the Chinese statement of July 31, 1963, and Chou En-lai's letter of August 2, 1963.

4. Text in *Peking Review,* VII, No. 43 (October 23, 1964), p. 6. Emphasis added to suggest Peking's possible indifference, at least on paper, to nonproliferation.

5. See the analysis by Morton H. Halperin, "Chinese Nuclear Strategy: The Early Post-Detonation Period," London: Institute for Strategic Studies, *Adelphi Paper,* No. 18, May 1965, p. 10.

6. Translation in *Peking Review,* VII, No. 48 (November 27, 1964), pp. 12–14.

7. Pressure from China kept the Soviet Union (like Malaysia) uncertain of being seated at the "Second Bandung" Conference in Algiers up to the moment when it was

put off due to Ben Bella's overthrow. For a penetrating analysis, see *Die Zeit*, June 18, 1965. See also the discussion of Chou En-lai's maneuvering before the conference in *The New York Times*, June 20, 1965, p. 4.

8. *Pravda*, July 16, 1965, p. 5; see also "Big Sell-Out at Helsinki," *Peking Review*, VIII, No. 26 (June 25, 1965), p. 29.

9. *Zëri i Popullit*, February 2, 1965, which included the text of a January 5, 1965 note from Warsaw to Tirana and other relevant correspondence. It remains an open question, however, whether Albania in this instance was being holier than the Chinese pope desired.

10. *Peking Review*, VI, No. 31 (August 2, 1963), pp. 7–8.

11. The analysis that follows is based in largest part on Soviet media and on comments transmitted by the New China News Agency. Since the comments themselves are sometimes ambiguous, and since they are not always reported in full by the Chinese, the views expressed by various governments may not fall so precisely into various categories as expressed here. Many of the relevant documents are reprinted in *Europa-Arkhiv*, No. 6 (March 25, 1965), pp. D127–46; for analysis, see *ibid.*, pp. D127 ff.; Ralph L. Powell, "China's Bomb: Exploitation and Reactions," *Foreign Affairs*, Vol. 43, No. 4 (July 1965), pp. 623–24; Morton H. Halperin, "Chinese Nuclear Strategy: The Early Post-Detonation Period," *loc. cit.*, p. 9; *The New York Times*, December 26, 1964, p. 14.

12. Interview with correspondent of the *Manila Times*, reported in *The New York Times*, October 29, 1964.

13. Speech to the General Assembly on December 7, 1964. ("Soviet Government Memorandum on Steps to Further Ease International Tension and to Limit the Arms Race," text in *Current Digest of the Soviet Press* [CDSP] XVI, No. 50 [January 6, 1965], pp. 9–11); see also *Le Monde*, December 9, 1964.

14. U.N. Document, DC/213/Add. 2, April 28, 1965.

15. This point was elucidated by Helmut Sonnenfeldt at the Airlie House Conference in 1965 and in his "The Chinese Factor in Soviet Disarmament Policy" in Morton H. Halperin, ed., *Sino-Soviet Relations and Arms Control* (Cambridge, Mass.: The M.I.T. Press, 1967), pp. 106–108.

16. *Pravda*, November 7, 1964.

17. On February 16, 1965, according to Chinese sources, Premier Kosygin submitted to Peking and Hanoi a formal proposal to convene a new international conference on the whole Indochina question. And on February 23, 1965 Moscow broached with de Gaulle the "question of calling an international conference without prior conditions" (*Red Flag* and *People's Daily*, November 11, 1965, translated in *Peking Review*, VIII, No. 46 [November 11, 1965], pp. 10–21, at pp. 15–17). But Peking charged also that the Kremlin had "wanted to send via China 4,000 men to be stationed in Vietnam . . . [and] to occupy and use one or two airfields in Southwestern China and to station a Soviet armed force of 500 men there" (Chinese Communist Party Central Committee letter to its Soviet counterpart quoted by Edward Crankshaw in *The Observer* [London], November 14, 1965; and Bernard B. Fall, "The Year of the Hawks," *The New York Times Magazine*, December 12, 1965, p. 48).

18. Halperin, *loc. cit.*, p. 5.

19. NCNA-English, February 6, 1965.

20. Premier Shastri failed in his attempt at the Conference to organize a mission to

Peking to persuade the Chinese not to test (*The New York Times,* October 8, 1964, pp. 1, 13). For documents of the Cairo Conference, see *Review of International Affairs* (Belgrade), XV, No. 350 (November 5, 1964).

21. Pakistan's reply in 1963 also discussed this alternative.

22. Mali has signed the Moscow Treaty, but Guinea and Albania have not.

23. Halperin, *loc. cit.,* p. 9.

24. Approximately one-sixth of the states establishing diplomatic relations with Peking from 1949 through 1965 did so during the period subsequent to the October 1964 test. In addition to China's nuclear status, however, the prospect of Chinese economic assistance also strengthened Peking's influence in Asia, Africa, and—for a time—in Cuba. In 1964 alone Communist China was reported to have extended $94 million in grants and credits, while in the entire preceding decade these had totaled only $138 million (*The New York Times,* August 16, 1965, p. 8). For a listing of the nations having diplomatic relations with Peking, with Taipei, or with neither, see A. M. Halpern, ed., *Policies Toward China: Views from Six Continents* (New York: McGraw-Hill Book Company, 1965), pp. 494–502.

25. In addition to East European, Chinese, and other Asian radio broadcasts, the following sources have been used: *Neue Züriche Zeitung,* May 19, 1965; *The New York Times,* May 15, 1965; *Le Monde,* May 18, 1965; *Boston Sunday Herald,* May 16, 1965, p. 42; plus press surveys of *Asahi Evening News, Nihon Keizai, Yomiuri,* and the *Japan Times.*

26. "Carry the Struggle against Khrushchev Revisionism through to the End," *People's Daily* and *Red Flag,* June 14, 1965 (Booklet issued by Peking: Foreign Languages Press, 1965), pp. 9–10.

27. Another hypothesis was that the bomb employed a fission-fusion process to attain its large yield, a fission trigger igniting the thermonuclear material. See *The New York Times,* May 15, 1966, p. 4E and May 21, 1966, p. 6.

28. See *London Times,* May 12, 1966; *Frankfurter Allgemeine Zeitung,* May 12 and 13, 1966.

29. *Asahi* and *Sankei,* May 17, 1966; *Asahi,* May 18, 1966.

30. Text of the Chinese statement in *The New York Times,* May 10, 1966.

31. *Pravda* (Moscow), May 10, 1966; *Rude Pravo* (Prague), May 11, 1966; *Borba* (Belgrade), May 12, 1966. The Yugoslav paper charged that the Chinese experiment "is motivated by an incomprehensible racial complex," but the only evidence cited was that Peking proclaimed its test necessary as a means of opposing "United States–Soviet collusion for maintaining a nuclear monopoly and sabotaging" the struggle of the oppressed peoples.

32. The following analysis is based on radio broadcasts; the *Frankfurter Allgemeine Zeitung,* May 11–16, 1966; and the *Peking Review,* IX, Nos. 21 and 22.

33. *Peking Review,* IX, No. 22 (May 27, 1966), p. 38.

34. Text in *Peking Review,* IX, No. 21 (May 20, 1966), pp. 5–12 at p. 8.

35. Not clear whether this is a quote or a paraphrase of the film commentary. See *Peking Review,* IX, No. 41 (October 7, 1966), p. 31.

36. *Ibid.,* pp. 31–32.

37. *Peking Review,* IX, No. 45 (November 4, 1966), p. 27.

38. *Ibid.,* pp. 24–26.

39. Peking did not formally classify these individuals into those from the Soviet

and those from the non-Soviet orbit, but it did observe a de facto separation, marked by a subtitle "Love Chairman Mao All the More." See *ibid.;* also IX, No. 46 (November 11, 1966), pp. 28–29.

In a somewhat unusual step for the U.N. Secretary-General, U Thant expressed his regret at the Chinese test (and at a Soviet underground test one day before). "Any atomic explosion anywhere at any time is to be regretted," he said, noting that the General Assembly had urged in 1965 that all atomic tests be suspended (*The New York Times,* October 29, 1966, p. 3).

40. *The New York Times,* December 31, 1966.

41. Text in *The New York Times,* December 29, 1966, p. 12.

42. See the report on the foreword to the Japanese edition of Alice L. Hsieh's *Communist China's Strategy in the Nuclear Age* in *The New York Times,* May 31, 1966, p. 3. The foreword was written before the third Chinese test, after which Chinese claims mounted.

43. See "The Mortal Enemy Must Pay for Its Old and New Crimes," editorial, *Liberation Army Daily,* May 13, 1966, in *Peking Review,* IX, No. 20 (May 13, 1966), p. 6.

44. See Cyrus Sulzberger in *The New York Times,* February 5, 1967.

45. Stanley Hoffmann, "Nuclear Proliferation and World Politics" in Alastair Buchan, ed., *A World of Nuclear Powers?* (Englewood Cliffs, N.J.: Prentice-Hall, 1966), p. 105.

CHAPTER IX

1. In spring 1967 it appeared that France's submarine-launched missiles would be equipped initially with 500 kiloton atomic warheads and later with megaton thermonuclear ones (*The Washington Post,* March 30, 1967, p. H1). While France was developing a range of small atomic arms, she did not expect to test a thermonuclear device until 1968 (*The New York Times,* April 14, 1967, pp. 1, 13).

2. *The New York Times,* January 27, 1967, pp. 1, 10; *The Christian Science Monitor,* January 27, 1967, p. 2.

3. *The New York Times,* December 16, 1965, p. 1.

4. William Beecher, "China ICBM Force Likely in Three Years," *The New York Times,* February 5, 1967, p. 77.

5. McNamara's 1967 estimate held that the Chinese missiles expected in the mid-1970s were not likely to possess "great reliability, speed of response, or substantial protection against attack."

6. Despite a "near-famine" economy, China was spending 10 percent of her gross national product on defense. Already, McNamara noted, China had the largest land army in the world—2,300,000 men—and an air force of 1,500 planes. Recently, he went on, China had begun experiments with rocket-launching submarines. See *The New York Times,* December 16, 1965, p. 1; also "Gelbe Gefahr für Europa?" *Die Zeit,* December 24, 1965, p. 8.

7. Caravelle transport planes were discussed initially, but the follow-on could have included Mirage bombers. Both planes contained U.S. navigational equipment, the sale of which to communist countries would probably be prohibited by the Battle Act.

8. September 29, 1966.

9. This "birthright" was claimed for Germany by former Defense Minister Strauss.

See *The Washington Post,* December 1, 1965, p. A21; see also Harry B. Ellis, "Rising nationalism may influence Bonn," *The Christian Science Monitor,* September 23, 1965, p. 1F.

10. See Theo Sommer, "The Objectives of Germany," in Alastair Buchan, ed., *A World of Nuclear Powers?* (Englewood Cliffs, N.J.: Prentice-Hall, Inc., 1966), pp. 39–54. A similar point emerges from the survey research of West German elites conducted by Karl Deutsch and his associates for the U.S. Arms Control and Disarmament Agency.

11. *Pravda* (Bratislava), October 24, 1964, p. 5.

12. Australia's representative to the General Assembly in 1965 stressed his government's displeasure that the Moscow Treaty had not become universally binding and had not been made to prohibit underground testing. Criticizing Paris as well as Peking for not signing the test ban treaty, Mr. Shaw noted also that he had been "shocked and surprised by the apparent degree of acceptance amongst representatives in this Committee of the assumption that Peking has some sort of right or prerogative to remain outside the test ban treaty and to proceed to develop a nuclear arsenal (U.N. Doc. A/C 1/PV. 1385, November 25, 1965, pp. 40–41)."

Privately, Australian and New Zealand officials began to ask about the adequacy of the ANZUS Pact and SEATO in future situations when Chinese missiles could reach to the United States. Washington's Pacific allies, like those in Europe, came face-to-face with the possibility of wanting to control their own deterrent.

For a discussion of some of the problems posed by the Chinese bomb, see *Nuclear Dispersal in Asia and the Indo-Pacific Region* (Canberra: Australian National University, the Australian Institute of International Affairs, 1965 Defense Studies Project, February 1965); see also Shane Paltridge, "Australia and the Defense of Southeast Asia," *Foreign Affairs,* Vol. 44, No. 1 (October 1965), pp. 49–61.

13. The following analysis of Japanese attitudes draws heavily on Kei Wakaizumi, "Japanese Attitudes toward the Chinese Nuclear Programs," in *Sino-Soviet Relations and Arms Control, Collected Papers* (2 vols., Cambridge, Mass.: Harvard University, 1966), II; and by the same author, "The Problem for Japan," in Buchan, *A World of Nuclear Powers?* pp. 76–88. For a more general survey, see Sadako Ogata, "The Japanese Attitude Towards China," *Asian Survey,* August 1965, reprinted in *Survival,* VII, No. 9 (December 1964), pp. 328–33; also Shigeharu Matsumoto, "Japan and China: Domestic and Foreign Influences on Japan's Policy," in A. M. Halpern, ed., *Policies Toward China: Views from Six Continents* (New York: McGraw-Hill, 1965), pp. 123–65.

14. Foreign Office Statement in *Yomiuri Shimbun,* October 17, 1964.

15. Speech of Foreign Minister Shiina on October 23, 1964, to the Liberal Democratic Party Steering Board.

16. Speech of Foreign Minister Shiina on October 22, 1964, in *Yomiuri Shimbun,* October 22, 1964.

17. See especially Prime Minister Sato's remarks at the National Press Club in Washington on January 13, 1965.

18. Proposal of Dr. Morinosuke Kashima, Chairman of the Liberal Democratic Party Foreign Affairs Research Committee, in a speech at the House of Councillors plenary session on January 29, 1965.

19. *Asahi Shimbun,* October 29, 1964. Ironically, however, it was the first mission to Peking by a delegation of the Japan Socialist Party that was compelled to protest

the Chinese nuclear test. (This visit from October 15 through October 30, 1964 coincided with gala celebrations for the success of China's first nuclear test). See also Sadako Ogato, *loc. cit.*, *Survival*, p. 330.

20. From an article by Goh Muramatsu, Assistant Professor at Rikkyo University, in a book entitled *The Security of Non-Nuclear Japan*, compiled and published by the Current Problems Research Institute in June 1965.

21. The question was stated:

The recent situation of Asia is much disturbed as the result of the outbreak of the Vietnam trouble. What steps should we take to protect the peace and security of Japan?

The full spectrum of reply was:
  (1) Arm Japan with nuclear weapons 2.6%
  (2) Strengthen the present U.S.–Japan
        Security system 10.1%
  (3) Maintain the present status 20.3%
  (4) Abolish the U.S.–Japan Security Treaty and neutralize Japan,
        with no armament 24.7%
  (5) Others 4.1%
  (6) Don't know and unanswered 38.2%

22. *The New York Times*, November 28, 1965, p. 13; see also *Time*, December 10, 1965, p. 41. For a Chinese evaluation, see "Japanese Militarism on the Road Back," Parts I and II, *Peking Review*, VIII, No. 50 (December 10, 1965), pp. 5–8 and No. 51 (December 17, 1965), pp. 18–20.

23. Harrison E. Salisbury in *The New York Times*, August 19, 1966.

24. *Ibid.*

25. *Ibid.*, August 19 and 26, 1966.

26. Wakaizumi, "The Problem for Japan," *op. cit.*, p. 86.

27. For background on India's nuclear development, see, e.g., *Die Zeit*, November 26, 1965, p. 6; also *The Christian Science Monitor*, January 29, 1966, p. 4.

28. *The Christian Science Monitor*, November 2, 1965, p. 1.

29. *Ibid.*, September 23, 1965, p. 5.

30. Interview with Homi J. Bhabha in *The New York Times*, November 29, 1965, p. 8. Some Indian leaders, however, warned in 1965 that China would be able to mount an airborne nuclear attack on India in eighteen months (*Washington Post*, June 1, 1965, p. A13).

31. In Czechoslovakia in 1966 the author heard speculation that the Chinese had sabotaged the plane in which Mr. Bhabha was flying to Europe, but an Indian businessman told the author that a relative had been displaced from the same flight in order to make room for Mr. Bhabha, who showed up at the last minute.

32. *The Christian Science Monitor*, August 2, 1966; see also the report by Harrison E. Salisbury in *The New York Times*, August 18, 1966; and Sisir Gupta, "The Indian Dilemma," in Buchan, *op. cit.*, pp. 55–67.

33. According to the Institute for Strategic Studies, power reactors already operating or under construction by late 1965 would produce enough plutonium to make 236 bombs a year in India and progressively smaller numbers in Canada, West Germany, Italy, Japan, Belgium, Sweden, Czechoslovakia, down to ten in The Netherlands. Other countries coming up in nuclear development included Israel, Egypt, Switzerland, and Norway (*The New York Times*, January 22, 1966, p. 26 m).

34. See Karl Birnbaum, "The Swedish Experience," in Buchan, *op. cit.*, pp. 68–78.

35. This reluctance provoked an attack upon Brazilian and Argentinian "militarists" in a radio broadcast from Warsaw in English on April 23, 1966. A few days earlier Chile and Venezuela sided with Brazil and Argentina in demanding adequate guarantees from nuclear powers as a condition for the establishmnet of a Latin American atom-free zone. The major book on the subject is Alfonso Garciá Robles, *The Denuclearization of Latin America* (New York: Taplinger Publishing Company, 1967).

36. Cuba refused in 1965–67 to take part in negotiations on a Latin American atom-free zone or to sign any treaty on that subject so long as the United States retained the Guantanamo Naval Base and continued an aggressive policy to Cuba. Among its various motives, the Castro government may have wanted to keep open the option of permitting Soviet nuclear forces again to be stationed in Cuba.

37. See Leonard Beaton, "Capabilities of Non-Nuclear Powers," in Buchan, *op. cit.*, p. 38; and by the same author, *Must the Bomb Spread?* (Middlesex, England: Penguin Books, Ltd., 1966) and *The Struggle for Peace* (New York: Frederick A. Praeger, Inc., 1967).

38. Report of the Committee on Arms Control and Disarmament of the National Citizens Commission, White House Conference on International Cooperation, 1965, Part I, p. 9.

CHAPTER X

1. The inspection issue was particularly complex with respect to West Germany, which had accepted inspection by Euratom under the terms of the 1954 agreements on West European Union, allowing Germany to rearm and enter NATO. Bonn resisted in 1967 proposals that Euratom inspection be supplanted or at least supplemented by that of the International Atomic Energy Agency (IAEA). The United States tried to work out a compromise solution whereby Euratom inspection would be regarded as carried out in behalf of the IAEA or on a transitional basis prior to inspection by the IAEA itself. See also Chapter XI.

On conditions (a) to (d), see statement by India to the U.N. Disarmament Commission, May 4, 1965 (U.N. Doc. DC/PV.75, May 4, 1965, p. 5); also U.N. Doc. A/C.1/PV.1384, November 24, 1965, pp. 11–20; on items (e) and (f), see *The New York Times*, November 1, 1966; on Bonn's concern with item (g), see *The Christian Science Monitor*, February 8, 1967, p. 4. On all the items see the list of UN and ENDC documents referenced in Working Paper ENDC/221 submitted by Italy on March 6, 1968.

2. Such suspicions, voiced, e.g., in *The Washington Post* (June 1, 1965, p. A13) were expressed also by a Soviet publication in 1966 (A.N. Shevchenko, *Problema razoruzheniia na sovremennom etape* [Moscow: Znanie, Mezhdunarodnaia Seriia, No. VII, 1966], pp. 11–12). The author denied that the Soviet Union wanted to keep up an exclusive atomic club, but argued that a more radical approach to the disarmament problem was not currently feasible; he specifically asked whether those who demand disarmament measures beyond a nonproliferation treaty were not trying to obstruct agreement.

In early 1966 both Moscow and Washington expressed the view that no attempt should be made to make the nonproliferation treaty part of a larger package (*The New York Times*, March 4, 1966).

3. Ambassador Trivedi declared: "The first priority is the task of making the Moscow Treaty universally binding. We have requested and we have urged, we have

deplored and we have condemned; but neither our displeasure nor our appeals have borne any fruit. The international community cannot, I submit, continue to remain helpless and impotent in the teeth of such defiance and will be obliged to examine what it can do to insure that the health of humanity is not periodically attacked by the death-dealing debris of radioactive fallout" (U.N. Doc. A/C.1/PV.1384, November 24, 1965, pp. 13–15).

4. The problem was further complicated by the publicity given in 1965 to the fact that U.S. atomic weapons were already assigned to German, French, and other NATO forces. The nuclear warheads assigned to West Germany alone possessed an explosive power far exceeding all the explosives used in World War II. American controls over the weapons, both on planes and in separate stockpiles, were reported at times to exist "more in principle than in fact" (John W. Finney, "We are Already Sharing the Bomb," *The New York Times*, November 28, 1965, p. E3). Secretary McNamara asserted that "the nuclear component of the NATO deterrent" consisted in late 1965 of 5,000 U.S. warheads stored on European soil in support of Atlantic alliance forces, and that it would be increased by 20 percent in the next six months (*The New York Times*, November 28, 1965, p. 1). Soviet opposition to what Moscow called de facto proliferation had been expressed earlier in the year at the Eighteen-Nation talks (ENDC/PV.207, August 13, 1965, pp. 24–29). For its part, the United States had earlier asked for Soviet assurances that Moscow would keep strict control over nuclear warheads for missiles given to East Germany and other East European armies. William C. Foster referred in particular to the Soviet-made missiles paraded by East German troops on May 8, which, Foster said, could carry nuclear warheads a distance of up to 100 miles (*The New York Times*, May 25, 1965). For a report that Moscow might formalize a plan for nuclear sharing or consultation with her East European Allies, see *The Washington Post*, October 30, 1965.

5. For an example of a Soviet denunciation of the MLF so sophistic as to imply greater concern with subverting NATO than with halting proliferation, see Tsarapkin's remarks in ENDC/PV.220, August 3, 1965, pp. 32–41.

6. Chancellor Erhard and President Johnson issued a communiqué on December 21, 1965, that killed the MLF by not mentioning it. There was no pledge, as in the past, to keep working for the early formation of an allied nuclear force. Instead they agreed to continue talking in the future on Bonn's desire for a more "appropriate" part in the West's defensive system. The communiqué declared that Bonn had no intention of acquiring or desire to acquire national control over atomic weapons, but Germany reportedly suggested that several non-nuclear states share in the financing and management of a force of ten U.S. and British missile-carrying submarines, an idea to which London was cool.

Other signs of varying interpretations occurred when German and U.S. spokesmen disagreed on (a) whether alliance problems took precedence over nonproliferation or whether there was no conflict between them; and (b) whether a more appropriate role for Germany in Western defense necessarily included physical control over nuclear weapons. For text of the communiqué, see *The New York Times*, December 22, 1965, p. 10. For Erhard's insistence that the solution for Germany's defense must include a physical element as well as a political restructuring, see *Die Zeit*, December 24, 1965, p. 1.

7. Plans for the establishment of the Consultative Committee were reported in May 1965. The Committee's structure took shape in September and October, and in November it was announced that it would probably consist of three subcommittees: one on nuclear planning, one on the exchange of data and intelligence, and one on

communications. Washington and London (and probably Paris, if it chose) would sit on all subcommittees, and Bonn on the first.

Official sources denied that the Consultative Committee was a substitute for multilateral sharing, but the Citizens Committee on Arms Control and Disarmament chaired by Jerome B. Wiesner advised the White House to halt and reduce the buildup of nuclear weapons in Central Europe and focus instead on creating for Germany a greater role in strategic planning. The citizens' report also recommended "more fruitful involvement of the principal NATO allies in discussions of disarmament and arms control" (Section IV of the report).

8. Reports out of Moscow in December 1965 hinted that the Kremlin would not view a NATO-planned and guided nuclear force as an insurmountable obstacle to a nonproliferation treaty, provided Bonn's finger were kept off the trigger. Moscow itself showed signs of interest in working out with the Warsaw Treaty member-states a permanent consultative committee possibly dealing with nuclear strategy. If such an arrangement came about, the apparent symmetry with NATO might permit the Kremlin to tolerate better the Consultative Committee. However, British Foreign Secretary Michael Stewart was reported unable in December 1965 to learn in Moscow what the Soviet Government meant by opposing any plan whereby West Germany had "access to decisions" on the use of nuclear missiles. And on the eve of the ENDC negotiations in January 1966, contradictory estimates of Moscow's attitude to the Consultative Committee were circulating in Washington.

9. Plans agreed to in September were announced only in December 1966. Even then spokesmen for London and Washington disagreed as to whether the new program ruled out a hardware solution. (See *The Christian Science Monitor*, December 15, 1966; *The New York Times*, December 17, 1966.)

10. Erhard's downfall, while rooted in domestic economic problems, was precipitated by his visit to Washington in which he gained little concession either on the issue of nuclear sharing or on the requirement for German purchases of military equipment made in America. See, e.g., Walter Lippmann's column on November 22, 1966 "Bonn's Crisis Made in the U.S.A."; for a view that minimizes Erhard's troubles with Washington, comments by Deutschlandfunk on September 29, 1966; a view stressing that "the White House and McNamara have prevailed on all points where purely American interests were involved. . . ." *Neue Ruhr Zeitung*, September 29, 1966. Comments rather critical of the Erhard-Johnson meeting appeared also in *Bayern-Kurier*, September 28; *Die Welt*, September 29; *Frankfurter Rundschau*, September 29. One of the more positive appraisals appeared in *Die Zeit*, October 4, 1966.

11. For an example of Soviet vitriol on U.S. policy in Vietnam, see U.N. Doc. DC/PV.87, May 24, 1965, pp. 16–27.

12. "New Directions in Arms Control and Disarmament," *Foreign Affairs*, Vol. 43, No. 4 (July 1965), pp. 587–601.

13. Shortly after Harriman's departure, *Pravda* declared (on August 8, 1965) that Moscow was "ready for talks and agreements in the interest of peace, freedom, and independence of peoples."

14. See, however, the Conference resolution on Vietnam, in *Pravda*, July 16, 1965, p. 5.

15. See also *The Christian Science Monitor*, December 14, 1965, pp. 1, 15.

16. *The New York Times*, January 26, 1966, p. 14. Radio broadcasts from Moscow and Warsaw, however, took an opposite tack and predicted a dark future for the

ENDC talks because of the continuing Vietnamese war and the persistent efforts to give Bonn at least indirect control over nuclear weapons.

17. *Izvestiia* on June 22, 1966 stated firmly that Moscow did not demand the withdrawal of U.S. troops from Vietnam as a condition for a nonproliferation treaty. See also the earlier statement by Soviet negotiator Tsarapkin cited in *The New York Times*, January 26, 1966.

18. Broadcast from Moscow in Albanian, February 28, 1966; for a contrary view on Soviet participation in the ENDC, see, e.g., *Peking Review*, IX, No. 8 (February 18, 1966), p. 12.

19. Speech by Leonid Brezhnev at a Soviet-Polish friendship meeting on October 15, 1966, commenting in part on President Johnson's address of October 7, 1966.

20. On the historical development of China's declaratory policy, see Oran R. Young, "Chinese Soviet Views on the Spread of Nuclear Weapons," in Morton H. Halperin ed., *Sino-Soviet Relations and Arms Control* (Cambridge, Mass.: The M.I.T. Press, 1967), pp. 13–72.

21. Chinese statement of August 15, 1963, in Griffith, *The Sino-Soviet Rift*, pp. 346–47; statement of November 18, 1963, in *ibid.*, p. 486.

22. See, e.g., speech by Liao Cheng-chih, August 1, 1963, in *People of the World, Unite, for the Complete, Thorough, Total and Resolute Prohibition and Destruction of Nuclear Weapons!* (Peking, 1963), pp. 69–70.

23. Chinese statement of August 15, 1963, in Griffith, *op. cit.*, p. 347.

24. *People's Daily* editorial, August 9, 1962, in *SCMP* 2799, August 15, 1962, p. 22.

25. The line was that China had been compelled to develop her own atomic bomb because of the threat to her from U.S. imperialism (which was condemned for "proliferating" its weapons to Europe and the Far East). China's mastering of nuclear weapons would "encourage" the revolutionary struggle around the world, but Peking would never be the first to use the bomb. The oppressed peoples would achieve liberation "by relying on their own struggles and also through mutual aid. . . ." The "atomic bomb is a paper tiger," Peking declared, avowing that "China will neither commit the error of adventurism nor the error of capitulationism" (Statement of October 16, 1964, in *Survival*, VII, No. 1 [January–February 1965], pp. 3–9).

26. See, e.g., Chou En-lai's greeting to the World Conference against Atomic and Hydrogen Bombs in Tokyo, *Peking Review*, VII, No. 31 (July 30, 1965), p. 4. On the Tokyo conference, see *Neue Züricher Zeitung*, August 5, 1965, p. 22.

27. *Peking Review*, VIII, No. 5 (January 29, 1965), p. 7. One analyst suggested that Peking was planning to "supply Indonesia with enough enriched uranium to permit her to explode a nuclear device" (E. R. Zilbert, "The Chinese Nuclear Explosion, N-Nation Nuclear Development and Civil Defense," Santa Monica, Cal.: Rand, P-3074, April 1965, p. 2).

28. *Peking Review*, VIII, No. 6 (February 5, 1965), pp. 6 ff. The Indonesian delegation included army generals and was welcomed by, among others, Lo Jui-ching, Chief of the General Staff of the Chinese Army.

29. "Chinese-Indonesian Joint Communiqué," *Communist Area*, Research Department of Radio Free Europe, January 30, 1965; see also Tad Szulc's commentary on Chen Yi's November 1964 visit to Jakarta, "Sukarno Build-Up Linked to Peking," *The New York Times*, January 8, 1965, pp. 1–2. Late in 1964 Brig. General Hartono, Chief of the Indonesian army arsenal, had forecast that Indonesia would explode her own atomic bomb by the end of 1965. See *The New York Times*, August 5, 1965.

30. The four-hour meeting on September 29, 1965, was attended by nearly three

hundred Chinese and resident foreign correspondents. Text in *Peking Review*, VIII, No. 41 (October 1965), pp. 7–14.

31. *Ibid.*, pp. 8–9.

32. *Peking Review*, VIII, No. 47 (November 19, 1965), p. 20.

33. *Peking Review*, IX, No. 1 (January 1, 1966), p. 15.

34. In the same vein, Peking's severe criticism on November 11, 1965 of Soviet policies assailed the Kremlin for plotting with Washington "for 'the prevention of nuclear proliferation' and similar so-called 'disarmament' measures in an effort to maintain the monopoly of the two nuclear overlords, the Soviet Union and the United States, against China and all other independent countries" (*Peking Review*, VIII, No. 46 [November 11, 1965], pp. 13–14). Peking's main concern seemed to be that U.S.–Soviet collaboration might be directed against China.

35. In addition to the November 15, 1966 statement cited in note 36, see especially the Joint Statement of China and Albania, May 11, 1966, in *Peking Review*, IX, No. 21 (May 20, 1966), pp. 5–12; Chou En-lai's speech in the same issue, pp. 16–17; the Chinese position at an executive meeting of the World Council of Peace in Budapest in March, reported in *ibid.*, IX, No. 16 (April 15, 1966), p. 15; Chou En-lai's message to the 12th World Conference Against Atomic and Hydrogen Bombs in Japan, given in *ibid.*, IX, No. 32 (August 5, 1966), pp. 15–16.

36. Observer, "Another Deal between the Two Nuclear Overlords, the U.S. and the Soviet Union," *People's Daily*, November 15, 1966, translated in *Peking Review*, IX, No. 47 (November 15, 1966), pp. 34–35. This article addressed itself to the resolution on nonproliferation put forward at the General Assembly by the Soviet Union, which the United States and other nations then co-sponsored, a measure discussed in Chapter XI.

37. *Ibid.*

38. A correspondent for *Yomiuri* (Tokyo) wrote from Peking on November 26, 1965, that China saw the U.N. resolution on the World Disarmament Conference as a diplomatic victory, but that Peking would attend only the kind of summit conference proposed by China since July 31, 1963. For China's apparently definite refusal to attend the World Disarmament Conference, see Reuters and Kuala Lumpur Domestic Service in English, December 1, 1965; *Le Monde* and *The New York Times*, December 2, 1965. As late as June 1966, however, rumors emanating from Cairo had it that the Chinese might attend a World Disarmament Conference on three conditions: (a) that France participated; (b) that Kuomintang representatives were excluded; and (c) that time be allotted to permit completion of a series of nuclear tests already planned.

39. The idea that China and the United States might exchange such pledges (without any corollary agreements) appeared in Chinese proposals immediately following the October 1964 test (see *Peking Review*, VII, No. 44 [October 30, 1964], pp. 6–7). China's representative at the Ambassadorial talks in Warsaw broached the proposal again privately, but it was rejected since no controls were provided (*Frankfurter Allgemeine Zeitung*, May 13, 1966). Chou En-lai said the U.S. rejection compelled China to continue testing (*Peking Review*, IX, No. 21 [May 20, 1966], p. 17).

40. Mexico and other sponsors of the plan had hoped that Peking would at least be noncommittal, if only in the hope of winning Latin American support for seating Communist China at the United Nations. China seems to have given its reply to the Mexican Ambassador to Cairo; the text of the Chinese statement was later circulated

as a U.N. document. See *The New York Times*, October 2, 1966, p. 27. Moscow's position was that it would respect "all denuclearized zones that might be established, provided other nuclear powers are willing to assume the same obligations."

41. NCNA International Service in English, May 18, 1966.

42. *Peking Review*, IX, No. 21 (May 20, 1966), p. 11.

43. *People's Daily*, October 16, 1966, translated in *Peking Review*, IX, No. 43 (October 21, 1966), p. 21; the argument was anticipated in a note in *Peking Review*, IX, No. 42 (October 14, 1966), p. 3.

44. High-ranking Japanese were told privately in late 1964–65 that Japan would not be safe if she remained allied with the United States, while an independent Japan could expect good relations with China. Even if Japan embarked on her own nuclear program for defensive purposes, China would not object. Some Chinese even suggested the possibility of future Sino-Japanese collaboration in the nuclear field.

CHAPTER XI

1. Draft resolutions were slow to emerge at the U.N. Disarmament Commission, until five appeared in rapid succession: (1) a Soviet draft on the withdrawal of foreign troops and foreign military bases; (2) a Soviet draft for a convention on prohibiting the use of nuclear weapons; (3) a U.S. draft on the next arms control steps to be taken (a comprehensive test ban treaty; a nonproliferation agreement; a halt to all production of fissionable materials for weapons use; a freeze on strategic nuclear vehicles; a return to negotiations at the ENDC); (4) a thirty-six power draft calling for a world disarmament conference; and (5) a twenty-nine power draft on next disarmament steps. The Soviet drafts had so little support that Moscow withdrew them on June 15, 1965, and Washington obliged by withdrawing its draft as well.

Attention then turned to the twenty-nine power draft. The attitudes that different states took to portions of the draft proved most revealing. India had proposed a preamble "deploring" current nuclear tests and the failure to reach a comprehensive test ban. A roll-call sustained the preamble by a vote of 71 to 12, with 18 abstentions. The negative votes came from ten communist countries (not including Rumania) plus Cambodia and Pakistan. Another separate vote was asked on the operative paragraph regarding nonproliferation, chiefly because the communist states wanted a different formulation to ensure no transfer of nuclear weapons to military alliances. This paragraph too was retained by a vote of 71 to 1, with 25 abstentions. The resolution as a whole passed by a vote of 83 to 1 (Albania) with 18 abstentions— among them ten from the communist states, four from African states (Algeria, Burundi, Guinea, and Mali), and France. All 18 abstaining states had already shown their interest in retaining Peking's favors. Soviet delegate Fedorenko noted that the resolution contained some non-Soviet priorities if not anti-Soviet elements, since it embodied some Western and nonaligned priorities and no Soviet ones. For further analysis, see Homer A. Jack, "The U.N. Disarmament Commission, 1965," Boston: Unitarian Universalist Association, 1965, mimeo.

2. ENDC/162, August 17, 1965.

3. Moscow's attitude toward the MLF had, of course, been repeatedly expressed; see, e.g., the Soviet notes to Washington and Bonn in *Pravda*, January 19, 1965. See also the report of the Geneva talks in *The New York Times*, July 31, 1965. On Britain's draft proposal circulated before the U.S. text was announced, see *The New York Times*, July 27, 1965.

4. *The New York Times*, August 18, 1965. Other papers, however, such as the

Washington Post, approved the U.S. draft treaty for providing a reasonable compromise solution. For William C. Foster's defense of the U.S. proposal, see his statement at the 228th plenary session of the ENDC, August 31, 1965, replying to questions posed by Ambassador Tsarapkin on August 17, 1965.

5. See Homer A. Jack, "The Eighteen-Nation Disarmament Committee, 1965," Boston: Unitarian Universalist Association, 1965, mimeo.

6. See U.N. Documents A/5976 and A/C.1/L.338.

7. See Zbigniew Brzezinski, "Moscow and The M.L.F.: Hostility and Ambivalence," *Foreign Affairs,* Vol. 43, No. 1 (October 1964), pp. 126–34.

8. These resolutions dealt with "The Urgent Need for Suspension of Nuclear and Thermonuclear Tests," "Nonproliferation of Nuclear Weapons," "Declaration on the Denuclearization of Africa," "Question of General and Complete Disarmament," and "Question of Convening a World Disarmament Conference."

9. This resolution, as noted in Chapter XII, evoked a Soviet abstention in protest against its approval of "improved possibilities for international cooperation in the field of seismic detection"—a principle Moscow maintained would unnecessarily complicate negotiations to halt nuclear testing.

10. The only disarmament resolution turned down by the Assembly vote called for "Publicizing the Transfer of Arms." This draft resolution met opposition from Saudi Arabia, from proponents of national-liberation wars, and from some countries which argued the resolution needed further study. Though encouraged by the United States to have the resolution considered later by the ENDC, Malta forced a vote by the Assembly which defeated it by an unrecorded tally of 18 in favor, including the U.K., 19 opposed, including the Soviet bloc, and 39 abstaining, including the United States.

11. U.N. Doc. A/6097, November 11, 1965, pp. 5–6.

12. Among the states voting affirmatively: Brazil, Nationalist China, India, Israel, Japan, Mexico, South Africa, Tanzania, Zambia; Against, none. Abstaining: Cuba, France, Guinea, Pakistan, Rumania. Absent: Cambodia, Congo (Brazzaville), and Mali.

13. For the Soviet resolution, see U.N. Documents A/5976 and A/C.1/L.338; for the United States text, see A/C.1/L.337.

14. Press Release SG/SM/395; GA/3119, November 19, 1965, p. 2.

15. U.N. Doc. A/PV.1335, September 24, 1965, p. 26.

16. U.S.S.R. Mission to the United Nations, Press Release #53, December 24, 1965, p. 5.

17. For background and text, see Report of the First Committee A/6119, November 25, 1965; also statement by the Secretary-General, Press Release SG/SM/398; GA/3122, November 29, 1965.

18. *The New York Times,* November 24, 1965, p. 1.

19. Thus, for example, Moscow submitted a draft resolution to the U.N. Disarmament Commission in May 1965 calling for the prohibition of nuclear weapons and, for this purpose, the convening of a world disarmament conference not later than the first half of 1966 (DC/219, May 27, 1965).

20. *The New York Times,* December 2, 1965, p. 1; *The Washington Post,* December 2, 1965, p. 1.

21. For an uncompromising Chinese view on the conditions for Peking's participa-

tion in the United Nations, see the editorial in *People's Daily*, November 19, 1965, in *Peking Review*, VIII, No. 48 (November 26, 1965), pp. 15–18.

22. "The U.N.—A Market-Place for U.S.–Soviet Political Deals," *Peking Review*, IX, No. 1 (January 1, 1966), pp. 13–17.

23. For background and text, see Report of the First Committee, A/6127, December 2, 1965. The declaration had been endorsed by the Organization of African Unity in July 1964.

24. For background, see Report of the First Committee, A/6129, December 2, 1965.

25. A/C.1/PV.1387, November 26, 1965, p. 41.

26. Early in 1966 the Soviet Government issued conflicting signals as to its estimate of the prospects for a nonproliferation agreement. See the relatively optimistic appraisal in *Pravda*, January 10, 1966, and the pessimistic account given by TASS International Service in English, January 27, 1966.

27. Report of the Committee on Arms Control and Disarmament, National Citizens Commission, White House Conference on International Cooperation, Section II-C; recommendation I-3.

28. The phrasing of his 1966 pledge was, however, slightly more qualified: "The nations that do not seek national nuclear weapons can be sure that *if they need* our strong support against some threat of blackmail, they will have it [emphasis added]. See *The New York Times*, January 28, 1966; October 19, 1964.

29. U.S.S.R. Mission to the United Nations, Press Release #3, February 3, 1966; *The New York Times*, February 3, 1966, pp. 1, 16.

30. There was also a report, unverified and probably untrue, that Moscow had indicated a willingness to provide a nuclear guarantee in at least one specific circumstance—to protect the United Arab Republic in the event that Israel produced or acquired nuclear weapons. This offer was allegedly made by a high-level Soviet military delegation headed by Marshal Andrei A. Grechko, First Deputy Minister of Defense, visiting Cairo in December (*The New York Times*, February 4, 1966, pp. 1, 12).

While Grechko was reported to have told Cairo that Moscow objected in principle to nuclear proliferation, the Soviet Union (like the United States) continued to supply conventional weapons to the Middle Eastern and North African arms race. Thus, Soviet rockets were paraded in Algeria in December—a sign that Moscow had accepted Ben Bella's fall, and refused to leave the field to Peking or Washington (*Die Zeit*, December 24, 1965, p. 8).

31. For an outspoken critique, see *Rheinischer Merkur*, February 18, 1966.

32. *Asahi*, February 14, 1966.

33. See the discussion below of U.N. Resolution 2135A (XXI) adopted November 17, 1966.

34. *The New York Times*, March 23, 1966.

35. Jeremy J. Stone, private communication.

36. *The New York Times*, March 30, 1966; for the U.S. rebuttal, see *Frankfurter Allgemeine Zeitung*, April 2, 1966.

37. *The New York Times*, October 12, 1966, pp. 1, 10.

38. Adopted on November 4, 1966 by 110 to 1, with 1 abstention, there was no

roll-call vote in the plenary, but in the First Committee, where the vote was recorded, the major threshold powers—India, Japan, Israel, Sweden, and the U.A.R.— joined in voting for the proposal, as did France—her first positive vote on a disarmament issue since 1962. Only Albania voted negatively, while Cuba abstained. See "Renunciation by States of Actions Hampering the Conclusion of an Agreement on the Nonproliferation of Nuclear Weapons," Report of the First Committee, U.N. Doc. A/6496, November 2, 1966; General Assembly Resolution 2149 (XXI) adopted November 7, 1966.

39. "Nonproliferation of Nuclear Weapons," Report of the First Committee, U.N. Doc. A/6509, November 14, 1966; resolution 2153 (XXI) adopted November 18, 1966 by a vote of 97 to 2, with 3 abstentions. Albania and the Central African Republic voted against; the Democratic Republic of the Congo, France, and Iceland abstained. Nineteen states did not vote. (These counts, and those for other General Assembly resolutions in 1966, are from Homer A. Jack, "Disarmament at the 21st U.N. General Assembly" (Boston: Unitarian Universalist Association, 1967, mimeo.), pp. 27 ff.

40. Resolution 2153B (XXI) adopted November 17, 1966 by a roll-call vote of 48 to 1, with 59 abstentions.

41. Ambassador Trivedi explained that India favored the resolution on security guarantees because it endorsed the principle, expressed in General Assembly resolution 2028 (XX) in 1965: that a treaty on nonproliferation must be seen as a step toward general disarmament, more particularly nuclear disarmament; that, in his words, "it is not an isolated, limited, lopsided problem of further proliferation, or the emergence of additional nuclear weapons countries. . . ."

India opposed the conference of non-nuclear powers for the same reason that she favored the resolution calling for security guarantee: the resolution implied the need for preconditions to a nonproliferation treaty, while the conference would deal with these matters only after the treaty was signed.

Pakistan replied that the non-nuclear countries had to meet separately in order to create and direct new energies toward their common problems; to ensure communications over and above those taking place within the ENDC.

Yugoslavia explained that she abstained on the Pakistani motion because the conference would deal with too narrow a problem; Belgrade favored continued attempts to establish a world disarmament conference in which China would take part. See debate in the General Assembly on November 17, 1966, A/PV.1469; Trivedi quote at pp. 13–15.

42. "Question of General and Complete Disarmament," Report of the First Committee, U.N. Doc. A/6529, November 24, 1966; resolution 2162 (XXI) adopted December 5, 1966 by 91 to 0, with 4 abstentions.

43. U.N. Doc. A/6529, November 24, 1966; see also the more detailed report on December 5, 1966, in U.N. Doc. A/PV.1484.

44. See the debate on December 5, 1966, U.N. Doc. A/PV.1484; resolution 2165 (XXI) adopted December 6, 1966 by 94 to 0, with 10 abstentions.

45. See, e.g., the debate on November 17, 1966, U.N. Doc. A/PV.1469; resolution 2160 (XXI).

46. Resolution 2162 (XXI) adopted unanimously December 5, 1966.

Of the many disarmament measures proposed at the General Assembly in 1966, only two failed to come to a vote. One was the Polish and Ukrainian proposal to call upon all states to refrain from sending aircraft carrying nuclear weapons beyond national frontiers. A second proposal was one submitted by Iran, Morocco, Tunisia, Tanzania, and the Ivory Coast specifying means by which resources devoted to armaments could be limited and transferred to development assistance programs (see debate on November 4, 1966, U.N. Doc. A/PV.1458). As noted, however, the Soviet draft on foreign bases was for the most part replaced by another text before a vote was taken.

47. "Question of Convening a Conference for the Purpose of Signing a Convention on the Prohibition of the Use of Nuclear and Thermonuclear Weapons," Report of the First Committee, U.N. Doc. A/6532, November 29, 1966; resolution 2164 (XXI) adopted December 6, 1966 by 80 to 0, with 23 abstentions.

48. *Seventh Annual Report of the U.S. Arms Control and Disarmament Agency* (Washington, D.C., U.S. Government Printing Office, 1968), p. 8.

49. *Ibid.*, p. 6.

50. ENDC/192 and ENDC/193, both dated August 24, 1967.

51. ENDC/195, August 30, 1967.

52. See "Interim Report to the United Nations General Assembly and the United Nations Disarmament Commission (Recommended by the co-Chairmen)," ENDC/208, December 7, 1967.

53. A/RES/2346 (XXII).

54. ENDC/210, dated January 18, 1968, although the letter was dated January 11.

55. A/RES/2286 (XXII).

56. The Treaty had been signed only by Mexico and Brazil as of April 1, 1968. Text and protocols in *Seventh Annual Report, op. cit.,* pp. 49–61. As of May 1968, the United States and the U.K. had signed the second protocol, while the other nuclear powers refrained.

57. A/RES/2289 (XXII).

58. A/RES 2342A (XXII) and A/RES/2342B (XXII).

59. A/RES/2343 (XXII).

60. A/RES/2344 (XXII).

61. ENDC/192/Rev.1 (the U.S. draft) and ENDC/193/Rev.1 (the Soviet draft). The following analysis is based on documents kindly made available by the U.N. Secretariat; on the excellent booklet by Arthur Larson, *Questions and Answers on the Spread of Nuclear Weapons* (Durham, North Carolina: Rule of Law Research Center, Duke University School of Law; and New York: Educational Committee to Halt Atomic Weapons Spread, April 1968); and "Statements and Documents Related to the Non-Proliferation Treaty," Office of Public Affairs, U.S. Arms Control and Disarmament Agency, 1968.

62. See, e.g., O. Grinev, "Progress in Geneva," *Pravda*, August 27, 1967, p. 4; also John W. Finney, "Nuclear Compromise," *The New York Times*, January 20, 1968, p. 8. According to the U.S. Arms Control and Disarmament Agency, the U.S. delegate in Geneva informed the White House at 4:25 a.m. on January 18, 1968, that the co-chairmen had reached final agreement on a draft treaty and that a complete draft treaty was to be submitted to the ENDC later that day (*Seventh Annual Report, op. cit.,* p. 3).

63. See Paul Wohl in *The Christian Science Monitor*, March 14, 1968.

64. ENDC/199, October 19, 1967.

65. ENDC/223/Rev.1.

66. For the text of the draft resolution, see ENDC/222; for comments by the U.S., Soviet, and U.K. delegates, see ENDC/PV.375, March 11, 1968.

67. See Larson, *op. cit.,* pp. 29–30.

68. See also, for example, Ashok Kapur, writing from Washington, "Big Power Opposition to Indian Nuclear Arms" and "Should India Sign Nuclear Treaty?" *The Hindu* (Madras), February 4 and 5, 1968.

69. ENDC/224, Annex A.

70. Such sentiments appeared, e.g., in *Die Welt* (February 24), *Frankfurter Rundschau* (February 23), *Frankfurter Allgemeine* (February 27), and *Stuttgarter Zeitung* (February 23). The foreign editor of *Die Zeit,* however, commented (February 24): "There is no need for us to indulge in shadow-boxing with the spectres of hypothetical contingencies—Russian inspectors swarming through our factories, all our most advanced research and development withering away, Germany dropping to the level of an agricultural state. Some people may be obsessed by such nightmares, but there is nothing in the text of the treaty draft to justify them." The *Hessische Allgemeine* of Kassel also warned on February 26 that undue emphasis on Bonn's objections to the treaty "would strengthen American isolationism."

71. See "No Nuclear Arming by Japanese Militarism is Permissible," by Commentator, *People's Daily,* April 5, 1968, reprinted in *Peking Review,* No. 16 (April 19, 1968), 17–18.

72. See, e.g., Lincoln P. Bloomfield, *Western Europe to the Mid-Seventies: Five Scenarios* (Cambridge, Mass.: M.I.T. Center for International Studies, A/68–3, 1968); and Walter C. Clemens, Jr., "The Future of the Warsaw Pact," *Orbis* (Winter 1968), pp. 996–1033.

CHAPTER XII

1. Assembly Resolution 1665 (XVI), "Prevention of Wider Dissemination of Nuclear Weapons," adopted unanimously on December 4, 1961; similar resolutions had been adopted on November 20, 1959 (1380 [XIV]) and December 20, 1960 (1576 [XV]).

2. See Thomas W. Wolfe, *Soviet Strategy at the Crossroads* (Cambridge, Mass.: Harvard University Press, 1965).

3. A front-page story by William Beecher in the *Wall Street Journal,* July 26, 1965, began: "Missile-Killing Gains; Chances for Go-Ahead on the Nike-X System Seem to Be Improving; New Technology Cuts Cost, Chinese Nuclear Capability Adds to Sense of Urgency; Odds 60–40 for 1966 Start?" See also George A. W. Boehm, "Countdown for Nike-X," *Fortune,* November 1965, pp. 133 ff; *U.S. News and World Report,* November 29, 1965, p. 66; *Jane's All the World's Aircraft, 1965–1966* (New York: McGraw-Hill, 1965), pp. 442–43.

4. See Jeremy J. Stone, "Containing the Arms Race," *Bulletin of the Atomic Scientists,* September 1965, pp. 18–21. Walter F. Hahn and Alvin J. Cottrell, "Ballistic Missile Defense and Soviet Strategy," *Orbis,* LX, No. 2 (Summer 1965), pp. 316–37.

5. See, e.g., N. Talensky, "Anti-Missile Systems and Disarmament," *International Affairs,* No. 10 (October 1964), pp. 14–19, published simultaneously in *Mezinarodni politika* (Prague) and in *Bulletin of the Atomic Scientists,* February 1965, pp. 26–29. As early as 1961 both Khrushchev and Malinovsky boasted that Soviet scientists had solved the problem of destroying missiles in flight (*Izvestiia,* September 9, 1961; *Pravda,* October 25, 1961). In May 1965 Soviet television viewers saw the firing of an

ABM and its interception of an ICBM at an unspecified altitude, as well as scenes showing installations of ABM defenses including testing stations, computer centers, and launch sites. Western observers, however, believed the television film did not show recent developments but rather tests of at least three years earlier (*The New York Times*, May 11, 1965). Shortly thereafter, on August 7, 1965, the East German *National Zeitung* (p. 6) printed a photo of a Soviet antimissile missile and asserted that Soviet ABM Technology was superior to American. And in September 1965 a leading Soviet military journal printed an article that argued: "Victory in war is determined not merely by the character of weapons but by the *relationship of forces* of the combatant sides. . . . It is possible that new means of war, capable of reliably parrying the enemy's nuclear strikes, will be developed." From these and related assumptions, the author challenged the view often expressed in both the West and the Soviet Union that general war cannot be "won" in any meaningful sense (Lt. Col. E. Rybkin, "War and Policy," *Kommunist Vooruzhennykh Sil,* excerpted in *Survival,* VIII, No. 1 [January 1966], pp. 12–16). For Western analyses, see Hahn and Cottrell, *loc. cit.;* Wolfe, *op. cit.;* pp. 189–99; and Fritz Ermarth, "The ABM Decision," *Radio Free Europe Research, Communist Area, Munich,* December 8, 1965, mimeo.

In a related field, in August 1965 the commander of the Soviet antiaircraft defense corps noted that the USSR had "adequate means to detect and destroy any aircraft of any size and at any altitude, even the lowest ones." He granted, however, that it was "extremely difficult to detect in time aircraft at heights of 50 to 100 meters" (Air Vice Marshal Vladimir Sudets interview in *Nedelia* reported in *The Washington Post,* August 15, 1965).

6. In the fall of 1966 the Soviet military press intensified its calls for improving civil defense preparations. In late October 1966 Soviet newspapers prominently displayed in article by Marshal Chuikov, chief of civilian defense, entitled "There Is a Defense against the Nuclear Weapon." And on November 22, 1966, *Red Star* criticized indifference and delays in implementing instructions to prepare Soviet towns and villages against an "imperialist" atomic attack. Whether the "imperialists" in question might be Chinese or Western was not indicated.

7. Department of Defense estimates indicated that the highest casualties China could inflict on the United States by 1975 would be six to twelve million fatalities, whereas a small fraction of U.S. delivery vehicles surviving a Soviet first strike could, if directed against China, kill fifty million Chinese and destroy half of Chinese communist industry. See Joseph I. Coffey, "The Anti-Ballistic Missile Debate," *Foreign Affairs,* Vol. 45, No. 3 (April 1967), p. 407.

8. *Ibid.,* p. 408. See also J. I. Coffey, "The Chinese Question and ABM Deployment," Study Paper No. 6, Office of National Security Studies, Bendix Systems Division, Ann Arbor, Michigan, September 1965; Jerome B. Wiesner, *Where Science and Politics Meet* (New York: McGraw-Hill, 1965), pp. 288–96; also Stone, *loc. cit.,* Hahn and Cottrell, *loc. cit.*

9. See, e.g., the remarks of Secretary of State Rusk in "United States Armament and Disarmament Problems," *Hearings before the Subcommittee on Disarmament of the Committee on Foreign Relations, United States Senate, Ninetieth Congress, First Session,* February 3, 6, 7, 28, and March 1, 2, 3, 1967 (Washington: U.S. Government Printing Office, 1967), p. 169.

10. See excerpts from statement before a House Armed Service subcommittee on January 25, 1966, *The New York Times,* January 26, 1966, p. 10.

11. *The New York Times,* December 1, 1965, p. 1.

12. First reported in *The New York Times,* November 24, 1965, p. 1.

13. Report of the Committee on Arms Control and Disarmament of the National Citizens' Commission prepared for the White House Conference on International Cooperation [November 29–December 1, 1965] (New York: United National Association of the United States of America, 1966), recommendation III-B.

14. See *The New York Times,* December 1, 1965, pp. 1, 16; *The Washington Post,* December 2, 1965, p. A8.

15. See *The New York Times,* November 26, 28, December 4, 1965; *The Washington Post,* November 30, 1965; *The New Republic,* Vol. 153, No. 24 (December 11, 1965, pp. 5–6).

16. See Jack Raymond in *The New York Times,* December 1, 1965, pp. 1, 14.

17. See *The New York Times,* November 28, 1965, p. 5E; also *New Statesman,* December 31, 1965, pp. 1019–20.

18. "Discussion at the Round Table," Radio Moscow, December 8, 1965.

19. *Cincinnati Enquirer,* June 20, 1967; see also *U.S. News and World Report,* July 3, 1967, p. 36.

20. The following is based largely on the testimony of John S. Foster, Cyrus R. Vance, Earle G. Wheeler, and others in "United States Armament and Disarmament Problems," *loc. cit.,* supplemented by articles in the public press.

21. Testimony of Earle G. Wheeler, *ibid.,* p. 89. See also Richard J. Whalen, "The Shifting Equation of Nuclear Defense," *Fortune,* June 1, 1967, pp. 85 ff.

22. *The New York Times,* December 9, 1966.

23. See Hanson W. Baldwin, "Soviet Antimissile System Spurs New U.S. Weapons," *The New York Times,* February 5, 1967, pp. 1, 76. The article was criticized by Dr. John Foster in response to a query by Senator Claiborne Pell ("United States Armament and Disarmament Problems," *op. cit.,* p. 21). For comments on the role of the military-industrial complex, see Jerome B. Wiesner, "The Cold War Is Dead, but the Arms Race Rumbles On," *Bulletin of The Atomic Scientists,* June 1967, pp. 6–9.

24. John Erickson, "The Fly in Outer Space: The Soviet Union and the Anti-Ballistic Missile," *The World Today* (March 1967), p. 108, extrapolating in part from the periodic reports entitled *The Military Balance* [title varies] issued by the Institute for Strategic Studies, London.

25. McNamara statement to the press, November 10, 1966; Vance statement in "United States Armament and Disarmament Problems," *op. cit.,* p. 56.

26. Vance statement, *ibid.,* p. 61; also *The Christian Science Monitor,* June 22, 1967, p. 7.

27. The need to study methods of waging "small-scale wars that the imperialist may ignite" is urged in both the first (1962) and second (1963) editions of *Military Strategy,* edited by V. D. Sokolovskii (*Voennaia Strategiia* [Moscow: Voenizdat] 1st ed., pp. 214–15; 2nd ed., p. 234). The second edition adds the clarification that "limited wars include all types of wars in which conventional as well as tactical nuclear weapons are used, and also local [civil?] wars." See p. 93. See also Lieutenant-General Zav'ialov in *Kraznaia Zvezda,* March 31, 1967.

28. Erickson, *loc. cit.,* p. 109; Keith Bush, "New Soviet Budgetary Data Point to Increased Defense Spending," Radio Liberty Dispatch, December 7, 1966; Fritz Ermarth, "The ABM Race," Radio Free Europe, December 13, 1966; "Soviet Military Politics under Brezhnev and Kosygin," Radio Free Europe, May 17, 1967.

29. "United States Armament and Disarmament Problems," *op. cit.*, p. 84.

30. Table adapted from Vance statement, *ibid.*, p. 46; For Brennan's analysis, see his "New Thoughts on Missile Defense," *Bulletin of the Atomic Scientists*, June 1967, p. 12. His calculations lead to the conclusion that "a fixed sum to be spent on the strategic forces of one side will have the same immediate effect on the nuclear balance—considered as a difference in fatalities—whether it is spent on offensive or defensive forces."

31. For initial reports on some of these possibilities, see *The New York Times*, May 31, 1967, pp. 1, 28; July 4, 1967, pp. 1, 2.

32. This table and the next table are adapted from Vance statement in "United States Armament and Disarmament Problems," *op. cit.*, pp. 40, 46.

33. McNamara statement, November 10, 1966; also Vance statement cited above, p. 49.

34. *The New York Times*, February 22, 1967, p. 1.

35. *Ibid.*, February 21, 1967, p. 5; TASS International Service in English, February 20, 1967. Kurochkin's claims regarding ABM capabilities were not so explicit in the transmission of Moscow Domestic Service at 1430 GMT February 20, 1967. For a detailed Soviet account on the possibilities of "war with rockets," see N. F. Shibaev, *Bor'ba s raketami* (Moscow: Voenizdat, 1965).

36. A U.S. reporter noted that "Wall Street is interested in the prospect that the United States may not be able to postpone the Nike program any longer, now that it is believed the Soviet Union is building an antimissile-missile system." Some 3,000 companies were already involved in the Nike-X development program as contractors. See Robert A. Wright, "Nike-X Missile System Arouses New Interest among Investors," *The New York Times*, December 25, 1966, pp. 1, 9.

37. The freeze might pertain to numbers of missiles if not to their characteristics (penetration aids, etc.).

38. See the review of U.S. positions in 1964 in Memorandum of the United States on Measures to Stop the Spread of Nuclear Weapons, Halt and Turn Down the Arms Race, and Reduce International Tension, U.N. Document, DC/214 Add. 1, April 29, 1965, pp. 1–15.

39. See, e.g., the statement by Mr. Tsarapkin in ENDC/PV.182, April 9, 1964, pp. 35–46, esp. p. 42. The basic outline of Soviet positions in 1964 and 1965 was contained in Memorandum by the Soviet Government on Measures for the Further Reduction of International Tension and Limitation of the Arms Race, U.N. Doc. A/5827, December 7, 1964; also issued as DC/213/Add. 2, April 28, 1965. The memorandum urged agreement on the following measures:

1. Reduction of military budgets by 10–15 percent.
2. Withdrawal or cutback of foreign troops stationed in alien countries.
3. Dismantling of foreign military bases.
4. Prevention of the further spread of nuclear weapons whether by direct or indirect access, either directly or through military alliances.
5. Prohibition of the use of nuclear weapons.
6. Establishment of denuclearized zones in Central and Northern Europe, the Balkans, Africa, the Indian Ocean, the Near and Middle East "and other regions of the world" (nothing said specifically about Asia or Latin America).
7. Destruction of bombers.
8. Banning of underground nuclear weapons tests.

9. Nonaggression pact between the NATO and Warsaw Treaty States.
This list contained the same nine items proposed by Moscow in January 1964
(*Pravda,* January 29, 1964, p. 1) with two exceptions: first, the December list
reflected the October 1964 Chinese position by calling for a prohibition on the use of
nuclear weapons, substituting this for an appeal in January for measures to prevent
surprise attack; second, the order of the proposals was altered in the following manner
(December item listed first, followed by the January number): 1, 3; 2, 1; 3, 2; 4, 6;
5 (prohibition of nuclear weapons), 7 (surprise attack); 6, 5; 7, 8; 8, 9; 9, 4. Thus
the most radical change between January and December was the downgrading of a
nonaggression pact from item 4 to 9.
The revised Soviet draft treaty on general and complete disarmament was issued on
April 28, 1965 as U.N. Doc. DC/213/Add. 1. Article 5 provides for a Soviet and U.S.
"nuclear umbrella."

40. U.N. Doc. A/PV.1334, September 23, 1965, p. 37.

41. *The New York Times,* October 28, 1965, pp. 11–12.

42. Qualitative improvements in existing and planned missiles, including their
being fitted with multiple war heads, facilitated such thinking.

43. Sections III-C and III-D; see discussion and recommendations.

44. *The Christian Science Monitor,* October 4, 1965, p. 10C.

45. Surveys by the AEC and IAEA provided the following figures on reactors in
the three countries as of mid-1966:

Czechoslovakia:	1	research reactor, 2 mw thermal
	1	power reactor under construction, 150 mw elec, due to go critical in 1967 or 1968
Poland:	3	research reactors: one zero output, one 1-10 kw thermal, and one 2 mw thermal
	1	research reactor "planned" (30 mw thermal)
	1	power reactor "planned" to go critical in 1975, 200 mw electrical
West Germany:	18–21	research reactors (a variation in IAEA and AEC figures), of which 5 or 6 are 1 mw thermal or larger
	10	research reactors under construction
	2	power reactors in operation; 15 and 50 mw electrical
	6	power reactors under construction, and 3 more "planned," making a total of 9

"Foreign Reactor List," U.S. Atomic Energy Commission, Program and Reports
Branch, Division of International Affairs, March 1, 1966 (an unofficial listing);
International Atomic Energy Agency, Annual Report of the Board of Governors to the
General Conference, 1 July 1965–30 June 1966, Report GC (X)/330 (Vienna: IAEA,
July 1966). See also *East Europe,* XVII, No. 5 (May 1968), pp. 3–12.

46. Similarly, Washington indicated in September 1965 its willingness to continue
the atoms-for-peace program in Indonesia for five more years, provided Jakarta
accepted IAEA controls. Contrary to this trend, however, France began construction
of a reactor in Spain without any explicit provision for safeguards, although French
officials bravely contended they would never contribute to the spread of atomic
technology for military purposes.

47. On November 1966 representatives of 50 nations were shown a once-secret
U.S. reactor that produced plutonium until it was shut down in 1964. They saw a

demonstration of a technique worked out by the U.S. Atomic Energy Commission for verifying that a plutonium reactor had not been placed back in operation. No communist states sent representatives, although all U.N. members received invitations. Presumably the Soviet Union did not want to incur a reciprocal responsibility.

48. The U.S. delegation to the General Assembly's First Committee stated in the fall of 1966 that Washington favored improved cooperation between IAEA and EURATOM to develop "a single, world-wide safeguard system whose effectiveness is ensured by the participation of all states."

49. The Soviet Union agreed in September 1965 to an improvement in IAEA safeguards to ensure that nuclear facilities and material under IAEA supervision were not diverted for military purposes.

50. Report by the Washington Center of Foreign Policy Research.

51. *The New York Times,* July 29, 1966.

52. Rumania, however, voted with the majority of 92 states, as did the United States; Albania cast the sole negative vote; France joined Cuba and the Soviet bloc in abstaining. Red China's special friends, Cambodia and Congo (Brazzaville), did not vote. Mali, however, voted affirmatively, as did Nationalist China.

53. The resolution apparently referred to U.S. and Swedish proposals for international cooperation in the establishment of seismic detection and of identification networks.

54. Tsarapkin's remarks are in U.S. Doc. A/C.1/PV.1386, November 26, 1965, p. 41; see report of the First Committee, A/6124, December 2, 1965.

55. *The New York Times,* October 17, 1965, p. 34; *The Tech* (Cambridge, Mass., M.I.T.), October 20, 1965, p. 11. For parallel progress in the elaboration of seismic identification systems in the United Kingdom and in India, see *The Christian Science Monitor,* January 15, 1966, p. 4 and U.N. Doc. A/C.1/PV. 1384, November 24, 1965, p. 17. For background, see William C. Foster's remarks in ENDC/PV.229, September 2, 1965; the report of a symposium at M.I.T., *The New York Times,* December 4, 1964, p. 8E; also Walter C. Clemens, Jr., *Automated Inspection of Underground Nuclear Testing* (Santa Barbara, Calif., General Electric Defense Programs Operation, TAAO 62–5, December 1962).

56. A/C.1/PV.1385, November 25, 1965, pp. 56–60.

57. Resolution on the Urgent Need for Suspension of Nuclear and Thermonuclear Tests, adopted December 3, 1965.

58. Press Release SG/SM/400; GA/3129, December 3, 1965.

59. The U.A.R. proposal was made to the ENDC on August 17, 1965 and reiterated in the General Assembly debate on October 7, 1965 (A/PV.1351, p. 43). India endorsed the idea on October 12, suggesting that the threshold be lowered as a result of the continuing exchange of scientific data and other negotiations (A/C.1/PV.1384, p. 38). Moscow's support was registered, e.g., on September 24, 1965 (A/PV.1335, p. 18); and on November 26, 1965 (A/C.1/PV.1386, p. 42). (The very frequency of these offers might point to certain propagandistic purposes in the third world.)

60. A/C.1/PV.1385, November 25, 1965, pp. 58–62; for Moscow's rebuttal, see A/C.1/PV.1385, November 26, 1965, pp. 32–36.

61. An anthology of essays resulting from the meeting, however, contains little discussion of a comprehensive test ban and nothing about the erstwhile accord in

Canada. See Alastair Buchan, ed., *A World of Nuclear Powers?* (Englewood Cliffs, N.J.: Prentice-Hall, 1966), where the divergencies in the U.S. and Soviet viewpoints are summarized by Lord Chalfont, pp. 127–29.

62. "Urgent Need for Suspension of Nuclear and Thermonuclear Tests," Report of the First Committee, U.N. Doc. A/6530, November 25, 1966.

63. John W. Finney, "A Test in Big Cave May Hide Effects," *The New York Times,* December 30, 1966.

64. Another complication resulted from U.S. concern that civilian nuclear states (such as India) "could not possibly develop the capability of detonating nuclear devices for peaceful purposes without, by so doing, acquiring the capability of detonating nuclear bombs." For this reason the United States urged that the proposed nonproliferation pact be "equally applicable" to nuclear weapons and to nuclear explosives for peaceful projects. Washington argued that any treaty "must prohibit the dissmination to, or the manufacture by, non-nuclear weapon states of peaceful nuclear explosives." In exchange for this concession, the military nuclear powers would contract to undertake any atomic blasting for peaceful purposes required by countries that forswear the possession of nuclear explosives (*The New York Times,* August 10, 1966, p. C3). Other states proposed that such services should be provided by the IAEA instead of by the nuclear military powers. But India's Ambassador Trivedi objected to all these proposals saying that "this is the first time it is suggested that there should be nonproliferation in science and technology."

65. "Support systems" include reconnaissance, command and control, geodetic and other satellites.

66. General Assembly Resolution 1884 (XVIII): Stationing Weapons of Mass Destruction in Outer Space, October 17, 1963. The resolution was adopted by acclamation. The gentleman's agreement was announced in New York on October 3 by Soviet, U.K., and U.S. negotiators.

67. This is the basic Soviet as well as official U.S. position. But one Soviet scholar has written that the agreement in New York and the General Assembly resolution provided "distinctive" or "original" (*svoebraznye*) forms of international law,"legally binding for the countries participating in them." See G. P. Zhukov in G. P. Zadorozhnyi, ed., *Kosmos i problema vseobshchego mira* (Moscow: Nauka, 1966), p. 29.

68. This view was expressed succinctly and authoritatively for the United States on September 5, 1962, by the Deputy Secretary of Defense, Roswell Gilpatric. See *Documents on Disarmament, 1963* (Washington: Government Printing Office, 1964), p. 537.

69. *The New York Times,* May 10, 1965, p. 1; November 9, 1965, p. 5. Moscow cooperated by giving data on the missile to *Jane's All The World's Aircraft, 1965–1966.* See p. 446.

70. Part of his analysis was based on an essay in the West German newspaper, *Die Welt.* See Col. Gen. Vladimir Tolubko in *Za rubezhem,* September 1965; see also the article by East German Julius Mader, "U.S. Militarist Plans in Space," *International Affairs* (Moscow), XI, No. 8 (August 1965), pp. 54–58.

71. Leonov added that after "many space laboratories" had been established, "with crews periodically changed," the Soviet Union expected to give attention to "a spaceship to the moon, and a landing on the moon." See the editorial, "Space Plans

and Defense," *Philadelphia Inquirer,* September 19, 1965; also *The Washington Post,* September 17, 1965, p. A3.

72. *The Christian Science Monitor,* October 13, 1965.

73. General Major Engineer-Technical Service, Georgi I. Pokrovsky, Professor at the Zhukovsky Military Air Engineering Academy, Doctor of Technical Science.

74. *Krasnaia Zvezda,* February 12, 1966.

75. The following periodicals were cited, but usually without reference to specific articles or dates: *Air Force, Aviation Week, Missiles and Rockets, Army, Astronautics,* and *U.S. News & World Report.*

76. General Major of Aviation B. Teplinsky, retired, "The Strategy of Cosmic Adventures," *Krasnaia Zvezda,* April 23, 1966.

77. *The New York Times,* August 26, 1965.

78. U.N. Doc. A/PV.1334, September 24, 1965, pp. 42–45.

79. *The New York Times,* May 8, 1966.

80. *Ibid.,* June 1, 1966, p. 22; June 18, 1966, p. 11. U.N. Doc. A/6352.

81. See U.S. Mission to the United Nations, Press Release, "Text Agreed in Meeting Working Group of the Legal Subcommittee," 9 August 1966.

82. International Cooperation in the Peaceful Uses of Outer Space: Report of the Committee on the Peaceful Uses of Outer Space, U.N. Doc. A/6621, December 17, 1966.

83. For the text of the treaty and its interpretation by the executive and legislative branches of the U.S. Government, see "Treaty on Outer Space," *Hearings Before the Committee on Foreign Relations, United States Senate,* on Executive D, 90th Congress, First Session, March 7, 13, and April 12, 1967 (Washington: U.S. Government Printing Office, 1967).

84. Such as the articles regarding liability, ownership, and registration.

85. Because countries such as Japan and Australia, where the United States has tracking stations, objected to an obligation to grant equal rights to the Soviet Union, Article X merely requires that signatories to the treaty "consider on a basis of equality any requests by other States Parties to the Treaty to be afforded an opportunity to observe the flight of space objects launched by those States.

"The nature of such opportunity for observation and the conditions under which it could be afforded shall be determined by agreement between the States concerned."

86. In a related event—plans to hold a U.N. conference on international cooperation in outer space—the United States was successful in blocking a formula that would "invite all States to participate in the Conference." Instead, the resolution invited all U.N. members, states members of specialized agencies, states parties to the International Court of Justice, "and states that the General Assembly decides specifically to invite to participate in the Conference." The "all states" formula, proposed by Ethiopia, Guinea, India, Indonesia, Iraq, the U.A.R., and Yugoslavia, was defeated by a vote of 31 in favor, 44 against, with 15 abstentions. Of the 30-some states absent during the vote, many—such as Indonesia and Albania—would have approved the more inclusive formula. See "International Co-operation in the Peaceful Uses of Outer Space: Report of the Committee on the Peaceful Uses of Outer Space," U.N. Doc. A/6621, December 17, 1966, pp. 3–8.

87. See *The New York Times,* January 18, 1967, p. 7 and *ibid.,* January 22, 1967,

p. 4; also Nicholas E. Golovin, "The Nth Country's Problem in Space Exploration," *Bulletin of the Atomic Scientists,* XXII, No. 10 (December 1966), pp. 13–17.

CHAPTER XIII

1. This divergence has been repeatedly illustrated, e.g., in the famous editorial, "Long Live Leninism!" *Red Flag,* No. 8 (April 16, 1960), translated in G. F. Hudson, Richard Lowenthal, and Roderick MacFarquahar (eds.), *The Sino-Soviet Dispute* (New York: Praeger, 1961), pp. 82–112.

Peking's views were refuted, e.g., in Khrushchev's speech to the Third Congress of the Rumanian Workers Party on June 22, 1960: "The thesis, enunciated at the 20th and 21st Congresses of our Party, that war is not inevitable in our time has immediate bearing on the policy of peaceful coexistence. The tenets on imperialism that Lenin advanced still hold true; they serve as before, and will go on serving, as a lodestar for us in our theory and practice. But it must not be forgotten that Lenin's tenets on imperialism were put forward and developed by him decades ago, when many phenomena that have now become decisive for the development of the historical process and for the entire international situation did not exist."

Khrushchev warned: "Comrades, when it comes to this question we must not now repeat mechanically what Vladimir Il'ich Lenin said about imperialism many decades back, and again and again reiterate that imperialist wars are inevitable until socialism has won all over the world" (*Pravda,* June 22, 1960).

2. The basic materials used to document the historical evolution of Soviet and Chinese views prior to 1963 are cited in the notes. Much of the analysis of the recent positions of the two sides derives from their polemics in 1963–64, particularly as found in the Chinese Communist Party Central Committee letter of June 14, 1963, to the Central Committee of the CPSU and the latter's open letter of July 14, 1963, to all party organizations and communists in the U.S.S.R. The study takes account also of the Chinese and Soviet statements cited in previous chapters, particularly those dealing with the nuclear test ban and the utility (or disutility) of collaboration with the capitalist adversary, and with documents of 1965–68, such as the major article of Chinese Defense Minister Lin Piao written to commemorate the Twentieth Anniversary of China's triumph over Japan, "Long Live the Victory of People's War!" *Peking Review,* VIII, No. 36 (September 3, 1965), pp. 9–30.

The Chinese letter of July 14 is reprinted in the *Peking Review,* VI, No. 25 (June 21, 1963), pp. 6–22, together with the CPSU Central Committee letter of March 30 (pp. 23–32), to which the Chinese letter responds. References to four other Soviet and seven Chinese statements issued from December 1962 through March 1963, may be found in the June 14 letter (*Peking Review,* V, No. 25 ([June 21, 1962], p. 21).

An earlier version of the following analysis appeared in the author's "The Sino-Soviet Dispute—Dogma and Dialectics on Disarmament," *International Affairs* (London), Vol. 41, No. 2, (April 1965), pp. 204–22.

For further discussion of these matters, see, e.g., Raymond L. Garthoff, *Soviet Military Policy: A Historical Analysis* (New York: Praeger, 1966), chaps. X and XI.

3. For documentation, see Frederic S. Burin, "The Communist Doctrine of the Inevitability of War," *American Political Science Review,* LVII, No. 2 (June 1963), pp. 334–54.

4. *Ibid.*

5. This point in the June 14, 1963, letter was explicitly stated also, for example, in

Red Flag's "Long Live Leninism!" in April 1960 (Hudson *et al., op. cit.*, pp. 97–100). For the most articulate (if exaggerated) communist attack on Peking's aggressive tendencies, see Edvard Kardelj, *Socialism and War: A Survey of Chinese Criticism of the Policy of Coexistence* (London: Methven & Co., Ltd., 1961).

6. *Peking Review*, IX, No. 4 (January 21, 1966), p. 6.

7. Khrushchev's expression of the unavoidability of such wars is quoted in Part 2 of the July 14, 1963, Soviet letter. Peking's views are argued in "The Differences Between Comrade Togliatti and Us," *Red Flag*, No. 3–4 (March 4, 1963), reprinted in *Peking Review*, VI, No. 10–11 (March 15, 1963). Point 14 of Peking's June 14, 1963, letter assures that such wars will not "lead to a world conflagration."

8. In the words of China's Defense Minister in 1965: "The Khrushchev revisionists maintain that a single spark in any part of the globe may touch off a world nuclear conflagration and bring destruction to mankind. If this were true, our planet would have been destroyed time and time again. There have been wars of national liberation throughout the twenty years since World War II. But has any single one of them developed into a world war?" The Chinese Defense Minister also reiterated that the "principal contradiction" in the contemporary world is that between the revolutionary peoples of Asia, Africa, and Latin America, on the one hand, and the imperialists headed by the United States on the other (Lin Piao, *loc. cit.*, pp. 27, 25–26).

9. While Moscow has shown much greater interest than Peking in bringing the Vietnamese conflict to a halt, direct Soviet military aid to Hanoi has included ground-to-air missiles. On several occasions Moscow has offered to send volunteers to fight in Vietnam if requested by Hanoi (Edward Crankshaw, *The Observer* [London], November 14, 1965, p. 5).

Additional Chinese statements on the question of Soviet aid to Vietnam may be found in *Peking Review*, IX, No. 4 (January 21, 1966), p. 26 and *ibid*. IX, No. 19 (May 6, 1966), pp. 25–26. For the Soviet side, Ambassador Fedorenko told a Stanford University audience in March 1967 that the United States and Communist China seemed to have joined forces to work for the same end in Vietnam, i.e., more warfare.

10. This interpretation is gathered primarily from material in the *Peking Review*, IX, No. 4 (January 21, 1966), pp. 18–22. Articles on the conference in *World Marxist Review* in the first months of 1966 did not give such details, but indicated the validity of the peaceful coexistence resolution (endorsed "overwhelmingly") for inter-state relations, though not for inter-class struggle. See, e.g., J. M. Fortuny, A. Delgado, M. Salibi, "The Tri-Continental Conference," *World Marxist Review*, IX, No. 3 (March 1966), pp. 21–24, which also defends the coexistence resolution as confirming the theses of the Twentieth Congress of the CPSU.

11. See Part II of the July 14, 1963 Soviet letter and Points 13 and 16 of the June 14, 1963 Chinese letter. This position was upheld also in *Red Flag*'s "Long Live Leninism!" in 1960 (Hudson *et al., op. cit.*, pp. 97–100).

12. Lin Piao, *loc. cit.*, p. 28.

13. For Malenkov's statement, see *Pravda*, March 13, 1954; for discussions of Soviet military strategy, see Herbert S. Dinerstein, *War and the Soviet Union* (Rev. ed.; New York: Praeger, 1962); Raymond L. Garthoff, *Soviet Strategy in the Nuclear Age* (Rev. ed.; New York: Praeger, 1962); see also the recent collection edited by Vasilii D. Sokolovskii, *Soviet Military Strategy*, annotated by Herbert S. Dinerstein, Leon Gouré and Thomas W. Wolfe (Englewood Cliffs, N.J.: Prentice-Hall, 1963).

14. Part II of the July 14 Soviet letter specifically attacks the Chinese view of the

consequences of nuclear war, quoting from the expression in "Long Live Leninism!" *Red Flag* (April 1960), a view which was repeated in the *People's Daily* attack on "Comrade Togliatti" on December 31, 1962, reprinted in *Peking Review*, VI, No. 1 (January 4, 1963), p. 12. For Chinese and Soviet versions of Mao Tse-tung's remarks in November 1957 on the consequences of atomic war, see the documents in William E. Griffith, *The Sino-Soviet Rift* (Cambridge, Mass.: The M.I.T. Press, 1964), pp. 376 and 445.

15. Lin Piao, *loc. cit.*, p. 28.

16. See "Whence the Differences? A Reply to Thorez and Other Comrades," *People's Daily*, February 27, 1963, reprinted in *Peking Review*, VI, No. 9 (March 1, 1963), p. 13; "More on the Differences between Comrade Togliatti and Us," *Peking Review*, VI, No. 10–11 (March 15, 1963), pp. 25–26; the basic idea is repeated in Point 15 of Peking's June 14, 1963 letter.

17. See George Quester, "On the Identification of Real and Pretended Communist Military Doctrine," *Journal of Conflict Resolution*, X, No. 2 (June 1966), pp. 172–79.

18. Mao Tse-tung as well as Stalin is quoted on the indecisiveness of nuclear weapons in "More on the Differences between Comrade Togliatti and Us," *loc. cit.*, p. 26.

19. Lin Piao, *loc. cit.*, pp. 26–27.

20. See, e.g., the decisions of a People's Liberation Army Political Conference reported in *Peking Review*, IX, No. 4 (January 21, 1966), p. 5.

21. See especially Chinese statements following the third, fourth, and fifth nuclear tests in 1966. A typical statement of more general praise held that: "Mao Tse-tung's thought is the acme of Marxism-Leninism in the present era. . . . Once the world's people master Mao Tse-tung's thought, which is living Marxism-Leninism, they are sure to win their emancipation, bury imperialism, modern revisionism and all reactionaries lock, stock and barrel, and realize communism throughout the world step by step" (*Peking Review*, XI, No. 24 [June 10, 1966], p. 7).

22. *Peking Review*, IX, No. 23 (June 3, 1966), p. 12; "Indonesian reactionaries put a noose around their necks; no good end awaits those who hire themselves out to U.S. imperialism, collude with Soviet revisionism and oppose communism, China and the People," *ibid.*, IX, No. 37 (September 9, 1966), p. 36; "The Robber's Neck and the People's Nooses," *ibid.*, IX, No. 46 (November 11, 1966), p. 27.

23. This comment was included in Ambassador Wang Kuo-Chuan's statement at the 131st meeting of Chinese-U.S. talks in Warsaw, which was published, Peking explained, because of deliberate leaks by Washington to the press. Text in *Peking Review*, IX, No. 38 (September 16, 1966), p. 7. He added: "Should you dare to impose war on the Chinese people, we will surely take you on and keep you company to the end" (p. 9).

24. From a speech by Yao Wen-yuan, identified as a member of the group in charge of the Central Committee of the Chinese Communist Party, in *Peking Review*, IX, No. 45 (November 4, 1966), pp. 14–15.

25. In response to an alleged U.S. violation of Chinese air space, Peking declared: "We are in full battle array. If you must have a test of strength, then come on! The iron fists of the 700 million Chinese people will definitely crush all aggressors to pulp" (*Peking Review*, IX, No. 39 [September 23, 1966], p. 26); see also *ibid.*, IX, No. 4 [January 21, 1966], p. 6.

26. The areas of agreement and disagreement concerning the issues of capitalist-communist relations discussed here are expounded at length in Points 14–16 of the June 14, 1963 Chinese letter and throughout the Soviet reply on July 14, especially in Part 2, where the "conclusions" of the Twentieth Party Congress are reiterated.

27. See Point 16 of the Chinese letter of June 14, 1963 and the conclusion of Part 2 in the Soviet reply on July 14, 1963.

28. *The Fundamentals of Marxism-Leninism* (Moscow: Foreign Languages Publishing House, 1960), pp. 614 *et seq.* This has been the Soviet position since the Twentieth Party Congress in 1956; see *The New York Times*, February 15, 1956. It is alluded to briefly in Part 4 of the July 14, 1963 Soviet letter.

29. *Peking Review*, IX, No. 14 (April 1, 1966), pp. 24–25; *ibid.*, IX, No. 16, (April 15, 1966), pp. 23–29. In 1966–67 Soviet doctrine moved away from emphasis on the all-people's state, and toward theoretical justification of centralized, orderly government. Similarly, the Chinese Government seemed at times to recoil from the problems inherent in some of its anarchistic movements.

30. Point 16 of Peking's June 14, 1963 letter. But Soviet spokesmen have expressed concern also lest Moscow's peace offensive reach too far. Thus, Cosmonaut Gagarin, probably expressing a common anxiety among the Soviet military, told a Komsomol group that "sometimes, while making propaganda for peaceful coexistence, we forget about military-patriotic upbringing and the necessity to train young people to defend our motherland with arms in hand. . . . From time to time one can hear a Philistine say that there is no need for the military, there is no need for the army, and that in general there will be no war. . . . Struggle is not only possible, it is being waged . . . with weapons in hand. Vietnam is an example of this, Vietnam where our people too are fighting heroically [*gde geroicheski srazhaiutsia i nashi liudi*] (speech by Yu. A. Gagarin to the Komsomol Central Committee plenum held December 26–28, 1965, broadcast by the Russian Domestic Service on January 8, 1966).

31. For documentation and further discussion of the stages of Lenin's thinking on disarmament, see Walter C. Clemens, Jr., "Lenin on Disarmament," *Slavic Review*, XXIII, No. 3 (September 1964), pp. 504–25.

32. V. I. Lenin, *Leninskii Sbornik* (Moscow: Gospolizdat, 1959), XXXVI, pp. 451–54; see also the documents published for the first time in *Pravda*, April 12 and 22, 1964. Chicherin drew up what he called a "broad pacifist programme," which included disarmament proposals for presentation at the 1922 Genoa Conference; Lenin, from his bedside, indicated his approval. See Clemens, "Lenin on Disarmament," *loc. cit.*

Moscow also brought from obscurity the recollection of Lenin's wife Krupskaia that in 1918 and again in 1920–21 the Soviet leader had talked earnestly with her about the possibility of an end to all war as a result of the increasing destructiveness of military technology (N. K. Krupskaia, *O Lenine: sbornik statei* [Moscow, 1960], p. 41).

33. The Soviet letter could draw sustenance from Friedrich Engels' contributions in *Vorwärts*, Nos. 51–56, 58–59 (March 1–10, 1893).

As if to demonstrate the feasibility of disarmament, Moscow has revised its line on the economic consequences of disarmament for capitalist economies also. Since 1959 Soviet economists (following Khrushchev's lead) have argued that disarmament would be an unmixed blessing for all economies—socialist, underdeveloped and capitalist. The arms industry, it is now argued, is not a necessary or even a useful prop for capitalist economies, but a brake on their progress. It is the least militarized capitalist economies—the Japanese and the West German—which have the fastest growth rates. For a brief discussion of the recent evolution of Soviet views on the consequences of disarmament for capitalist economies, see Herbert Ritvo, "Internal Divisions on Disarmament in the U.S.S.R." in Seymour Melman (ed.), *Disarmament: Its Politics and Economies* (Boston: American Academy of Arts and Sciences, 1962), pp. 222–24. The major Soviet work expressing the new line is Igor S. Glagolev (ed.), *Ekonomicheskie problemy razoruzheniia* (Moscow: Academy of Sciences, 1961). For references to Soviet periodical literature on this subject, see Walter C. Clemens, Jr., *Soviet Disarmament Policy, 1917–1963: An Annotated Bibliography of Soviet and Western Sources* (Stanford, Calif.: The Hoover Institution, 1965), pp. 77–86. A recent book that takes up economic and other factors in disarmament is *SSSR, SShA i razoruzhenie*, ed. V. Ia. Aboltina (Moscow: Nauka, 1967).

34. Peking grants that "the possibility of banning nuclear weapons does indeed exist"—not because of the imperialists' love of humanity, but owing to popular pressure and the imperialists' own "vital interests." Further: "It is possible to reach certain agreements through negotiation by relying on the correct policies of the socialist countries and the pressure of the people of all countries." But Peking adds, and Moscow would concur, that "necessary compromises" between socialist and imperialist countries "do not require the oppressed peoples and nations to follow suit and compromise with imperialism and its lackeys" (Point 15, Chinese letter of June 14, 1963; see also Part 2 of the Soviet letter of June 14, 1963).

35. *China Youth*, February 16, 1960, quoted in Dan N. Jacobs and Hans H. Baerwald, eds., *Chinese Communism: Selected Documents* (New York: Harper Torchbooks, 1963), p. 164.

36. Quoted in Hudson *et al., op. cit.,* pp. 98, 105.

37. Jean Kanapa, "General and Complete Disarmament Is the Urgent Need of Our Time." *World Marxist Review,* May 1962, pp. 21–27.

38. The same point was made by Boris E. Shtein, the Secretary to the Soviet delegation to the League of Nations disarmament negotiations, in discussing Lenin's works with the author in 1958–59 at Moscow University. These discussions took place before the Chinese attacks became explicit with the publication of "Long Live Leninism!" in April 1960. But the sensitivity of the issue can be seen from the fact that Shtein apparently endeavored to keep from the author the text of Lenin's well-known treatise on communist morality, contained in his speech to the Third All-Russian Congress of the Communist Union of Youth on October 2, 1920, printed frequently in Komsomol literature and appearing most recently in V. I. Lenin, *Polnoe Sobranie Sochinenii* (5th ed., Moscow: Gospolizdat, 1963), Vol. 41, pp. 298–318.

39. "Two Different Lines on the Question of War and Peace—Comment on the Open Letter of the Central Committee of the CPSU (5)," by the editorial departments of *People's Daily* and *Red Flag*, November 18, 1963, in *Peking Review*, VI, No. 47 (November 27, 1963), pp. 6–16.

40. Paradoxically, Soviet use of Leninist disarmament tactics tends to obstruct the realization of the very arms controls that seem to be a goal of Kremlin strategy. The employment of disarmament negotiations as a sounding board for Soviet propaganda inevitably raises doubts about the sincerity with which the U.S.S.R. seeks a reduction or limitation of armaments. The Russian leaders might like to have it both ways, but it may be impossible to achieve an agreement with the West while at the same time scoring propaganda coups against the West. A major address by Khrushchev to Soviet Party Leaders on January 6, 1961 indicated the First Secretary's strong commitment to Lenin's second stage. Khrushchev recalled that, prior to the Genoa Conference in

1922, Lenin "pointed to the necessity of establishing contact with those bourgeois circles that gravitate toward pacifism, 'be it even of the poorest kind.' He said that in the struggle to preserve peace we must also use sensible representatives of the bourgeoisie" (*Kommunist*, No. 1, January 1961, pp. 23–24).

Because of the suspicions it arouses, the speech and its handling in the communist press provide an example of the self-defeating character of Moscow's bifurcated approach to disarmament. An analysis of the speech was requested by a U.S. Senate Subcommittee. The resulting testimony emphasized the lengths to which communist propaganda will go to impress favorably peace-minded people abroad. The speech's English translation in the *World Marxist Review* (January 1961) left out or altered many of the more hard-line aspects of Khrushchev's remarks. The above quotation from Lenin, for example, was rendered: "In the struggle for peace, he [Lenin] said we should not overlook the saner representatives of the bourgeoisie." The replacement of "use" (or "utilize") by "overlook" strips from Lenin's remarks much of their original cynical opportunism (Stefan T. Possony, *Analysis of the Khrushchev Speech of January 6, 1961*. Hearing before the Subcommittee to Investigate the Administration of the Internal Security Act and Internal Security Laws of the Committee on the Judiciary, U.S. Senate, 87th Congress, 1st session [Washington, D.C.: U.S. Government Printing Office, 1961]; see esp. Appendix IV by Natalie Grant, p. 18).

CHAPTER XIV

1. See also Richard C. Snyder, M. W. Bruck, and Burton Sapin, eds., *Foreign Policy Decision Making* (New York: The Free Press of Glencoe, 1962); James N. Rosenau, ed., *International Politics and Foreign Policy* (New York: The Free Press of Glencoe, 1961).

2. Clyde Kluckhohn and Alfred L. Kroeber, *Culture: A Critical Review of Concepts and Definitions* (Cambridge: Peabody Museum of American Archeology and Ethnology, 1952); Harry Hoijer, ed., *Language in Culture* (Chicago: University of Chicago Press, 1954); Talcott Parsons and Edward A. Shils, eds., *Toward a General Theory of Action* (Cambridge: Harvard University Press, 1951).

3. See, e.g., Harold D. Lasswell, *Psychopathology and Politics* (Chicago: University of Chicago Press, 1930); Calvin S. Hall and Gardner Lindzey, *Theories of Personality* (New York: John Wiley, 1965); Raymond B. Cattell, *Personality: A Systematic, Theoretical, and Factual Study* (New York: McGraw Hill, 1950); David C. McClelland, ed., *Studies in Motivation* (New York: Appleton-Century-Crofts, 1955).

4. On nationalism, e.g., Hans Kohn, *The Idea of Nationalism*, (New York: Macmillan, 1961); on ideology, see, e.g., Zbigniew Brzezinski, *Ideology and Power in Soviet Politics* (New York: Praeger, 1962); also Kurt Mannheim, *Ideology and Utopia; An Introduction to the Sociology of Knowledge* (New York: Harcourt, Brace, 1936).

5. See, e.g., Karl Lewin, *Field Theory in Social Science* (New York: Harper & Row, 1951); Harold D. Lasswell, "Why Be Quantitative," in Lasswell, Nathan Leites and associates, *Language of Politics* (Cambridge: The M.I.T. Press, 1965), pp. 47–48; Stanley Hoffmann, "International Relations: The Long Road to Theory," *World Politics*, XI (1959), pp. 346–77; Walter C. Clemens, Jr., ed., *World Perspectives on International Politics* (Boston: Little, Brown and Co., 1965), pp. 1–37.

6. See Chapter I, where reference is made to Alexander L. George, *Propaganda Analysis* (Evanston, Illinois: Row, Peterson and Co., 1959), especially pp. 58–59.

7. Stanley Hoffmann, "Nuclear Proliferation and World Politics," in Alastair

Buchan, ed., *A World of Nuclear Powers?* (Englewood Cliffs, New Jersey: Prentice-Hall, 1966), p. 102; see also Karl Deutsch, "The Future of World Politics," *Political Quarterly*, Vol. 37, No. 1 (January–March 1966), p. 15.

8. One authority has commented: "For a century controversy has raged over the relative weight of 'material' and 'ideological' factors in the social and political process. This controversy has been sterile of results, though the propaganda resonance of 'dialectical materialism' has been enormous." The main technical problem for the scholar has been to measure the ideological factor and correlate it with material factors more readily quantified. "It is as though you put people in an environment called material—and presto!—their ideas change in a predictable way; and if they do not, the failure is ascribed to an ideological lag of some kind." While studies of the material factor have been operationalized, those of the ideological elements have been "qualitative, impressionistic and conjectural" (Lasswell, *loc. cit.*, p. 47). Lasswell's critique applies with much force to the materialist hypothesis presented here; in defense of this hypothesis, however, it is (a) probabilistic and relative rather than determinist and absolute; (b) limited, at least in this stage, to the behavior of two states in a specific time frame; (c) based on a series of case studies.

9. Mao Tse-tung, "Problems of War and Strategy," *Selected Military Writings of Mao Tse-tung* (Peking: Foreign Language Press, 1963), p. 272.

10. See the epilogue to *War and Peace*.

11. Hans J. Morgenthau, *Politics Among Nations* (3rd ed., New York: Alfred A. Knopf, 1960).

12. Walt W. Rostow, *The Stages of Economic Growth* (Cambridge: University Press, 1960).

13. For conflicting views on this question in Soviet policy, see the essays compiled by Alexander Dallin, *Soviet Conduct in World Affairs* (New York: Columbia University Press, 1960) and by Ivo J. Lederer, ed., *Russian Foreign Policy* (New Haven and London: Yale University Press, 1962). On continuity in Chinese policy, see, e.g., Amaury de Riencourt, *The Soul of China* (Rev. ed.; New York: Harper & Row, 1965), p. xviii.

14. The value of searching for this handle is argued, e.g., in Lincoln P. Bloomfield, *The United Nations and U.S. Foreign Policy* (Rev. ed.; Boston: Little, Brown and Co., 1967).

15. See John W. Spanier and Joseph L. Nogee, *The Politics of Disarmament: A Study in Soviet-American Gamesmanship* (New York: Praeger, 1962), evaluated at greater length by the author in the *American Political Science Review*, LVIII, No. 3 (September 1963), pp. 678–80.

16. Whether the weight of material forces will increase in the future is unclear. On the one hand, technology reduces the distances between all states, friends and foes alike, making isolation more a fiction and interdependence more a reality. In this context, the military advantages accruing to technology and economic development may raise the political utility of a rich nation's military capability vis-à-vis less developed ones. On the other hand, the advantages of the superpowers may be reduced by such possible developments as (a) nuclear proliferation leading to a number of new power centers; and (b) the difficulties—military, political, and moral—of using or even threatening one's full military power.

17. On the extremes traditional to Russian thought and action, see, e.g., Geoffrey Gorer and John Rickman, *The People of Great Russia* (New York: W. W. Norton and

Company, Inc., 1962). The "fundamental impression" made by a traditional Chinese "is that he is moderate." But "the most conservative nation in history has [now] become the most radical. . . ." See Ch'u Chai and Winberg Chai, *The Changing Society of China* (New York: The New American Library, 1962), p. 230.

18. For further discussion, see Walter C. Clemens, Jr., "Ideology in Soviet Disarmament Policy," *Journal of Conflict Resolution,* VIII, No. 1 (March 1964), pp. 8–9.

19. Daniel Bell, "Marxism-Leninism: A Doctrine on the Defensive; The 'End of Ideology' in the Soviet Union?" in Milorad Drachkovitch, ed., *The Aspects and Paradoxes of Contemporary Marxism* (New York: Praeger, for the Hoover Institution, 1966).

20. For further development of this concept, see Brzezinski, *Ideology and Power in Soviet Politics,* pp. 66–70.

21. See introduction by Brzezinski and Alexander Dallin in Dallin, ed., *Diversity in International Communism* (New York: Columbia University Press, 1963), pp. xxvii–xxix. See also Robert V. Daniels, "The Chinese Revolution in Russian Perspective," *World Politics,* XII, No. 2 (January 1961), pp. 210–30. For reasons why Peking and Moscow are likely to disagree in their assessments on the "nature of the epoch," see Donald S. Zagoria, *The Sino-Soviet Conflict, 1956–1961* (Princeton, N.J.: Princeton University Press; London: Oxford University Press, 1962), pp. 13–20.

22. See also George H. Quester, "On the Identification of Real and Pretended Communist Doctrine," *Journal of Conflict Resolution,* X, No. 2 (June 1966), pp. 172–79.

23. Clemens, "Ideology in Soviet Disarmament Policy," *loc. cit.,* pp. 8–9.

24. Lincoln P. Bloomfield, Walter C. Clemens, Jr., Franklyn Griffiths, *Khrushchev and the Arms Race* (Cambridge, Mass.: The M.I.T. Press, 1966).

25. The announcement of the conference in 1921 brought about a shift in the Soviet line, so that Moscow for the first time approved the usefulness of disarmament negotiations. Moscow's motive, however, probably had more to do with a desire to take part in the conference because it would deal also with Far Eastern and Pacific problems. Soviet participation was denied, however, Washington declaring that it would look after the interests of Russia. Indeed, U.S. pressure proved to be instrumental in securing Japanese withdrawal from Siberia in later 1922; but the Soviet regime was nevertheless very bitter toward the conference as a whole.

26. For the July 1921 statement of the Soviet Government's interest in the conference, see *Sovetskii Soiuz v bor'be za mir: sobranie dokumentov i vstupitel'naia stat'ia* (Moscow, 1929), pp. 131–32. See also the "Theses on the Forthcoming Washington Conference" drawn up by the Communist International Executive Committee in August 1921, in Jane Degras, ed., *The Communist International, 1919–1943: Documents* (London: Oxford University Press, 1956), I, 285 ff.; for the views of the President of the Communist International on the work of the Conference, see Zinoviev's statement of January 23, 1922, in Xenia J. Eudin and Robert C. North, *Soviet Russia and the East, 1920–1927: A Documentary Survey* (Stanford, California: Stanford University Press, 1957), p. 222; for a collection of articles analyzing the conference, see *Ot Vashingtona do Genui* (Moscow: Vysshii Voennyi Redaktsionyi Sovet, 1922). For documentation on the Soviet counterproposals at the 1922 Genoa Conference, see Walter C. Clemens, Jr., "Lenin on Disarmament," *Slavic Review,* XXIII, No. 3 (September 1964), pp. 509–16. For the documents of the Washington Conference, see U.S. Department of State, *U.S. Treaty Series* No. 671.

27. See the July 31, 1963, "Statement of the Chinese Government Advocating the Complete, Thorough, Total and Resolute Prohibition and Destruction of Nuclear Weapons [and] Proposing a Conference of the Government Heads of All Countries of the World," *Peking Review*, VI, No. 31 (August 2, 1963), pp. 7–8; see also the Chinese Government's "comment" of August 15, 1963, on the Soviet Government's statement of August 3, 1963, both of which are reprinted in *Peking Review*, VI, No. 33 (August 16, 1963), pp. 7–19.

28. *Pravda*, August 21, 1963; *Izvestiia*, August 22, 1963. For a similar interpretation by Western officials, see *The New York Times*, August 16, 1963, p. 1.

29. The argument that follows is based in part on the author's "Peking, Moscow, and the West in a Warless World," in Walter C. Clemens, Jr., ed., *Toward a Strategy of Peace* (Chicago: Rand McNally, 1965), pp. 133 ff.

30. A revised version of the March 1962 Soviet draft incorporating this and other modifications was circulated by the U.N. Secretariat on September 24, 1962, as U.N. Doc. A/C.1/867. Whereas the September 1962 proposal would have extended a nuclear umbrella for the United States and the Soviet Union into the second stage of GCD, Gromyko proposed on September 19, 1963, that the umbrella be retained until the end of the third and final stage. Text, e.g., in *Bulletin of the Atomic Scientists*, XIX, No. 9 (November 1963), p. 43.

31. On the problem of militia-type forces in the process of disarmament, see Walter C. Clemens, Jr., "The Soviet Militia in the Missile Age," *Orbis*, VII, No. 1 (Spring 1964), pp. 101–104.

32. This position was affirmed by Peking not only after the 1963 Moscow Treaty, but also after China had entered the atomic club in 1964. See *Peking Review*, VI, No. 31 (August 2, 1963), pp. 7–8, and *ibid.*, VII, No. 43 (October 23, 1964), p. 5.

33. Zoppo, "The Test Ban: A Study in Arms Control Negotiation," *op. cit.*, pp. 429, 446, 449.

34. Bloomfield, Clemens, Griffiths, *op. cit.*

35. For further elaboration of this thesis, see Robert C. Tucker, *The Soviet Political Mind* (New York: Praeger, 1963).

36. See, e.g., Harold J. Berman, "Soviet Law Reform and Its Significance for Soviet International Relations," in *Law, Foreign Policy, and the East-West Détente*, ed. Edward McWhinney (Toronto: University of Toronto Press, 1965), pp. 3–17.

37. For development of this idea, see Robert C. North, "Soviet and Chinese Goal Values: A Study of Communism as a Behavior System," in *Unity and Contradiction: Major Aspects of Sino-Soviet Relations*, ed. Kurt London (New York: Praeger, 1962), pp. 62–63.

38. "The Sino-Soviet Split in Perspective," *The Annals of the American Academy of Political and Social Science* (January 1964), p. 8.

39. The decline of ideology, Bell has suggested, offers the possibility for an end to politics *à outrance*, to the war of beliefs, to the struggle to the death, at least on the rhetorical level, between the Soviet and Western systems. Apart from the cohesive impact on those systems of the rising threat from China, as doctrinaire certitudes fade, new attitudes may emerge and new forms of discussion appear. See Bell, *loc. cit.*, footnote 58.

40. See Cyril A. Zebot, *The Economics of Competitive Coexistence: Convergence Through Growth* (New York: Praeger, 1964), especially pp. 138 ff. For an argument that parallel evolution rather than political convergence may be expected in the

United States and Soviet Union, see Zbigniew Brzezinski and Samuel P. Huntington, *Political Power: USA/USSR* (New York: The Viking Press, 1964); for a Soviet attack on the theory of "convergence" see *Kommunist*, No. 13 (September 1962), pp. 110–19; and, more recently, the criticism in "Anti-Sovietism: One of the Main Trends in the Ideology of Imperialism Today," *Kommunist*, No. 7 (July 1965). Many such Soviet comments have been elicited by Western interpretations of the Soviet and East European economic reforms since the mid-1960s. For a Soviet analysis of recent developments in "capitalist economics," see *Sorevnovanie dvukh sistem* (Moscow: Nauka, 1967).

41. "Concerning Mao Tse-tung's Talk with a Group of Japanese Socialists," *Pravda*, September 2, 1964, p. 2.

42. The supposition that Khrushchev was at least partially concerned with inhibiting violence in the third world was reinforced by the Soviet proposal in July 1964 for the establishment of a U.N. peacekeeping force composed of contingents from non-permanent members of the Security Council but subject to it. See Chapter V.

43. In a major address to the U.N. General Assembly in 1965 the Soviet Foreign Minister condemned four times the attempts by outside powers to influence by "diktat" the affairs of states in the Western or Eastern Hemispheres. Perhaps meaning to cast a plague on both houses, he condemned not only U.S. "aggression" in Vietnam but also "third parties who would only see advantages for themselves in India and Pakistan getting bogged down still deeper in mutual enmity, for this would weaken each of them and make them prone to foreign influence and diktat" (U.N. Doc. A/PV.1335, September 24, 1965, pp. 7–32 at p. 11).

Developments in late 1965-early 1966 also demonstrated for Peking the difficulties in influencing the policies of governments such as the Indonesian and Cuban. On the historical development of the Soviet and Chinese strategies toward the third world, see Kurt Müller, *Über Kalkutta nach Paris?* (Hannover: Verlag für Literatur und Zeitgeschehen, 1964); also Uri Ra'anan, "Tactics in the Third World: Contradictions and Dangers," *Survey*, No. 57 (October 1964), pp. 26–37.

44. These divergencies are set out in the Chinese and Soviet Statements of June 14 and July 14, 1963, and are analyzed in Scalapino, *loc. cit.*, pp. 7–11.

CHAPTER XV

1. China's economic recovery after the debacle of the Great Leap Forward was slow and uneven. While considerable success was registered in modernization of military equipment, CIA analysts concluded that industrial production in 1965 was almost 20 per cent below the 1960 level (*The New York Times*, March 7, 1967, p. 7).

2. Among the indicators: (a) the intensifying and apparently more effective U.S. effort in Vietnam; (b) the vacuous nature of Peking's threats to New Delhi during the Kashmir conflict between India and Pakistan; (c) the upsurge in anti-Chinese feeling in Africa, leading to the expulsion from various countries of Chinese representatives and whole legations in 1965 and early 1966; (d) the refusal of the planned Second Afro-Asian Conference to exclude the U.S.S.R. or to focus on condemning U.S. aggression (the decision to put off the conference indefinitely appeared due more to conflicts within the third world than to China's refusal to attend); (e) Peking's loss of influence in Havana—as evidenced in the departure of Che Guevara, in Castro's insistence on holding an Asian, African, Latin American Conference (with Soviet participation) in January 1966, and in Peking's subsequent reduction of sugar imports and rice exports in trade with Cuba; and, perhaps most important, (f) in the

suppression of the PKI and Sukarno's regime in 1965–66 by Indonesian army officers.

3. Morton H. Halperin, "Is China Turning In?" (Cambridge, Mass.: Harvard University Center for International Affairs, Occasional Papers in International Affairs, No. 12, December 1965); see also the comments by others and Halperin's rejoinder, pp. 17–34; see also Richard Eder, "Peking's Frustration," *The New York Times,* August 16, 1965, p. 8; Erwin D. Canham, "Peking's Foreign Setbacks," *Christian Science Monitor,* November 1, 1965, p. 18.

Ithiel de Sola Pool noted that generalized descriptions of policy such as "turning inward," "turning outward," "liberal," "conservative," etc., may constrict one's perception of the richness of reality if they are the concepts of the observer—not of the actor. Pool argued, however, that Halperin's categories were useful, because the debate over world revolution versus building socialism in one country is part of the theoretical framework the Chinese learned in their formative years (*ibid.,* pp. 25–26). Shulman, however, cautioned, first, that short-term setbacks may have only a transient effect on Chinese policy decisions; and second, that analogies from Soviet experience were precarious: Moscow reacted to adversity in 1921 with moderation abroad, but in 1928 with a turning-in accompanied by greater militancy abroad (*ibid.,* p. 30).

4. A study of Soviet policy from 1917 to 1921 indicates that in relatively dark hours the Bolsheviks tended to believe that their revolution depended on and would be saved by a German revolution, but that when the survival of the Bolshevik regime clearly depended upon its own efforts, the Russian communists wrote off foreign assistance as neither imminent nor necessary for the near- or middle-term (Walter C. Clemens, Jr., "Bolshevik Expectations of a German Revolution, 1917–1921," Columbia University, Russian Institute Essay, 1957).

5. *Peking Review,* VIII, No. 36 (September 3, 1965), pp. 9–30.

6. The question is the more complex in that some of the ideas Lin Piao claimed to have lifted from the "vast treasure house" of Mao Tse-tung's thinking were taken almost textually from a resolution of the defunct Comintern. The "rural-city" dichotomy was presented to the sixth Comintern congress in 1927 by the then secretary-general of the Chinese Communist Party, Chiu-pai, and incorporated into the 1928 program of the Communist International: "The importance of the colonies and semi-colonies in the transition period stems from the fact that they are in some way the world's rural areas as opposed to the industrial countries, which play the role of the city of the world." A further complication is that the Comintern program itself was drafted by Nikolai Bukharin, who during the great purge was executed as a "Japanese spy," although one of his major crimes in Stalin's eyes was that he (like the Chinese) believed that the peasantry had to be brought along for the revolution to succeed. Significantly, the Comintern thesis was attacked by Jewish Communist Solomon Z. Lozowsky in November 1928 on the ground that: "If we say that the colonies form the world's village, the question of the dictatorship of the proletariat is automatically discarded . . . the proletariat disappears as the leading class" (a precursor to the present Soviet contention that the main contradiction in the modern world is between socialism and capitalism, as contrasted with the Chinese view that the main revolutionary front is between all oppressed peoples and imperialism). The Comintern origin of Lin's theory was reportedly discoverd by Branko Lazitch, editor of the French biweekly *Est & Quest.* It was then exploited by Boris N. Ponomarev, head of the international department of the CPSU Central Committee, at a conference in Prague late in 1965 of 35 Communist Parties, where he used the information to deflate Peking's claim to new and original leadership of the communist movement.

See Paul Wohl, "Peking Echoes 1927 Comintern," *Christian Science Monitor,* November 11, 1965, p. 15. But the basic ideas expressed by Lin have been explicit in Chinese strategic writing since 1958 and were explicitly stated on behalf of Peking over a year before Lin's speech. See Donald S. Zagoria, "China's Strategy: A Critique," *Commentary,* XL, No. 5 (November 1965), p. 63.

7. For an interpretation that portrays Lin Piao's statement as Peking's *Mein Kampf,* see Neal Sanford, "Peking's Manifesto," *Christian Science Monitor,* October 9, 1965, p. 15, reporting on the assessment of Cyrus R. Vance, U.S. Deputy Secretary of Defense. See also G. Alpin in *International Affairs,* No. 6 (June 1968).

8. Tang Tsou and Morton H. Halperin, "Mao Tse-tung's Revolutionary Strategy and Peking's International Behavior," *American Political Science Review,* LIX, No. 1 (March 1965), pp. 98–99; also Tang Tsou, "Mao Tse-tung and Peaceful Coexistence," *Orbis* (Spring 1964), pp. 36–51.

9. Radio broadcast of October 1, 1939, reprinted in Churchill, *The Gathering Storm* (Boston: Houghton-Mifflin, 1948), p. 449.

10. For a study of similarities and differences between the Soviet and Chinese revolutions, see Robert Vincent Daniels, "The Chinese Revolution in Russian Perspective," *World Politics,* XII, No. 2 (January 1961), pp. 210–30.

11. For discussion of "relative stages-of-growth" and the problems of peace and aggression, see Walt W. Rostow, *The Stages of Economic Growth* (Cambridge: University Press, 1960), Chaps. VIII and IX.

12. Lin Piao, *loc. cit.,* p. 28.

13. Mao's government appears for some time to have been obsessed with a concern that the next generation of Chinese leadership may capitulate to revisionism, and in 1965 issued statements calling for the perpetuation of revolutionary élan, if necessary for thousands of years. See, e.g., *The New York Times,* April 18, 1965; "Special Information Note" [U.S. Department of State], March 1, 1965, No. 73. One Chinese article predicted that the upsurge of China's economy "will inevitably give rise to a certain number of bourgeois 'intellectual aristocrats' who will ride high above the workers and peasants, and constitute a social basis engendering revisionism." The title of the article suggested the remedy: "The Revolutionary Road for China's Intellectuals," *Peking Review,* VIII, No. 51 (December 17, 1965), p. 12. A Chinese statement at the outset of the Cultural Revolution held that those who hoped the CPR would evolve like the U.S.S.R. were "living in a fool's paradise," because new cadres were already growing up and being trained. It cautioned, however, that the building of socialism and communism would take five to ten more generations. See *Peking Review,* IX, No. 10 (March 4, 1966), p. 3.

Bibliographical Note

The note references of this study provide a general guide to useful sources, as well as an indication of the sources of the particular information cited. A complete bibliography would necessarily cite literature from several fields of study, but many works are reviewed in the publications of the Office of External Research, U.S. Department of State—particularly in *Studies in Progress or Recently Completed: Arms Control and Disarmament*. Other useful bibliographies are published by the U.S. Department of State; the U.S. Arms Control and Disarmament Agency; and by strategy and peace research centers such as those in Canada, Norway, Sweden, and West Germany.

A guide to the bibliographies and to other relevant sources may be found in the author's *Soviet Disarmament Policy, 1917–1963; An Annotated Bibliography of Soviet and Western Sources* (Stanford, Calif.: The Hoover Institution, 1965). Methodological problems are discussed in the introduction to that work, and in the section "On Analyzing Soviet Disarmament Policy" by Lincoln P. Bloomfield, Walter C. Clemens, Jr. and Franklyn Griffith in *Khrushchev and the Arms Race: Soviet Interests in Arms Control and Disarmament, 1954–1964* (Cambridge, Mass.: The M.I.T. Press, 1966), the bibliography of which supplements that of *Soviet Disarmament Policy*. Further discussion of the methodological problems encountered in the preparation of *Khrushchev and the Arms Race* and the present study may be found in the author's "Underlying Factors in Soviet Disarmament Policy: Problems of Systematic Analysis," *Papers, Peace Research Society (International)*, Vienna Conference (1966), pp. 51–70. See also the useful bibliographies in *Intercom* (Foreign Policy Association), X, No. 1 (January–February 1968), pp. 31–80 and in the generally informative booklet by Arthur Larson, *Questions and Answers on the Spread of Nuclear Weapons* (Durham, N.C.: Rule of Law Research Center, Duke University School of Law and New York: Educational Committee to Halt Atomic Weapons Spread, April 1968), pp. 80–82.

For additional background and bibliographical references on topics related to the present study, the following recent sources are recommended.

First, two anthologies that treat many of the same subjects as the present book (sometimes reaching rather different conclusions) but which have a wider general scope: Morton H. Halperin (ed.), *Sino-Soviet Relations and Arms Control* (Cambridge, Mass.: The M.I.T. Press, 1967); and Raymond L. Garthoff (ed.), *Sino-Soviet Military Relations* (New York: Praeger, 1966).

On international communism, William E. Griffith, *Sino-Soviet Relations, 1964–65* (Cambridge, Mass.: the M.I.T. Press, 1967); Zbigniew Brzezinski, *The Soviet Bloc,* Rev. ed. (Cambridge, Mass.: Harvard University Press, 1967).

On Soviet military affairs, Raymond L. Garthoff, *Soviet Military Policy: A Historical Analysis* (New York: Praeger, 1966).

On Chinese military affairs, the still useful volume by Alice L. Hsieh, *Communist China's Strategy in the Nuclear Era* (Englewood Cliffs, N.J.: Prentice-Hall, Inc., 1962); Morton H. Halperin, *China and the Bomb* (New York: Praeger, 1965); and the periodical *The China Quarterly*.

On Soviet arms control policy, Alexander Dallin *et al, The Soviet Union and Disarmament: An Appraisal of Soviet Attitudes and Intentions* (New York: Praeger, 1965); and *Khrushchev and the Arms Race, op. cit.*

On China and disarmament, Morton H. Halperin and Dwight H. Perkins, *Communist China and Arms Control* (New York: Praeger, 1965). References to studies undertaken at Columbia University and the Hoover Institution to update and carry forward research on arms control problems related to the Soviet Union and Communist China may be found in *Seventh Annual Report of the U.S. Arms Control and Disarmament Agency* (Washington, D.C.: U.S. Government Printing Office, 1968), pp. 17, 25.

On arms control and strategy generally, see the introduction by Morton H. Halperin, *Contemporary Military Strategy* (Boston: Little, Brown & Company, 1967); the more theoretical treatment of Kenneth E. Boulding, *Conflict and Defense* (New York: Harper and Brothers, 1962); and the strategic estimates and analyses of the Institute for Strategic Studies in London. See also *Report of the Secretary-General on the Effects of the Possible Use of Nuclear Weapons and on the Security and Economic Implications for States of the Acquisition and Further Development of These Weapons,* U.N. General Assembly, A/6858, 10 October 1967.

Analysis of arms control matters also requires a reading of the proposals and discussions recorded in the documents of the Eighteen Nation

Disarmament Committee, the United Nations General Assembly, and other negotiating forums. For a useful guide, see *The United Nations and Disarmament, 1945–1965* (United Nations: Office of Public Information [1967]). See also the documentary collection compiled by V. M. Khaitsman, *50 let bor'by SSSR za rozoruzhenie* (Moscow: Nauka, 1967).

An examination of current arms control problems as well as a set of policy recommendations endorsed by a number of specialists, many of them with governmental experience, may be found in the *Report of the Committee on Arms Control and Disarmament, National Citizens' Commission,* prepared for The White House Conference on International Cooperation (New York: United Nations Association, 1966) and in *Stopping the Spread of Nuclear Weapons: A Report of a National Policy Panel Established by the United Nations Association of the U.S.A.* (New York, 1967).

A discussion of methodological problems associated with the study of Chinese arms control policy may be found in Davis B. Bobrow, "Old Dragons in New Models," *World Politics*, XIX, No. 2 (January 1967), pp. 306–19. In the growing literature on comparative studies of communist systems, see Robert C. Tucker, "On the Comparative Study of Communism," *World Politics*, XIX, No. 2 (January 1967), pp. 242–57. A valuable sourcebook is Chester J. Cheng, ed., *The Politics of the Chinese Red Army: A Translation of the Bulletin of Activities of the People's Liberation Army* (Stanford, Calif.: The Hoover Institution, 1966).

Among periodicals, in addition to *The China Quarterly* recommended earlier, the following are particularly useful: *Asian Survey; Current Digest of the Soviet Press; Foreign Affairs; International Affairs* (London); *International Affairs* (Moscow); *Journal of Conflict Resolution; New Times; Orbis; Peking Review; Slavic Review; Survey; World Marxist Review*.

The news analyses from listening posts in Munich and Hong Kong have become extremely useful, not only for spotting specific information but for the often incisive interpretations of the many trained analysts there.

While a number of libraries have become important centers of documentation on the subjects of this study, the Hoover Institution is unique for its concentration of relevant materials and the ease with which they can be consulted. The International Communism Project of the M.I.T. Center for International Studies is particularly notable for its wide collection and indexing of current periodical and radio broadcasts.

Appendix A

RESOLUTION ADOPTED BY THE GENERAL ASSEMBLY
[on the report of the First Committee (A/7016/Add.1)]
2373 (XXII). *Treaty on the Non-Proliferation of Nuclear Weapons*

The General Assembly,

Recalling its resolutions 2346 A (XXII) of 19 December 1967, 2153 A (XXI) of 17 November 1966, 2149 (XXI) of 4 November 1966, 2028 (XX) of 19 November 1965 and 1665 (XVI) of 4 December 1961,

Convinced of the urgency and great importance of preventing the spread of nuclear weapons and of intensifying international co-operation in the development of peaceful applications of atomic energy,

Having considered the report of the Conference of the Eighteen-Nation Committee on Disarmament, dated 14 March 1968,[1] and appreciative of the work of the Committee on the elaboration of the draft non-proliferation treaty, which is attached to that report,[2]

Convinced that, pursuant to the provisions of the treaty, all signatories have the right to engage in research, production and use of nuclear energy for peaceful purposes and will be able to acquire source and special fissionable materials, as well as equipment for the processing, use and production of nuclear material for peaceful purposes,

Convinced further that an agreement to prevent the further proliferation of nuclear weapons must be followed as soon as possible by effective measures on the cessation of the nuclear arms race and on nuclear disarmament, and that the non-proliferation treaty will contribute to this aim,

Affirming that in the interest of international peace and security both nuclear-weapon and non-nuclear-weapon States carry the responsibility of acting in accordance with the principles of the Charter of the United Nations that the sovereign equality of all States shall be respected, that

[1] A/7072.
[2] *Ibid.*, annex I.

the threat or use of force in international relations shall be refrained from and that international disputes shall be settled by peaceful means,

1. *Commends* the Treaty on the Non-Proliferation of Nuclear Weapons, the text of which is annexed to the present resolution;

2. *Requests* the Depositary Governments to open the Treaty for signature and ratification at the earliest possible date;

3. *Expresses the hope* for the widest possible adherence to the Treaty by both nuclear-weapon and non-nuclear-weapon States;

4. *Requests* the Conference of the Eighteen-Nation Committee on Disarmament and the nuclear-weapon States urgently to pursue negotiations on effective measures relating to the cessation of the nuclear arms race at an early date and to nuclear disarmament, and on a treaty on general and complete disarmament under strict and effective international control;

5. *Requests* the Conference of the Eighteen-Nation Committee on Disarmament to report on the progress of its work to the General Assembly at its twenty-third session.

1672nd plenary meeting,
12 June 1968.

ANNEX

Treaty on the Non-Proliferation of Nuclear Weapons

The States concluding this Treaty, hereinafter referred to as the "Parties to the Treaty,"

Considering the devastation that would be visited upon all mankind by a nuclear war and the consequent need to make every effort to avert the danger of such a war and to take measures to safeguard the security of peoples,

Believing that the proliferation of nuclear weapons would seriously enhance the danger of nuclear war,

In conformity with resolutions of the United Nations General Assembly calling for the conclusion of an agreement on the prevention of wider dissemination of nuclear weapons,

Undertaking to co-operate in facilitating the application of International Atomic Energy Agency safeguards on peaceful nuclear activities,

Expressing their support for research, development and other efforts to further the application, within the framework of the International Atomic Energy Agency safeguards system, of the principle of safeguarding effectively the flow of source and special fissionable materials by use of instruments and other techniques at certain strategic points,

Affirming the principle that the benefits of peaceful applications of nuclear technology, including any technological by-products which may be derived by nuclear-weapon States from the development of nuclear explosive devices, should be available for peaceful purposes to all Parties to the Treaty, whether nuclear-weapon or non-nuclear-weapon States,

Convinced that, in furtherance of this principle, all Parties to the Treaty are entitled to participate in the fullest possible exchange of scientific information for, and to contribute alone or in co-operation with other States to, the further development of the applications of atomic energy for peaceful purposes,

Declaring their intention to achieve at the earliest possible date the cessation of the nuclear arms race and to undertake effective measures in the direction of nuclear disarmament,

Urging the co-operation of all States in the attainment of this objective,

Recalling the determination expressed by the Parties to the 1963 Treaty banning nuclear weapon tests in the atmosphere, in outer space and under water in its Preamble to seek to achieve the discontinuance of all test explosions of nuclear weapons for all time and to continue negotiations to this end,

Desiring to further the easing of international tension and the strengthening of trust between States in order to facilitate the cessation of the manufacture of nuclear weapons, the liquidation of all their existing stockpiles, and the elimination from national arsenals of nuclear weapons and the means of their delivery pursuant to a treaty on general and complete disarmament under strict and effective international control,

Recalling that, in accordance with the Charter of the United Nations, States must refrain in their international relations from the threat or use of force against the territorial integrity or political independence of any State, or in any other manner inconsistent with the Purposes of the United Nations, and that the establishment and maintenance of international peace and security are to be promoted with the least diversion for armaments of the world's human and economic resources,

Have agreed as follows:

Article I

Each nuclear-weapon State Party to the Treaty undertakes not to transfer to any recipient whatsoever nuclear weapons or other nuclear explosive devices or control over such weapons or explosive devices directly, or indirectly; and not in any way to assist, encourage, or induce any non-nuclear-weapon State to manufacture or otherwise acquire nuclear weapons or other nuclear explosive devices, or control over such weapons or explosive devices.

Article II

Each non-nuclear-weapon State Party to the Treaty undertakes not to receive the transfer from any transferor whatsoever of nuclear weapons or other nuclear explosive devices or of control over such weapons or explosive devices directly, or indirectly; not to manufacture or otherwise acquire nuclear weapons or other nuclear explosive devices; and not to seek or receive any assistance in the manufacture of nuclear weapons or other nuclear explosive devices.

Article III

1. Each non-nuclear-weapon State Party to the Treaty undertakes to accept safeguards, as set forth in an agreement to be negotiated and concluded with the International Atomic Energy Agency in accordance with the Statute of the International Atomic Energy Agency and the Agency's safeguards system, for the exclusive purpose of verification of the fulfilment of its obligations assumed under this Treaty with a view to preventing diversion of nuclear energy from peaceful uses to nuclear weapons or other nuclear explosive devices. Procedures for the safeguards required by this article shall be followed with respect to source or special fissionable material whether it is being produced, processed or used in any principal nuclear facility or is outside any such facility. The safeguards required by this article shall be applied on all source or special fissionable material in all peaceful nuclear activities within the territory of such State, under its jurisdiction, or carried out under its control anywhere.

2. Each State Party to the Treaty undertakes not to provide: (a) source or special fissionable material, or (b) equipment or material especially designed or prepared for the processing, use or production of special fissionable material, to any non-nuclear-weapon State for peaceful purposes, unless the source or special fissionable material shall be subject to the safeguards required by this article.

3. The safeguards required by this article shall be implemented in a manner designed to comply with article IV of this Treaty, and to avoid hampering the economic or technological development of the Parties or international co-operation in the field of peaceful nuclear activities, including the international exchange of nuclear material and equipment for the processing, use or production of nuclear material for peaceful purposes in accordance with the provisions of this article and the principle of safeguarding set forth in the Preamble of the Treaty.

4. Non-nuclear-weapon States Party to the Treaty shall conclude agreements with the International Atomic Energy Agency to meet the requirements of this article either individually or together with other States in accordance with the Statute of the International Atomic Energy Agency. Negotiation of such agreements shall commence within 180 days from the original entry into force of this Treaty. For States depositing their instruments of ratification or accession after the 180-day period, negotiation of

such agreements shall commence not later than the date of such deposit. Such agreements shall enter into force not later than eighteen months after the date of initiation of negotiations.

Article IV

1. Nothing in this Treaty shall be interpreted as affecting the inalienable right of all the Parties to the Treaty to develop research, production and use of nuclear energy for peaceful purposes without discrimination and in conformity with articles I and II of this Treaty.

2. All the Parties to the Treaty undertake to facilitate, and have the right to participate in, the fullest possible exchange of equipment, materials and scientific and technological information for the peaceful uses of nuclear energy. Parties to the Treaty in a position to do so shall also cooperate in contributing alone or together with other States or international organizations to the further development of the applications of nuclear energy for peaceful purposes, especially in the territories of non-nuclear-weapon States Party to the Treaty, with due consideration for the needs of the developing areas of the world.

Article V

Each Party to the Treaty undertakes to take appropriate measures to ensure that, in accordance with this Treaty, under appropriate international observation and through appropriate international procedures, potential benefits from any peaceful applications of nuclear explosions will be made available to non-nuclear-weapon States Party to the Treaty on a non-discriminatory basis and that the charge to such Parties for the explosive devices used will be as low as possible and exclude any charge for research and development. Non-nuclear-weapon States Party to the Treaty shall be able to obtain such benefits, pursuant to a special international agreement or agreements, through an appropriate international body with adequate representation of non-nuclear-weapon States. Negotiations on this subject shall commence as soon as possible after the Treaty enters into force. Non-nuclear-weapon States Party to the Treaty so desiring may also obtain such benefits pursuant to bilateral agreements.

Article VI

Each of the Parties to the Treaty undertakes to pursue negotiations in good faith on effective measures relating to cessation of the nuclear arms race at an early date and to nuclear disarmament, and on a treaty on general and complete disarmament under strict and effective international control.

Article VII

Nothing in this Treaty affects the right of any group of States to conclude regional treaties in order to assure the total absence of nuclear weapons in their respective territories.

Article VIII

1. Any Party to the Treaty may propose amendments to this Treaty. The text of any proposed amendment shall be submitted to the Depositary Governments which shall circulate it to all Parties to the Treaty. Thereupon, if requested to do so by one third or more of the Parties to the Treaty, the Depositary Governments shall convene a conference, to which they shall invite all the Parties to the Treaty, to consider such an amendment.

2. Any amendment to this Treaty must be approved by a majority of the votes of all the Parties to the Treaty, including the votes of all nuclear-weapon States Party to the Treaty and all other Parties which, on the date the amendment is circulated, are members of the Board of Governors of the International Atomic Energy Agency. The amendment shall enter into force for each Party that deposits its instrument of ratification of the amendment upon the deposit of such instruments of ratification by a majority of all the Parties, including the instruments of ratification of all nuclear-weapon States Party to the Treaty and all other Parties which, on the date the amendment is circulated, are members of the Board of Governors of the International Atomic Energy Agency. Thereafter, it shall enter into force for any other Party upon the deposit of its instrument of ratification of the amendment.

3. Five years after the entry into force of this Treaty, a conference of Parties to the Treaty shall be held in Geneva, Switzerland, in order to review the operation of this Treaty with a view to assuring that the purposes of the Preamble and the provisions of the Treaty are being realized. At intervals of five years thereafter, a majority of the Parties to the Treaty may obtain, by submitting a proposal to this effect to the Depositary Governments, the convening of further conferences with the same objective of reviewing the operation of the Treaty.

Article IX

1. This Treaty shall be open to all States for signature. Any State which does not sign the Treaty before its entry into force in accordance with paragraph 3 of this article may accede to it at any time.

2. This Treaty shall be subject to ratification by signatory States. Instruments of ratification and instruments of accession shall be deposited with the Governments of the Union of Soviet Socialist Republics, the United

Kingdom of Great Britain and Northern Ireland and the United States of America, which are hereby designated the Depositary Governments.

3. This Treaty shall enter into force after its ratification by the States, the Governments of which are designated Depositaries of the Treaty, and forty other States signatory to this Treaty and the deposit of their instruments of ratification. For the purposes of this Treaty, a nuclear-weapon State is one which has manufactured and exploded a nuclear weapon or other nuclear explosive device prior to 1 January 1967.

4. For States whose instruments of ratification or accession are deposited subsequent to the entry into force of this Treaty, it shall enter into force on the date of the deposit of their instruments of ratification or accession.

5. The Depositary Governments shall promptly inform all signatory and acceding States of the date of each signature, the date of deposit of each instrument of ratification or of accession, the date of the entry into force of this Treaty, and the date of receipt of any requests for convening a conference or other notices.

6. This Treaty shall be registered by the Depositary Governments pursuant to article 102 of the Charter of the United Nations.

Article X

1. Each Party shall in exercising its national sovereignty have the right to withdraw from the Treaty if it decides that extraordinary events, related to the subject matter of this Treaty, have jeopardized the supreme interests of its country. It shall give notice of such withdrawal to all other Parties to the Treaty and to the United Nations Security Council three months in advance. Such notice shall include a statement of the extraordinary events it regards as having jeopardized its supreme interests.

2. Twenty-five years after the entry into force of the Treaty, a conference shall be convened to decide whether the Treaty shall continue in force indefinitely, or shall be extended for an additional fixed period or periods. This decision shall be taken by a majority of the Parties to the Treaty.

Article XI

This Treaty, the Chinese, English, French, Russian and Spanish texts of which are equally authentic, shall be deposited in the archives of the Depositary Governments. Duly certified copies of this Treaty shall be transmitted by the Depositary Governments to the Governments of the signatory and acceding States.

IN WITNESS WHEREOF the undersigned, duly authorized, have signed this Treaty.

Done in _____ at _____ this _____ day of _____.

Appendix B

RESOLUTION 255 (1968)
Adopted by the Security Council at its 1433rd meeting on 19 June 1968

The Security Council,

Noting with appreciation the desire of a large number of States to subscribe to the Treaty on the Non-Proliferation of Nuclear Weapons, and thereby to undertake not to receive the transfer from any transferor whatsoever of nuclear weapons or other nuclear explosive devices or of control over such weapons or explosive devices directly, or indirectly; not to manufacture or otherwise acquire nuclear weapons or other nuclear explosive devices; and not to seek or receive any assistance in the manufacture of nuclear weapons or other nuclear explosive devices,

Taking into consideration the concern of certain of these States that, in conjunction with their adherence to the Treaty on the Non-Proliferation of Nuclear Weapons, appropriate measures be undertaken to safeguard their security,

Bearing in mind that any aggression accompanied by the use of nuclear weapons would endanger the peace and security of all States,

1. *Recognizes* that aggression with nuclear weapons or the threat of such aggression against a non-nuclear-weapon State would create a situation in which the Security Council, and above all its nuclear-weapon State permanent members, would have to act immediately in accordance with their obligations under the United Nations Charter;

2. *Welcomes* the intention expressed by certain States that they will provide or support immediate assistance, in accordance with the Charter, to any non-nuclear-weapon State Party to the Treaty on the Non-Proliferation of Nuclear Weapons that is a victim of an act or an object of a threat of aggression in which nuclear weapons are used;

3. *Reaffirms* in particular the inherent right, recognized under Article 51 of the Charter, of individual and collective self-defence if an armed attack occurs against a Member of the United Nations, until the Security Council has taken measures necessary to maintain international peace and security.

Index

Further information on the position of an asterisked entry on major issues of arms control and nuclear strategy can be found by referring to the table of contents, the tables on pages 142–43, the discussion on page 89, and the following index entries: Conference of non-nuclear-weapon countries; Nonproliferation treaty; Nuclear proliferation; Nuclear test ban; Nuclear tests; Nuclear-free zones; World disarmament conference.

* See (also) note preceding Index

* See (also) note preceding Index

* *See* (*also*) *note preceding Index*

* *See (also) note preceding Index*

* See (also) note preceding Index

* See (also) note preceding Index

* *See (also) note preceding Index*